CIVIL
RELIGION
in POLITICAL
THOUGHT

CIVIL RELIGION *in* POLITICAL THOUGHT

Its Perennial Questions
and Enduring Relevance in
North America

Edited by

RONALD WEED &
JOHN VON HEYKING

The Catholic University of America Press

Washington, D.C.

Library of Congress Cataloging-in-Publication Data
Civil religion in political thought : its perennial questions
and enduring relevance in North America / edited by
Ronald Weed and John von Heyking.
p. cm.
Includes bibliographical references and index.
ISBN 978-0-8132-1724-6 (cloth : alk. paper)
1. Civil religion—North America.   2. Religion and
politics—North America.   I. Weed, Ronald L.
II. Heyking, John von.   III. Title.
BL98.5.C58 2010
322′.1097—dc22
2009030748

Contents

Foreword

University of Tennessee at Chattanooga

This collection of essays is both welcome and extremely timely. The term "civil religion" has become such an object of reflexive contempt among those who employ it, who generally see in it only a form of dangerous idolatry, that the term's analytical and descriptive purposes seem to have been forgotten. But such a dismissive position, although having the advantages of perfect clarity, fails to do justice to reality, and more particularly to the enduring needs of actual human beings living in real communities. There are good reasons to be profoundly wary of civil religion. But there are equally good reasons to be respectful of it. These essays are alive to both sets of reasons and serve as an outstanding prolegomenon to further discussion of the subject.

Civil religion originally refers to the way in which a particular set of political/social arrangements come to acquire an aura of the sacred, thereby elevating their stature and enhancing their stability. It can serve as a point of reference for the shared faith of the entire state or nation, focusing on the most generalized and widely held beliefs about the history and destiny of that state or nation. It is rarely entirely spontaneous or entirely invented, and is more likely to be some combination of the two. But it plays an important role in social cohesion, providing much of the glue that binds together a society through well-established symbols, rituals, celebrations, places, and values, endowing the society with an overarching sense of spiritual unity—a sacred canopy, in Peter Berger's words—and a focal point for shared memories of struggle and survival. Although it borrows extensively from the society's dominant religious tradition, it is not itself a highly particularized religion, but instead a somewhat more blandly inclusive one, into whose highly general stories and propositions those of various faiths can read and project what they wish. It is, so to speak, a highest common denominator.

The tendency to overlap, and even conflate, the realms of the religious and the political has hardly been unique to North American life and history. Indeed, as these essays show, the achievement of a stable relationship between the two constitutes one of the perennial tasks of social existence. But in the West, the immense historical influence of Christianity has had a lot to say about the particular way the two have interacted over the centuries. From its inception, the Christian faith insisted upon separating the claims of Caesar and the claims of God—recognizing the legitimacy of both, though placing loyalty to God above loyalty to the state. The Christian was to be *in* the world but not *of* the world, living as a responsible and law-abiding citizen in the City of Man while reserving his ultimate loyalty for the City of God. Such a separation and hierarchy of loyalties, which sundered the unity that was characteristic of the classical world, had the effect of marking out a distinctively secular realm, although at the same time confining its claims.

In the United States, this dualism has often manifested itself as an even more decisive commitment to something called "the separation of Church and State," a slogan that is taken by many to be the cardinal principle governing American politics and religion. Yet the persistence of an energetic American civil religion, and of other instances in which the boundaries between the two becomes blurred, suggests that the matter is not nearly so simple as that. There is, and always has been, considerable room in the American experiment, and in any liberal-democratic order, for the *conjunction* of religion and state. This is a proposition that committed religious believers and committed secularists alike find deeply worrisome—and understandably so, since it carries with it the risk that each of the respective realms can be contaminated by the presence of its opposite number. But it is futile to imagine that the proper boundaries between religion and politics can ever be fixed once and for all, in all times and cultures, separated by an abstract fiat. Instead, their relationship evolves out of a process of constant negotiation and renegotiation, responsive to the changing needs of the culture and the moment.

We seem to be going through just such a process at present, as the renegotiation of boundaries continues fast and furious. Consider, for example, the case that recently came before the U.S. Supreme Court involving

whether the words "under God" in the Pledge of Allegiance violate the establishment clause of the First Amendment. (An issue that will undoubtedly be revisited in the years to come.) Or the many similar cases, most notoriously that of Judge Roy Moore in Alabama, involving the display of the
Ten Commandments in courthouses and other public buildings. Or the
intentions behind U.S. President Bush's faith-based initiative, which extends an effort begun in the Clinton administration to end discrimination
against religious organizations that contract to provide public services. Or
the contested status in all of North America of the institution of marriage,
which has always been both a religious and a civil institution, a process that
could lead not only to same-sex marriages but to the legalization of polyga-
mous and other nontraditional marital unions, and to a sharp distinction
between marriage as a civil institution and marriage as a religious one. A
multitude of issues are in play, and it is hard to predict what the results will
look like when the dust settles, if it ever does.

Experience suggests, however, that when it comes to the question of civil religion, we would be well advised to steer between two equally dangerous extremes, which can serve as negative landmarks in our deliberations
about the proper relationship between religion and the nation-state. First,
we should avoid total identification of the two, which would in practice
likely mean the complete domination of one by the other—a theocratic or
ideological totalitarianism in which religious believers completely subordinated themselves to the apparatus of the state, or vice versa. A great deal of
attention has been paid to this danger of civil religion—that the political
civil order would become all-religious or the religious order become all-
political, two superficially different cases that have in common their tendency to conjoin moral power and political power, endowing moral righteousness with the power of the state and vice versa. And the attention paid
to this danger is always justified.

But second, and equally important, but perhaps less well articulated: we
should not aspire to a total segregation of the two, which would in practice
bring about unhealthy estrangement between and among different kinds of
citizens in our North American nations, leading in turn to extreme forms
of sectarianism, otherworldliness, cultural separatism, and Gnosticism—a
state of affairs in which religious believers will regard the state with pure
antagonism, and the state will return the favor. We already see dramatic
glimpses of this in the efforts to stigmatize orthodox Christian views as

"hate crimes," but the greatest dangers may manifest themselves in more subtle ways, in a long process of mutual disengagement and estrangement and distrust.

None of these things are necessary or inevitable. Religion and the nation are inevitably entwined, and some degree of this entwining is a good thing. As Robert Bellah and others have observed, it is a good thing for our loyalties to the nation-state to be qualified by their being subject to a higher moral criterion: to being "under judgment." It is also true, human nature being what it is, that religious institutions (being subject, like all human institutions, to imperfection and excess) generally benefit from being checked by the existence of secular institutions, particularly of a secular state, which legitimately requires its own sources and tokens of loyalty. We are not searching for a steady state, but for a delicate and ever-adjusting equilibrium.

But how are we to reconcile all these different, and seemingly incompatible, imperatives, and give each its due? A good place to start would be with the reinvigoration of our discussion of civil religion. And a good place to start on that indispensable task is to be found . . . right here, in the essays that follow.

Acknowledgments

This volume is the product of sustained collaboration among scholars in political science, philosophy, history, and religious studies. The early work on some of these essays originated from a summer workshop in 1996 on the theme of political theory and constitutionalism lead by Dr. Graham Walker at the University of Notre Dame. The Pew Foundation provided generous support for the workshop, as well as for a conference at the Catholic University of America on the topic of civil religion.

Some of the work on this volume was supported through a fellowship at New College, Edinburgh, which provided research resources and support during the later phase of its preparation. Dr. Oliver O'Donovan offered numerous suggestions and feedback on the project. A faculty research grant from Tyndale University College and the clerical assistance of Will Kinchlea and Brad Longard were very helpful in the final stages of the manuscript preparation. David Mwangi, Amy Gabriel, and Ryan Eras also offered valuable research support and editorial work at earlier stages of the project. Special thanks are due to the anonymous referees with the Catholic University of America Press and James Kruggel, acquisitions editor, who provided excellent help at every stage of the process.

CIVIL
RELIGION
in POLITICAL
THOUGHT

Introduction

RONALD WEED &

JOHN VON HEYKING

Civil religion has been a political and theological problem of enduring concern across the centuries because of both the potency of its promises and the intractability of its hazards. Indeed, recent appeals to religion by former U.S. president George W. Bush and controversies over the Pledge of Allegiance demonstrate the endurance of civil religion in contemporary politics. There is a rich heritage of philosophical, theological, and political reflection on the problem that extends at least as far back as Plato's *Laws*.[1] This volume includes essays on significant philosophical, theological, and political expressions of civil religion from a wide variety of sources in the Western intellectual and political tradition. With essays on ancient, medieval, and modern political philosophers, and essays on major statements and figures from the United States and Canada, this volume demonstrates why civil religion is an enduring political phenomenon.[2] The philosophical and

1. The concept of civil religion has its roots in Varro's threefold distinction of pagan theology: mythical, natural or philosophic, and civil or political (as reported by Augustine, *City of God*, VI–VII.).

2. This volume covers a wide spectrum of thinking on civil religion, but it obviously cannot provide a comprehensive overview of the topic in the history of political thought. In addition to the thinkers presented here, the reader should also consult the following primary sources: Aristotle, *Politics* V.11, VI.8; John of Salisbury, *Politicraticus*, Bk. 5; Marsilius of Padua, *Defensor Pacis*, Discourse I; Girolamo Savonarola, "Treatise on the Constitution and Government of the City of Florence," in *Humanism and Liberty: Writings on Freedom from Fifteenth-Century Florence*, trans. and ed. Renee Neu Watkins (Columbia: University of South Carolina Press, 1978); Machiavelli, *The Discourses* I:11–15, II,: 2,5; *The Prince* VI, VII, XI, XII, XXV, XXVI; Giambattista Vico, *New Science*, pars. 334, 342, 360, 364, 366, 385, 390, 990; Benedict Spinoza, *Tractatus Theologico-Politicus*, especially chaps. 3, 6.40, 8.46; John Locke, *The Reasonableness of Christianity*; Samuel Pufendorf, *Of the Nature and Qualifications of Religion in Reference to Civil Society*; Montesquieu, *The Spirit of the Laws*, Books 24–25; David Hume, *Dialogues Concerning Natural Religion*; Immanuel Kant, *Religion Within the Limits of Reason Alone*; G. W. F. Hegel, *Elements of the Philosophy of Right*, par. 270; *Reason in History*, III. 3d; "The Positivity of the Christian Religion," in *Early Theological Writings*, trans. T. M. Knox (Philadelphia: University of Pennsylvania Press, 1975), I.21; Adam Smith,

theological reflection that comprises this legacy brings with it a relevance to our contemporary situation that this volume emphasizes. The essays in this volume blend historical and philosophical reflection with concern for contemporary political problems. They show that the causes and motivations of civil religion are a permanent fixture of the human condition, though some of its manifestations and proximate causes have shifted in an age of multiculturalism, religious toleration, and secularization. The essays serve as a reminder that all political societies function within some unquestioned assumptions and commitments. The topic of civil religion turns our attention to the realm of action, where human beings have little choice but to disclose the unexamined faith within which their lives unfold.

What is civil religion and how should it be understood? Civil religion seems to have as many definitions as it has interlocutors. However, the interpretations fall within an identifiable range of shared observations and explanations. We begin by suggesting a thumbnail distinction between political and theological causes of civil religion, though, for reasons explained here and throughout the volume, this thumbnail distinction gives way to a deeper unity of political and religious experience. One view of civil religion is that it is an acknowledged set of beliefs, drawing on familiar religious symbols and language, that sustains and reinforces a society's moral-political beliefs. Plato, Spinoza, Bacon, Locke, and Rousseau emphasize this dimension. Another interpretation of civil religion ascribes more significant theological motivations, though it garners power by political means and maintains itself in political forms. This version of civil religion arises out of some overlapping theological consensus within the society and, consequently, cultivates a wider recognition of its bond with God and His providence, often adopting the language of a national destiny and world-historic sacred purpose. Some features of this view occur in certain ancient Roman and medieval thinkers, while its other features are manifest variously in later figures such as Machiavelli, Hegel, and certain American Puritan writers. Both views of civil religion highlight its theological and political features and mark two poles

---

The Theory of Moral Sentiments, part III, section V; Karl Marx, On the Jewish Question; John Stuart Mill, "The Utility of Religion" and "Theism" in Three Essays on Religion (Amherst, NY: Prometheus Books, 1998); Max Weber, Protestant Work Ethic and the Origins of Capitalism; Weber, "Social Psychology of the World Religions" and "Religious Rejections of the World and Their Directions" both in From Max Weber: Essays in Sociology, ed. H. H. Gerth and C. Wright Mills (Oxford: Oxford University Press, 1958); Carl Schmitt, Political Theology; Emile Durkheim, The Elementary Forms of Religious Life, trans. Karen E. Fields (New York: Free Press, 1995), 418–448; John Dewey, A Common Faith; John Rawls, A Theory of Justice.

of interpretation between which the views of other thinkers may be found and the phenomenon itself may be manifested. Both dimensions or views can be present in the same interpretation. The primary difference between them is that in the former, civil religion sustains the moral and political life of a political society without making claims for other societies, while the language of Providence and world-historic role in the latter frequently suggests a unique, vanguard, or imperial political self-understanding.

Both views of civil religion also suggest a reason why it is such a permanent problem. Why do societies appeal to the divine? According to both interpretations of the problem, there are political and theological motivations for this appeal. Politically motivated appeals to civil religion recognize its enormous political power that rulers may tap into, as they draw from the spiritual allegiance of its citizenry. Rulers achieve their own aims by persuading their citizens that they best foster their own theological aims, as they help realize their country's political goals. In contrast, theologically motivated appeals to civil religion already recognize an allegiance to the divine that some portion of its citizenry hopes to celebrate and augment by political means. The essays in this volume treat different aspects of both interpretations of civil religion, especially as they illuminate the following consideration. Civil religion in all of these forms expresses an enduring need for the divine, whether it is the citizenry's need for the divine that provides political power for those who capitalize upon it or a religious citizenry's desire to absorb the political community at large into a wider theological destiny. This need for the divine becomes manifest in civil religious forms and is ineradicable.[3] For this reason, the enduring need for the divine continues to give rise to civil religion, though the forms in which it occurs have changed as some of its political and theological contexts have changed.

The past fifty years has seen numerous scholarly studies on civil religion. Sociologists, historians, religious studies scholars, theologians, and political scientists have conducted most of this work. Scholars have sought to define and explain the phenomenon of civil religion according to the contours of these respective disciplines. For example, Robert Bellah has been one of its

3. There are a wide range of figures covered in the volume who have very different ways of understanding and addressing the problem of civil religion and so also the enduring need for the divine that gives rise to it. While many of these figures disagree about the nature of this need, nearly every one of them recognizes the significance of this dependence whether understood as social utility, psychological need or ontological dependence of creature to creator.

most? influential analysts and has invited a very welcome reconsideration of civil religion as a phenomenon, especially in its American historical and cultural context.[4] One characteristic feature of his work as a sociologist has been his attention to the complexities and internal logic of religious and political associations across the political and religious spectrum. His supporters and critics alike recognize how well he classifies and interprets the attitudes and behavior of such groups without reducing their motivations to merely economic or class considerations or inflating their religious and political dimensions to the exclusion of other factors.[5] He also recognizes the limitations of secularization theory, prominent among sociologists, that predicts religion to become increasingly private and individualistic as society becomes more secular. Secularization theory fails to explain the phenomenon of civil religion. While this kind of treatment of civil religion is welcome, relevant, and attentive to many aspects of the phenomenon, its empirical focus often overlooks the philosophical reasons why such expressions of civil religion occur.

Among religious studies scholars, Martin Marty offers perceptive analyses of civil religion that capture some important religious and political features of the phenomenon.[6] For example, he distinguishes priestly and

4. Some relevant and representative contributions include: "Civil Religion in America," *Daedalus* 96 (1967): 1–21; "American Civil Religion in the 1970's," in *American Civil Religion*, ed. Russell E. Richey and Donald G. Jones (New York: Harper & Row, 1974), 255–272; *The Broken Covenant: American Civil Religion in Time of Trial* (New York: Seabury Press, 1975); *Varieties of Civil Religion* (New York: Harper & Row, 1980); "Public Philosophy and Public Theology in America Today," in *Civil Religion and Political Theology*, ed. Leroy S. Rouner (Notre Dame, Ind.: University of Notre Dame Press, 1986), 79–97.

5. See Robert Bellah, "Conclusion: Competing Visions of the Role of Religion in American Society," *Uncivil Religion: Interreligious Hostility in America,* ed. Robert Bellah and Frederick E. Greenspahn (New York: Crossroad, 1987), 219–232. Some of social scientists who were favorable to his approach included: Donald Jones and Russell E. Richey, eds., *American Civil Religion* (New York: Harper & Row, 1974); Phillip E. Hammond, "The Sociology of American Civil Religion: A Bibliographic Essay," *Sociological Analysis* 37 (1976): 169–182; Ronald C. Wimberly, "Testing the Civil Religion Hypothesis," *Sociological Analysis* 37 (1976): 341–352; Ronald C. Wimberly, Donald A. Clelland, Thomas C. Hood, and C. McCurdy Lipsey, "The Civil Religion Dimension: Is It There?" *Social Forces* 54 (1976): 890–900; Phillip E. Hammond, *The Sacred in a Secular Age: Toward Revision in the Scientific Study of Religion* (Berkeley: University of California Press, 1985); Jeffrey C. Alexander, ed., *Durkheimian Sociology: Cultural Studies* (Cambridge: Cambridge University Press, 1988). Some of the critics of his suitability of his approach and understanding of civil religion included: Richard K. Fenn, "Toward a New Sociology of Religion," *Journal for the Scientific Study of Religion* 11 (1972): 16–32; John F. Wilson, "The Status of Civil Religion" in *The Religion of the Republic,* ed. Elwyn A. Smith (Philadelphia: Fortress, 1974).

6. *A Nation of Behavers* (Chicago: University of Chicago Press, 1976); "Eight Approaches toward Understanding Public Religion and Politics in America" in Blumhofer, *Politics, Religion, and*

prophetic strains of civil religion.[7] His prophetic variety of civil religion appropriates the religious language of prophecy to highlight the progress of social and political change toward a future of greater peace and justice. He associates a priestly version of civil religion with a religious language that promotes and preserves "American values." While this distinction captures some important features of civil religion, his analysis is restricted to the United States and also does not address significant historical and philosophical analyses of civil religion. As a result, its analysis remains too embedded in the contemporary American political terminology of liberal versus conservative to provide a more philosophically grounded diagnosis of its causes.

Political scientists have tended to focus on the United States. For example, Jürgen Gebhardt's study of the American Founding, as well as the work of Ellis Sandoz, has focused on the manner in which American political self-understanding relies on a wide range of philosophical and theological sources to represent itself as a manifestation of order under God.[8] Other scholars focus on particular institutions of American government, including the Constitution and the presidency. Representative examples of this can be seen in Richard Pierard and Robert Linder's book *Civil Religion and the Presidency*[9] and Sanford Levinson's *Constitutional Faith*.[10] These are detailed studies of particular institutions as they are altered by civil religious phenomena, but they do not consider the broader political and theological causes, motivations, and uses of civil religion.

There are also a number of illuminating studies of civil religion through particular figures in the history of political philosophy. Some good examples of such work include Michael Zuckert's essay on "Locke and the Prob-

the American Experience (Tuscaloosa: University of Alabama Press, 2001); Civil Religion, Church, and State (Munich, Germany: K. G. Saur, 1992); Marty and Moore, Politics, Religion, and the Common Good: Advancing a Distinctly American Conversation about Religion's Role in Our Shared Life (San Francisco: Jossey-Bass, 2000); Religion and Republic: The American Circumstance (Boston, Mass.: Beacon Press, 1987).

7. "Two Kinds of Two Kinds of Civil Religions" in American Civil Religion, ed. Russell E. Richey (New York: Harper & Rowe, 1974), 139–160.

8. Jürgen Gebhardt, Americanism: Revolutionary Order and Societal Self-Interpretation in the American Republic, trans. Ruth Hein (Baton Rouge: Louisiana State University Press, 1991); Ellis Sandoz, A Government of Laws: Political Theory, Religion, and the American Founding (Columbia: University of Missouri Press, 2002); Sandoz, Republicanism, Religion, and the Soul of America (Columbia: University of Missouri Press, 2006).

9. Robert D. Linder and Richard V. Pierard, Civil Religion and the Presidency (Grand Rapids: Zondervan, 1988).

10. Sanford Levinson, Constitutional Faith (Princeton: Princeton University Press, 1989).

lem of Civil Religion," Sanford Kessler's book *Tocqueville's Civil Religion: American Christianity and the Prospects for Freedom,* or Ronald Beiner's essay "Machiavelli, Hobbes and Rousseau on Civil Religion."[11] Recently, the most sustained philosophical effort to understand civil religion is that of Eric Voegelin, whose works, including *Political Religions, New Science of Politics,* the eight-volume *History of Political Ideas,* and the five-volume *Order and History,* examined the various ways societies in human history have symbolized themselves as reflections of divine and cosmic order.[12] Voegelin developed a historically informed philosophical anthropology and general theory of political society, whereas the essays in this volume more narrowly consider civil religion as a separate concept whose connections with other strata of political reality can only be implied.

This volume aims to draw from the theoretical resources of figures like these and in the spirit of this scholarship. But this volume draws from a wider range of figures, spanning ancient, medieval, and modern periods. Moreover, this volume makes the case that drawing from such divergent traditions of thought on civil religion reinforces its status as a permanent problem and so offers a better framework for understanding its manifestations, especially across new settings and contexts.

While civil religion is usually associated with societies that precede Enlightenment rationalism, the essays in this volume demonstrate its enduring appeal in contemporary times. The problem of civil religion confronts three interlocking trends in contemporary society: secularization, multiculturalism, and religious toleration. Civil religion, in most of its forms, aims to cultivate a more unified social bond. But this aim is complicated by some of the dilemmas of modernity. The advances of highly technological and politically progressive commercial societies bring about a society that is allegedly more rational and secular, and therefore seemingly no longer in need of religion to bind it together. Yet, secularization inspires a countermovement to preserve the identities and traditions of particular groups,

---

11. Michael Zuckert, "Locke and the Problem of Civil Religion," in *The Moral Foundations of the American Principle,* ed. Robert Horowitz (Charlottesville: University Press of Virginia, 1979); Sanford Kessler, *Tocqueville's Civil Religion: American Christianity and the Prospects for Freedom* (Albany: State University of New York Press, 1994); Ronald Beiner, "Machiavelli, Hobbes, and Rousseau on Civil Religion," *Review of Politics* 55 (1993): 617–638.

12. Eric Voegelin, *The Political Religions; The New Science of Politics; and Science, Politics, and Gnosticism, in Modernity Without Restraint, Collected Works of Eric Voegelin,* vol. 5, ed. Manfred Henningsen (Columbia: University of Missouri Press, 2000); *History of Political Ideas, Collected Works,* vols. 19–26; *Order and History, Collected Works,* vols. 14–18.

often religiously based, and multiculturalism and religious toleration are the political strategies used to achieve this end. In this sense, the promise of mass rationality becomes more questionable as quests for more basic and immediate bonds of particularity intensify. Moreover, the promise of mass rationality is itself an act of faith because it has roots in Enlightenment hopes in unlimited progress and an "end of history."

The failure of secular society, with mass rationality, to satisfy fully its citizens' desire for meaningful community produces a crisis in citizenship. Citizens find meaningful community in their particular religious and ethnic communities, but not necessarily in their political community except insofar as it serves the utilitarian purpose of leaving their particular community alone. The failure of secular society to integrate fully the human personality into a schema of citizenship produces a crisis of citizenship, that in turn produces a crisis of political unity. Secular society has difficulty expressing political unity in terms other than utility, which inspires attempts to articulate political unity in nonutilitarian terms. Civil religion is a major example of such an attempt and explains why in modernity, it is frequently evoked by critics of utilitarian political ethics (i.e., Jean-Jacques Rousseau, and, somewhat ironically, John Stuart Mill). The essays in this volume consider whether contemporary expressions of civil religion are simply attempts by particular religious or ethnic communities to project their values onto the whole of society, whether secular societies must appeal to "premodern" symbols and values to produce civil religion, or whether secular societies are capable of generating their own symbols and values for civil religion. The scope and magnitude of secularization in the West has compounded a need for the divine and has fueled manifestations of civil religion in these new forms, especially as its older forms lose currency and viability in the culture.[13]

The first set of essays in the volume draw from the works of great figures in the history of political philosophy. Each essay considers the problem of civil religion and why that figure considers it to be such a permanent prob-

13. See Peter L. Berger, *The Desecularization of the World: Resurgent Religion and World Politics* (Grand Rapids, MI: Eerdmans, 1999); Peter Emberley, *Divine Hunger: Canadians on Spiritual Walkabout* (Toronto: HarperCollins Canada, 2002); Joshua Mitchell, "The Trajectories of Religious Renewal in America: Tocquevillean Thoughts," in *One Nation Under God?*, ed. R. Bruce Douglass and Joshua Mitchell (Lanham, MD: Rowman and Littlefield, 2000); Pippa Norris and Ronald Inglehart, *Sacred and Secular: Religion and Politics Worldwide* (Cambridge: Cambridge University Press, 2004); John von Heyking, "Secularization: Not Dead Yet, But Never What it Seemed," *International Studies Review* 7 (2005): 279–84.

lem. These essays explore how the need for the divine becomes manifest in civil religious forms and seem to be an intractable condition of political life. According to both interpretations of civil religion, there are theological and political motivations for civil religion. The first set of essays illuminates those bases for civil religion.

In V. Bradley Lewis's essay "Gods for the City and Beyond: Civil Religion in Plato's *Laws*," he raises the problem of civil religion by first challenging what may be our modern, North American assumptions about civil religion. By taking seriously Plato's *Laws* and its classical Greek context we are also better able to understand both a premodern rationale for civil religion and the more modern motivation of separating the religious and political spheres. The ancient city was sacred space and recognized little distinction between religion and civil religion. Plato depicts the Magnesian city in his *Laws* as a realistic city—one that seems a world away from the beautiful city in speech of the *Republic*. Yet, Plato accepts and works from the inextricably civil religious context of the historical polis. Accordingly, he elaborates the sacred parts of the city, the organization of celebrations and sacrifices, the arrangement of temples, the purposes of priesthoods and other religious functions. In contrast, the Athenian stranger goes beyond this, discussing the content of the beliefs that citizens should profess (or at least not deny publicly). Along these lines, Plato has the Athenian stranger introduce more substantive philosophical questions concerning the nature of the city and soul and so anticipates the introduction of the city of philosophy. The civil religion of the *Laws,* therefore, aims to do what conventional civil religion may achieve in terms of civic unity and virtue. But this civil religion also aims beyond itself to a separate and more transcendent dimension of religion.

While Plato's treatment of civil religion presents both a rationale for the usefulness of civil religion and its philosophical and religious limitations, St. Augustine offers a Christian critique of civil religion that becomes one of the most decisive and influential critiques of civil religion. It therefore offers a motivation for the separation of church and state that some modern philosophers and theologians appeal to, albeit for more distinctively modern reasons. In Matthias Riedl's essay "Truth versus Utility: The Debate on Civil Religion in the Roman Empire of the Third and Fourth Centuries" he provides some background to the debates on civil religion that preceded and anticipated Augustine's critique. A primary term in these disputes that certain Latin apologists highlighted was *vera religio* (true religion). Roman writers such as Cicero, Varro, Seneca, and Livy treated civil religion chiefly as a function of political utility. But Christian writers saw in the practice of civil religion an overriding theological compromise and so offered considerable objections to the alleged necessity of Roman civil religion. At the same time, they found it important to reply to objections that the new Christian religion would undermine the unity of Roman society and the piety of its citizens. His essay surveys thinkers frequently overlooked by scholars, including Minucius Felix, Tertullian, Arnobius, Lactantius, and Ambrose of Milan, as well as late ancient proponents of the pagan cult such as Symmachus. He elucidates both their arguments and the historical situation that gave rise to their arguments. He pays special attention to the shift from the third-century Christian emphasis upon the truth of the Gospel and the virtue of Christian citizens to a post-Constantinian emphasis upon Christianity as an essential alternative to the pagan cult and its foundation for civic virtue and political order.

Once this context for Augustine's thought on civil religion has been prepared in terms of the background both preceding it and following it, the volume directly turns to his critique of civil religion. David Bobb's essay "The Humility of True Religion: Augustine's Critique of Roman Civil Religion," offers a treatment of books 1–4 of the *City of God,* considering his claim that the Roman civil religion was both false and ineffective in its political aims. The essay also surveys Augustine's response to the objection that Christianity enfeebles political rule and fuels political disunity. Bobb argues that the success of Augustine's response turns on the quality of his critique of civil religion. Moreover, this critique depends on Augustine's argument for the central dependence of true virtue upon true religion. Bobb maintains that Augustine's emphasis on the "mirror of princes," though often criticized, conveys a substantial political dimension in Augustine's thought that thereby enhances his critique of civil religion.

In the modern period, the problematic disjunction between truth and utility in civil religion, recognized by Augustine, takes on different forms. In this period, the problem of civil religion is not so much the specter of an explicit paganism that risks absorbing Christian allegiances into civil religious alliances. Rather, the problem of civil religion is manifested as a political response to the specter of religiously inspired conflict and disorder. One option that emerges is to reduce this disorder by strongly separating religion from public life. Another response to that problem is not so much to separate religion from public life, but rather to minimize the potentially divisive impacts of religion on public life by diluting or dividing religion. On the other hand, the presence of religion in public life, however mitigated it may be, retains a potential for a related extreme—religious citizens may use their influence to augment or expand the influence of their religious traditions by political means. To the extent that religion is impossible to separate fully from public life, the latter options become more plausible manifestations of civil religion. So, either religion tends to become weakened, compromised, and, consequently, co-opted for political reasons as a more politically salutary force or it maintains its strength and integrity. But if religion maintains its integrity and is allied with power, it may expand the scope of its religious power and objectives through political means. Religion may drive politics or become a tool of politics.

Many of the early modern thinkers treated in this volume aim to present religion on terms that make it more palatable to scientific progress, tolerant, and a source of political unity rather than a source of division. Travis Smith's contribution, "Forgiving Those Not Trespassing against Us: Hobbes and the Establishment of the Nonsectarian State Church," traces Thomas Hobbes's usage of religious ideas in his political thought, drawing attention to his intentional secularization of key Christian concepts for the purpose of persuading the faithful to be peaceable. Smith counters the tendency to interpret Hobbes's teaching on civil religion as somewhat authoritarian, by illuminating a somewhat easygoing or democratic form of spirituality as the basis of civil religion. Civil religion serves Hobbes's modern view that freedom is the core of human psychology, and so civil religion, which must be cultivated through indirect methods, serves as a way of promoting Hobbes's natural law teaching. Paradoxically, Hobbes wishes to depoliticize religion (i.e., remove legitimacy of ecclesiastical interference) by completely politicizing it by transforming Christian doctrine of forgiveness into a watered-down teaching on justice where people are indifferent toward one another. Hobbes's deepened politicization of religion would make public religious appeals not only illegitimate, but also strange to the ears insofar as Hobbes's teaching is meant to educate people into regarding uniquely prophetic voices as illegitimate as well as unintelligible. Like George Orwell, Smith explains why wishing someone Merry Christmas in a Hobbesian society provokes controversy. While Hobbes crafts a civil religion to fit with modern science, he differs from later secularization theorists such as Auguste Comte or Sigmund Freud by casting doubt that religion can be removed from the heart of man. Religion is part of human nature, and people would resist attempts to compel belief in secularization as much as they should resist attempts to compel religious belief.

David Innes, in his essay, "Civil Religion as Political Technology in Bacon's *New Atlantis*," offers a discussion of the civil religion present in Francis Bacon's *New Atlantis:* a pious, patriotic civilization of questionable orthodoxy modeled on the New Jerusalem of Christianity. Innes points out that on first impression, one might think that Bacon's purpose in writing the *New Atlantis* was to show an idealized community in which the new science was wholly compatible with the reigning established religion of his day, Anglicanism. Stripping away the layers of belief and disbelief, Innes calls this impression into question, arguing instead that Bacon's community is not founded on an idealized Anglicanism, but rather on a civil religion. As Innes points out, this civil religion manifests Bacon's understanding that religion is, itself, a feature of human life, and that this feature must be recognized and commanded in a scientific civilization.

In Ronald Weed's essay "Jean-Jacques Rousseau on Civil Religion: Freedom of the Individual, Toleration, and the Price of Mass Authenticity," he reflects on Rousseau's claim that the presence of revealed religion in society tends to foster conflict whether through intolerance or disunity. Rousseau thought that the public presence of religion induced a kind of spiritual competition between it and the state, culminating in either a state-controlled civil religion or the domination of political life by revealed religion. Rousseau entertained the following alternatives as a solution: a strong separation of a publicly expressed church from the state or a more private and interiorized transformation of the church. According to Rousseau either of these solutions would only generate greater social disunity. So, for him the unity of civil society was so important that he considered it better to seek social unity precisely by drawing from the spiritual force of a publicly expressed religion rather than separating it or privatizing it. He thought that some form of a civil religion would promote the unity that he thought was so urgent for society.

While Rousseau is also well known for his very positive treatments of religious individualism and authenticity such as in his *Reveries of the Solitary Walker* and his masterpiece *Emile*, it is unclear that he saw them as models that were good for society. Rather, he thought mass authenticity, especially in its religious forms, would increase intolerance and conflict more than it would minimize it. Weed argues that Rousseau's model of religious authenticity does not reduce the conditions for conflict between religion and public life, but rather heightens the competition between them. The modification of the public features of religion into a more politically diffuse and interiorized religion is no less public and no less intolerant. Moreover, the model of romantic religion described by Rousseau is a greater instrument of intolerance and conflict precisely because of its more interior and private status. In this form, it supplies more dynamic opportunities for passive intolerance and prejudice.

In the remaining essays, we turn to the North American context of civil religion. Doug Kries, in "Alexis de Tocqueville on 'Civil Religion' and the Catholic Faith," considers the role that equality and its wider democratic ethos may play in the emergence of civil religion. In this essay, Kries discusses Tocqueville's account of civil religion in America and his treatment of the possible tensions between Catholicism and democracy as a case study of the former. The essay initially considers Tocqueville's views on the problem of civil religion generally. Although Tocqueville seems to think that religion is in some sense natural to humanity, he also thinks that religious expression differs from regime to regime. He implies that civil religion is a fundamental problem for politics. But since Tocqueville is most concerned with the problems in democratic regimes, the essay turns to civil religion as a problem in democracy. One way that Tocqueville considers this problem is through his treatment of the relationship between Catholicism and democracy. Although these two are usually placed in juxtaposition, Tocqueville argues that there is a fundamental affinity between the two. This section discusses how this affinity makes Catholicism a suitable civil religion for democrats and the considerable dangers in such a union. Examples of the latter can be seen through the enmity between Catholicism and democracy in France during Tocqueville's time. The essay then turns to how Catholicism may serve as a civil religion in the U.S. In Tocqueville's view, Catholicism is able to work as a civil religion in America because of specifically American developments. The conclusion discusses how recent developments in the United States on the problem of religion imply that the United States is heading for the "French arrangement" that Tocqueville lamented, rather than the solution that Tocqueville advocated.

The theoretical difficulty of a strong separation of religion from public life is implicit in a number of the figures examined in the first half of the volume, and is taken seriously even by those who aim for that strong separation. Jeff Sikkenga illuminates this difficulty in the American context. In his essay, "Rational Theology: Thomas Jefferson and the Foundation of America's Civil Religion" he elucidates some of the theological and anthropological dimensions of the religious establishment debate in Virginia.

The history of the United States demonstrates that religious liberty was not always of central importance to Americans. Successive communities supported established churches, and individual citizens held the belief that it was the responsibility of the state to limit religion. Against this backdrop, the writings of Thomas Jefferson on his opposition to the establishment of Anglicanism in Virginia become all the more striking. In the Virginia Statute of Religious Freedom, Jefferson articulates the view that the separation of church and state assumes a particular theological position. His opponents agreed, arguing that the question of disestablishment was itself a theological debate engaging two radically different understandings of human nature and the relation between human beings and God. In this chapter, Sikkenga outlines Jefferson's own view of religious liberty as well as the view of his detractors, with special attention to the theologico-political underpinnings of those views. In so doing, Sikkenga draws attention to an often overlooked aspect of the founding of American civil religion.

The next essay reconsiders the more recent American context for civil religion. Tom Powers examines the current state of the First Amendment and its status as an allegedly secular precept of American political life. In his essay, the "Unsettling Faith: The Radicalization of the First Amendment and Its Consequences" he maintains the First Amendment shapes the place of religion in America, but it is also an apparently sacred principle of a liberal political order. Powers raises the question of whether, in an era of postmodernism, we can comfortably aspire to an ideal of religious liberty and the separation of church and state that amounts to little more than an article of "constitutional faith," as Sanford Levinson has characterized it. According to Powers, the fact that the rational basis for this ideal—an ideal that was originally conceived by the leading modern rationalists—is now very much in question suggests that such a political faith is at very least quite paradoxical. This broader problem is framed against a backdrop of apparent doctrinal chaos in the First Amendment jurisprudence of the U.S. Supreme Court that has cultivated an ethos of critique among scholars and jurists alike. Powers concludes that while the critics of the First Amendment do identify valid causes for concern, they nevertheless overstate the difficulties we face and neglect important evidence that suggests the vitality of the liberal political order.

Joseph Knippenberg turns his attention to the person and presidency of George W. Bush in his essay "The Personal Is (Not?) the Political: George W. Bush's Vocation and America's." Confronting both the proponents and the critics of Bush, Knippenberg argues that it is overly simplistic to reduce the Bush presidency to an outgrowth of evangelicalism. With special attention to both biographical and critical sources, Knippenberg identifies and discusses key aspects of Bush's sense of calling and responsibility. He then considers how Bush's religious worldview—which highlights God's sovereignty, human finitude, and human fallibility—informs his understanding of America's place in history and the world. Knippenberg contends that there is always some danger of overreaching pride and idolatry that is associated with any purely civil religion. Nevertheless, Bush's own sense of God's sovereignty actually works against this tendency, thereby moving him and the nation toward a greater humility.

Preston Jones shifts the focus of the volume from European or American versions of civil religion to focus on Canadian society.[14] By considering Canada, his essay and the final one, by John von Heyking, illuminate an alternative path for civil religion within the context of Anglo-American constitutionalism. In his essay, "Sacred Words, Fighting Words: The Bible and National Meaning in Canada, 1860–1900," Jones turns his attention to both French- and English-speaking Christians in the late nineteenth-century. He argues that these Canadians frequently used Scripture as a political tool, and occasionally as a political weapon. With special attention to both French and English public figures, Jones argues that the scriptural language used by these figures was used primarily to further secular power and prestige, rather than to further a particularly theological agenda, and to enhance Anglo dominance over the western part of the country.

Despite frequent observations that Canada is more secular and progres-

14. This volume limits itself to the Anglo-American tradition of civil religion on the North American continent. While it would be worthwhile to include coverage of civil religion in the Mexican context, it would be difficult to capture the full complexity of North American civil religion within the confines of a whole volume let alone the second half of this volume.

sive than the United States (thereby making it more "European"), John von Heyking, in his essay, "Civil Religion and Associational Life under Canada's 'Ephemeral Monster': Canada's Multi-Headed Constitution," finds that the 1982 Canadian Charter of Rights and Freedoms has created a characteristically "postmodern" democratic faith and civil religion among segments of the population. Heyking considers how numerous Canadian commentators, jurists, legal scholars, and politicians view the Charter as marking the inauguration of a new era in Canadian history, and view the Charter and the Supreme Court as an instrument to bring about a progressive civilization where Canadian identity, which has long been difficult to determine, gets identified as the new "secular religion" of human rights. Heyking argues this democratic faith is characteristic of the Enlightenment faith in progress, and draws upon Tocqueville's critique of the democratic egalitarianism and statism to analyze key court cases and evocations of national symbols.

One

The Legacy of Civil Religion in the History of Political Philosophy

Gods for the City and Beyond

Civil Religion in Plato's *Laws*

V. BRADLEY LEWIS

Plato's teaching on civil religion in the *Laws* reflects the complexity of that dialogue's more general themes and, indeed, those of Plato's political philosophy as a whole. The foremost of those themes is the possibility of a politics consistent with the highest human potential. This theme is most present in those dialogues concerning the trial and death of Socrates and in the *Republic*. There it is pursued largely from the Socratic perspective and plainly asks whether and how the philosopher can pursue his way of life, which aims to understand "all time and all being," within the city, which, even in the practically impossible ideal considered there, is necessarily limited.[1] The *Laws* starts from a considerably more obviously political perspective. It takes that perspective more seriously than any other Platonic dialogue, and it is perhaps for that reason that Socrates is absent from it. The *Republic* takes as its theme the life of philosophy; it is preeminently about the soul and, as Leo Strauss has remarked, largely abstracts from the body.[2] The *Laws* reintroduces the body: it envisions a city governed not by wisdom in the form of philosophers who neither have families nor own property, but by laws administered by men who are also the heads of families and thus the owners of property.[3] Such a city is said to be second-best

1. *Republic* 486a. The limitations I have in mind are spatial and temporal, indicated by the acknowledgement that Kallipolis too will have to fight wars (373d–e) to protect a specific piece of territory endowed with a significance grounded in a patently untrue myth (414b–e).

2. *The City and Man* (Chicago: Rand McNally, 1964), 109.

3. *Laws* 739a–e. Hereafter, I will cite the text of the *Laws* parenthetically by Stephanus page and, where precision is wanted, also line numbers. I have used the text of Édouard des Places, S.J., and Auguste Diès in *Platon: Oeuvres Complètes*, 4th ed., vols. 11–12 (Paris: Les Belles Lettres, 1992; the current text of books 11–12, in vol. 12, part 2, is only in a 2nd edition of 1976). Translations are

(*deuterōs*, 739a4, 807b6–7). This second-best, compromised, bodily city is also a religious city.[4] The religion is a civil religion because it is so closely bound to the particular goods, practices, and institutions of the Magnesian city and includes conventional religious elements as well as a civil theology that deploys philosophical arguments.[5] The civil theology is important in that it both supports the conventional practices and thus the order of the city, but also points beyond the second-best. The dual character of religion articulates Plato's teaching about the limits of reason in human affairs. The civil religion of the laws exposes the extent to which the city cannot be all soul and all intellect. At the same time, the civil religion indicates ways in which the city's limits can be transcended by the human beings who inhabit it and opens onto speculative philosophical theology. The gods of the city are for the city, but they point beyond themselves.

In what follows, I examine the civil religion as it unfolds in the dialogue: first, its role in the critical theoretical introduction that is the dialogue's first three books, then according to its articulation in three stages as (1) the conventional practical sense of festivals, sacrifices, priesthoods, and related institutions meant to support the unity of the city and the authority of its laws; (2) the more symbolic sense that I will call its "cosmic representational" aspect; and (3) its transition to civil and then philosophical theology. These three stages or facets of the civil religion of the *Laws* are related to one another and illustrate the great project of a city and regime that could succeed as a city and also be consistent with and open to the highest human possibilities. The religion of the Magnesian city points in both directions. While a number of commentators have seen the civil religion of

those of *The Laws of Plato,* translated, with notes and an interpretive essay by Thomas L. Pangle (New York: Basic Books, 1980), with some modifications.

4. The philosophical city of the *Republic* is not wholly without a religious aspect; however, religion there is largely confined to the content of stories about the gods used in the education of the warrior class. Such stories are said to be false (376e–377a) and seem designed largely to support the patriotism and self-restraint of the soldiers; indeed much of the discussion is negative, that is, it concerns things in conventional poetry and mythology that should be eliminated (377e; cf. 378c, 380bc). One might say, adopting Augustine's Varronian division of theology between the poetic, civic, and philosophical (*On the City of God,* 6.6; 8.5), that the *Republic* concerns itself primarily with the rejection of the poetic theology, but only gestures at the civil and philosophical, the relationship between which is a central concern of the *Laws.*

5. The city proposed in the *Laws* is referred to as the Magnesian city or the city of the Magnesians, although the source of the name is never explicitly stated. See 848d, 860e, 919d, 946b, 969a; cf. 704a. Glenn R. Morrow, *Plato's Cretan City: A Historical Interpretation of the "Laws"* (Princeton, N.J.: Princeton University Press, 1960), 30–31, suggests that Plato may have had in mind that the location of the new city would be that of a much older now-abandoned city called Magnesia.

the *Laws* as emblematic of a Platonic betrayal of Socrates, I think a careful examination of its elements reveals it to be an attempt to manage or mitigate the tensions between philosophy and the city, to honor both Socrates and the city as much as possible.

The *Laws* is divided into roughly four unequal parts. The first three books constitute a critical-theoretical introduction to the problem of legislation: what legislation is and on what basis it should be undertaken. At its conclusion Kleinias, a Cretan, reveals that he has been charged with leading a commission established by his native Knossos and drafting legislation for a prospective colony. He asks his interlocutors, Megillos, a Spartan, and a nameless Athenian "stranger," to help him do this as a kind of test of the theoretical principles articulated in their initial discussion. Books 4 through 7 constitute the basic constructive discussion in which the particulars of the settlement project are discussed and a basic set of laws and institutions is proposed. Where the theoretical principles governing the goals of the regime, its form as a regime, and the education it will promote are discussed abstractly in the first three books, those themes are taken up again constructively in books 5, 6, and 7, with book 4 providing initial information about the proposed settlement. Books 8, 9, and 10 treat sources of resistance to law grounded in the human soul as divided into parts: *eros, thumos,* and *logos* (desire, spiritedness, and reason), and the law's response to those psychic challenges. This reflects without precisely repeating the so-called tripartite psychology of the *Republic.* Finally, book 12 constitutes a conclusion that returns to the basic Platonic question of the compatibility of the city with the highest human possibility, philosophy, through the Athenian stranger's proposal of that novel institution, the nightly meeting (*nukterinos sullogos*).[6]

Before discussion of the dialogue, a historical note is in order. Many scholars have noted both the more realistic political character of the *Laws* relative to the *Republic* and its heavier emphasis on religion.[7] This confluence of political realism and religious detail makes perfect historical sense, for the Greek *polis* rested on sacred ground. Indeed, to speak of *civil* religion in the historical context of the Greek *polis* is to commit a redundancy: there was no other kind. Religion was necessarily civil and the city was necessarily religious. The modern distinction between a political and a religious sphere was unknown to the classical Greeks. With its sacred groves, temples, calendar of obligatory public sacrifices and festivals, and its roster of public officials who often acted as priests, the *polis* was an essentially and pervasively religious community just as it was a political community, and these two aspects interpenetrated one another at almost every point. Christianne Sourvinou-Inwood has written that the "Greek *polis* articulated religion and was itself articulated by it; religion became the *polis'* central ideology, structuring, and giving meaning to, all the elements that made up the identity of the *polis,* its past, its physical landscape, the relationship between its constitutive parts."[8]

The City, Laws, and Gods

Eric Voegelin characterized the *Laws* as a "religious poem,"[9] and, in one sense at any rate, the description is apt: the action of the dialogue is liter-

---

most distinguished students of classical Greek religion, writes of the *Laws* that it "presents a state in which the realities of the Greek polis come much more to the foreground than in the earlier, utopian project of the *Republic.* Though only second best in the eyes of the philosopher, the state of the *Laws* is filled to the brim with the manifold reality of what actually existed; it is the most comprehensive literary account of the Greek polis we have, including its religion." *Greek Religion,* trans. John Raffan (Cambridge, Mass.: Harvard University Press, 1985), 333. On the specifically religious character of the *Laws* see also, e.g., Friedrich Somsen, *Plato's Theology* (Ithaca, NY: Cornell University Press, 1942), 132; Thomas L. Pangle, "The Political Psychology of Religion in Plato's *Laws,*" *American Political Science Review* 70, no. 4 (1976): 1059; R. F. Stalley, *An Introduction to Plato's "Laws"* (Oxford: Blackwell, 1983), 166; George Klosko, *The Development of Plato's Political Theory* (London: Methuen, 1986), 231; Harvey Yunis, *A New Creed: Fundamental Religious Beliefs in the Athenian Polis and Euripidean Drama,* Hypomnemata 91 (Göttingen: Vandenhoeck and Ruprecht, 1988), 29–30; Andrea Nightingale, "Writing/Reading a Sacred Text: A Literary Interpretation of Plato's *Laws,*" *Classical Philology* 88, no. 4 (1993): 279–300; Malcolm Schofield, "Religion and Philosophy in the *Laws,*" in *Plato's "Laws": From Theory into Practice, Proceedings of the VI Symposium Platonicum, Selected Papers,* ed. Samuel Scolnicov and Luc Brisson, 1–13 (Sankt Augustin: Academia Verlag, 2003).

8. "What Is *Polis* Religion?," in *The Greek City from Homer to Alexander,* ed. Oswyn Murray and Simon Price (Oxford: Clarendon Press, 1990), 295–322, 304–5. Sourvinou-Inwood's whole article is very helpful, as is her "Further Aspects of *Polis* Religion," *Annali, Instituto orientale di Napoli: Archeologia e storia antica* 10 (1988): 259–74; and François de Polignac, *Cults, Territory, and the Origins of the Greek City State,* trans. Janet Lloyd (Chicago: University of Chicago Press, 1995).

9. See above, note 7.

ally a kind of religious pilgrimage. The three interlocutors meet on the road from Knossos to the cave and temple of Zeus on Mt. Ida in Krete (625b).[10] The very first word of the *Laws* is "god." The Athenian stranger asks his two companions who is credited with the laying down of the Kretan laws, "god or some human being?" The Athenian notes that Zeus is given credit for the Kretan legislation in the Homeric myth according to which Minos, his son, was instructed by him (624a–625a).[11] This points back to another Platonic dialogue, the *Minos.*

There the Kretan laws are said to be the best because they are the oldest, and their ancient provenance is related to their origin in Zeus. The *Minos* illuminates the opening of the *Laws* in other ways.[12] The *Minos,* often treated as an introduction to the *Laws,* is centrally concerned with the question, "What is law?" But it concludes with a discussion of Minos as legendary origin of the Kretan laws. This seems strange, since Minos was an ancient enemy of the Athenians, who demanded annual human sacrifices. Socrates argues that this is a myth from Attic tragedy[13] and that the Homeric epic tradition paints a very different portrait. There Minos is seen as a son and student of Zeus who legislates in light of divine tutelage.[14] The impasse between these rival accounts can be broken when we consider a third tradition about Minos: that of the historians. They saw Minos primarily as an iron-fisted ruler who brought peace and eventually prosperity and civilization to the Mediterranean basin through his development of a navy and war against pirates.[15]

The initial claim of both the Kretan and the Spartan is that their regimes were granted divine legislation; however, the Athenian soon induces them to admit that their more detailed understanding of their laws is, at best, faulty. They hold that Minos legislated with one overwhelming end in mind: victory in war (625e–626b). The Athenian holds that Minos was correct to have legislated in an orderly and purposeful way, contrasting this to the disorderly practice of other cities (630e–631a, 635e), but argues

10. For the probable location of the cave and temple of Zeus see Glenn R. Morrow, *Plato's Cretan City,* 27–28.

11. *Odyssey,* 9.178–79.

12. I have discussed the *Minos* in much greater detail in "Plato's *Minos:* The Political and Philosophical Context of the Problem of Natural Right," *Review of Metaphysics* 60 (2006): 17–54.

13. Euripides's lost play, *Kretans,* seems to have said this.

14. *Iliad* 13.449, 14.321; *Odyssey* 11.568, 19.178–79.

15. Thucydides 1.4, 8; Diodorus of Sicily 4.60–61, 5.78; Strabo 10.4.8–9, 5.19.

against victory in war as the proper end. He induces the two Dorians to engage with him in a fresh inquiry into the nature and purpose of legislation "according to nature" (*phusei*, 627d; cf. 966b). In other words, a good legal code is one that aims at the right goal and proceeds in the right order toward that goal, and both the goal and the order are true according to nature.

Given the importance of the goal of laws it is remarkable that the Athenian seems intentionally to fudge that goal, which he says in some places is simply virtue (705e–706a, 770c–e, 771a, 836d, 853b, 963a) or the "whole of virtue" (630c, e, 632e, 688a–b), but at other times friendship (627e, 628b, 640c–d, 627a, 698c, 743c) or peace (628c). The goal is later characterized as a compound of "freedom, prudence and friendship" (693b, c, e, 694b, 701d). This last seems most revealing: friendship describes the unity of the city, and unity is a political goal of the highest order since its opposite, faction (*stasis*), is often described as the greatest misfortune that can befall a city (628b, 629d, 744d, 856b, 945e). Freedom here indicates both the freedom of the city from domination by others and the freedom of citizens within the city, but a freedom that must also be balanced by authority (693d–e, 697c–d, 701e), the source of which is indicated by the third goal, prudence or intelligence (689b, 690b–c).

On closer inspection, then, what may seem to be fudging is something more. The different goals suggested for the city and its laws are all necessary, but also in tension with one another. The most adequate legislation for a city is one that navigates and manages these tensions with an awareness that the simply highest goal may need to be diluted or alloyed by naturally lower goods.[16] We can see this most plainly by considering one important episode in the first book. The Athenian stranger begins his inquiry by asking his interlocutors about the aim of some of their institutions, which elicits from Kleinias the thesis that success in war is the highest aim of legislation. The Athenian dialectically challenges that view by getting the Kretan to admit that the source of strife between cities is rooted in the source of strife between neighborhoods, households, and individuals, and ultimately within individuals. To use the celebrated formulation of Solzhenitsyn, the line between good and evil runs through the heart of every human being.[17]

---

16. Cf. Strauss, *The Argument and the Action of Plato's "Laws,"* 9.

17. Alexandr Solzhenitsyn, "Repentance and Self-Limitation in the Life of Nations," in *From*

Real victory, then, is victory of the better over the worse parts of oneself (626e). With Kleinias's approval of this counter-thesis (perhaps because it remains at the problematic level of simple victories and defeats: consider 627b, 638a–b, 641c), the Athenian returns to the question of the city itself (avoiding the issue of relations between cities) and suggests that in any city it would be common for the unjust and bad to outnumber the just and good citizens. As an analogy the Athenian suggests the case of a family and the corresponding thesis that the unjust brothers would likely outnumber the just. Real superiority could not simply be a question of victory, since one would expect the more numerous and therefore stronger to prevail. How could we properly describe such a family and indeed a city as genu- inely "superior to itself"?

It is at this point that the Athenian suggests that the three look to the correctness of laws "according to nature." Who, the Athenian asks, would be the better judge between the brothers: one who destroyed the bad and set the good up to rule themselves; one who allowed all to live, but ar- ranged things so that the good would rule and the bad would willingly be ruled; or one who allowed all to live "reconciling them by laying down laws for them for the rest of time and thus securing their friendship with one another" (627e4–628a3)? Kleinias readily accepts the third option as best. But it is not clear that it is *simply* best. Indeed, the Athenian refers to the third option as "the judge who is third with respect to virtue" (627e3–4). The first option would secure the most undiluted virtue, since only the just would remain, but it would make the city's freedom less secure against ene- mies. The second option would preserve more freedom and ensure the rule of virtue, but by splitting the city into fixed divisions of ruler and ruled it would preclude or severely limit friendship as an end. The third option ac- cepts less operative virtue in the interest of both freedom and friendship by way of the rule of law. The rule of law, then, is a kind of compromise. There are better and worse compromises, however. What sort of compromise is the law code proposed here?

Shortly after this episode, having criticized a number of aspects of the Kretan legislation, the Athenian tells Kleinias what the legislator should have said. The laws should have followed the natural order of goods. The

---

Under the Rubble, edited by Solzhenitsyn and trans. by A. M. Brock, et al. (Boston: Little, Brown, 1975), 108.

good things, he says, are of two kinds: the human and the divine. The human goods are health, beauty, strength, and wealth; the divine goods are prudence, moderation, justice, and courage. "All of these last goods," the Athenian says, "are by nature [*phusei*] placed prior in rank to the first, and this is also the way they should be ordered by the legislator" (631b–d). The divine goods thus are the virtues and the first of them is variously stated as prudence (*phronēsis*, 631c6, 632c5) or intelligence (*nous*, 631b7, d5, 632c6). The human goods look to the divine goods, and the divine goods follow intelligence. So according to the strictly natural order, intelligence or prudence is first.[18] If the whole of virtue were the undiluted end of the regime, intellect would rule unconstrained—and this the Athenian clearly affirms later in the dialogue, in the ninth book:

[N]o law or order is stronger than knowledge, nor is it right for intelligence to be subordinate, or a slave, to anyone, but it should be ruler over everything, if indeed it is true and really free according to nature. But now, in fact, it is so nowhere or in any way, except to a small extent. That is why one must choose what comes second, order and law—which see and look to most things, but are incapable of seeing everything. (875c6–d5)

The rule of law, then, is itself a compromise of sorts, albeit a practically necessary one. In the regime of the *Laws,* however, the spirit of compromise goes even further, since the law is intended to serve as common ground between the naturally better and worse elements of the city. Thus the fudging of ends is a necessary compromise intended to make the city maximally viable, that is free, and this partly because of the civic friendship among its unequal inhabitants, but as open to the leadership of intelligence as possible consistent with the first two ends as embodied in law. Beyond this the city makes possible the cultivation of intelligence for its own sake in ways related to the civil religion, as we shall see below.

The *Laws,* then, represents a far more direct and "realistic" kind of political inquiry than the *Republic* and makes its center of concern law itself, both the act of legislation and the nature of law and the practicalities of the rule of law. It is this last point that returns us directly to the issue of religion. Recall that the dialogue begins with a question about the source of the Kretan laws and the answer that the source is Zeus mediated by

18. I have discussed the Platonic idea of natural right in detail in "'La raison qui entreprend de se faire loi': nature et loi dans *les Lois* de Platon," in *Droit naturel: relancer l'histoire,* ed. and trans. Xavier Dijon (Brussels: Bruylant, 2008), 101–32.

Minos. The source of law is said to be a god mediated by the work of a semi-divine lawgiver. The *Laws* repeats the view that Minos "got together" with his father, Zeus, every nine years and was guided by his oracles in legislating (624b). As noted above, this matter is taken up in more detail in the *Minos*, where Zeus's relationship to Minos is explicitly characterized as educational: Zeus acted as a "sophist" toward Minos, and his royal scepter is said to symbolize education rather than simply power.[19] One can say that where the opening premise of the dialogue is Minos legislating under the guidance of Zeus, the actual unfolding of the dialogue reveals a kind of reflection of the myth: Kleinias (with the help of Megillos) will legislate under the guidance of their philosophical tutor, the Athenian stranger. The dialogue presents to us what the myth does not, that is, the original education, an act of guiding intelligence.

The myth itself, however, is not discarded, or at least not wholly discarded, for the notion of a divine origin of legislation is maintained—indeed, more than maintained: it is made a fundamental premise of the city. Shortly after elaborating the natural order of goods and legislation and thus implicitly criticizing the actual Kretan laws, the Athenian implies a further criticism of an actual Kretan practice and, realizing this, remarks that such criticisms may recur, but that there should be no discomfort with this:

Because, given that what pertains to your laws has been put together in a measured way, one of the finest is the law that does not allow any of the young to inquire which laws are finely made and which are not, but that commands all to say in harmony, with one voice from one mouth, that all the laws are finely made by gods; if someone says otherwise, there is to be paid no heed to him at all. And yet if some old man has been thinking over something in your laws, he is to make such arguments before a magistrate and someone his own age, with no young person present. (634d7–e6)

The passage is extraordinary in that it suggests one of the main themes of the *Laws* in a very compressed space: the city's laws require the strength that comes from belief in a divine origin but, at the same time, must be subject to correction. The solution is that the city as a whole must affirm always that laws are the product of divine craftsmanship and therefore perfect, and the young are never even to criticize them. However, old men are encouraged to think about how they may be improved and to approach

---

19. *Minos* 319c, 320d. For detailed discussion see my "Plato's *Minos*."

magistrates about these matters discreetly and in a way that poses no threat to the laws. This foreshadows the device introduced in the tenth book and explained at greater length in the twelfth whereby such moderate criticism of the regime is to be accomplished, the "nightly meeting" (*nukterinos sullogos*, 908a, 909a, 960b–968e).

The nightly meeting, composed of the chief magistrates of the city, is specifically charged with the consideration of improvements to the laws of the city, but also with meeting foreign visitors and with philosophical inquiry into the nature of the virtues, the existence of the gods, and any other subjects that would bear on the city. It is then a kind of institutionalized forum for wide-ranging philosophical inquiry, but one that operates out of public view.[20] The ordinary people of the city are said repeatedly to believe and to be required to believe that the laws are made by gods (645b–c, 653d, 657a–b, 664b–c, 696b; cf. 762e).

The nightly meeting and the problem it is introduced to address are even more directly foreshadowed by the well-known institution of drinking parties (reformed *symposia*) discussed in the first two books of the *Laws,* and often thought to be a perplexing divagation.[21] The drinking parties have a liturgical context: after introducing them in the first book with resistance from Kleinias and Megillos, the Athenian provides that context in the second book in his first discussion of an institutionalized religious practice. The necessary moral education provided by the city, he says, tends to slacken over time, and so the gods have introduced festivals as times of rest in order to lessen this tension. "They have given as fellow celebrants the Muses, with their leader Apollo, and Dionysus" (653d3–4). The main activity in the festivals is choral performance of sacred music and dance (657a–b), and the citizens are divided into different choruses by age. The oldest men belong to a chorus dedicated to Dionysus, and rather than sing, they talk and drink wine (664d–666c). The purpose of this body, however, goes beyond rest and religious devotion.

The Athenian had earlier stated that the goal of the city's education was to make children feel the same joys and pains as an old man (659d–e)— indeed, the role of the old in the rule of the city is a constant theme. Nevertheless, a characteristic vice of the old is inflexibility in the face of chang-

20. I have discussed the operations of the nightly meeting at length in "The Nocturnal Council and Platonic Political Philosophy."

21. Annie Larivée, "Du vin pour le Collège de veille? Mise en lumière d'un lien occulté entre le Choeur de Dionysos et le *nukterinos sullogos* dans les *Lois* de Platon," *Phronesis* 48 (2003): 29–53.

ing circumstances. This is explicitly recognized by the (elderly!) Athenian, who says that wine is a drug given by Dionysus that "heals the austerity of old age" (666b6).[22] The laws of the city and its other institutions—especially those concerned with education—must have an authority sufficient to ensure their preservation. This authority is a function of age and, related to this, divine sanction and even establishment. The naturally true, the reasonable, is supported by this kind of authority, but the characteristic defect of such authority is inflexibility. Wine is a remedy for the "hardness" (literally "sclerosis," *sklērotēs,* 666c1) of old age. Wine here serves as a kind of metaphor for philosophy, introduced into the city later by way of the nightly meeting.[23]

Thus does the authority of reason have a place from which it can address the authority of age. This is all neatly symbolized by the Dionysian chorus, a liturgical body intended to check the defects of sacred tradition. The nightly meeting is a body of officials that will inquire into the nature of the soul and the gods while also dealing with the threat posed to the city by a rejection of its laws and traditions as a result of the rejection of the gods. This issue is taken up later in this chapter. The next section will look at the constructive aspects of the Magnesian city's religion after the three interlocutors have agreed to translate the theoretical principles of the first three books into practice in the rest of the dialogue.

The Civic Cult of the Magnesians

The regime proposed in the *Laws* aims to establish a second-best city, one characterized by the rule of law intended to promote reconciliation between the different human types who inhabit the city and to protect in it a kind of balance of the goods of freedom, friendship, and prudence. Since the many will have some say (limited, but real and important, as suggested by the principle of mixture) and thus influence in the city,[24] the purely

22. The age of the interlocutors is frequently mentioned: see 625b, 634d, 635a, 658d–e, 685a, 712b, 752a, 769a, 770a, 799d, 821a, e, 892d–e. Thomas Pangle has written that the "drama in the *Laws* is the greatest psychological-political study of old age that has ever been undertaken." *The Laws of Plato,* 393. Cf. Schofield, "Religion and Philosophy in the *Laws*," 4–6.

23. That wine represents philosophy was suggested by Strauss in *The Argument and the Action of Plato's "Laws,"* 21–22, 35–36.

24. Morrow, *Plato's Cretan City,* 229–33, characterizes the regime as "aristocracy with the approval of the people," after the phrase used to describe the ancestral constitution of the Athenians in *Menexenos* 238d.

rational character of the city is diluted, and the rule of law as distinct from unlimited intelligence is strengthened by its rooting in the gods. This idea is reinforced early in the constructive part of the discussion, indeed, in the discussion of the city's constitution or regime (*politeia*) in the forth book.

The Athenian stranger asks Kleinias and Megillos to describe the regimes of their two cities. They fumble around with the usual categories of democracy, oligarchy, aristocracy, monarchy, and tyranny, but are unable to give precise answers. The Athenian replies with a criticism of the whole notion of regimes as conventionally understood: these are really forms of despotism, rule by factions, not real political regimes (712c–713a). The regime should rather be named for "the god who truly rules as despot over those who possess intellect (*nous*)." When asked by Kleinias to name this god, the Athenian tells a myth about the age of Kronos, when human beings were ruled well by daimons appointed by Kronos. "Kronos understood that, as we have explained, human nature is not at all capable of regulating the human things, when it possesses autocratic authority over everything, without becoming swollen with insolence and injustice" (713c4–8). The meaning of the myth is explained by the Athenian thus:

> What this present argument is saying, making use of the truth, is that there can be no rest from evils and toils for those cities in which some mortal rules rather than a god. The argument thinks that we should imitate by every device the way of life that is said to have existed under Kronos; ... we should obey whatever within us partakes of immortality, giving the name law to the distribution ordained by intelligence. (713e3–714a1)

This is the Athenian stranger's basic explanation of the rule of law, a foundational principle of the Magnesian city. Rule by men is to be replaced by rule by god, which means rule by intellect couched as divine law. It is for this reason that the chief magistrates of this city are not called "rulers" (*archontes*), as in most *poleis,* but Guardians of the Laws (*nomophulakes,* 752e).

The civil religion constitutes a public recognition of the status of the law and a practical means for strengthening it. The main aspects of the city are rooted in religious practices and ideas. In the most basic sense, the city is spatially said to be connected to the gods in its plan and construction and even as a kind of reflection of divine intelligence. The regime of the city is also grounded in an imitation of the divine, and the city's officials and public acts are surrounded by religious ceremony. Similarly, the education of the citizens, especially the continuing membership of the citizens in the choruses mentioned above, has powerful religious aspects meant to strengthen their commitment to the regime and laws and to promote the city's basic goals.

One can distinguish three different levels related to the civil religion of the Magnesians. First, there are the common and conventional religious practices similar to those one would find in historical *poleis*.[25] At the opposite pole there is the theology of the tenth book, with its arguments for the existence of the gods and the priority of soul and in its description of the work of the nightly meeting. Between these two, mediating between them, is what I shall call, for lack of a better word, the "cosmic representational" aspect of civil religion. It serves to place the institutions and practices of the city in a larger context of meaning and order that, while not strictly philosophical, is symbolic and points toward the sorts of inquiries undertaken by philosophy, thus linking the ordinary life of the city to the highest human possibility. This cosmic representational aspect is not unique, but the *Laws* seems to be the most developed account of it in the literature of classical political philosophy.[26] After a review of the more conventional aspects of civic piety, an examination of the cosmic representational aspect of the city follows in the next section, and then a discussion of civil theology.

There is a significant dramatic emphasis on the importance of piety early in the discussion: I noted above that the first word of the *Laws* is literally "god" and that the entire inquiry begins as one about the origins of a divine law code. Near the beginning of the actual constructive discussion of legislation in the fourth book—a new beginning of the whole dialogue—just after hearing about the material conditions of the territory to be settled and just prior to a discussion of the regime of the proposed colony, the Athenian utters a prayer, invoking a god and asking him to take part in the discussion of the "ordering of the city and the laws" (712b4–6).[27]

The invocation of the god is appropriate particularly in this city since, as the Athenian says later in the seventh book, "One should live out one's days playing at certain games—sacrificing, singing, and dancing—with the result that one can make the gods propitious to oneself and can defend

25. See above, note 8.

26. The most well-known exposition of this aspect of politics is probably the work of Eric Voegelin, e.g., *The New Science of Politics* (Chicago: University of Chicago Press, 1952), especially chaps. 1–2; and *Order and History*, vol. 1, *Israel and Revelation* (Baton Rouge: Louisiana State University Press, 1956), especially pp. 1–110. See also vol. 3, *Plato and Aristotle*, 250–53.

27. This sentence, like the first sentence of the first book, begins with the word "god" (*theos*).

oneself against enemies and be victorious over them in battle" (803b–c). This indicates a connection between the religion of the city and two of the goals noted above, its freedom and its friendship. Certainly the Athenian clearly emphasizes the role of religious practices in forging friendship and solidarity among the citizens, thus promoting the maximum feasible unity of the city: the festivals provide for interaction between citizens, making them well known to one another, and "there is no greater good for a city than that its inhabitants be well known to one another" (738d–e, see also 759b, 771d, 816d).

The civic importance of festivals and sacrifices is underscored by their number: the Athenian specifies that there will be some important sacrifice performed by some official every day of the year (828b) as well as at least twelve major religious festivals in honor of the gods of each of the city's twelve tribes and including sacrifices, choral performances, and musical and gymnastic contests (828c, cf. 771d). There will also be additional sacrifices determined according to traditional formulae and the Delphic Oracles (738b–c, 759c, 828a, 848d).[28]

In addition to the festivals and sacrifices, other more standard civic functions are freighted with religious ceremony and significance. Especially important here are marriages, elections, and trials. Marriage is always a kind of mediating institution between the individuals, their families, and the larger civic community, and this is emphatically the case among the Magnesians. Marriage is included among the "sacred things" (ta hiera, 771a6) discussed very early in the actual legislation. The prelude to the marriage law enjoins marriage as both a sacred obligation and one crucial to the good of the city (772a6–773c2). Young people are primarily exposed to potential mates at festivals with choral dancing (771e–772c) so that the very origins of their relationship are surrounded with religious activity, and the marriage ceremony itself is a sacrifice (784b). Procreation is regulated in a similar fashion: norms regulating sexual conduct and procreation are evidently communicated by way of the festivals with their edifying choral performances (783a–b), and actual procreation is monitored by a group of women who meet in the temple of Artemis, the traditional goddess of

---

28. The details and mechanics of these typical cult practices are discussed in detail with much comparative information in Olivier Reverdin, *La Religion de la Cité Platonicienne* (Paris: Boccard, 1945), Part 2; Morrow, *Plato's Cretan City,* ch. 8; and Marcel Piérart, *Platon et la Cité grecque: Théorie et realité dans la Constitution des "Lois"* (Bruxelles: Académie Royale de Belgique, 1974), ch. 9.

childbirth (784a–b). Once children are delivered, their names are then recorded in temples (785a).

The election procedures for the city's chief magistrates, the thirty-seven Guardians of the Laws (*nomophulakes*) are described in detail. The election is lengthy, highly consensual, and steeped in religious ritual. Citizens carry tablets with the names of proposed candidates (and that of the person proposing the candidate) to the most honored temple in the city and place them on the altar. For the next month others can remove the names of candidates they think unsuitable. After this the top three hundred names are displayed together to the citizens, and candidates are proposed from these names in the same manner. At the end of this second round, the top one hundred candidates are selected. Finally, citizens are to carry the names of their favored candidates from among this group to the altar, walking between the parts of sacrificed animals, and the top thirty-seven vote-getters are appointed after a scrutiny (753c–d). The Minister of Education, said to be "by far the greatest of the highest offices in the city" (765e2–3), is elected from among the Guardians of the Laws by all the magistrates of the city by secret ballot in the Temple of Apollo (766b).

Judges are elected in a similar fashion. The system of courts in the Magnesian city is somewhat unusual, but fits with one of the chief aims of the city's laws: unity and friendship. Disputes between citizens are first taken to local arbitration boards and reach proper courts (established for each of the city's twelve tribes) only if two initial sets of arbitration boards fail to achieve a settlement (766d–767b, 956b–c). So actual courts with judges are a last resort.[29] The judges for these courts are selected in a meeting held in an unspecified temple of all the officials of the city with terms of office of a year or more. After swearing oaths to the god of the temple they select one judge from each category of official to serve for one year. Other officials are expected to witness the trials and monitor the judicial process (767c–e). Court houses themselves will be built on sacred ground, near the chief temples, and special mention is made of those courts that will hear homicide and other capital cases (778c), and whose judgments in cases of temple

---

29. This arrangement, which in the first instance favors informal settlement, but in the final instance relies on professional judges, is also likely intended to suggest a sharp contrast to the large raucous Athenian popular courts. See, e.g., 876b–e. This process, as initially described, seems to refer to civil courts, but there is a later passage (915c) suggesting that criminal cases will proceed in the same way, and that in these cases the local citizen courts will operate somewhat like a grand jury.

robbery (a capital crime) are deposited in the altar of Hestia and confirmed by a sacred oath among the judges (855c–856a). Those who are summoned to testify in trials must also swear religious oaths (936e–937a, 948b–c), as must judges in all cases (948e).

In considering the officialdom of the city, it remains to discuss the audit (*euthuna*). The audit was an Athenian procedure (common among other cities as well) in which magistrates were examined prior to finishing their terms of office to see that they had committed no official abuses, especially with respect to public funds. The procedure had two stages in the fourth century: a first involving examination of officials' financial records by boards of auditors and public advocates and a second involving a more general examination of their conduct in office carried out by officials called *euthunoi,* who seem to have had fairly broad discretion in conducting investigations and preferring charges.[30] The importance of the office of auditor is indicated by the Athenian stranger's reference to them as "rulers over rulers" (*tōn archontōn archonta,* 945c1) and "superior in virtue" to the magistrates: they are the guardians of the guardians and are said to be responsible for no less than preventing the dissolution of the regime. Their selection takes place at the beginning of winter, when the entire city assembles on ground sacred to the Sun and Apollo to choose three men, who are then to nominate men whom they consider "best in every way." The three "best men" are chosen by a procedure of repeated proposals and examinations and are dedicated to Apollo and the Sun. The procedure is repeated until a total of twelve auditors are chosen, who will then live in the sacred precinct of Apollo and the Sun. In addition to their auditing duties, these officials function as priests of Apollo and the Sun and participate with places of honor at all other important sacrifices and festivals. It is from among these men that the chief official is chosen whose name will mark each year. They also receive preeminent burial honors in the city (945b–948b).[31] These officials, then, are among the most important in the city and are vested with great religious authority and ceremony.

In addition to specific established priesthoods, nearly all of the city's

30. See Marcel Piérart, "Les *euthunoi* athéniens," *Antiquité classique* 40 (1971): 526–73; S. C. Todd, *The Shape of Athenian Law* (Oxford: Clarendon Press, 1993), 112–14.

31. Indeed, the discussion of the burial honors of the auditors is much more extensive than that of comparable posthumous honors for any other official, thus indicating their importance. Reverdin, *La Religion de la Cité Platonicienne,* 151–58, discusses this in detail.

magistrates are assigned priestly functions, and, as noted earlier, there is to be some important sacrifice to be carried out each day, so there are many priestly duties to go around.[32] It remains to discuss briefly one other institutional and legal feature of the civil religion: its relation to criminal law by way of the punishment of impiety.

Impiety (*asebeia*) was an actionable crime in classical cities. It usually included actions thought to violate specific cult practices or to pollute or injure sacred spaces or persons. Temple robbery, oath breaking, and violation of sacred truces or asylum in temples were all typical acts of impiety punishable by law.[33] Specific laws against impiety were certainly on the books in classical Athens, but their content is murky.[34] The *Laws* most likely includes some actual Athenian provisions, although, as Saunders notes, the Athenian is selective and rather cursory in his discussion of these ordinary forms of impiety.[35] The Athenian states, for example, that innovation in the songs and dances performed at religious festivals can be prosecuted as impiety (799b), as can falsifying messages from Magnesia to other cities (an offense against Hermes, 941a). Impiety is mentioned most frequently in connection with murders of a particularly heinous type: those involving relatives. Any kind of killing involves ritual pollution; however, killing family members is the one type for which one can be prosecuted also for impiety (868d–869a). Even the burial of one convicted of such a crime is considered impious (871d). Failure to have children is also considered evidence of impiety (877e).

While contemporary Athenian laws against impiety appear largely to have been directed against specific practices, that is, to the specification of the mechanics of ritual, the Athenian stranger seems more concerned with protecting the sacredness of relationships among persons within the city and making religious practices as public as possible. One can see this in the discussion of public sacrifices and festivals above, as well as in the somewhat unusual ban placed on private shrines (910b–d). The public character of religious practice and its connection to the unity of the city are paramount. A related but special case of impiety concerns the regulation not

---

32. See Morrow, *Plato's Cretan City*, 411–34.

33. Burkert, *Greek Religion*, 274.

34. See Douglas M. MacDowell, *The Law in Classical Athens* (Ithaca, NY: Cornell University Press, 1978), 197–200; S. C. Todd, *The Shape of Athenian Law*, 307–10.

35. Trevor J. Saunders, *Plato's Penal Code: Tradition, Controversy, and Reform in Greek Penology* (Oxford: Clarendon Press, 1991), 303–4.

just of actions, but of words and beliefs. This is discussed in the infamous tenth book of the *Laws* and will be treated later in this chapter.

The City as Image of the Whole

By the "cosmic-representational" aspect of the city I mean the way in which the city itself serves as a kind of image of the cosmos, the order of the whole, for its inhabitants. That the Magnesian city has this aspect is made clear in a number of general programmatic statements by the Athenian stranger, but even more so by his descriptions of the physical layout of the city. In the fourth book, just after having discussed many of the concrete characteristics of the territory and settlers for the new city (and after his mythical justification for the rule of law as the rule of a god), the Athenian suggests an inaugural speech addressed by the lawgivers to the citizens:

Sirs, let us address them, the god, just as the ancient saying has it, holding the beginning and the end and the middle of all the beings, completes his straight course by revolving according to nature (*perainei kata phusin periporeuomenos*). Following him always is justice, avenger of those who forsake the divine law. He who is going to become happy follows Her, in humility and orderliness. But anyone who is puffed up with boastfulness, or who feels exalted because of riches or honors or good bodily form accompanied by youth and mindlessness, anyone whose soul burns with insolence and hence regards himself as needing neither ruler nor any leader but rather considers himself capable of leading others, is left behind, abandoned by the god. (715e7–716b1)

One is enjoined to follow the god (and later to imitate Him, 716c–d; cf. 792d) in the orderliness of one's life. The god follows a regular course and revolves "according to nature." This refers back to the order of goods, stated in the first book, led by prudence (*phronēsis*) and intelligence (*nous*), and prefigures the discussion of the gods in the tenth book. There the Athenian argues for the priority of soul and intellect to matter and identifies the gods with the former. The account is sketchy and repeatedly qualified (e.g., 865a5, 896c6, 896d2–3, 896d8, 897c3–8; and see discussion in the next section), but the intent is clear: to associate the order of the laws with the order of intelligence that informs the whole. When the Athenian suggests to Kleinias an image (*eikon,* 897e1) of *nous,* it is that of a sphere turning on a lathe, that is, of revolution (898a–b).[36]

36. Both the qualifications and the inability of the Athenian Stranger to explain directly the

Why is this the most adequate image of intelligence for mortals to imagine? The overpowering sense one gets from the Athenian's description of the motion of intelligence is *sameness:* the motion is "according to what is the same," "in the same way," "in the same place," "around the same things," "to the same things," and is "according to one reason (*logos*) and order" (898a8–b1).[37] The essence of the image lies in its intimations of eternity, perfection, order, and unchangeability. Similarly, the regularity of the motion is opposed to the arbitrariness or randomness that many wrongly attribute to the motion of the stars and planets. Non-arbitrary and non-random motion is principled, and principle implies intelligence.[38]

The physical order of the city, its social organization, and the laws that regulate its material constitution reflect this image and thereby aim to communicate and reinforce it.[39] In the fifth book, the Athenian specifies that the city should be constructed as close to the center of the territory as possible. At its center will be a sanctuary to Hestia, Zeus, and Athena. This sacred center will be surrounded by a wall and called the Acropolis (745b). Hestia was the sacred hearth fire maintained in the household and also in a place of great honor in Greek *poleis.* She is a shadowy figure with none of the rich mythology that accompanies other gods, but stands for the preservation of the family and for the unity of the city.[40] One important aspect of Hestia is that she never acquired the full status of a personal deity, but is fully embodied in the sacred fire. Therefore she does not move. As we shall see, the city and its institutions are repeatedly given a kind of immobility, a permanence and unchangeability. Zeus, of course, is the chief cosmic god in the pantheon. Athena is a symbol of Athens, but she was also widely associated with civic virtue, especially in war, as well as of the arts.[41]

---

motion of intelligence to Kleinias remind one—intentionally, I take it—of Socrates's inability to directly explain the science of dialectic and thus of the good to Glaucon, settling on a poetic image that is said to be a "child of the good" (*Republic* 533a, cf. 506d–507a), and perhaps also to Socrates's turn to speeches in *Phaedo* 96a–99d.

37. Cf. also 741a–b and note E. B. England's remarks in his commentary, *The Laws of Plato,* the text, edited with notes, introduction, etc. (Manchester: University Press, 1921), ad 898a8; and Solmsen, *Plato's Theology,* 147n20.

38. A very helpful discussion of the symbolization and argument here is Edward N. Lee, "Reason and Rotation: Circular Movement as the Model of Mind *(Nous)* in Later Plato," in *Facets of Plato's Philosophy,* ed. W. H. Werkmeister, 71–102, *Phronesis* Supplementary, vol. 2 (Amsterdam: Van Gorcum, 1976). Cf. Voegelin, *Plato and Aristotle,* 251.

39. See Marcel Piérart, *Platon et la Cité grecque,* 15–36; and Anissa Castel-Bouchouchi, "L'Espace civique: le plan de la Cité des *Lois,*" *Revue Philosophique* 190 (2000): 21–39.

40. Burkert, *Greek Religion,* 170.

41. Ibid., 139–43.

From this center the city radiates outward, divided into twelve parts, which include both urban and rural sections of the territory and are said to be divided equally by reference to the richness of the soil (745c). The territory as a whole (excluding the acropolis) is divided into 5,040 allotments (*klēroi*), each assigned to a full citizen for the support of his family. The estates have both urban and rural components, again, equal with respect to the richness of the soil. Each estate also has two houses: one in the city and one in the country (745c, e). Clearly one aim of this system is to establish the ruling class of the city as a kind of landed aristocracy, each member of which has both urban and rural property and interests as a way of promoting the unity of the city. The economic basis of the city is said more than once to be essentially agricultural (743d, 949e), with artisans and traders available to provide necessities, but denied citizenship (846d–e, 761d, 842c 849b–d, 919d–920a).

The 5,040 estates are divided into twelve groups, each of which (1) is constituted a tribe (*phulē*), (2) is also equal by reference to quality of land, (3) is considered the estate (*klēros*) of one of the twelve Olympian gods (745d–e, 771d), and (4) has two altars, one rural and one urban, to which sacrificial processions will be made, two a month (771d). Such ceremonies will, the Athenian says, both please the gods and promote kinship among the citizens (771d). Morrow observes that Plato's assignment of each tribe to an Olympian god is a "notable innovation." The ten Athenian tribes were named for heroes, as were tribes in other *poleis*. The import of the proposal is, Morrow writes, "[t]o place the primary organization of the state under the direct patronage of the highest gods, moreover, who are not merely local in their significance but worshipped by the entire state. This is both to make more sacred and inviolable the tribal divisions, and at the same time to take away some of the divisiveness that might accompany them."[42] This is no doubt true. However, it seems even more important that this division is meant to be a kind of image of the ordered cosmos meant to encourage the citizens to see themselves as parts of that larger order. The number of allotments, 5,040, is repeatedly emphasized (737e–738a, 740d–e, 745e, 746d, 771a, 771c, 877d, 919d, 929a), and the number's chief advantage is said to be its large number of divisors: all numbers one through twelve, excepting only eleven (771c). Most importantly, the number can be divided

---

42. Morrow, *Plato's Cretan City*, 435. Cf. E. B. England, *Laws of Plato*, ad745d8, and 771d4.

by twelve as can each twelfth. This relates it to the twelve tribes: "Each part must be understood as a sacred entity, a gift of the god, corresponding to the months and to the revolution of the whole (*tou pantos periodō*). That is why every city is naturally (*sumphuton*) led to sanctify these divisions" (771b6–c1). Later, in the seventh book, which is mostly concerned with the education of the citizens, the Athenian points out the importance of mathematics for war, household management, the management of the city, and for understanding the "revolutions of divine things (*periodois tōn theiōn*), the stars, sun and moon" (809c7–8). Every city, the Athenian says, must make arrangements based on these things concerning "the ordering of the days into the revolutions (*periodous*) of the months, and the months in each year, so that each of the seasons, sacrifices, and festivals will receive its due for itself according to the sequence of nature (*kata phusin*), will keep the city alive and awake, will render honors to the gods, and will make the humans more prudent in these matters" (809d2–7). The characteristics of the physical arrangement of the city, then, provide an image of the whole. The citizens participate in that whole through their civic life, and thus the city becomes a kind of point of access to the divine through its symbols and institutions. Crucial to the reflection of cosmic order is the number twelve: the city's parts relate to the structure of the cosmos as related to the months of the year and thus to the sun.[43] This aspect is emphasized dramatically in the fact that the dialogue is said to take place near the solstice (683c) and that the actual legislation begins at high noon (722c–d).

One aspect of this already mentioned but stressed repeatedly in the text is the unchanging character of the city's practices and institutions. Certainly the main example of this is the stability of the law itself, which is frequently mentioned, as is the difficulty that should be attached to changing it (960c–d). The estates assigned to citizens are always to number 5,040 and their size is never to be altered (740b, 855a). The explicitly religious festivals and sacrifices are also made unchangeable (738c–d, 816c–d), as are marriage customs (772c–d) and the games to be played by children (797a–c). In addition to these things, the Athenian stranger frequently warns against the danger of innovation generally (758c, 797d–e, 950a, 952e–953a). One might also mention in this regard the respect for old age and even the tastes of the old described in the *Laws* (690a, 879c, 917a, 927b, 931a, 964e–965a).[44] All

43. See Voegelin, *Plato and Aristotle*, 251–53.
44. See above, note 22.

of these things support the idea that the city has a perfection that mirrors and participates in the completeness and permanence of the whole.

This cosmic representational aspect of the religion of the Magnesians adds something to the civil religion described above. There the unity of the city was primary. Recall the three primary ends of the laws: freedom, friendship, and prudence. The unity of the city promoted by the civic cult is a means to maintain the freedom of the city. It is also related to the third and higher aim of prudence or intelligence. The civic cult is linked to the cosmic representational character of the city and its religion, and this points beyond the purely terrestrial political character of the city. It situates the city and its inhabitants in the order of the whole by way of ritual and symbol. But it also points beyond this to the life of philosophy as the quest for knowledge of the whole. Here, however, we see again the tensions in the city's pursuit of the three goals: since the pursuit of truth itself is trans-political, it is not simply congruent with the unity or even the freedom of the city, although it cannot do without these things. The city's religion points beyond the city to philosophy, but philosophy is in tension with the city, and this raises the possibility of more serious conflict between the two. That conflict was obviously central to Plato's concerns since it was the great drama in the life and death of Socrates. The next section considers the Magnesian city's management of this tension.

Gods beyond the City

One of the most extraordinary and frequently discussed features of the *Laws* is the Athenian's proposal for the establishment of a body of officials (and their younger aides) to convene at night (to be precise, he suggests just before dawn, 951d, 961b) for the purposes of meeting with those convicted of impiety, as well as for discussing reform proposals for the city and philosophical problems such as the unity of the virtues and the existence of the gods (908a, 909a, 960b–968e). This body, which the Athenian sometimes refers to as the "nightly meeting," is indeed an innovation of the first importance, for it attempts to address the problem of the relationship of philosophy to the city. It is the culmination of this effort, but the effort itself is indicated long before the nightly meeting's first explicit appearance in the tenth book. As noted above, the nightly meeting is foreshadowed by the discussion of the Dionysian chorus in the second book. The meeting itself is described by the Athenian in the twelfth book as providing for "complete security forever" (*sōtērian . . . teleōs aei*, 960b8) for the Magnesian city. There he explains in some detail the meeting's various activities. When the body is first introduced, however, it is in conjunction with the punishment of impiety.

As was noted previously, the *Laws* evinces a concern not only with impious actions (conventional in Greek *poleis*), but with beliefs. A concern with the beliefs of the citizens is introduced very early in the first book of the *Laws,* when the Athenian approvingly notes the Kretan law forbidding the young to criticize the city's laws and institutions, but allows such criticism by the old among themselves (634d–e). Later in the second book the Athenian says that the lawgiver should "seek only the convictions which would do the greatest good for the city, and he should discover every device of any sort that will tend to make the whole community speak about these things with one and the same voice, as much as possible, at every moment throughout the whole of life, in songs and myths and arguments" (663e9–664a6). In introducing the discussion of impiety in the tenth book, the Athenian begins with "unrestrained and insolent (*hubreis*) things done by the young" (884a6–7), the worst of which offend sacred things. Such acts are soon explained as manifestations of a deeper problem, namely, incorrect beliefs about the gods:

> No one who believes in gods according to the laws has ever voluntarily done an impious deed or let slip an illegal utterance unless he is suffering one of three things: either this, which I just said, he doesn't believe; or, second, he believes they exist but that they do not think about human beings; or, third, he believes they are easily persuaded if they are brought sacrifices and prayers. (885b4–9, cf. 948c)

There follows a long discussion of these three propositions, which is, in fact, the most extensive philosophical theology of the classical period. While it is beyond the scope of this paper to discuss the theology in detail, we can note some of its features that bear on the question of civil religion. First, the discussion itself is initially constructed not as a dialogue between the Athenian stranger and his two Dorian interlocutors, but between the lawgiver and a young atheist/heretic. The imaginary young man asks the lawgiver not simply to regulate or punish, but rather to persuade and teach (885d–e).[45] And the Athenian secures Kleinias's permission to do so by dis-

---

45. See on this Pangle, "The Political Psychology of Religion in Plato's *Laws*," 1061–62.

cussing the arguments in detail with the prospect of their being recorded for future study (890e–891a). Thus these ideas about the gods are preserved in the city precisely in the context of a rational inquiry and not simply as dogma (I say more about this below).

Second, the theological arguments are said by the Athenian to relate precisely to the threat that the laws will be undermined by unbelievers (891b) and indeed to constitute the "noblest and best prelude on behalf of all the laws" by no less than Kleinias (887c1–2). This is clearly true if it is essential that the city's laws and institutions have a divine origin. Third, when the account begins to unfold, the first issue is transformed from an argument for the existence of the gods into an argument for the priority of the soul to the body.[46] This seems precisely related to the discussion of the natural order of goods described by the Athenian stranger in the first book as the very foundation of the legal code (631b–d). The gods, then, stand for the soul and its goods—the highest of which is prudence or intelligence—as the highest aim of the city.[47]

Fourth, while the theology of the tenth book is sometimes described as dogmatic and thought to be a function of Plato's betrayal of Socrates in favor of theocratic authoritarianism, one must be struck by the qualifications and tentativeness evinced by the Athenian in laying out the arguments about the gods.[48] This can be illustrated by looking more closely at one portion of the Athenian's account. The argument for the priority of soul is essentially an argument from motion. The power of self-motion implies life, and life, the Athenian suggests, implies the presence of soul. The Athenian seems particularly concerned to relate soul to the movements of the heavenly bodies against what many took to be the atheistic intentions of pre-Socratic philosophers such as Anaxagoras to explain the heavens in purely naturalistic and indeed materialistic terms. The key to the Athenian's argument is the *orderly* motion of stars and planets. Such orderly movement shows that "soul has come into being prior to body, and that

46. See on this Edward C. Halper, "Soul, Soul's Motions, and Virtue," in *Plato's "Laws": From Theory into Practice*, 257–67.

47. This point is discussed in more detail below.

48. For the dogmatic view see, e.g., George Grote, *Plato and the Other Companions of Sokrates*, 3d ed. (London: John Murray, 1875), 3:409–12; George H. Sabine, *A History of Political Theory*, rev. ed. (New York: Henry Holt, 1950), 84–85; E. R. Dodds, *The Greeks and the Irrational* (Berkeley and Los Angeles: University of California Press, 1951), 207–10, 215–16, 224; John Gould, *The Development of Plato's Ethics* (Cambridge: Cambridge University Press, 1955), 109; George Klosko, *The Development of Plato's Political Theory* (London: Methuen, 1986), 232–33.

body is second and later, being ruled, while soul rules, according to nature (*kata phusin*)" (896c1–3; cf. 892c2–5).

Now the Athenian introduces intelligence (*nous*) into the discussion. Earlier it was mentioned in the context of the argument of the atheists, who held that it was not prior to matter (889c5, 892b4), but that nature was random in its character. In other words, the earlier argument attempted to separate nature from intelligence. Now, having secured Kleinias's agreement that soul rules body "according to nature," the Athenian reconnects the two by suggesting a hierarchy of psychic motion. Soul leads all things in heaven and earth through its own motions called wishing, investigating, supervising, deliberating, forming correct and false opinions, fearing, hating, desiring, and all motions related to these. Such motions control a second class of motions that are peculiar to bodies, such as growth, decay, separation, and coalescence, and these in turn control physical properties like heat, cold, heaviness, lightness, hardness, softness, light, darkness, bitterness, and sweetness (896e8–897b1; cf. 892b4–9, 896c9–d3). The Athenian concludes that soul makes use of all of these, and, "whenever it takes as a helper intelligence (*nous*), it guides (by teaching or training, *paidagōgei*) all things to what is correct and happy" (897b1–3).[49] And when soul associates with ignorance (*anoia*) the opposite occurs.

Two things are striking here: first, as suggested above, this seems directly related to the order of lawgiving that follows the natural order of goods in the first book, with *nous* at the head (631b; cf. 683b, 710b, 713e, 716a, 718b, 742d–e, 790b, 858d). Second, the Athenian stranger repeatedly phrases his account as conditional: "if this is so" (896a5), "if soul should manifestly be older than body" (896c6), "if indeed soul came to be before body" (896d2–3), "if indeed we are to set it down that it [soul] was the cause of everything" (896d8). And he concludes with one more:

If, you amazing man, we should say, the whole path and motion (*phora*) of heaven and of all the things in it has the same nature as the motion, revolution, and calculations of intelligence and moves in a kindred way, then it is clear that one must say that the best soul supervises the whole cosmos and leads it along such a path as that one. (897c3–8; cf. 892a–c)

---

49. I have omitted from my quotation a much disputed phrase from the text, which does not affect its sense important to my account. If there is any text at all there that is genuine, it associates *nous* with the gods. See England, *Laws of Plato* ad 897b1, and the apparatus criticus in Diès's Belles Lettres text ad 897b2.

What I am suggesting by pointing to the tentative and conditional nature of the argument is that it does not present itself as any kind of conclusive demonstration. Indeed, following on the heels of the imaginary dialogue with the young unbeliever, it seems like an invitation for one to inquire into these matters. This impression is only strengthened when one considers the importance the Athenian stranger attributes to the study by citizens of Magnesia of astronomy, which he explicitly connects to piety (809c–d, 817e, 818c, 820e–822c, 886a–d, 897c, 898d, 966e–967a), against the idea— with terrible consequences for Socrates—that rational inquiry about the heavenly bodies necessarily implies atheism.[50]

Finally, and this is the fifth element of the theology of the tenth book that I want to emphasize, one must consider the punishment prescribed for those convicted of impiety based on the three propositions noted above. This again has led to the view that Plato betrays Socrates and becomes Meletus in the *Laws*. The details of the account, however, suggest otherwise.[51] Genuine unbelievers are confined not in the ordinary prison, but in an institution called the "moderatorium" (*sophronistērion*) located near the place of the nightly meeting (908a). They are confined there for five years, during which time they can speak only to the officials who constitute the nightly meeting, who will, "consorting and discussing with them, admonish them for the safety of their souls" (909a4–5). Not much is said about one's time in the moderatorium. Beyond confinement itself, the punishment is conversation with the most influential (and, one imagines, interesting) people in the city. Given the name, the hoped-for outcome of confinement may simply be moderation (recall the context of impiety in the "hubristic" acts of the young), as distinct from any kind of real recantation, but it could also be a genuine change of mind. Moreover, one wonders how such conversations might affect the members of the nightly meeting itself. One is led to the possibility that this very odd institution and this very odd form of punishment may be intended to reinforce and influence one another.[52]

What about those who are not moderated? After five years a judgment is made about the inmate. While the text is not entirely clear, one can suppose that those who either are convinced of their error or are simply willing

50. *Apology of Socrates* 18a–e.
51. For more detail see Lewis, "The Nocturnal Council and Platonic Political Philosophy," 3–5.
52. I suggest this in ibid., as does Pangle's interpretive essay in *Laws of Plato*, 503–4.

to be silent about such matters in public will be released.[53] The fate of those who are unconvinced or unwilling to keep quiet is unclear—their confinement could go on indefinitely. Those who are released, but who repeat the offense and are convicted a second time are to be put to death (909a). It seems unlikely that Socrates would ever be accused of violating the law laid down by the Athenian stranger, at least given what he says in his own defense in Plato's *Apology of Socrates*.[54] Socrates never committed any public acts of impiety like those described in the *Laws,* nor did he give voice to the heretical opinions proscribed there. Had Athens been governed under the legal code devised by the Athenian stranger, even if Socrates had been convicted of impiety, his punishment would have been to live out his remaining years in philosophical conversation with men whose legal duty it was to study just those questions to which he devoted his own life of inquiry.

I have tried to show in this section how the civil religion of the Magnesian city opens onto the civil theology exemplified in the tenth book of the *Laws* and how the practices and institutions there described attempt to manage the ineliminable tension between philosophy and the city. The civil religion of public cult practices is connected to a civil theology grounded in the propositions that there are gods, that the gods take an interest in human affairs, and that they cannot be bribed by prayers and sacrifices. Such a theology supports both the laws and the city's imaging of the cosmic order, but also opens onto a more genuinely philosophical piety: inquiry into the existence and nature of the gods and the soul for its own sake, as the very perfection of the soul.

Conclusion

The philosopher and former president of the Italian Senate, Marcello Pera, has recently proposed that Europe adopt a "Christian civil religion" as a means of explaining and protecting such central goods as human dignity, the integrity of the traditional family, and tolerance.[55] The proposal was

---

53. This is the (plausible, I think) view of England, *Laws of Plato,* ad 909a7; see also Saunders, *Plato's Penal Code,* 309–310.

54. Cf. Strauss, *The Argument and the Action of Plato's "Laws,"* 2, against Yunis, *A New Creed,* 72.

55. "Letter to Joseph Ratzinger," in Joseph Ratzinger and Marcello Pera, *Without Roots: The West, Relativism, Christianity, Islam,* trans. Michael F. Moore (New York: Basic Books, 2006), 94–96.

made in a dialogue with then Cardinal Joseph Ratzinger (now Pope Benedict XVI) and in response to what Pera takes to be a debilitating cultural, moral, and political relativism and deracination that renders the West particularly vulnerable to the forces of radical Islamists. That relativism and deracination was, he thinks, exemplified in the European Union's refusal to recognize the continent's Christian heritage in the preamble to its draft constitutional treaty, but has its origins in some tendencies of the Enlightenment and especially in recent postmodernist thought.[56] The West's current cultural and political maladies, then, are a result of the popularization of certain philosophical currents.

It was this very issue that Plato took as his central concern in the *Laws:* how can the city and philosophy best live together? The issue occupied Plato in many other works, especially the *Republic,* where it is approached in a different way. In the *Laws,* he gives the city its due, adopts its perspective through many dramatic devices. He imagines a city based on the rule of law, backed by tradition and the authority of those deeply formed by the laws and extra-legal practices that make up that tradition. At the roots of the city are the gods as its putative legislators, partners in festival and sacrifice, ultimate enforcers of justice, and the object of its prayers, but also of its speculative thought. The city itself is a condition of human life, an image of the order of the whole, and a means of one's connection to the whole. It includes within itself a place for philosophy that aims to be supportive of and consistent with its explicitly political goals. The project, we are repeatedly warned, is difficult and fraught with risk. In the end, the Athenian says that it amounts to a gamble (968e–969a; cf. 708d, 752b). But the massive scope and intricate structure of his longest work suggests that Plato thought it a chance worth taking, at least in speech.

Is the possibility of civil religion open to us, as Pera suggests? The role in Christianity (and Islam, as well) of revelation—the claim that God Himself has spoken—would seem to pose a great challenge to such a project. It requires genuine faith and not simply practice to sustain it.[57] Nevertheless, even beginning to address such a proposal as well as understanding its context requires the guidance of the tradition of political philosophy at the beginning of which is Plato's *Laws* and the civil religion of the Magnesians.

---

56. Pera, "Relativism, Christianity, and the West," in ibid., 15–22, 27–38.

57. One should note in this respect then-Cardinal Ratzinger's notably qualified response to Pera's proposal, "Letter to Marcello Pera," in ibid., 119–21.

2

Truth versus Utility

The Debate on Civil Religion in the Roman Empire of the Third and Fourth Centuries

MATTHIAS RIEDL

One of John Stuart Mill's late essays is entitled "The Utility of Religion" and starts as follows: "It has sometimes been remarked how much has been written, both by friends and enemies, concerning the truth of religion, and how little, at least in the way of discussion or controversy, concerning its usefulness."[1] A few lines later, he adds: "The utility of religion did not need to be asserted until the arguments for its truth had in a great measure ceased to convince."[2] Mill is right in one respect; truth and utility are two essentially different ways of looking at religion. But he is wrong to claim that the question of the utility of religion arises later in history than the question of its truth. Both questions have a 2,000-year-old history in Western civilization.

The first major clash between the two perspectives happened in the third and fourth centuries A.D., when a new Latin-speaking Christian intelligentsia started to question the rationale behind Roman civil religion. However, if we read the literature of early Western Christianity we are confronted with a curious phenomenon, namely the seemingly irreconcilable difference between the picture of the pagan cult, as drawn by Christian authors of this period, and the picture of non-Christian religiosity, as presented to us by modern scholarship. Regardless of whether we read the earliest documents of Latin apologetic literature, such as Tertullian and

---

1. John Stuart Mill, *Three Essays on Religion* (Amherst, Mass.: Prometheus, 1998), 69.
2. Ibid., 70.

Minucius Felix, written around 200, or Augustine's *The City of God,* written in the early fifth century, the authors give us the impression that the pagans still worshiped Jupiter, Mars, Minerva, Venus, and all the other deities of the traditional polytheist pantheon. Modern historians, on the other hand, tell us that by the third century, the majority of the non-Christians in the Roman Empire had turned to what is generally known as "the oriental mystery cults," such as the Persian Mithras, the Egyptian Isis, and the variations of the Syrian solar cult. Only a small pagan minority, mostly members of the senate aristocracy, kept defending the cult of their ancestors. However, many of the Christian treatises show only minor concern for the mystery cults, which must have been a more serious rival in the competition for the religious orientation of the masses.[3] So the question arises: why, centuries after the decline of the republic and, in the case of Augustine, even decades after the supposed Constantinian or Theodosian turns, did republican civil religion remain the chief frame of reference of the religio-political debates?

The solution to the problem seems to be that the chief enemy the authors had in mind was indeed the small pagan aristocracy. But this is again a phenomenon that requires explanation. I can offer two preliminary answers: First, because of the exoteric character of the gospel, Christianity sought to conquer the public sphere, where it confronted not the mystery cults but Roman civil religion. Second, a literary controversy was possible only with pagans who, to a certain extent, had enjoyed the same education. Almost all Christian authors were educated as pagans and converted to Christianity as adults, Ambrose of Milan being one of the few exceptions. Tertullian and Minucius Felix started their careers as lawyers, and Arnobius, Lactantius, and Augustine as rhetoricians. Since both sides shared the same educational background they drew most of their categories and examples from the classics, first of all Varro, Cicero, Sallust, Livy, and Virgil—except the latter, all authors praised the pious cult of the earlier republican times and regarded their own time as an era of religious crisis.

3. The book *De errore profanarum religionum* by Firmicus Maternus seems to be a remarkable exception since it provides detailed reports about the mystery cults. Although the title might suggest otherwise, the book does not belong to the context of the pagan-Christian debate. Rather, it aims to inform the Christian successors of Emperor Constantine the Great about the existing pagan cults, which, in the eyes of the author, the emperors are obliged to destroy (Firmicus Maternus, *The Error of the Pagan Religions,* trans. Clarence A. Forbes, Ancient Christian Writers 37 (New York: Newman Press, 1970)).

In this intellectual controversy, it appears that the main argument of the pagans for the preservation of the civil religion is its political utility. The Christians, on the other hand, insist on the truth of their revelation, which does not allow them to support the official cult. Yet, as I intend to show, the dividing lines between the proponents of utility and the proponents of truth are not as clear as they appear at first sight. Instead of giving a survey of the relevant literature, which would necessarily remain rather general and superficial, I offer two examples, which do not cover all aspects of the debate on civil religion in the third and fourth century but seem representative of two distinct historical situations: the dialogue *Octavius* by Minucius Felix illustrates the defensive character of the apologetic literature in the pre-Constantinian era, whereas the debate between Symmachus and Ambrose over the altar of victory shows the pagan defenders of civil religion struggling against the power of the new Christian elites.

Minucius Felix

The dialogue *Octavius* was written by the otherwise unknown author Minucius Felix in the first half of the third century. The opening scene describes the author and his two friends, the Christian Octavius and the pagan Caecilius, promenading along the beach of Ostia near Rome. As they leave the city and pass an image of Serapis, an Egyptian god recently added to the pantheon of the official cult, the pagan makes a gesture of veneration. Octavius, the Christian, immediately accuses him of superstition, and so the discussion starts. The dialogue is, of course, not the protocol of a discussion that actually happened, and probably it was read only by Christians. However, I am convinced that it reflects a real debate. Written in a time when the Christians were still a minority, it provided arguments that Christian intellectuals could use to defend themselves and to convince others. For this purpose, Minucius Felix had to draw a realistic picture of the pagan intellectual.

Before the pagan Caecilius, who gives the first speech in the dialogue, begins his attack on Christianity, he praises the utility of civil religion. His main argument is the close relation between the receptivity of the Roman cult for new gods and the military success of the empire:

[Rome] has propagated its empire beyond the paths of the sun, and the bounds of the ocean itself; in that in their arms they practice a religious valor; in that

they fortify their city with the religions of sacred rites ... ; in that, when be-
sieged and taken, all but the Capitol alone, they worship the gods which when
angry any other people would have despised; and through the lines of the Gauls
... they move unarmed with weapons, but armed with the worship of their religion; while in the city of an enemy, when taken while still in the fury of victory,
they venerate the conquered deities; while in all directions they seek for the gods
of the strangers, and make them their own. . . . Thus, in that they acknowledge
the sacred institutions of all nations, they have also deserved their dominion.[4]

Caecilius concludes that the traditional cult had always protected and
strengthened the city. However, its receptivity and tolerance reaches its limits when it comes to Christianity. The way Caecilius describes the dangerous character of the Christian community includes almost all common ste-
reotypes. He accuses the Christians of gathering in secret meetings, where
they perform cruel sacrifices, including the worshiping of animals and the
killing of children, as well as abnormal sexual practices, especially incest.

Yet the far more interesting fact is that the vocabulary used for these
accusations includes a number of key words that would have been immediately understood by every educated contemporary. Caecilius asserts that
the Christians "establish a herd of a profane conspiracy [*profana coniuratio*]
which is leagued together by nightly meetings ... not by any sacred rite
[*sacrum*], but by sinful crime [*piaculum*]."[5] According to a modern editor
of the dialogue, this is "the almost standard jargon to describe contemp-
tuously any clandestine religious sect."[6] Caecilius also says: "I know not
whether these things are false; certainly suspicion is applicable to secret
and nocturnal rites."[7] The expression "secret and nocturnal rites" (*occulta
et nocturna sacra*) is literally taken from the thirty-ninth book of Livy's Roman history, as are the opposition of *sacrum* and *piaculum* and a number of
other concepts.[8]

In this book, Livy reports on the scandal of the Bacchanals that occurred four hundred years earlier, after the Second Punian War.[9] We can

---

4. Minucius Felix, *Octavius,* trans. G. W. Clarke, Ancient Christian Writers 39 (New York:
Newman Press, 1974), 6,2–3. Latin quotes are taken from Minucius Felix, *Octavius,* Lateinisch–
Deutsch ed., ed. Bernhard Kytzler (München: Kösel, 1965).

5. Ibid., 8,4.   6. Ibid., note 106.

7. Ibid. 9,4.

8. Livy, *Ab urbe condita* XXXIX,8 and XXXIX,18.

9. Ironically, the Christian Firmicus Maternus uses the persecution of the Bacchants as an ex-
emplary model for measures that the Christian emperors of the Constantinian dynasty should take
against the pagan cults (Firmicus Maternus, *De errore profanarum religionum,* VI,9).

learn from the work of Minucius that contemporary pagans attempted to construe a parallel between the Bacchanals and the Christian gatherings. The motive is easily discerned. Before (under Emperor Decius) systematic persecutions of the Christians were enacted, the Roman authorities and most emperors hesitated to bring Christians to trial because such measures lacked legal grounds.[10] Worshiping the "wrong" god was not a crime. If, however, the anti-Christian propaganda could successfully show that the case of the Christians equals the case of the Bacchanals, it would have provided a justification for judicial measures. The case of the Bacchanals was widely regarded as the precedent for religious persecution; and the authoritative historian, Livy, confirmed that the persecution was a necessary and legitimate means for protecting the social and religious order of the Roman republic.

Livy tells us that in 186 B.C., a consul conducted investigations into the Bacchanals and presented the following results before the senate: A certain time after the Bacchanals were introduced in Rome as a cult for female initiates, a priestess altered the rules. Henceforth, rites were performed secretly at night, and male adolescents were initiated to the cult:

From the time when the rites were held promiscuously, with men and women mixed together, and when the license offered by darkness had been added, no sort of crime, no kind of immorality was left unattempted. There were more obscenities practised between men than between men and women. . . . To regard nothing as forbidden was among these people the summit of religious achievement. . . . There was . . . a vast number of initiates, and by this time they almost made up a second people.[11]

After further official inquiries, the senate issued a decree. Due to fortunate circumstances, the text of that decree was handed down to us and is preserved on a bronze tablet, currently located in the *Kunstgeschichtliche Museum* in Vienna. We can therefore be certain that the core of Livy's story is based on facts. Recent archaeological discoveries have shown that exactly at this time a temple dedicated to Bacchus was violently destroyed.[12] We

---

10. Jochen Bleicken, *Verfassungs- und Sozialgeschichte des Römischen Kaiserreiches,* vol. 2, 3rd ed. (Paderborn: Schöningh 1994), 167–74.

11. Livy, *Ab urbe condita* XXXIX,13, in Livy, *Rome and the Mediterranean. Books XXXI–XLV of the History of Rome from Its Foundation,* trans. Henry Bettenson (London: Penguin, 1976).

12. Mary Beard, John North, and Simon Price, *Religions of Rome,* 2 vols. (Cambridge: Cambridge University Press, 1998), 1:93.

do not know how many people were actually killed, exiled, or put in jail during the persecutions, but they must have been in the thousands.[13] In the end, the cult was more or less eliminated.

The senatorial decree and Livy's account give us a number of reasons why the Bacchanals were unacceptable. At the same time, they reveal deep insights into the character of Roman civil religion. It is obvious that truth was not an issue, since the senators did not doubt the existence of the god Bacchus. Certainly the senators could not neglect the stories about excessive drunkenness and abnormal sexual practices. However, their main concern was the novelty that the Bacchants constituted a religious community of their own.[14] Traditionally, the most important religious community of Rome was the Civitas, the community of the citizens, itself. A clear distinction between religion and politics was unknown. The aristocratic families who dominated politics throughout the republican era also held most of the important priesthoods and supervised the *sacra publica*, sacred public affairs.[15] Their political influence was enormous. According to their specific responsibilities, the different religious authorities, the *pontifices*, the *augures*, and the *haruspices*, were consulted before virtually every political decision.[16] The college of the pontiffs also controlled the non-public area of the Roman religion, the *sacra privata*, the worship of the family gods. At the beginning of a speech Cicero once gave before the college of the pontiffs, he summed up the religio-political order of the republic:

Among the many divinely-inspired expedients of government established by our ancestors, there is none more striking than that whereby they expressed intention that the worship of the gods and the vital interests of the state should be entrusted to the direction of the same individuals (*eosdem et religionibus deorum immortalium et summae rei publicae praeesse voluerunt*), to the end that citizens of the highest distinction and the brightest fame might achieve the welfare of religion by a wise administration of the state, and of the state by a sage interpretation of religion (*religiones sapienter interpretando rem publicam conservarent*).[17]

13. Livy says, "more than 7,000 men and women were involved in the conspiracy"; and "[t]he people executed outnumbered those who were thrown into prison" (Livy, *Ab urbe condita* XXXIX,17–18, 412–13).

14. John A. North, *Roman Religion* (Oxford: Oxford University Press, 2000), 65.

15. Ibid., 21–34.

16. Ibid., 29–30.

17. Cicero, *De domo sua* I,1, in Cicero, *The Speeches*, trans. N. H. Watts, Loeb Classical Library (Cambridge and London: Harvard University Press/William Heinemann, 1965), 133.

From this perspective, it is understandable that a religious group, which established its own leadership, its own loyalties, and its own funds, was unacceptable. Therefore, the senate decreed, in the case of the Bacchanals:

No man shall be a priest. No man nor woman shall be a master. None of them shall seek to have money in common. No one shall seek to appoint either man or woman as master or acting master, or seek to create mutual guarantees. No one shall seek to perform rites in secret, nor shall anyone seek to perform rites in public or private or outside the city, unless he . . . is given permission with a senatorial decree, so long as not less than one hundred senators are present when the matter is considered.[18]

To us moderns, this decision might appear to be a purely political decision in order to eliminate competing elites. Yet, as Livy tells us, the Bacchanals were seen as a threat not just against the political order of the city, but also against religion.[19] In fact, the two charges were inseparable. According to the British historian J. A. North, there "is a sense in which the gods and goddesses of Rome were citizens belonging to the city just as much as the human citizens and participating in its triumphs and defeats as well as in its rituals."[20] Moreover, the relations between gods and humans were described in exactly the same terms as the social relations between the citizens, such as between patrons and clients. One of the key concepts is *procuratio,* care. A recent study on social relations in the Roman Republic describes the concept as follows: "Cicero and other authors frequently use the terms *procuratio* (or variants) to denote political responsibilities or to describe the care of the gods over human affairs. By far the most attestations of the term *procurator* denote anyone who takes care (*procurare*) of the affairs of others, regardless of whether these affairs are economic, social, political or religious."[21]

In other words, the Roman citizen experienced his existence as participation in a system of care. Cicero, the Homo Novus, offers the most profound intellectual penetration of the existence of the Roman aristocrat. In his *Republic,* the hero Scipio says that there is one single task (*opus*) he in-

18. Cited from Beard, North, and Price, *Religions of Rome,* 2:291; for the Latin text see *Fontes Iuris Romani Anteiustiniani. Pars Prima: Leges,* ed. Salvator Riccobono (Florence: S.A.G. Barbèra, 1968), 240–41.

19. Livy, *Ab urbe condita* XXXIX,16.

20. North, *Roman Religion,* 37.

21. Koenraad Verboven, *The Economy of Friends: Economic Ascpects of Amicitia and Patronage in the Late Republic* (Brussels: Éditions Latomus, 2002), 230.

herited from his parents, namely the care for and administration of the Res Publica (*procuratio atque administratio rei publicae*).[22] But also on the other levels of the social order, virtually including the gods, care for others was more or less identical with the meaning of existence. The Patres Familias cared for their families, the patrons for their clients, the patricians for the Res Publica, and the gods for the welfare of the citizens and the success of the political and military leaders. In this order, there was no place for a religion that constituted an alternative society, a second people (*alter populus*), as Livy writes,[23] whose purpose was not the care for the family or the Res Publica but the individual experience of the divine and happiness in the afterlife.[24] In the eyes of the senators, the cult therefore ruined the commonwealth, the families, the religion, and, first of all, the virtue that bound all elements of the Roman order together: piety (*pietas*), the dutifulness and loyalty to parents, patrons, ancestors, and gods, to all the authorities on whose care one depends. We find exactly the same charge in the dialogue of Minucius Felix. The pagan Caecilius sums up his accusations with the conclusion that Christians are an impious community (*impia coitio*).[25]

According to an old myth, polytheism is by definition tolerant, and monotheism is the origin of intolerance. The Bacchanals, however, provide a good example for the limits of polytheistic toleration and help us to understand the suspicion of Christian communities. Religious toleration is, in the first place, not a question of polytheism or monotheism. Toleration is possible as long as the constitutive self-understanding of a society is not endangered, as long as the logic of the political order, from which the dominant part of the society derives the meaning of its existence, is not questioned. Exactly this happened in Rome, when Bacchants and Christians established communities seeking otherworldly beatitude and establishing their own leadership, instead of trusting in the joint efforts of gods and patricians in securing the public good of the Civitas. Even though neither in the case of the Bacchanals nor in the case of the early Christianity was a political program clearly discernible, the establishment of an alternative social order could only be perceived as a conspiracy against the Res Publica.[26]

22. Cicero, *De re publica*, I,22,36.
23. Livy, *Ab urbe condita* XXXIX,13.
24. Concern for an otherworldly existence was, however, an important feature of the Dionysian mysteries already in the fifth century B.C. (Walter Burkert, *Antike Mysterien* (München: Beck, 1991), 27).
25. Minucius Felix, *Octavius* 9,1.
26. On the charge of conspiracy (*coniuratio*), see Wilhelm Nippel, "Orgien, Ritualmorde und

Yet if we take a closer look at the argumentation of Caecilius, we see that, despite all the praise for the traditional religion, something has been lost, and that is the experience of divine presence: "the mediocrity of human intelligence is so far from (the capacity of) divine investigation," he says, "that neither is it given us to know, nor is it permitted to search, nor is it religious to ravish, the things that are supported in suspense in the heaven above us, nor the things which are deeply submerged below the earth."[27] Caecilius concludes: "Thus either an uncertain truth is hidden from us, and kept back; or, which is rather to be believed, in these various and wayward chances, fortune, unrestrained by laws, is ruling over us."[28]

But, as so often, from skepticism follows almost naturally a conservative attitude that also applies to religion:

Since, then, either fortune is certain or nature is uncertain, how much more reverential and better it is, as the high priests of truth, to receive the teaching of your ancestors, to cultivate the religions handed down to you, to adore the gods whom you were first trained by your parents to fear rather than to know with familiarity; not to assert an opinion concerning the deities, but to believe your forefathers, who, while the age was still untrained in the birth-times of the world itself, deserved to have gods either propitious to them, or as their kings.[29]

It is easy to discern that the certainty about divine care is replaced by the experience of the ineffable vicissitudes of fortune. What remains for the pagan aristocrat is to insist on the tradition and the political utility of the ancient cult. History proves, Caecilius says, that the Roman religion is ancient (*vetusta*), useful (*utilis*), and wholesome (*salubris*).[30] Yet, it does not prove that the gods really exist. The question of truth is raised, but it finds no answer.

What I want to emphasize is that the questions of truth and utility were not meaningful questions in earlier republican times. The senatorial decree against the Bacchanals appealed neither to truth nor to utility but sought to protect the Civitas, the community of gods and citizens. The most important question of Roman religion was: How can we do justice to the gods? What can we do to be in good relations with the gods in order to deserve their care? When, at the end of the republic, the Roman aristocrats

Verschwörung? Die Bacchanalien-Prozesse des Jahres 186 v. Chr.," in *Große Prozesse der römischen Antike,* ed. Ulrich Manthe and Jürgen von Ungern-Sternberg (München: Beck, 1997), 68; R. A. Bauman, "The Suppression of the Bacchanals: Five Questions," *Historia* 39, no. 3 (1990): 342–43.

27. Minucius Felix, *Octavius,* 5,5. 28. Ibid., 5,13.

29. Ibid., 6,1. 30. Ibid., 8,1.

successively lost their political influence and their capability to take care of the Res Publica, they also lost their sense of the guiding assistance of divine care.

One of the possible reactions was skepticism. The literary model for this attitude, used by Minucius and many other authors of the period, was Cicero's dialogue *On the Nature of the Gods,* written after Cicero was removed from office and exiled.[31] It differs significantly from the treatment of religion in the speeches and treatises he wrote as a senator. As long as Cicero was allowed to care for the Res Publica, he professed the traditional creed of civil religion; whether he personally experienced the numinous forces he is speaking of is not important at this point. In his commentary on the soothsayers' responses to questions put to them by the senate, he says: "And, indeed, who is so witless that, when he gazes up into heaven, he fails to see that gods exist . . . ? Or, who, once convinced that divinity does exist, can fail at the same time to be convinced that it is by its power (*numen*) that this great empire has been created, extended, and sustained?"[32]

In *On the Nature of the Gods,* however, Cicero takes a skeptical view on religion; as he discusses the various opinions of the philosophers, however, he makes clear that, for reasons of political utility, neither the existence of the gods nor the civil religion may be publicly questioned.[33] But Cicero even sets limits on the esoteric philosophical discussion, since there is one philosophy that no responsible Roman could ever accept, namely, Epicureanism. The epicurean view that the gods exist, but do not care about humans, destroys all Roman order and virtue. Cicero writes: "There are and have always been philosophers who believe that the gods have no concern (*procuratio*) whatever with the affairs of man. But if this belief is true, what becomes of piety, of reverence and of religion (*quae potest esse pietas, quae sanctitas, quae religio*)?"[34]

The skeptic Cicero concludes the dialogue that we do not know the truth about the gods; but the Stoic idea of divine providence seems more likely to be true (*verisimilis*)[35] because it conforms best with the civil reli-

31. For Minucius's dependence on Cicero, see Carl Becker, *Der "Octavius" des Minucius Felix. Heidnische Philosophie und christliche Apologetik* (München: Beck, 1967), 10.

32. Cicero, *De haruspicum responsis oratio,* 9,19, trans. N. H. Watts, 341.

33. Cicero, *De natura deorum,* I,61.

34. Cicero, *De natura deorum,* I,3; cited from Cicero, *The Nature of the Gods,* trans. Horace C. P. McGregor. Penguin Classics (Harmondsworth: Penguin 1984), 70; cf. the more detailed refutation of Epicureanism in I,115–124.

35. Ibid., III,95.

gion, which has proved useful. This inconsistency between the esoteric and
the exoteric treatment of religion and this tension between philosophical
knowledge and political responsibility was clearly discerned by the Christian writers and used as a point of attack. In the dialogue of Minucius, the
Christian Octavius accuses his pagan counterpart of varying "at one time
from believing the gods, at another time to being in a state of hesitation on
the subject."[36] In *The City of God,* Augustine provides a variety of examples
for the inconsistent religious existence of pagan intellectuals. Varro wrote
that, if he could found the city anew, he would choose other gods. But
he held it necessary for the order of the city that the Romans worship the
gods of their ancestors. Cicero, who was an augur himself, laughed about
augury if he spoke to educated people.[37] Finally, Augustine cites Seneca's
lost *Dialogue on Superstition,* which displays exactly the same mixture of
skepticism and conservative *raison d'état* as we find it in the speech of the
pagan in Minucius Felix: "with respect to these sacred rites of the civil religion, Seneca preferred, as the best course to be followed by a wise man, to
feign respect for them in act, but to have no real regard for them at heart.
'All which things,' he says, 'a wise man will observe as being commanded
by the laws, but not as being pleasing to the gods.'"[38]

For reasons of political utility, this separation between public behavior
and private thought might have appeared as unavoidable to a pagan intellectual; for Christians, it was unacceptable. They were in possession of the
Gospel that revealed the true God. And therefore they had a true religion
(*vera religio*), a new concept that first appears in the writings of Minucius
Felix, Tertullian, and Lactantius. The basic truth that Christ revealed to
mankind is eternal life and eternal happiness in the beyond.[39] And from
this perspective all Roman gods are useless. Even if they are capable of fulfilling some earthly desires and of providing some temporal goods, they
are not in the position to grant eternal life. None of Christian writers of
the period ever said that the deities of the Roman Pantheon do not exist
at all; however, they lose their divine status and sink to the rank of demons. From the perspective of true religion, civil religion is simply a false

36. Minucius Felix, *Octavius,* 16,2.
37. Augustine, *City of God,* trans. G. E. McCracken, Loeb Classical Library (Cambridge,
Mass.: Harvard University Press, 1957), IV,31.
38. Ibid., VI,10.
39. Lactantius, *Epitome Divinarum institutionum,* ed. Eberhard Heck and Antonie Wlosok
(Stuttgart: Teubner, 1994), 47,1.

religion (*religio falsa*), as it is most clearly expressed in Lactantius.[40] From the perspective of truth, the old age of the Roman religion is no longer a criterion for its dignity. In his sketch of an ideal religious law, given in *The Laws,* Cicero prescribes: "No one shall have gods of his own, whether new or foreign, unless they have been officially brought in. In private they shall worship those gods whose worship has been handed down in its proper form by their forefathers. . . . They shall preserve the rituals of their family and fathers. They shall worship as gods those who have always been considered divine."[41] But now Lactantius asks: the religious customs might have been handed down from the ancestors for centuries; but what if the ancestors were foolish and mislead by demonic deceptions?[42] In the eyes of the Christian writer, all the considerations of Roman thinkers about the utility of religious traditions appear as mere opportunism.

Nevertheless, the political question remains unsolved in the texts of the pre-Constantinian period. The Christians defend themselves against the charge of cruel sacrifices and obscenities; but they have nothing to say in justification of the charge that they undermine the public order, except that they do not care. In his *Apologeticum,* Tertullian refutes the equation between Christians and illicit groups such as the Bacchants, but he also refuses any kind of political responsibility:

Ought not Christians . . . to receive not merely a somewhat milder treatment, but to have a place among the law-tolerated societies, seeing they are not chargeable with any such crimes as are commonly dreaded from societies of the illicit class? For, unless I mistake the matter, the prevention of such associations is based on a prudential regard to public order, that the state may not be divided into parties, which would naturally lead to disturbance in the electoral assemblies, the councils, the curiae, the special conventions, even in the public shows. . . . But . . . we have no pressing inducement to take part in your public meetings; nor is there anything more foreign to us than the affairs of the state.[43]

This contempt of politics, which differs decisively from the attitude of most Eastern Church Fathers, can be explained partly by the provenience of the

40. Ibid., 24.
41. Cicero, *De legibus,* II,19, in Cicero, *The Republic. The Laws,* trans. Neil Rudd. Oxford World's Classics (Oxford: Oxford University Press, 1998), 129–30.
42. Lactantius, *Epitome Divinarum institutionum,* 50,1; cf. Lactantius, *Institutiones Divines,* ed. Pierre Monat, Sources Chrétiennes 204 (Paris: Les Éditions du Cerf, 1973), V,19,3.
43. Tertullian, *Apologeticum,* 38, in Tertullian, *Apology,* trans. S. Thelwall, Ante-Nicene Fathers 3, American ed. (Grand Rapids, Mich.: Eerdmanns, 1989), 45.

authors. Minucius Felix, Tertullian, Lactantius, Cyprian, Arnobius, and Augustine were all Africans.[44] The early Muslim conquest of the Maghreb had the effect of almost completely removing from our consciousness the fact that, between the third and the fifth century, North Africa was the intellectual center of the West. At the periphery of the empire, among the Punic and Lybian populations of Africa Proconsularis, the attitude toward the empire and its representatives was highly ambiguous.

The Controversy over the Cult of Victory

Eric R. Dodds described the third century as "the age of anxiety."[45] In any case, it was a century with long periods of political chaos and disorder. Persians and Goths exercised pressure on the borders in the East and the North, which led to a successive militarization of the Empire. The so-called soldier emperors, who mostly came from the provinces, were enthroned by acclamation of the troops. The influence of the old Roman and Italian elites declined rapidly, especially in the military.[46] Yet, the political disorder can also be explained by the lack of a political theology that supported the imperial order. Some emperors tried more or less successfully to base their rule on the oriental cults they imported from their home countries. What these cults had in common was that they were not so much monotheistic as henotheistic; that is, they worshipped one highest god but recognized the existence of other gods. Finally, Constantine decided to base his rule on Christianity and transferred the capital of the empire to Constantinople, the new Christian Rome. It was Eastern Christian writers, first of all Eusebius of Caesarea, who developed an imperial theology in which truth and political utility merged into one. Most Christian theologians of the West, however, did not accept, or only reluctantly accepted, imperial theology—not only because of their African origin, but also because the Western Church had already developed its own political order, including an independent civil jurisdiction and an excellent system of social care. By the fourth century, this order already gradually replaced imperial institu-

44. Cf. Franz Georg Maier, *Die Verwandlung der Mittelmeerwelt* (Augsburg: Weltbild, 1998), 99.

45. Eric R. Dodds, *Pagan and Christian in an Age of Anxiety: Some Aspects of Religious Experience from Marc Aurelius to Constantine* (Cambridge: Cambridge University Press, 1990).

46. Arnoldo Momigliano, "Introduction: Christianity and the Decline of the Roman Empire," in *The Conflict between Paganism and Christianity in the Fourth Century*, ed. Arnoldo Momigliano (Oxford: Clarendon, 1964), 8–9.

tions. Consequently, the Church authorities were self-confident enough to refuse integration into the political order of the Empire. Bishop Ambrose of Milan, a powerful consultant to three emperors, made perfectly clear that the emperor is the highest earthly authority, but as a member of the Church he has to obey the bishop. This is the background of what was often perceived as the last great battle between Christian and pagan intellectuals in the West, the controversy over the Altar of Victoria.

In 382, Emperor Gratian decided that the Altar of Victoria, the goddess of victory, had to be removed from the curia, the building on the Forum Romanum where the sessions of the senate took place. Two years later, under Emperor Valentinian II, the rebellion of Maximus and a bad harvest caused a short-term revival of the pagan elites. They argued that the disasters were the revenge of the gods and regained some influence at the court of the emperor. Symmachus, a representative of the pagan party in the senate, wrote his *Third Relatio*. In this letter to Emperor Valentinian, he dares to demand no less than the restoration of the ancient cult, which, as he writes, had been so useful for the Res Publica.[47] Moreover, being a member of the college of pontiffs, he almost appears to be most concerned about the loss of all the tax and property privileges that the pagan priests had previously enjoyed. So he calls on the emperor to give them back.[48] In the *Third Relatio* we find all the arguments of political utility that we already know. The Altar of Victory, Symmachus says, ensures the morality and concord of the people and guarantees military success.[49]

But again something seems to have changed. Symmachus writes: "It is just that all worship should be considered as one. We look on the same stars, the sky is common, the same world surrounds us. What difference does it make by what pains each seeks the truth?"[50] "The divine Mind has

47. "Repetimus igitur religionum statum, qui rei publicae diu profuit." Symmachus, *Relatio III*, 3, in Richard Klein, *Der Streit um den Victoriaaltar. Die dritte Relatio des Symmachus und die Briefe 17, 18 und 57 des Mailänder Bischofs Ambrosius* (Darmstadt: Wissenschaftliche Buchgesellschaft, 1972), 100.

48. Symmachus, *Relatio III*, 11–18; cf. Richard Klein, "Die Romidee bei Symmachus, Claudian und Prudentius," in *Colloque Genevois sur Symmaque à l'occasion du mille six centième anniversaire du conflit de l'autel de la Victoire*, ed. F. Paschoud (Paris: Société d'Edition "Les Belles Lettres," 1986), 120. The emphasis on the financial issue is understandable given the fact that, as Ambrose correctly points out in his reply (*Epistula XVIII*, 8–16), the pagan cult could survive only on public subventions while the Church at this time received only minor subsidies. Cf. Hans von Campenhausen, *Lateinische Kirchenväter* (Stuttgart: Kohlhammer, 1986), 92.

49. Symmachus, *Relatio III*, 4–6.

50. Symmachus, *Relatio III*, 10, in Ambrose, *Some of the Principal Works of Ambrose*, trans.

distributed different guardians and different cults to different cities. As souls are separately given to infants as they are born, so to peoples the genius of their destiny."[51] This paganism is identical neither with the polytheist piety of the Roman republic nor with the skeptic conservatism of Cicero or the intellectuals of the Augustan age. Paradoxically, Symmachus justifies his polytheism with the monotheistic philosophy of Neo-Platonism.[52] Like the Christians, he appeals to truth. The providence of the divine Mind (*mens divina*) gave different cults to different peoples so that there would be a variety of ways to search for the divine truth.

Yet this political theology was not an intellectual construct of Symmachus. Just a few decades earlier the same mixture of Neo-Platonic metaphysics and polytheism had served as an ideological basis for the rule of Emperor Julian, commonly known as the Apostate. But Julian's religious policy was not apostasy; it was an innovative attempt to reconcile the ancient cult with imperial rule. In his *Against the Galileans,* Julian says: "Our writers say that the creator is the common father and king of all things, but that the other functions have been assigned by him to the national gods of the peoples and gods that protect the cities; every one of whom administers his own department in accordance with his own nature."[53]

Whether this political theology could have been a possible alternative to Christianity is an academic question. Its failure is a historical fact. Probably Neoplatonic philosophy was simply too sophisticated to convince the masses. The truth of Neoplatonic mysticism had to be sought by meditation and intellectual efforts, whereas the Christian truth was revealed and at hand. Bishop Ambrose was quite aware of this advantage. In his *Letter XVIII,* which addresses the emperor and comments on the *Third Relatio* of Symmachus, he writes: "By one road, says he [Symmachus], one cannot attain to so great a secret. What you know not, that we know by the voice of God. And what you seek by fancies, we have found out from the very Wisdom and Truth of God. Your ways, therefore, do not agree with ours."[54]

Of course, Symmachus does not restrict his argument to truth. *Accedit*

H. de Romestin, Nicene and Post-Nicene Fathers, Second Series X, reprint (Grand Rapids, Mich.: Eerdmans 1989), 414.

51. Symmachus, *Relatio III,* 8, in Ambrose, 415.

52. Cf. Manfred Fuhrmann, *Rom in der Spätantike. Porträt einer Epoche* (Munich: Artemis and Winkler, 1994), 73–75.

53. Cited from Arnoldo Momigliano, "The Disadvantages of Monotheism for a Universal State," *Classical Philology* 81, no. 4 (October 1986): 293.

54. Ambrosius, *Epistula XVIII,* 8, in Ambrose, 418.

utilitas are the two words, he hastens to add: "Here comes in the proof from advantage, which most of all vouches to man for the gods. For, since our reason is wholly clouded, whence does the knowledge of the gods more rightly come to us, than from the memory and evidence of prosperity? Now if a long period gives authority to religious customs, we ought to keep faith with so many centuries, and to follow our ancestors, as they happily followed theirs."[55]

This quotation, however, sounds much more like the skepticism of Cicero and the pagan in Minucius's *Octavius;* and it displays the traditional creed of civil religion. The main arguments for the traditional cult are its utility and its old age. Richard Klein, one of the leading Symmachus scholars, therefore warns not to overemphasize the Neoplatonic dimension of the *Third Relatio.*[56] The vast corpus of letters Symmachus left behind does not show any higher philosophical ambitions of its author. Even in the *Third Relatio,* Symmachus shows no major interest in theological disputes, since he concludes his remarks about the *Mens Divina* with the words: "but this discussion is rather for persons at ease."[57] This interpretation of Klein, which I am inclined to follow, lets the Neoplatonist argument appear as a concession to the contemporary intellectual discourse. However, it shows that Symmachus was more or less aware of the fact that his position was anachronistic. As a member of the senatorial aristocracy he identified the meaning of his existence with the care for the Res Publica, according to the *mos maiorum.* This self-image included the protection of the traditional cult. On the other hand, Symmachus had to accept that the senate had long ago lost its authority in religious matters, and he knew that religious policies were increasingly negotiated between the Church authorities and the imperial court. The fact that Symmachus addressed the emperor and his court in Milan instead of the senate in Rome was the clearest sign of the republican institutions' almost complete loss of power.

Undoubtedly, Symmachus was aware that all he could hope for was toleration. When he pleaded for the restoration of the ancient cult, he certainly did not expect the restoration of the ancient religio-political order.[58]

55. Symmachus, *Relatio III,* 8, in Ambrose, 415.

56. Klein, "Die Romidee bei Symmachus, Claudian und Prudentius," 123. Manfred Fuhrmann, on the other hand, thinks that the Neoplatonist dimension is essential to Symmachus's argument. Fuhrmann, *Rom in der Spätantike,* 73–75.

57. Symmachus, *Relatio III,* 10; transl. de Romestin, 415.

58. This become manifest in these sentences: "Let the rulers of each sect and of each opinion

The experience of decline is clearly articulated, when in the *Third Relatio* the personified Roma complains: "Have I been reserved for this, that in my old age I should be blamed? I will consider what it is thought should be set in order, but tardy and discreditable is the reformation of old age." In other words, Roma is simply too old to convert to Christianity. When Symmachus adds, "We ask, then, for peace for the gods of our fathers and of our country," it almost sounds as if he desired not much more than a decent and undisturbed retirement for the ancient gods and the pagan aristocracy.

There is, however, evidence that Christian aristocrats in the senate as well as in the council of the emperor showed sympathies for Symmachus's case. As modern scholars, such as Glen W. Bowersock, have pointed out, the leading class was not simply divided into pagans and Christians. Obviously, many Christian members of the senatorial aristocracy preserved, or, in case they were only newly promoted to the senatorial rank, adopted, the traditional self-image. Consequently, they were not inclined to destroy the cult of "their" ancestors.[59] The senatorial aristocracy still possessed a kind of class identity; friendship between Christian and pagan members was not unusual. In private life, even the two opponents Symmachus and Ambrose, the latter also stemming from the senatorial aristocracy, got along quite well. Therefore it is no surprise that, in the first place, the council of Valentinian II decided in favor of Symmachus.

Yet this was the moment for Bishop Ambrose to intervene. He wrote two letters to the young emperor of the West, who at this time was only fourteen years old. *Epistula XVII* was written before Ambrose had read the *Relatio* of Symmachus. The opening paragraphs appear like a manifesto of the catholic policy which was to govern the Western society in the following centuries:

As all men who live under the Roman sway engage in military service under you, the Emperors and Princes of the world, so too do you yourselves owe service to Almighty God and our holy faith. For salvation is not sure unless everyone worship in truth the true God, that is the God of the Christians, under Whose

---

be counted up; a late one [i.e. Julian the Apostate] practised the ceremonies of his ancestors, a later [Valentinian I] did not put them away. If the religion of old times does not make a precedent, let the connivance of the last [i.e. the emperors Valentinian I and Valens] do so" (Symmachus, *Relatio III*, 3, in Ambrose, 414). For a similar interpretation see Campenhausen, *Lateinische Kirchenväter*, 91.

59. Glen W. Bowersock, "Symmachus and Ausonius," in *Colloque Genevois sur Symmaque à l'occasion du mille six centième anniversaire du conflit de l'autel de la Victoire*, ed. F. Paschoud (Paris: Société d'Edition "Les Belles Lettres," 1986), 4–5.

sway are all things; for He alone is the true God, Who is to be worshipped from the bottom of the heart; for "the gods of the heathen," as Scripture says, "are devils." Now everyone is a soldier of this true God, and he who receives and worships Him in his inmost spirit, does not bring to His service dissimulation, or pretence, but earnest faith and devotion. And if, in fine, he does not attain to this, at least he ought not to give any countenance to the worship of idols and to profane ceremonies. For no one deceives God, to whom all things, even the hidden things of the heart, are manifest.[60]

In sum: the ruler is not sovereign, but subject to the will of the one true god (*deus verus*), who does not accept tolerance toward the pagan cult. To know the will of god, however, is the office of the bishop and not of the emperor. Should the emperor resist the will of the bishops they would refuse the Eucharist, and consequently his salvation would be endangered. "If it were a civil cause," Ambrose writes, "the right of reply would be reserved for the opposing party; it is a religious cause, and I the bishop make a claim. [. . .] Certainly if anything else is decreed, we bishops cannot contentedly suffer it and take no notice; you indeed may come to the church, but will find either no priest there, or one who will resist you."[61]

A few years later, when Theodosius ruled the Western Empire, the threat of excommunication proved to be a serious measure to discipline the ruler. The success of this policy of truth also meant the final defeat of traditional civil religion. Where the revelation of truth is accepted, the argument of utility does not count anymore, as Ambrose makes clear: "Ponder well, I pray you, and examine the sect of the heathen, their utterances, sound, weighty, and grand, but defend what is without capacity for truth."[62]

Conclusion

What we can observe in the texts of the third and fourth century is humans who seek for existential consistency, that is, consistency between experiences in the political and the numinous sphere. The polytheistic cult was the cult of the republic and, as Arnoldo Momigliano has shown, we do not find a theorist in this period who successfully achieved the reconciliation of traditional polytheism and imperial rule.[63] The multiplicity of

---

60. Ambrosius, *Epistula XVII*, 1–2, in Ambrose, 411–12.
61. Ambrosius, *Epistula XVII*, 13, in Ambrose, 413.
62. Ambrosius, *Epistula XVIII*, 2, in Ambrose, 417.
63. Momigliano, "Disadvantages of Monotheism," 296.

political responsibilities in the republic conformed to the multiplicity of responsibilities in a polytheist pantheon but conflicted with the experience that one emperor takes care of virtually the whole world. In this conflict, the questions of truth and utility gain relevance. The experience of universal political unity suggests unity in the numinous sphere, the existence of one true god who takes care of all mankind. In its turn, the experience of a one true divine ruler suggests a uniform imperial order. Under the same circumstances, the pagan elites, who did not want to partake in the religious transformation, emphasized the political utility of their cult. As we know, their efforts were ultimately futile. Augustine's *City of God* determined the self-understanding of the Western civilization for the next one thousand years. But if we take a closer look at the Church Father's terminology, we see that the symbolical cosmos of the ancient religion was not destroyed but was transformed under the signs of truth.

One could even say that Augustine, in a certain sense, achieved what seemed to be impossible, namely the reconciliation of truth and republic. Augustine speaks of the true religion (*vera religio*) worshiped by the true citizens (*cives veri*) in a truer city (*civitas verior*). The city of God is truer, because it is the mystical community of the true believers and not identical with any visible community. Political utility has not disappeared, but it is now completely secularized and restricted to the earthly city, the *civitas terrena*. At least in theory, religion is no longer useful for politics, but politics is useful for religion. It is to a large extent Ambrose's achievement that already Theodosius saw his highest office in protection of the Catholic Church and the unity of the orthodox faith.[64] In Augustine's mirror of princes, modeled upon the example of Theodosius, the emperor spreads Christianity over the world and destroys the pagan cults.[65] But the final goal of his life is not to achieve superiority in this world, but to dwell among equals in the heavenly city, which Augustine describes as the true republic.[66]

64. Charles N. Cochrane, *Christianity and Classical Culture: A Study of Thought and Action from Augustus to Augustine* (Indianapolis: Liberty Fund, 2003), 360–62.

65. Augustine, *The City of God*, V,24–26.

66. "True justice, however, exists only in that republic whose Founder and Ruler is Christ, if you please to call it too a republic, since we cannot deny that it is a people's estate" (Augustine, *The City of God*, II,21).

3

The Humility of True Religion

Augustine's Critique
of Roman Civil Religion

DAVID J. BOBB

In A.D. 410 the Eternal City was given a shocking reminder of its mortality. The Visigoth invasion of Rome prompted immediate accusations against Christians that the ascendancy of their faith in Rome had invited the catastrophic events of the early fifth century. Christianity enervated Rome's political strength and martial resiliency at the same time it offered no coherent political system of its own, Roman critics charged. Christianity sapped Roman *virtù* of its vitality. Saint Augustine counterattacked with vigor. The accusers of Christianity should look instead at their own vices, he countered, for the pride Romans took in their political and military edifice ensured not strength but weakness. It was only a matter of time, Augustine argued, before the entire structure would be toppled. Rome as the Eternal City was a deception of the highest order, a chimera constructed by demons bent upon obscuring the glorious truth revealed in the only true *civitas aeternas,* the City of God.

Roman civil religion, Augustine contended, was established to bind the people to the state. Pagan religious practices, which took the form of a "civil" religion because of the financial and political support offered by Roman authorities, were false, Augustine believed. *Contra Romanos* Augustine argued that it was not the humility of Christianity but the prideful assertiveness of Roman civil religion that precipitated Rome's demise. Founded on false religion, Roman civil religion proved weak glue for social and political cohesiveness. Against the pagans who saw humility as a vice—even more, the vicious source of the meekness that led to Rome's overthrow—Augustine hoped to establish its place as the pre-eminent virtue without which pride will enslave the souls of men and overrun their social and political institutions. Roman pride, Augustine argued, was rooted in their civil religion. Instead of blaming Christian meekness for the fall of Rome, Augustine adamantly insisted that Romans must instead examine their own civil religious failings.

Augustine concluded that pagan piety was a sham, as were all of the virtues that were thought by the pagans naturally to flow from their piety: self-sacrifice, pursuit of the common good, courage, temperance, prudence, justice, magnificence, and not least, magnanimity. Every virtue cherished by the Romans was in fact a vice—because every so-called virtue was divorced from *humilitas*. This did not mean, Augustine nonetheless claimed, that Roman accomplishments were without merit. Indeed, Augustine always was careful to give credit to the Romans for their impressive republican and even imperial accomplishments. Nonetheless, he argued that even the most outstanding Roman accomplishments were based upon a false foundation. Thus their accomplishments were falsely prized. Augustine's radical alternative required not a political goal that prized virtues for their service to the state, but rather the spiritual insight that if virtues were to be sustained as true they must be illuminated by *caritas,* animated by *humilitas,* and ordered according to *aeternitas.*

The Christian alternative, Augustine knew, seemed absurd to people puffed up with pride. That is why he realized that his task was to "convince the proud of the power and excellence of humility."[1] The immense difficulty with Augustine's task, from his perspective, was that the patients he wished to treat did not think they needed a doctor! Only *Christus medicus,* he believed, could heal souls inflamed by pride.

Augustine's Argument against the Diabolical Religion of Rome

The divine doctor, Augustine held, was uniquely capable of curing the infection of pride because only God could contend with its demonic cause. In book 9 Augustine analyzes the derivation of the word "demon" as part

---

1. Augustine, *City of God,* trans. Henry Bettenson (New York: Penguin, 1984), 5 (Preface). Hereafter cited as *City of God.*

of his discussion of the demonic omnipresence in Roman civil religion. Quoting 1 Corinthians 8:1, "Knowledge inflates: but love edifies," Augustine explains that knowledge requires charity in order to resist inflation. Augustine contrasts their pride with the humility of Christ: "Against this arrogance of the demons, to which mankind was enslaved as a deserved punishment, is set the humility of God, revealed in Christ. But the power of humility is unknown to men whose souls are inflated with the impurity of inflated pride. They resemble the demons in arrogance, but not in knowledge."[2]

The demons' possession of knowledge without charity causes them to be inflated with pride; they seek for themselves the honor properly paid only to God. They glimpse the truth but refuse to act on it because pride has overwhelmed them.

Man is enslaved to this same pride, for men share the demonic sin of attempting to rely upon their own knowledge, knowledge that they have severed from the love of God. Thinking that they gain liberation through autonomy, they actually enslave themselves. Both deny God the glory that is due only to Him. Augustine's long discussion of demons in the first part of the *City of God* is the major premise in his argument against Roman civil religion. Augustine's argument in the *City of God,* indicated in the preface to book 1, is "to convince the proud of the power and excellence of humility."[3] To accomplish this end, Augustine first must show that the Roman civil religion is the source of the damaging pride. Instead of bringing glory and honor to the empire, the civil religion instead caused its demise. It is not Christianity's humility and meekness that caused Rome's collapse, as many Romans alleged, but rather, Augustine counters, a diabolical pagan pride that led to Rome's demise.

Augustine's goal in the first five books in the *City of God* is to prove that the Roman religion, far from offering salutary political effects, actually welcomed a demonic rule that would preside over Rome's demise. The Roman gods did not protect Rome in its darkest hour because they were not beneficent beings but evil demons. Only Christianity, "the one true religion, had the power to prove that the gods of the nations are unclean demons."[4] The first five books focus on why Romans should not worship their gods for the purpose of securing temporal rewards. The next five

2. Ibid., 366 (IX.20).
3. Ibid., 5 (Preface).
4. Ibid., 294 (VII.33).

books, Augustine explains at the end of the fifth book, demonstrate that just as the Roman gods fail to provide earthly blessings, so too do they fail to provide for people in the life eternal.[5] This failure on the part of the Roman gods is not surprising, Augustine asserts as his underlying claim in the first ten books, because the "gods" are demonic, not divine.

The demons, Augustine avers, fashion a clever deception that because of their superior knowledge and conniving manner fools many men. The demonic deception is simply to fool mortals into believing that the demons are gods. Even more, they deceive men into believing that if the gods are sufficiently venerated and propitiated, the gods, in turn, will protect the people. In addition to temporal protection the gods can secure for men eternal felicity. The transformation of demons into "gods," Augustine insists, is nothing but a clever, ignoble lie.

Rome's reliance upon a civil religious lie was not surprising, Augustine argues, because Rome itself was ill-founded. A fratricide marked the founding of the earthly city, Augustine notes, referring to Cain's murder of Abel. The founding of Rome, the most visible instantiation of the City of Man, reflects this first founding, the murder of Abel. Pride prompted the bloodshed in both cases, for both Cain and his Roman counterpart, Romulus, the murderer of his brother Remus, acted with envy born of pride. The difference between the two founding fratricides, Augustine maintains, is that in the second the murdered brother, Remus, was as culpable as his murderer, Romulus, whereas Abel, Cain's victim, was innocent. Romulus and Remus "[b]oth sought the glory of establishing the Roman state, but a joint foundation would not bring to each the glory that a single founder would enjoy."[6] A desire to be *the* founder, a prideful assertion, motivated Romulus to kill his brother. His thinking was distorted by his disordered desire: "Anyone whose aim was to glory in the exercise of power would obviously enjoy less power if his sovereignty was diminished by a living partner."[7] The logic evident in this statement aptly summarizes what might be called the fundamental law of the City of Man: politics, like life, is a zero-sum game. The more one's fellow citizens have of something (glory, property, or power) the less there is available for others. The political state as exemplified in the Roman founding, birthed because of the original sin of pride, is beset by pride. Pride begets more pride until its weight is un-

5. Ibid., 224 (V.26).   6. Ibid., 600 (XV.5).
7. Ibid.

bearable. Augustine cites Rome as the prime example of this unfortunate truth: "And the lust for power, which of all human vices was found in its most concentrated form in the Roman people as a whole, first established its victory in a few powerful individuals, and then crushed the rest of an exhausted country beneath the yoke of slavery."[8]

The City of God and the City of Man are built on opposing loves. A citizen of the City of God loves God alone; a subject of the City of Man loves himself first, and in this selfishness loses himself in pride.[9] In the City of God divine love is the shared goodness that does not diminish despite the addition of more sharers. In the City of Man at its worst, it is confusion—not goodness—that is shared in common. Within the City of Man, it is a concern for property, a limited common good, that is shared. Augustine clarifies the chasm that separates the cities with reference to their founders: "Thus the quarrel that arose between Remus and Romulus demonstrated the division of the earthly city against itself; while the conflict between Cain and Abel displayed the hostility between the two cities themselves, the City of God and the city of men."[10] The quarrel between Cain and Abel symbolizes the splitting away of the City of Man from the City of God: it is the difference between the embrace of evil and the adherence to good. The story of Romulus and Remus reveals what transpired after human beings fell from grace and embraced evil, for in doing so they plunged themselves into a constant struggle for glory that is marked above all by the prideful assertion of self.

The Roman founding, for Augustine, serves as important evidence for the baleful effects of pride. Like all members of the City of Man, the Roman founders "prefer their own gods to the Founder of that City [God]."[11] A rotten foundation, Augustine holds, inevitably leads to collapse. To demonstrate this point Augustine asks the defenders of Roman religion to evaluate the foundation of their cause. Where was the evidence, Augustine asks, for the gods urging the noble behavior that is essential for the survival of good life in general and good political life in particular? When gathered to worship the gods, do the assembled faithful "hear the commands of the gods about the need to restrain avarice, to curb ambition, to put a check on lust" and other essential imperatives for temporal peace?[12] Far from it,

8. Ibid., 42 (I.31).
9. Ibid., 593 (XIV.28).
10. Ibid., 601 (XV.5).
11. Ibid., 5 (Preface).
12. Ibid., 54 (II.6).

Augustine thunders: the pagan religious rites are themselves the *source* of popular corruption, for people emulate the lascivious behavior of the gods. Augustine recalls one especially foul pagan show he witnessed as a young boy: "If these were sacred rites, what is meant by sacrilege? If this is purification, what is meant by pollution?"[13] Instead of helping to ennoble the Roman people their religion debased them. How could demons posing as gods be credited with protecting Rome when all they demanded of people was debauchery?

After his attack on the integrity of pagan religion, Augustine counters the pagan condemnation of Christianity with a rhetorical thrust of his own: the pagans, he claims, are inconsistent in their own recognition of divine assistance. When Rome flourished, and the religious partisans relished Rome's exalted status, they were quick to give credit to the gods. Yet when Rome fell from the dizzying heights to which it rose, those same partisans failed to blame their divinities. By their own internal logic, the pagans could not consistently fault the Christian God for the invasion of Rome when in similarly dire straits they earlier had refused to fault their own gods.

Augustine presses a much deeper point, however, than the *incoherence* of the pagan position, for his fundamental claim is that the Roman ideas of religion, prosperity, and justice are as false as the demons they called gods. The pagans are inconsistent, Augustine states, but they are more than that: they are wrong—even wickedly wrong—in their impious pride that exalts their false claims about virtue above all others. The Romans upheld certain standards, to be sure, but ultimately they were the wrong standards, not a surprising state of affairs given the evil guidance of the gods: "But the worshippers and lovers of those gods, whom they delighted to imitate in their criminal wickedness, are unconcerned about the utter corruption of their country. 'So long as it lasts,' they say, 'so long as it enjoys material prosperity, and the glory of victorious war, or better, the security of peace, why should we worry?'"[14] Romans adopted false criteria for prosperity as they were blinded by pride, Augustine indicates. Focused on lavish displays of material wealth, the Romans were blinded to the real causes of their corruption. As Augustine writes in book 2 of the *City of God,* "For in the ruin of the city it was stone and timber which fell to the ground; but in the lives of those Romans we saw the collapse not of material but of moral defenc-

13. Ibid., 52 (II.4).
14. Ibid., 71 (II.20).

es, not of material but of spiritual grandeur. The lust that burned in their hearts was more deadly than the flame which consumed their dwellings."[15]

According to Augustine, the Roman idea of religion turned out to be blasphemy, just as the Roman idea of prosperity was in fact vile enslavement. The understanding of justice that flowed from Roman civil religion likewise was deeply flawed, in Augustine's estimation. In chapter 21 of book 2 in the *City of God,* Augustine appeals to the authority of Cicero to buttress his case that the Romans were in a downward spiral. If his interlocutors are not willing to listen to Sallust, the Roman historian Augustine frequently cites to document the degeneracy of the Roman way of life, perhaps they will heed the pronouncements of Cicero, Augustine hopes. Cicero, Augustine says, never would have countenanced the feeble arguments of Augustine's contemporary critics, for Cicero himself observed the real downfall of Rome "long before Christ came in the flesh."[16]

For Augustine, the signal importance of Cicero's *De Republica,* a dialogue about Rome and the common good, is that the work, by asking its readers to inquire into the requisite elements of republican justice and the common good, helps to make the case that without true justice there is no common weal. Christianity's detractors do not have to rely upon Augustine's asseverations about the Roman confusion regarding justice and the common good, for the central argument was anticipated—by more than four centuries—by Cicero, one of the greatest friends of Roman liberty. Scipio, a key character in Cicero's dialogue, defines the community as "'an association united by a common sense of right and a community of interest.'"[17] If there is a systemic miscarriage of justice in the community—what amounts to tyrannical injustice of one, a few, or many—the conclusion must be not that the commonwealth has been corrupted but rather that it has ceased to exist. Augustine claims that the logical force of Cicero's argument should require honest thinkers of the fifth century to confront the question of whether true justice had *ever* prevailed Rome. His own view, he admits, is to answer the query in the negative, but with an important qualification: "Now it certainly was a commonwealth to some degree, according to more plausible definitions [than Scipio's]; and it was better ruled by the Romans of antiquity than by their later successors."[18] Augustine concludes chapter 21 by introducing a radical idea upon which he will ex-

15. Ibid., 49 (II.2).
17. Ibid., 73 (II.21).
16. Ibid., 74–75 (II.21).
18. Ibid., 75 (II.21).

pound much later in the book: "[T]rue justice is found only in that commonwealth whose founder and ruler is Christ," the "City of which the holy Scripture says, 'Glorious things are said about you, City of God.'"[19]

Augustine's comprehensive argument against pagan pride hinges upon humility because it is only with a humble heart that a person can see the difference between true and false religion, true and false prosperity, and true and false justice. The grace of God allows humility to reveal counterfeits wherever they may be, for in ripping away prideful masks the humble believer sees the truth of things. The most terrible tyranny for Augustine is not a political tyranny but tyranny of the soul. A soul is enslaved when it is chained to the passions, when instead of being ordered according to virtue it is disordered according to vice.

Pride's pernicious influence in the political realm is unavoidable, according to Augustine. This does not mean that pride's negative effects are overwhelming. Pride in politics is the political original sin, we might say, just as pride in the Fall of man was *the* original sin, in Augustine's view. Original sin vitiates but does not destroy man's capacity for goodness; so too does political original sin vitiate but not destroy the possibility for a certain measure of goodness, or virtuous accomplishment, *within* the sphere of politics.[20] Augustine's understanding of humility in its political dimension impels him neither to diabolize nor to divinize politics. Just as the quest for glory is not inherently evil, so too participation in politics is not inherently evil. Such participation, however, like any religious quest, must be directed towards truth.

"True" is a common adjective for Augustine because the entirety of his argument depends upon differentiating truth from its innumerable counterfeits. *Vera religio* is the only foundation that supports true virtue, and Christ is the only author of abiding goodness. To imagine that virtue— true virtue—can be supported by any other foundation is prideful folly. Neither philosophic autonomy nor political power is a sufficient support for true virtue.

---

19. Ibid. Augustine quotes Psalm 87:5.

20. For a fine development of this point, see John von Heyking, chapter 5, "Glory as a Proper End of Politics," in *Augustine and Politics as Longing in the World* (Columbia: University of Missouri Press, 2001).

Pride and the False Promise of Political Salvation

Civil religion, which Augustine holds is a flimsy substitute for true religion that elevates social and political utility over truth, also fails, he believes, to provide a foundation strong enough to support true virtue. Only God, Augustine emphatically states, is the author of Good. Civil religion promises to produce a kind of good that will work as societal cement. Civil religion often propounds a gospel of political salvation. Although the Roman civil religion Augustine attacked was not based upon any particular "good news," Augustine saw in it a profound danger, for it still held out the possibility of salvation—outside of Christ, and mediated by the state. Christianity was considered by its pagan critics so completely odious because it could not abide any part of the *theologia civilis.* The root problem of Christianity's dogmatic and uncompromising attack on civil religion, from their perspective, was its universalism. The many permutations of Roman civil religion that proliferated throughout the empire, despite vast differences in their pantheons and religious practices, all shared the similar goal of binding Roman citizens to the state. With its strident attack on civil religion and apolitical character, Christianity posed a grave threat to the political unity that could be forged by civil religion.

Augustine's expert witness, we might say, in his critique of Roman civil religion was the prolific author Marcus Terentius Varro (116–27 B.C.). According to Varro's account of the pagan pontiff Scaevola's categorization of the gods, the Romans relied upon three main traditions: the gods of the poets, the gods of the philosophers, and the gods of the statesmen.[21] A struggle in Rome existed between the representatives of these traditions, as each party vied for the predominance of its particular mode of religion. The mythic, philosophic, and civic traditions can never be completely separated, but Augustine follows Varro, who follows Scaevola, with this system of classification for purposes of his critique. Books 1–5 of the *City of God,* as we have indicated, are devoted to the problem of Roman religion as it pursues this-worldly solutions; books 6–10 are devoted to the problem of Roman religion as it pursues a solution to life after man's earthly existence. This outline is important here in that Augustine treats Varro's classification scheme in its fullness in books 6 and 7 of the *City of God.* As Ernest Fortin

21. *City of God,* 168 (IV.27).

explains, this is a telling move by Augustine, for it reveals much about the nature of Augustine's critique of civil religion in general.

According to Fortin, civil theology (or civil religion—the terms may be used interchangeably here), is in between the other two types, for "Even in its perfected state, it still presents itself as a compromise between the theology of the philosophers, which demands too much of the people, and that of the poets, which demands too little."[22] Philosophers, Augustine knew, wish to puncture the superstitious myths that surround all cults. They thereby demand too much of the people by expecting people to live as they do, in awareness of the death of the gods. The poets, despite their power to weave religiously charged tales that inspire stronger dedication to the gods and perhaps even heroic sacrifice to the state, have no real purchase on the peoples' lives. Mythic theology, as Fortin notes, ultimately must accede to the demands of the political authorities.[23] From a pagan perspective, an effective civil religion will bind the people to the state without binding them too zealously to religious truth. In short, it will make the people learn to love religion for its utility without their realizing that they are utilitarians.

For Augustine, this theology of utility yields nothing but futility! At the heart of civil religion is a lie. Nonetheless, in the hands of a capable and crafty philosopher a lie can be made to seem noble. In Augustine's account, Varro was circumspect enough not to reveal his own atheism, and "he also realized that most people would think more highly of themselves and aspire to greater deeds if they cherished the belief in their own divine descent."[24] Assuming the "perspective of the dutiful citizen," and not the scandalous philosopher, Varro sought subtle reforms of Roman religion that would strengthen its civic component. Augustine placed his analysis of Varro in the second half of his division of the first ten books because, as Fortin suggests, Augustine was aware that Varro's civic persona masked his real effort at transcendence of the noble lie he proffers for political gain.

For Augustine, Varro was an authority of immense stature: "he is so full of knowledge and ideas that in the kind of learning which we Christians call secular and the pagans call liberal he gives as much informa-

22. Ernest Fortin, "Augustine and Roman Civil Religion: Some Critical Reflections," in *Classical Christianity and the Political Order: Reflections on the Theologico-Political Problem, Ernest L. Fortin: Collected Essays,* vol. 2, ed. J. Brian Benestad (Lanham, Md.: Rowman and Littlefield, 1996), 92–93.

23. Ibid., 92.

24. Ibid., 93.

tion to the student of history as Cicero gives pleasure to the connoisseur of style."[25] To Augustine's readers, however, Varro appeared largely as an anachronism, and his depiction of Roman religion was seen as unrepresentative of contemporary practices. Augustine's reliance upon Varro obscured the pluralistic quality of Roman religious practice. For Fortin, there is an even deeper reason to question Augustine's invocation of Varro, for while Augustine "pokes fun at the pagan gods in general, Augustine is careful to avoid any direct assault on the last remnants of the old civil religion."[26] Is Augustine pulling his punches? Fortin offers a qualified "yes" to his own incisive question: "To assail civil religion frontally would have been to rob the community of whatever benefit it could conceivably derive from it in an age of mounting political turmoil and instability." Fortin sees a "prudent" move in Augustine's indirect and more general critique of Roman civil religion; in forgoing a direct assault on the contemporary Roman civil religion (which would come complete with the details of the Roman religious practice historians are quick to note Augustine fails to offer), Augustine recognized the power of tradition and the grip that habit held on Roman hearts.

In assailing older and perhaps even outmoded practices Augustine focused his reader on the incoherence and danger of civil religion in general. Fortin summarizes Augustine's strategy: "It is thus fair to say that Augustine's treatment of political theology is itself political, combining as it does an unflinching commitment to the truth with a deep sympathy for the failings of ordinary human beings."[27] Augustine's "political" effort, we might add, was born of a humble approach to politics that in giving the power of public opinion due regard nonetheless refused to be cowed by it. His claims against civil religion of any sort come not in defense of a stronger state or even greater political liberty. Rather, Augustine criticizes civil religion so that the truth civil religion counterfeits may be revealed in all of its glory: "Whereas it was not any terrestrial community that established true religion; it was true religion, without doubt, that established the Celestial City; and true religion is given to his true worshippers by the inspiration and teaching of the true God, the giver of eternal life."[28]

25. *City of God*, 229 (VI.2).
26. Fortin, "Augustine and Roman Civil Religion: Some Critical Reflections," 95.
27. Ibid., 97.
28. *City of God*, 232 (VI.4).

The dependence of true virtue on true religion is the decisive context in which Augustine's argument about Rome, justice, and Scipio's definition of commonwealth must be understood. When in book 19 of the *City of God* Augustine picks up his long-neglected thread from book 2, he concludes that true justice is never possible in the City of Man. Augustine defines justice as "that virtue which assigns to everyone his due."[29] If Rome, as Augustine holds he had earlier established, is founded on demon worship, he is compelled to ask, following his definition of justice, "Then what kind of justice is it that takes a man away from the true God and subjects him to unclean demons?"[30] Where God does not rule, Augustine writes, there can be no true justice.[31] This uncompromising stance about justice dictates the flow of the rest of the argument that revolves around the Ciceronian definition of the common weal. If Scipio's definition of the state, or commonwealth, is true, then Rome never was a commonwealth, for Scipio's definition of a commonwealth requires justice. No justice, no "common sense of right." "No common sense of right," no commonwealth.

Augustine's carefully elaborated argument, even in its relative simplicity, stands atop another argument, for Augustine's larger argument is that pagan virtue, lacking a solid foundation in God, is vice. This argument, *prima facie,* seems both despondent *and* utopian. It seems despondent because there is no possibility of justice on Earth. It seems utopian because justice is possible only in perfection:

Justice is found where God, the one supreme God, rules an obedient City according to his grace, forbidding sacrifice to any being save himself alone; and where in consequence the soul rules the body in all men who belong to this City and obey God, and the reason faithfully rules the vices in a lawful system of subordination; so that just as the individual righteous man lives on the basis of faith which is active in love, so the association, or people, of righteous men lives on the same basis of faith, active in love, the love with which a man loves God as God ought to be loved, and loves his neighbour as himself.[32]

If understood with humility, Augustine suggests, his argument is not despondent but hopeful. It is not utopian, moreover, because that which is hoped for is most certainly realized, according to Augustine—in the City of God.

---

29. Ibid., 882 (XIX.21).
31. Ibid., 891 (XIX.24).

30. Ibid., 882 (XIX.21).
32. Ibid., 890 (XIX.23).

True Virtue Is Impossible without True Religion

In the City of God there exists perfect parallelism between each individual's proper ordering of the body according to the soul's right desires and the proper obedience paid by every subject to God's rule. In the City of Man disordered desires are as rampant as they are perfect in the City of God. As Augustine explains, "Thus the virtues which the mind imagines it possesses, by means of which it rules the body and the vicious elements, are themselves vices rather than virtues, if the mind does not bring them into relation with God in order to achieve anything whatsoever and to maintain that achievement."[33] If God is not the sovereign ordering agent, the desires are destined to run amok.

But what about apparently noble individuals, those who seem capable of accomplishing good on their own accord, even if they pronounce themselves independent of outside assistance? Augustine's answer is unswerving: "For although the virtues are reckoned by some people to be genuine and honourable when they are related only to themselves and are sought for no other end, even then they are puffed up and proud, and so are to be accounted vices rather than virtues."[34] In what is arguably the most important part of Augustine's most elaborate argument—on which his entire idea of analyzing people and commonwealths according to love depends—Augustine repairs to the puffery of the proud. The phantasm of self-sufficiency, pride, is central to Augustine's argument. His claim is not complicated: the more obdurately human beings cling to the idea of self-creation and autonomy, the more their efforts to be virtuous will redound to viciousness. Augustine denies the possibility of moral neutrality or an agnostic, existential effort to fashion values from one's own resources. "For just as it is not something derived from the physical body itself that gives life to that body, but something above it, so it is not something that comes from man, but something above man, that makes his life blessed; and this is true not only of man but of every heavenly dominion and power whatsoever."[35]

A humble stance, Augustine affirms, is required to formulate true theology and sound political reflection. Humility, a virtue of great good, is a prerequisite of the other great virtues. To start anywhere else is to go awry. Augustine's unqualified denunciation of pagan virtue as vice seems

33. Ibid., 891 (XIX.25).   34. Ibid.
35. Ibid.

in itself a proud proclamation—perhaps even the haughty and overzealous exaggeration of an ideologue whose teaching will give rise to crusades against pagan and heretical vice. To critics with this view, who seize upon what they see as Augustine's utopian streak, his great error originates in his inability to grant pagans any credit for their virtue. His wholesale condemnation of paganism, punctuated by incessant rants about demons, gave rise to intolerance, the critics charge, in which only Christianity is allowed. Seeing demons everywhere, Augustine unleashed a whirlwind.[36] To understand better Augustine's position in light of these charges, it is essential for us to consider the mirror of princes Augustine offered as a guide for Christian princes, for this mirror offers a direct confrontation with the problem of pride in politics.

From Humility to the Heights: The Politics of Pride

Augustine's analysis of spiritual pride led him to reflect on pride in politics. The political realm attracts individuals who love power, so the danger of pride is omnipresent in politics. Pride, it seems, is endemic to political rule. The ruler puffed up with pride readily believes himself to be autonomous; because of the ruler's power his misbegotten and mistaken belief threatens widespread problems. Augustine maintains that if the ruler forgets that he is not God the ruler crowns himself god; the satanic deception at the Garden of Eden is replicated in the demonic deception of pagan rule disordered by the *libido dominandi*. Yet to the pagan ruler—and the defenders of the old pagan Roman order—it would seem only natural that a ruler, especially an emperor, should love glory above all other things. Pursuit of power is the very definition of nobility, the realization of true greatness. To deprive a ruler of the quest for glory and power and might is to empty politics of meaning.

In his vast corpus of sermons, letters, and theological polemics Augustine addresses the problem of pride using a variety of metaphors, including those relating to medicine, mountains, trees, and general references to high

36. James J. O'Donnell's recent "new biography" of Augustine is one example of this excoriation of Augustine. "We have created a world of textualized, external, objective truth," O'Donnell laments. "Augustine's fantasy world, the fantasy world of earliest Christianity, has come eerily to be real. If many of the *specific* propositions he entertained have been discarded, the cultural practice whose power he attests remains with us. . . . Don Quixote gets the last laugh." See James J. O'Donnell, *Augustine: A New Biography* (New York: HarperCollins, 2005), 208.

and low. All of Augustine's metaphors of height convey this simple message: if you are lowly and humble, God will raise you up. If you are high and mighty—yet proud—he will throw you down. Beware! "Pride imitates what is lofty," Augustine writes in the *Confessions*.[37] It is God who is Most High. "Proud people may laugh at me," Augustine writes later, at the beginning of book 4 of the *Confessions*. "As yet they have not themselves been prostrated and brought low for their soul's health by you, my God."[38]

Whether speaking of his own spiritual journey, or of political or philosophical manifestations of pride, Augustine's metaphors of height are ominous, packed with the threat that God's mercy will not endure forever. The tone of righteous indignation Augustine employed would not have been lost on the imperial minions, for whom their leader was a god. Augustine's frequent use of political language in his discussions of dizzying heights and precipitous falls similarly would have resonated with his audience—whether his congregation or his imperial- class correspondents. Augustine's message as conveyed in metaphors of height was heresy to the Roman civil religion: The emperor is not divine, nor is he by nature of his office even great. He is, on the contrary, in his pride, a mean creature, worthy only of divine condemnation. Only God, Augustine explains in a sermon preached between 425 and 430, sees "the high and mighty things" from their proper prospective, "from afar."[39] By this Augustine means that God alone is not prideful—and God is close to those who are humble. He is unreachable by those who are prideful. "How are you going to get to him?" Augustine asks his parishioners. "Will you look for a ladder?" No, Augustine answers, "Look for the wood of humility, and you have already got to him."[40] Only in throwing oneself before the cross, "the wood of humility," is God accessible. One cannot reach God, Augustine preaches elsewhere, by hoisting oneself up—but only by humbling oneself.[41] Augustine teaches that Christ makes the lowly high by lifting them up.[42] Speaking to his Christian audience, Augustine reminds them that God will give them "all the

37. Augustine, *Confessions,* trans. Henry Chadwick (New York: Oxford University Press, 1991), 31. Hereafter cited as *Confessions.*

38. Ibid., 53.

39. Augustine, "Sermon 70A," in *Sermons,* trans. Edmund Hill, in *The Works of Saint Augustine: A Translation for the 21st Century,* ed. John E. Rotelle, part 3, vol. 3 (Hyde Park, N.Y.: New City Press, 2003), 244. Hereafter cited as *Sermons.*

40. Ibid.   41. Ibid., "Sermon 351," vol. 10, 118.

42. Ibid., "Sermon 23A," vol. 2, 70.

high altitude [they] want."[43] Condescending to become human in the Incarnation, God has "to come down to our pride," Augustine writes in the *Confessions*.[44] He does so to overturn earthly hierarchies, vanquish pride, and exalt the humble.

It is impossible, Augustine believes, speaking on behalf of those "who are truly religious," for one "to have true virtue without true piety, that is without the true worship of the true God."[45] Virtue for the sake of "human glory" is not "true virtue." Nonetheless, "those who are not citizens of the Eternal City—which the holy Scriptures call the City of God—are of more service to the earthly city when they possess even that sort of virtue than if they are without it."[46]

What about those who are members of the City of God, we might ask: How are they of service to the earthly city? How *should* they be of service to the earthly city? Augustine offers an answer that provides the context in which he introduces his mirror of Christian princes: "As for those who are endowed with true piety and who lead a good life, if they are skilled in the art of government, then there is no happier situation for mankind than that they, by God's mercy, should wield power."[47] Augustine does not, it is important to see, suggest that piety is the only qualification for a Christian to rule. The ruler must be "skilled in the art of government." He must also, Augustine writes, be humble:

Yet such men attribute to the grace of God whatever virtues they may be able to display in this present life, because God has given those virtues to them in response to their wish, their faith, and their petition. At the same time they realize how far they fall short of the perfect righteousness, such as is found in the fellowship of the angels, for which they strive to fit themselves. However much praise and public approbation is given to the virtue which is engaged in the service of human glory, it is in no way to be compared to the humblest beginnings of the saints, whose hope has been placed in the grace and mercy of the true God.[48]

Humility requires three major duties of the ruler, for he must: (1) recognize the divine source of his abilities and the sovereignty of God; (2) admit his fallibility: men are not angels nor are they God; and (3) emulate the humility of the saints even as he realizes that his duties are different. Each of

43. Ibid., "Sermon 45," vol. 2, 256.
45. *City of God*, 213 (V.19).
47. Ibid., 213–14 (V.19).

44. *Confessions*, 13.
46. Ibid., 213 (V.18).
48. Ibid., 214 (V.19).

these three duties is necessary to keep himself from falling down the slippery slope to the desire for domination.

Humility serves as a check against man's impulse to pursue glory at the expense of virtue. Just as glory becomes debased when it is pursued for its own sake, so too are the cardinal classical virtues debased if they are pursued for the sake of glory. The Stoic philosophers who chastised the Epicureans for making the virtues slaves of pleasure give a good lesson to those who would make the virtues slaves to glory. Augustine took this lesson to heart and commended it to others, urging them to cleave to the golden mean so as to put glory in its proper place. In their criticism of the Epicureans the Stoics portrayed Pleasure as a "female voluptuary" given unwarranted obeisance in Epicurean thought so thoroughly that the virtues are made her slaves. "Glory may not be a female voluptuary," Augustine notes, "but she is puffed up with empty conceit; and it is most improper that the Virtues, with their solidity and strength, should be her servants."[49] For if the cardinal virtues are made the servants—really slaves—of glory, "then Prudence would exercise no foresight, Justice make no dispensations, Fortitude show no endurance, Temperance impose no moderation, except so far as to win man's approval, and to serve the ends of Glory and her inflated conceit."[50] Only humility can deflate glory when it is puffed up. Humility before God and men is a pre-emptive strike against the evil elevation of glory and the concomitant degradation of the other virtues.

Humility is the indispensable helpmate of the other virtues because it reminds men that while they must not illegitimately elevate glory they also must not "despise" it and ignore the opinions of others. He cares for others' opinions mainly so that when they observe him they see his "genuine piety" and thus, like him, wish completely to cleave to "the Truth."[51] As helpmate, humility assumes what seems like a secondary role. In reality, humility is primary and of great importance. It makes the other virtues possible by orienting a man's soul to their cultivation and consistent practice. By combating pride at every step, and pointing the way to the *telos* of the soul, humility, according to Augustine, is a guide without which a person easily is lost.

Humility gives steady witness to the fact that God governs in the affairs of men. Augustine poses the question in book 5 as to *why* God would

49. Ibid., 215 (V.20).   50. Ibid.
51. Ibid.

allow the Romans to rule. Their answer about why they *should* rule is born of pride, in Augustine's view, for their ready answer is that their excellence has earned them the right to rule. They are most worthy of praise because of their glorious deeds. Augustine's response to this claim, as we have seen, is to identify the incoherence and evil in what amounts to a boast. The Romans' answer is incoherent because their claim redounds to a desire for praise for the sake of praise, a craving for glory for the sake of glory, which because it forsakes virtue becomes an empty cycle of interminable grief. The Romans' answer is evil because it flouts God: forgetting they are not God, the Romans deify their glory, and then, later, deify their glorious rulers. Humility is the only true and effective response to the Roman boasts, for a humble stance yields the correct answer to the question of *why* the Romans were allowed to rule: "we must ascribe to the true God alone the power to grant kingdoms and empires. He it is who gives happiness in the kingdom of heaven only to the good, but grants earthly kingdoms both to the good and the evil, in accordance with his pleasure, which can never be unjust."[52] As Augustine explains further, "God himself gave dominion to the Romans without the worship of those gods to whose worship the Romans thought they owed their Empire."[53]

Augustine's Mirror of Christian Princes

Some political rulers, Augustine goes on to write at the outset of chapter 24, operate with that "confident expectation of eternal life," and for that reason they are *felices.* Their happiness, or blessedness, comes not because of conquest but rather is the result of humility. The highest good, as he explains with his mirror, flows from humility. "Lord, you alone exercise rule without pride, since you alone are truly Lord, and you have no master."[54] Pride in human beings is inescapable. Pride in politics is inevitable. The omnipresence of pride in daily life as well as politics means that humility is all the more necessary. Humility receives its strength from God. Every Christian ruler is wise, Augustine teaches, to be humble. This is the message of book 5's "mirror" of Christian princes, in which Augustine details twelve characteristics befitting the blessed, or happy, Christian ruler. In this "mirror" Augustine gives practical application to his long reflections

52. Ibid., 216 (V.21).   53. Ibid.
54. *Confessions,* 213.

on glory. Only God's rule is impervious to pride. All mortal rulers are subject to pride's powerful temptation, which promises that if they assert their self-sufficiency they, like the sun, can radiate a glory that is awesome to behold. Humility, as we have seen, recognizes that a ruler must not seek glory for its sake. He can, at best, reflect the glory of God.

Augustine's mirror of Christian princes should be understood with this idea of reflection in mind: the Christian ruler is to reflect all of the virtues exercised perfectly by God, with the knowledge that he, unlike God, never will be perfect. The Christian cannot be perfect, but this fact does not grant him license to be prideful. In fact, his primary task, we might say, is to submit his own pride to divine control. The Christian prince must, above all else, be a humble ruler. He must first be humble before God and then humble before his fellow men:

We Christians call rulers happy,

1. if they rule with justice;

2. if amid the voices of exalted praise and the reverent salutations of excessive humility, they are not inflated with pride, but remember that they are but men;

3. if they put their power at the service of God's majesty, to extend his worship far and wide;

4. if they fear God, love him and worship him;

5. if more than their earthly kingdom, they love that realm where they do not fear to share the kingship;

6. if they are slow to punish, but ready to pardon;

7. if they take vengeance on wrong because of the necessity to direct and protect the state, and not to satisfy their personal animosity;

8. if they grant pardon not to allow impunity to wrong-doing but in the hope of amendment of the wrong-doer;

9. if, when they are obliged to take severe decisions, as must often happen, they compensate this with the gentleness of their mercy and the generosity of their benefits;

10. if they restrain their self-indulgent appetites all the more because they are more free to gratify them, and prefer to have command over their lower desires than over any number of subject peoples; and

11. if they do all this not for a burning desire for empty glory, but for the love of eternal blessedness; and

12. if they do not fail to offer to their true God, as a sacrifice for their sins,
the oblation of humility, compassion, and prayer.[55]

Underlying all of the attributes a Christian ruler must possess is humility. With explicit mention of humility in the second and twelfth sections, the mirror is an apt summary of Augustine's teaching about the political importance of humility. Humility, we see again in the mirror, is the mean between two extremes: the ruler being puffed up with pride or smitten with "excessive," or false humility. Humility's companions, we see in the twelfth section, are compassion and prayer.

In its emphasis on humility the mirror acts as a reminder to political rulers that "they are but men." In the two planes of humility—vertical and horizontal—included in the mirror, this is the vertical plane of humility. Man is not God. A political ruler is a man. He is not God. This statement was radical in Augustine's day, despite the fact that by the time Augustine wrote the *City of God* Christianity had predominated in Rome for almost a century. It still was radical to suggest that the emperor should fear, love, and worship God, as Augustine does in the fourth statement of the mirror. In pronouncing the Christian emperor blessed only if he is humble—if he recognizes that he is not God—Augustine is responding to both pagans and Christians alike. To pagans who long for the days of divine emperors Augustine's answer is clear: imperial deification is the height of pride, and in his pride such a ruler-god will bring only evil to his people. To Christians who see the emperor not as God but as *the* salvific instrument of His divine will Augustine offers a rebuke of their pride. To suppose that the anointing of God entails a ruler to speak or act on behalf of God and then claim the credit for all the good things that accrue to his people is blasphemously prideful. It is an assertion unwarranted by the humility to which Christians, including historians and imperial officials, are called.

When a Christian ruler humbly puts himself in the service of God he is given certain duties by God. This is the horizontal plane of humility—the realm in which a ruler truly must be a public servant. Justice is the first imperative in Augustine's mirror. He does not expect the emperor to rule with perfect justice, for that is God's ability alone, but nevertheless Augustine enjoins just rule. Justice is possible, we might conclude from the fifth statement of Augustine's mirror, because the Christian emperor's eyes are fixed

55. *City of God,* 219–20 (V.24). The twelve parts of the mirror have been numbered for easy reference.

firmly upon the City of God. In order to love his earthly kingdom well the emperor must value it less than the kingdom without end. If he does not fear sharing his kingship, he will not cling to it at the expense of justice. The next four statements emphasize aspects of justice having mainly to do with equity. The Christian emperor must be merciful, Augustine states—in all things but especially when he is required to make "severe decisions." In stark contrast to the advice Niccolò Machiavelli offers princes, it is not enough for the Christian prince to merely act correctly or feign goodness, for in addition to acting correctly he must also act for the right reasons.[56] The Christian prince must be virtuous. Thus when a Christian emperor must "take vengeance on wrong" it should be "to direct and protect the state, and not to satisfy their personal animosity." In granting a pardon the emperor must not do so "to allow impunity to wrong-doing" (a miscarriage of justice), "but in the hope of amendment of the wrong-doer."

In a nod to the classical conception of tyranny, and in partial articulation of his notion of justice, Augustine insists that unlike the classical tyrant, who acts for his own self-aggrandizement, Christian emperors must "restrain their self-indulgent appetites all the more because they are more free to gratify them." In other words, their souls must be ordered so that "they have command over their lower desires." This command is what is important; command as is normally imagined in politics—"over any number of subject peoples"—is not a righteous desire for the Christian ruler. That desire for domination, as we have seen, grows from what Augustine in the eleventh statement calls the "burning desire for empty glory," which must always be eschewed in favor of "the love of eternal blessedness."

The twelfth and final statement of the mirror connects the vertical and horizontal planes, for in reminding Christian emperors of their sinfulness Augustine commends to them the necessity of sacrifice, which, in his formulation, takes three forms: humility, compassion, and prayer. Humility, at the head of this list, must prepare the way for compassion and prayer.

---

56. See Niccolò Machiavelli, chapter 18, "In What Mode Faith Should Be Kept by Princes," in *The Prince*, trans. Harvey C. Mansfield, 2nd ed. (Chicago: University of Chicago Press, 1998), 68–70. Machiavelli's mirror is the antithesis of Augustine's mirror. For a good comparison of Augustine and Machiavelli, see James V. Schall, "The 'Realism' of Augustine's 'Political Realism': Augustine and Machiavelli," *Perspectives on Political Science* 25, no. 3 (1996): 117–23.

"Shoddy Passages," Confusion, and
Incoherence? Augustine and His Critics

Book 5 of the *City of God* ends with consideration of specific Christian emperors Augustine sees as blessed. Even for scholars who recognize how much Augustine prizes humility, the locus of his highest praise—book 5's mirror of princes—is singled out for some of their harshest criticism. Peter Brown, for example, writes, "Augustine's summary of the virtues of a Christian prince, and his portraits of Constantine and Theodosius, are, in themselves, some of the most shoddy passages of the *City of God*."[57] Robert Markus seconds Brown's opinion.[58] For Brown, despite the passage's shoddiness, "in the framework of Augustine's ideas they are quite explicable." The framework, Brown explains, is mainly about ends, or purposes: "The Christian ruler differs from the pagan, not in the amount of power he wields, nor in the nature of the state which maintains; he differs only in his awareness of where this power stands in God's order, to what it is related, what ends it may serve."[59] The shoddiness lies in Augustine's bad history, presumably (Brown writes earlier that Augustine's account of the pagan versus the Christian ruler appears to the historian "somewhat unconvincingly"), or perhaps just in his argument per se. Augustine can be made by his commentators to be coherent, Brown and Markus concur, but his conclusions (or at least some of his conclusions) in book 5 are wrong, because they are based upon bad history.

Brown's indictment of Augustine's book 5 as full of slipshod scholarship seems to stem from Augustine's effort to move from the generally stated principles of the mirror to the specific cases of Constantine and Theodosius. Constantine and Theodosius, Brown seems to suggest, should not think that if they were to look into Augustine's mirror they would see themselves. Yet Augustine, in his description of both emperors, according to Brown and other critics of this section, seems to lavish too much praise on his imperial subjects. If, as is widely accepted in the scholarly literature, Augustine modeled his mirror on Theodosius, he erred grievously, many scholars conclude. Augustine was at worst incoherent, and at best, confused.

57. P. R. L. Brown, "Political Society," in *Augustine: A Collection of Critical Studies,* ed. R. A. Markus (Garden City, N.Y.: Anchor Books, 1972), 319.

58. R. A. Markus, *Saeculum: History and Society in the Theology of St. Augustine* (Cambridge: Cambridge University Press, 1970), 57.

59. Brown, "Political Society," 319.

Augustine's overview of the reigns of Constantine and Theodosius should be understood in light of Augustine's revolutionary teaching regarding humility. Furthermore, this overview must be considered in light of Augustine's Christian rhetoric, and the larger tasks he undertakes in the *City of God,* chief among which is to convince the proud that their pride is not only counterproductive, but more importantly, sinful. Imperial hubris was at a high point in the century that preceded Constantine's reign. Constantine was not a ruler one might describe aptly as humble, but Augustine does not do so in his two paragraphs about Constantine. His contention regarding Constantine is limited. Without effusive praise Augustine notes many of the honors bestowed upon Constantine, all of which are "worldly gifts" that are associated not with the attributes Augustine adumbrates in the mirror but rather with the accomplishments that are *not* the criteria for a Christian prince:

Constantine had a long reign, and as the sole Augustus he ruled and defended the whole Roman world; he was victorious, above all others, in the wars which he directed and conducted; fortune favored his efforts in the repression of usurpers; and he died of sickness and old age after a long life, leaving his throne to his sons.[60]

Compare this list to Augustine's earlier list of four accomplishments that are *not* the criteria for happiness in a Christian prince:

When we describe certain Christian emperors as "happy," it is not because they enjoyed long reigns, or because they died a peaceful death, leaving the throne to their sons; nor is it because they subdued their country's enemies, or had the power to forestall insurrections by enemies in their own land and to suppress such insurrections if they arose.[61]

Each of the benefits in the four statements "and other similar rewards or consolations in this life of trouble" are not the exclusive property of either pagan or Christian rulers. If pagans see any of these benefits it is because of God's mercy. Christian rulers, Augustine warns, should not "demand such blessings from [God] as if they represented the highest good."[62]

Augustine calls Constantine a Christian emperor, but he does not suggest that Constantine was ordained to be the perfect vessel for fulfilling God's will on Earth. In fact, Augustine underscores his emphasis: in cit-

---

60. *City of God,* 221 (V.26).
62. Ibid., 220 (V.24).

61. Ibid., 219 (V.24).

ing Constantine Augustine seeks to show that God both blesses Christian emperors *and* allows pagan emperors to rule. He blessed Constantine not because Constantine's Christian commitment *demanded* such a quid pro quo. That idea for Augustine is heresy! Rather, God blessed Constantine to demonstrate to believers (who should not believe that God was to be worshipped "for the sake of life eternal") that demon worship was not the only way to temporal success. Thus Augustine in this section rebukes the pagans for their worship of demons for the sake of the afterlife (a futile endeavor), but he also exhorts Christians not to despair when it seems that the demon-worshippers are being granted favor. Augustine's point is a foundational one, repeated time after time in his writings: the sun shines on the good and the evil. God's will cannot be grasped by humans, who in striving to connect temporal events to cosmic forces must turn away from the ideological temptation to identify temporal success with divine favor.

The lesson Augustine derives from the Constantinian example seems perfectly harmonious with our suggestion of Augustine's bedrock belief in the strength of humility. Augustine's point about humility in politics in his section on Constantine is deeper than any one individual, even as mighty a warrior-prince as Constantine. Augustine's point is that even as Christian rulers must display humility, so too should observers of politics be humble in their conclusions about God's actions in human history.

Augustine's silence about humility when he writes about Constantine stands as a subtle critique of Constantine. His major point about Constantine is surely a criticism of Constantine's court historians, for whom superlatives were always used to describe their master's glory. One example from Eusebius of Caesarea's "Oration" in praise of Constantine is typical of this overheated rhetoric:

Hence is our emperor perfect in discretion, in goodness, in justice, in courage, in piety, in devotion to God: he truly and only is a philosopher, since he knows himself, and is fully aware that supplies of every blessing are showered on him from a source quite external to himself, even from heaven itself. Declaring the august title of supreme authority by the splendor of his vesture, he alone worthily wears that imperial purple which so well becomes him. He is indeed an emperor, who calls on and implores in prayer the favor of his heavenly Father night and day, and whose ardent desires are fixed on his celestial kingdom.[63]

63. Eusebius Pamphilus, "The Oration of Eusebius Pamphilus in Praise of the Emperor Constantine," in *A Select Library of Nicene and Post-Nicene Fathers of the Christian Church*, second se-

Elsewhere Eusebius praises Constantine for his prudence, temperance, and wisdom. He possesses the "native virtues" accorded to one who is "divinely-favored."[64] Compared to Eusebius's praise of Constantine, Augustine's recognition of his reign is mild and understated. But even when Augustine's statement stands alone it might most accurately be read as a statement about the place of revelation in politics: Be humble, Augustine urges the Christian, and never claim that God grants temporal success merely because he is praised.

Augustine's central point in his treatment of Theodosius is even more explicitly related to humility, for in focusing on Theodosius's humiliation before Ambrose he emphasizes the emperor's fallibility. "But nothing could be more wonderful," Augustine exclaims, "than the religious humility [Theodosius] showed after the grievous crime committed by the people of Thessalonica."[65] Here Augustine refers to a reprisal taken by Theodosius against rioters in Thessalonica. Because of its severity the bishop Ambrose ordered the emperor to penance; Theodosius agreed and repented. "These and other good works of like nature, which it would take too long to recount, Theodosius took with him when he left the loftiest summit of power—which is nothing but a passing mist."[66] For those works he earned "eternal happiness," the gift God gives only to "the truly devout. But all the rest that this world offers, whether the peaks of power or the bare necessities of life, God dispenses freely to good and evil alike."[67] Even an emperor can be brought low, Augustine says. The added implication of Augustine's reference to temporal power as "nothing but a passing mist" is that *especially* an emperor needs to be brought low.

Augustine's emphasis on humility in his section on Theodosius is borne out even in Augustine's praise of Theodosius's willingness to "help the Church against the ungodly," by which Augustine means heretics.[68] Emphasizing the fact that this succor was offered "by just and compassionate legislation" and not in a spirit of revenge or severity, Augustine also notes that "Theodosius was more glad to be a member of that Church than to be ruler of the world."[69] In his actions against pagans, Theodosius was even

ries, vol. 1, ed. Philip Schaff and Henry Wace (Grand Rapids, Mich.: Eerdmans, 1979), 586. Eusebius of Caesarea (ca. 260–339), a polymath who wrote on many topics, was a heterodox bishop who wrote the "Oration," an unfinished hagiographic account of Constantine's reign.

64. Ibid., 584.   65. *City of God,* 223 (V.26).
66. Ibid.   67. Ibid.
68. Ibid.   69. Ibid.

less severe, for while he destroyed "pagan images" he "did not deprive them of their property."[70] Never does Augustine suggest here that it was Theodosius's duty as protector of the state to overthrow all pagan practices. Without here undercutting the logic of Christian establishment (as he would do elsewhere), nonetheless, Augustine does not offer it nearly so hearty an endorsement as he might have. With his emphasis on humility and compassion Augustine believes he is offering a corrective to the prevailing ideology of pagans and Christians alike. To pagans who wished for the return of a deified emperor (and the ouster of the Christian establishment) Augustine dismisses the old order as a false sacrifice to the god *Superbia*. To Christians his counsel, made even clearer later in his life, opposed their proclaiming the era of Constantine and Theodosius the dawn of a new Christian kingdom that will usher in an age of universal happiness, prosperity, and justice. Augustine's chief concern is the soul, not a regime.

The soul of a ruler matters to Augustine more than his regime because his governing actions must be themselves governed by a higher authority. But it is for the salvation of the ruler's soul Augustine is most concerned— not the salvation of the state. States, Augustine teaches, cannot enjoy salvation. Soulcraft is God's dominion alone. The ruler, if he is a Christian, should be aware of spiritual matters. He should be ready and willing, even, to act based upon Christian imperatives—but with the important understanding that these imperatives to act against heretics and pagans are not mandated because of an ideology. Even when Augustine praises the intervention of a Christian ruler against pagans or heretics he never suggests that the ruler has the ultimate ability to decide a person's salvation. That decision is God's alone. Augustine's advice for rulers of any kind, Christian or not, is to love glory moderately. The more an individual inordinately loves glory, the less will he ultimately enjoy true glory.

Augustine's warning to individuals about the perils of pride applies equally, he argues, to civil society. Even more, he emphasizes, Christians who are part of the Church must not think that their participation in the Church immunizes them from the dangers posed by pride. The Church must guard against its gospel being used as a substitute civil religion. If what we have argued is accurate, Augustine improperly is blamed as the father of "political Augustinianism." The trajectory of his thought is not to replace pagan civil religion with Christian civil religion; rather, Augustine

70. Ibid., 222–23 (V.26).

urges Christians to act in accordance with the good news that their salvation is spiritual, not political.

How, then, do *societies* generate sufficient civic virtue to hold together in political organization? Augustine displays neither enthusiasm nor disdain for what we call civic virtues; he seems content to admonish Christian rulers and citizens alike to act in the common good. Augustine is little concerned, it seems, that a polity will lack civic vigor. Instead of attacking Augustine for unleashing a politicized Christianity upon later generations, then, critics might more aptly ponder what precisely for Augustine is the source of civic virtue. Augustine's inattention to political forms, or regimes, suggests that for him the major political problem is excessive political pride. Given the transpolitical character of Augustine's Christianity, what is less clear in Augustine's thought is the status of patriotism, or pride in one's polity. Ordinate political pride, like ordinate love of glory, seems to be the prescription offered by Augustine. However, his agnosticism about political regimes leaves open the question of just how Christian citizens might justify even a moderate political pride.

Augustine emphasizes a kind of epistemic humility even as he represents a confidence in his faith that is jarring to modern rationalism. Politics does not determine man's destiny. Individual rulers are not forbidden from considering the souls of their subjects, or the citizens over whom they preside, but neither are they commanded to transform them. Rome's civil religious quest for immortality in the pursuit of glory demonstrates for Augustine that the more Rome strives to be eternal, the further it removes itself from the true Eternal City.

4

Forgiving Those
Not Trespassing against Us

Hobbes and the Establishment of the
Nonsectarian State Church

TRAVIS D. SMITH

The Matter of Religious Disagreement

Hobbes writes as if he expects disagreement to turn into violence swiftly and surely (v:3).[1] "Rage," he says, follows from "vehement opinion of the truth of anything, contradicted by others" (viii:19). Great disagreements are often manifestations of competing claims to rule. Ordinary disagreements are taken for indications of idiocy, indictments of immorality, or allegations that one is a perpetrator or victim of duplicity. Religious disagreements are especially volatile. Like Socrates says in Plato's *Republic,* the hatefulness of finding falsehoods deep inside oneself regarding the greatest questions is unrivaled.[2] Disagreements regarding religious matters are readily interpreted as condemnations, adverse judgments regarding the condition of a man's innermost being and his likely ultimate destination, and not merely harmless accusations of folly. Confronted by another who differs with respect to the

An earlier version of this chapter was presented at the 2006 Canadian Political Science Association annual conference. The author expresses his gratitude to Arash Abizadeh, Leah Bradshaw, Jim Crimmins, Bryan Garsten, John von Heyking, Joanna E. Miller, John W. Seaman, and Joanne Wright for their comments on previous drafts, Loren Lomasky and the participants of the February 2006 Liberty Fund colloquium on "Rights, Responsibility, and Religion: Religious Belief and Liberty in Hobbes, Spinoza, and Locke" for their conversation, and his research assistant, Nina Valiquette.

1. All parenthetical citations in this chapter refer to Thomas Hobbes, *Leviathan,* ed. Edwin Curley (Indianapolis: Hackett, 1994), including the "Review and Conclusion" (R&C) and text translated from the Latin edition (OL).

2. Plato, *The Republic of Plato,* trans. Allan Bloom (New York: Basic Books, 1968), 382a–b.

divine, a man faces the possibility that his convictions are hogwash and his authorities are shams. That one's ancestors, kinfolk, and coreligionists are all suckers is a prospect made all the more unpalatable in proportion to how much has been endured and sacrificed for God's sake. In order to avenge one's own, fortify one's faith, please God, and secure heavenly rewards, religious disagreement is frequently met with violence. Silencing, subduing, or converting others are longstanding methods of assuaging a man's anxieties regarding all that is holy. It is as if the greatness of God (and by lucky association, the greatness of the godly) shall be confirmed by the enormity of deeds done desperately in His name (or in the case of the godless, the greatness of Man, by deeds done in rebellion against any idea of the divine).

Hardly encouraging men to discover lies in their souls, Hobbes wants them generally oblivious to the possibility that there might be some crisis there, something in need of correction.[3] I will argue that Hobbes would welcome a superficial diversity of opinion regarding matters divine, diversity being unavoidable anyway and potentially also advantageous, so long as a fundamental, underlying agreement could be arranged. Accordingly, Hobbes devises a model of religious toleration,[4] but not one that is based on cultivating any great learning or refined qualities of character among men. It is toleration grounded in sentiments such as tamed pride and rela-

---

3. Contrast Plato, *Gorgias,* trans. Donald J. Zeyl (Indianapolis, Ind.: Hackett, 1987), 470c.

4. That Hobbes's teaching is friendly to toleration, see also Alan Ryan, "Hobbes, Toleration and the Inner Life," in *The Nature of Political Theory,* ed. David Miller and Larry Seidentop (Oxford: Clarendon Press, 1983), 197–218; Alan Ryan, "A More Tolerant Hobbes," in *Justifying Toleration: Conceptual and Historical Perspectives,* ed. Susan Mendus (Cambridge: Cambridge University Press, 1988), 37–59; Richard Tuck, "Hobbes and Locke on Toleration," in *Thomas Hobbes and Political Theory,* ed. Mary G. Dietz (Lawrence: University Press of Kansas, 1990), 153–71; J. Judd Owen, "The Tolerant Leviathan: Hobbes and the Paradox of Liberalism," *Polity* 37, no. 1 (2005): 130–48; and Edwin Curley, "Hobbes and the Cause of Religious Toleration," in *The Cambridge Companion to Hobbes's "Leviathan,"* ed. Patricia Springborg (Cambridge: Cambridge University Press, 2007), 309–34. For the argument that Hobbes does not intend to teach toleration, but Spinoza and Locke are nonetheless able to tease it out, see Mark Lilla, *The Stillborn God: Religion, Politics, and the Modern West* (New York: Alfred A. Knopf, 2007), 74–103, 218. That profound differences distinguish Hobbes and Spinoza despite some outward similarity, see Noel Malcolm, "Hobbes and Spinoza," in *Aspects of Hobbes* (Oxford: Clarendon Press, 2002), 27–52. Curley argues at length that "[t]he affinities between Hobbes and Spinoza are really quite deep" ("Hobbes and the Cause of Religious Toleration," 315). I, too, tend to find that the bulk of the *TPT* is effectively prefigured in *Leviathan.* Comparing these two works, the difference in attitude substantially outweighs the difference in argumentation. Whereas Spinoza affects hyper-rationality, Hobbes is more poetical, showing more affection for the comic and greater sensitivity to the tragic. Exasperated and condescending, Spinoza barely tolerates man's folly. Hobbes is obviously unimpressed but more forgiving. Hobbes jeers, but Spinoza sneers.

tive indifference to others masquerading as respect for them. It involves an enlightened supposition of mutual impotence, generates an easy faith in easygoing divinities, and depends on crafting a civil religion that looks and feels like the absence of a civil religion.

Notwithstanding the unlimited authority of the civil sovereign to command his subjects to worship in whatever manner pleases him, even "contrary to their own consciences" (xxiv:7), Hobbes's guiding counsel to sovereigns is to lay off. Compounding the difficulty of persuading sovereigns to restrain themselves, subjects must also learn that they should not want their own religion overtly politicized. Where the prevailing religion of the people is such that they generally expect or demand official modes of public worship, proceeding prudently requires moderately accommodating their appetites while reeducating them (xlvii:18). Hobbes is hopeful regarding the possibility of this reeducation, but he does not imagine that it will be a quick and easy process. The minds of men have been "tainted" by the influence of interfering powers that must be subordinated, reformed, and made cooperative (xxx:6; cf. xxvii:31, 35; xxx:14; xlvi:13–14; OL-xlvii:29; R&C:16). Men are conformed to religious liberty gradually, not all at once.

"If I had written in uncorrupted hearts, as on a blank tablet, I could have been briefer," laments Hobbes (OL-xlvii:29). His account of the Christian Commonwealth in part 3 of *Leviathan* is tailored to his contemporaries, a prudential accommodation of his theoretical teaching to practical necessities. Its logic puts the meaning of a Christian Commonwealth in question and points toward the possibility of a nonsectarian commonwealth. It has application beyond Christendom because the requirements of peaceable living among men are everywhere the same. Indeed, Hobbes dispenses with the concept of Christendom by pointing out that there is no catholic church (xxxiii:24; xxxix:5; xlii:124; App. ii:22), whatever the creeds of men contend. Thought through, the very expression "Christian Commonwealth" makes as much sense in the here and now as "incorporeal substance" (cf. iv:21). The Christian revelation teaches that there is no Kingdom of God in this world (apart from ancient Israel, now long gone) until Christ establishes the one and only upon his Second Coming (xli:1, 6).[5] A sovereign may of course nevertheless proclaim his commonwealth to be Christian, and his subjects would remain formally obliged to outwardly

---

5. The future has "no being," however, and the past exists only "in the memory" (iii:7). Moreover, we should not heed prophecies regarding promised miracles "long deferred" (xxxii:8).

conform, although the disparity between the pretense and the reality of his regime would always constitute a palpable inconvenience and potential source of destabilization. God, however, is ultimately indifferent to modes of public worship (cf. xlv:12), and civil sovereigns should be likewise. When it comes to requiring, permitting, or proscribing religious behavior, they should consider only what is necessary to maintain "the common peace and security" (xxiv:7).

Indirect Civil Religion

While Hobbes sees many advantages to a monarchical form of government (xix:4–9), his portrait of humanity is exceedingly democratic in character. All men are to be governed as if they are but clever problem-solvers driven by idiosyncratic desires, seeking to satisfy them while avoiding things considered hurtful (iii:4–5; vi:4), as this comprises "the felicity of this life" (vi:58; xi:1). Men can never be wholly satisfied, but in their relatively free pursuit of personal satisfactions they may be pacified. As people are happier when they attain their satisfactions through their own "lawful industry" (xxx:1; cf. xvii:13), a civil sovereign should maximize and protect his subjects' liberties as much as "peaceable, sociable, and comfortable living" (xv:40) allows, even though he has the right to micromanage their lives. As is apposite to the democratization of mankind, any given man's standards of wisdom, justice, or what is worthy of love, derivative of his peculiar passions, experiences, pleasures, and interests, "can never be true grounds of any ratiocination" (iv:24; cf. vi:3–4; viii:14). Hobbes levels the intellects of men, declaring, "all men by nature reason alike, and well, when they have good principles" (v:16; cf. xiii:2)—meaning those Hobbes identifies, which begin by reducing men to a brute equality (xiii:1). Human spiritedness is harnessed toward the pursuit of effective powers and away from vain considerations of honor or glory. Rather than engaging in an ennobling pursuit of justice, men are simply expected to refrain from injustice so as to avoid punishment.

Deploying this democratic conception of mankind, Hobbes reworks religion, suppressing its claims to wisdom and glory and stressing its capacity to satisfy appetites. He ends up recommending that an underlying premise and shared purpose should be allowed to wear a variety of raiment. Religious quarrels will be resolved best not by enforcing a particularistic creed, but rather by instilling unanimity of opinion regarding the relative irrelevance of religious disagreements. His religious teaching is usually understood as unifying church and state by establishing a single, explicit civil religion with prescribed public rituals and offices, in conformity with the denomination of the sovereign's preference. However, in light of his teaching as a whole, it is unlikely that Hobbes would defer indifferently to the arbitrary preferences of sovereigns regarding an issue of such monumental consequence. As it happens, nonsectarianism is not a complete departure from the common view of his teaching. It remains fully consistent with his insistence that there should be a single public view regarding the tenets and practices of religion. This arrangement would not in practice allow people total freedom to believe and do what they will in the name of religion. It would shape people's habits and attitudes, transform their speech and rituals, and depend on legal protections, institutional arrangements, regulatory policies, and judicial actions.[6]

Hobbes's conception of philosophy is technological (v:17; xlvi:1). If he recommends a kind of religious toleration then he must be confident that it would work perfectly well if it were properly constructed. It must befit his idea of natural right, according to which those who attain power and prove that they truly know how to retain it deserve to wield it,[7] a doctrine that Hobbes obscures somewhat by positing as his initial premise each man's equal natural right to self-preservation (xiv:1). Might that endures is might well used, and it is best exercised indirectly so that men who do not want to feel dominated do not feel dominated—hence Hobbes's theory of representative government. Right rule requires an attentive cultivation of ap-

---

6. It may seem difficult to reconcile Hobbes's apparent approval of laws that "exacteth a pecuniary mulct of them that take the name of God in vain" (xxviii:18) with denominational disestablishment, but taking the name of God in vain would then come to encompass any appeal to God in order to justify one's public behavior. There would be laws prohibiting discrimination on religious grounds in mundane affairs, such as the printing of pamphlets or the renting of halls. In theory, the civil sovereign could go so far as to adjudge the charitable programs, ceremonial practices, qualifications for ordination, and rules for higher appointment within religious associations unconstitutional. Devout adherents to nonsectarianism will make pious use of courts and tribunals to revoke legislation, reform institutions, and chastise individuals and associations. Fines and damages will be levied. Even Hobbes's preference for public worship over private (xxxi:35) is perfectly conformable to a nonsectarian commonwealth. It has no less of an interest in endorsing public displays of devotion to its principles. It will encourage the prayerful repetition of opinions that celebrate harmless diversity in a "uniform" (xxxi:37) public voice. Its subjects will praise themselves and exalt their state for its official indifference to religion.

7. Hobbes's articulation of this view is more adept than Thrasymachus's and more earnest than Glaucon's. Plato, *Republic,* 340a–c, 358e–359b.

pearances as much as it does tangibles. It must seem indomitable to outsiders and yet not seem oppressive to insiders. Might used poorly will be lost, and the sovereign who loses his power has no basis upon which to claim that it ought to be given back. By whatever means a sovereign comes by his power, the rule that sustains his right remains the same: he must rule as if his power were a self-interested gift of each and every subject under him (xxviii:22)[8]—meaning his actual subjects, with their many imperfections and limited malleability, not an idealized abstraction from humanity or some imaginary community yearning for revolutionary transformation. Now, people will always differ in their opinions regarding religion. They will always regard their beliefs as their own, and free, and (paradoxically) they will always resist any attempt to control them. No man would or should choose for his sovereign one who would "endeavour, both by terror and persuasion, to make him violate his faith" (xlii:131). It is therefore ill-advised for a sovereign to treat his subjects in a way that makes them feel like their faith is under direct assault. They should feel free to claim to believe what they want, while being trained to repress belligerent beliefs.

The entanglement of religion and politics is inescapable, though it may be made covert. Politics is never truly subordinate to religion. There is no "spiritual power" held by certain men separable from and superior to the "temporal power" (xxix:12, 15; xxxix:5; xlii:80, 123). Sovereigns may privilege certain churches or religious orders under the law, but never out of deference to some prior or superior claim held by them. Religion may be explicitly subordinated to politics through a formally established church (xlii:80). When this works satisfactorily, given the complicity of the ruled, it produces an outward unity of politics and religion. Even then, Hobbes discourages direct attempts to tamper with the minds of men who seem to stray from what is publicly authorized. Where there is no established church, however, there is still always a rule emanating from the sovereign authority governing religious speech and activity. Retaining final authority over all religious matters, the civil sovereign's job as "supreme pastor" (xlii:68–72; cf. xxxix:5), as well as "sovereign prophet" (xxxvi:20), "sole messenger of God" (xl:7), authenticator of miracles (xxxvii:13), and judge and censor of all doctrines (xvii:13; xxiii:6; xxxviii:5; xl:4; xlii:67), are not forfeited should he refrain from establishing an organized church.[9] The sovereign

8. Travis D. Smith, "On the Fourth Law of Nature," *Hobbes Studies* 16 (2003): 84–94.
9. Although Hobbes indicates that sovereigns who happen to be Christian "oblige themselves

has then but determined that the divine powers are not displeased when he protects the bodies of men without trying to save their souls, restricts religious behavior for secular reasons alone, shies away from endorsing particular miracles and prophets, and teaches his subjects toleration. As it was not Christ who made kings pastors (xlii:67), a sovereign does not cease to be his people's pastor by rejecting Christ or merely distancing himself from Him through abstract formalities. A commonwealth without an official religious affiliation must still educate its subjects so that an underlying agreement about what the divine does not require or forbid is cultivated and consolidated.[10] Official interpreters must still be appointed and official interpretations provided (xviii:9; xxiii:6; xxvi:21, 26; xxix:6; xlii:73). The main thing that Hobbes expects men to come to agreement on is the idea that men cannot be expected to agree on anything except the desirability of survival and therefore the need to get along. In recommending that the rules that conduce to their mutual survival, the laws of nature, deserve to be called divine (Intro:1; xv:41; xxvi:24; xxxi:36; xxxiii:22; xlii:37, 131; xliii:5, 22), Hobbes delivers unto men the basis of a universal civil religion without a formal church.

If he deems them reasonable, a sovereign may, at his own discretion, recognize or establish practices of accommodation for religious groups that are calculated to safeguard the civil order and foster social integration. In principle, however, churches have the same status as any other association among men (xxii:16; xlii:69, 110; xliv:10; xlvii:7), meaning that their members and leaders have no prior right to claim special privileges or exemptions. Oaths do nothing to create or enhance a man's obligations (xiv:33), nor do the alleged commands of his conscience (vii:4; xxiv:7; xxvii:30; xxix:7). A man cannot oblige himself to do something contrary to the civil law simply because he promises God that he will do it (xiv:23; xviii:3). Per-

---

(by their baptism) to teach the doctrine of Christ" (xlii:92), we later learn that this sort of obligation holds only if one supposes that "the civil government be ordained as a means to bring us to a spiritual felicity" (xlii:124). Even then, each sovereign judges for himself what his self-imposed obligation entails. If he heeds Hobbes's counsel, the doctrine that he teaches will be lukewarm, lax, and infused with the spirit of ecumenism. To forgo interventions in the faith of others *is* to impart the doctrine of Hobbes's Christ. Strictly speaking, only natural persons receive baptism, whereas sovereignty is an "artificial soul" (Intro:1). The idea of a sovereign's baptism is therefore somewhat strange. The distinction between natural and artificial persons is what should enable a man to believe that God forbids something while abstaining from legislating on the basis of that conviction in his office as sovereign representative.

10. A self-identified Christian sovereign is entirely in the right and on the mark should he remind his Muslim subjects that theirs is a religion of peace and only blasphemers pretend otherwise.

mitting actions done contrary to the law in the name of conscience, under pretense of enthusiasm, or on account of some text or preacher only serves to give additional men pretexts and precedents. Religion could function as an extenuating factor only when examples of impunity have encouraged imitators to make recourse to faith in order to justify violating the law, but this would be no different from other situations in which a "presumption of mercy" is born of a failure to uphold the laws (xxvii:32). Going after those who use their religion in order to excuse unlawfulness in worldly dealings is to be regarded as criminal prosecution, not religious persecution. That said, their punishment is undeniably entangled with a determination that their conception of the will of God is terribly mistaken.

Against Religious Claims to Rule

If you should show Hobbes a self-proclaimed Kingdom of God on earth, or any endeavor to manufacture one before Christ Himself returns in glory (xxxviii:5, 23), he will show you a conspiracy. Christ and his apostles never sought to seize worldly authority (xli:5; xlii:68, 131). On its own terms, Scripture establishes no civil laws (xxxiii:1; xlii:47). Scripture is not self-interpreting, and every law or institution established in its name is a fabrication of those men who have interpreted it. The Roman Church's claim to stand in for the Kingdom of God in the interim is a transparent power-seeking and moneymaking scheme (xii:32; xlvii:2), the work of "crafty ambitious persons" (ii:8) comprising *"a confederacy of deceivers"* (xliv:1; cf. xlvii:17). The political ambitions of Calvinists are just as noxious (xxix:8; xliv:17; xlvii:4). According to John Aubrey's *Life of Hobbes,* Hobbes was an equal-opportunity critic of the priestly class—Roman, English, and Genevan alike—calling them all "cheats" and tracing their lineage as such back to Aaron.[11] Men have been everywhere manipulated by those who invent gods and spirits in order to prey on the common man's "fear of things invisible" (xi:26–27; cf. xii:20). In truth, men will be able to offer direct obedience to God only when they find themselves indisputably residing in the prophesied, miraculous Kingdom of God (xxxi:39). Until then, they should stop allowing themselves to be bullied and bled by those who adorn themselves with God's favor.

11. John Aubrey, *Life of Hobbes,* in Hobbes, *Leviathan,* lxviii. Check out Exodus 32. Hobbes traces several contrived ideas of the Roman Church to ancient Jewish thought (viii:25; xl:14; xlv:4; xlvi:10, 12).

Hobbes's principal complaint about the Roman Church has to do with its interference in the political life of nations. A civil sovereign is at liberty to make the Roman rites and those alone permissible in his commonwealth, but Rome acquires no rightful authority over him and his subjects thereby (xlii:70, 80). So long as Rome is sure to meddle in civil business, however, establishing the Roman cult is plainly unwise. Similarly, Hobbes can offer no principled objection to the establishment of presbyterian worship when the presbytery attains sovereignty. Its establishment is nevertheless regrettable insofar as its inability to become what it promises to be contributes to its eventual demise. It is better for every nation to have its own church, and one that concedes that the Kingdom of God is not of this world and cannot be constructed or hastened through human effort. Every commonwealth constitutes its own church in principle anyway (xxxiii:24; xxxix:4–5; xlii:79–80), although many states ruinously fail to recognize this. Hobbes supports the Church of England as established by his king (OL–Ded.Let.; xxxi:1; OL-xlvii:28; R&C:14).[12] He also finds himself at liberty to criticize its institutions and interpretations insofar as his criticisms are not expressly contradicted and therefore forbidden by his civil sovereign (xxii:15).

His criticisms reveal that a nationalized, established church with prescribed creeds and ceremonies is not simply best, but at best second- or third-best. Better than granting any single church direct authority over religious matters within the commonwealth would be to allow every subject the freedom to worship as he would, within the law, constraining every man's religion equally in the abstract. Only religious activities that disturb the peace should be treated prejudicially, because every activity that disturbs the peace must be treated with prejudice. Every religion should teach peaceable living at all times, and not simply after the whole nation or world has been made to submit. The desire to see the whole world submit to one's own religion is the neurotic, furthermost consequence of the apprehension that it might be false, inducing a need to manufacture concrete proof that it must be true. Thus, it is not enough to persuade sovereigns not to impose

12. Aubrey reports that Hobbes "declared that he liked the religion of the Church of England best of all other"—a dutiful yet peculiar formulation that does not resound with deep commitment. Aubrey, *Life of Hobbes*, lxviii. In his *Prose Autobiography*, Hobbes boasts that he attended church though he was not compelled by law or fear. In Hobbes, *Leviathan*, lxv. Given that he defines religion as having its origins in fear (vi:36), Hobbes apparently attends church for other reasons. In his *Verse Autobiography*, Hobbes is pleased that "The clergy at Leviathan repines," adding, "'tis hoped by me, That it will last to all eternity." Lines 265, 271–72, in Hobbes, *Leviathan*, lx. Eternity for Hobbes means endless linear time (xlvi:22; cf. xi:6; n.b. xxix:1; xlvii:1).

a religion. Subjects must be persuaded not to insist on having a religion imposed on them—or rather, people must be persuaded not to insist on imposing their own religion on others. Men must be released from both priestly masters and private zeal.

Private zeal can lead a man to think that he may or must kill someone else in the defense of and for the glory of God (R&C:10–11). Martyrs exhibit zeal at its worst. They may seem courageous, taking courage merely to be "contempt of wounds and violent death" (R&C:2). Underneath, they perceive the fragility of their faith and fear its untruth. Frustrated that the world does not flatter them by conforming to their will, they lash out at and flee from it. Out of this sad, irresponsible self-indulgence, conjuring God on their side, they promise themselves incomparable rewards for succumbing to weakness. Nothing is so "unmanly" (xviii:3; cf. xxi:16) as seeking martyrdom. Martyrs are like big babies or little girls.[13] Nobody should believe that God wants anyone to die or kill for Him. God is not impressed by self-sacrifice (xxxi:36) (which is ironic, if men are supposed to imitate Christ), and breaking any law for His sake is always a sin (xliii:23). The celebration of martyrdom is but a seditious stratagem used by those who hope to gain some illegitimate advantage by tricking others into immolating themselves (xlvii:12). The hope of the nonsectarian regime is that by neither endorsing nor menacing any religion, men will not gesture toward its downfall with such histrionics.

With a striking rhetorical question, Hobbes draws attention to the foolishness of religious persecution. Giving it a moment's reflection should lead the reader to concede that Hobbes's insight is right while the ways of the world are wrong. He asks,

But what infidel king is so unreasonable as, knowing he has a subject that waiteth for the second coming of Christ (after the present world shall be burnt),

13. Empirical evidence shows that "women, who are supposed to be listeners, mistake disagreement in conversation for hostility." Harvey C. Mansfield, *Manliness* (New Haven: Yale University Press, 2006), 30. In those who would be martyrs or make use of them, Mansfield sees both an excess and defect of manliness, observing, "though they say they are pious, they use the name of God to strengthen and serve their own will, not to direct it." Ibid., 236. If the data cited by Mansfield is accurate, then Hobbes would have impetus to welcome the ordination of women. Their inclusion should result in greater consensus, or at least less open debate among the clergy. According to Hobbes's own principles, Queen Elizabeth certainly had the right to administer all of the sacraments. She simply abstained of her own volition (xlii:78a; App. iii:34). We should disregard Hobbes's specious deference to 1 Corinthians 14:34–35. St. Paul can insist that women are prohibited from preaching, but it really is not up to him (xlii:72).

and intendeth then to obey him (which is the intent of believing that Jesus is the Christ), and in the meantime thinketh himself bound to obey the laws of that infidel king (which all Christians are obliged in conscience to do), to put to death or to persecute such a subject? (xliii:23)

Of course, there would be a long list. And not only infidel kings are so unreasonable. Although Hobbes's teaching is intended to apply to all times and places, he is acutely aware that throughout history men have abused religion to misuse political power. His position is that religious persecution is always unreasonable—as in, ultimately detrimental to its practitioner—as long as religious men are willing to live together law-abidingly. Imagine, from Hobbes's point of view, the trials mankind would have been saved from, if only a certain Roman potentate had not been complicit in the persecution and execution of a certain peace-loving religious personage.

Religion Made Easy

Hobbes would homogenize and tame the most politically salient aspects of religion while allowing relatively isolated individuals, disinclined to dispute details designated as optional personal preferences, a superficial variety of religious experiences. To this end, he is ready with extensive counsel for the reformation of doctrines and institutions. Protestant Christianity is his raw material, but what he is up to is hardly specific to seventeenth-century Christianity in England. Hobbes's effort to reinterpret and restructure Christianity has greater kinship with Plato's political-philosophical recommendations for refashioning the religion of the Greeks in books 2 and 3 of the *Republic* than with the lesser proposals for reforming the faith inundating his own era. (Consider, for example, his rendering of the afterlife as neither too fearsome nor paradisiacal (xxxv:1–13; xxxviii:1–25).) Hobbes knows full well that his contemporaries—church officials and other preachers, especially—will take his teaching personally and misconstrue him rather than be corrected by him (cf. xliii:24; R&C:13), but he is talking past and well beyond them more than he is talking to or against them. To be sure, his book is "occasioned by the disorders of the present time" (R&C:17),[14]

14. To situate Hobbes's positions on religious issues within their historical context, see Jeffrey R. Collins, *The Allegiance of Thomas Hobbes* (Oxford: Oxford University Press, 2005); and Jon Parkin, *Taming the Leviathan: The Reception of the Political and Religious Ideas of Thomas Hobbes in England 1640–1700* (Cambridge: Cambridge University Press, 2007).

but Hobbes is much too well versed in the languages, literature, and long history of mankind for the terms and debates of his own time to delimit the range of his thinking or the extent of his ambition. The tumults of seventeenth-century England offer him an opportunity to contemplate the theological-political problem as a whole, something rarely so vividly on display, as well as to intervene, so as to shape the world to come.

Reexamining doctrines regarding what is needful in this life and what to expect in the next, reworking the virtues of the faithful, remodeling ecclesiastical offices, revisiting the history of the church, and even raising questions about the origins, status, and purposes of the Scriptures themselves, Hobbes's reinterpretation of Christianity leaves little untouched. Because the Scriptures as a whole are not "perspicuous" and there can be no "infallible science" of reading them, it would be "a sign of folly" to accept any prefabricated interpretation of them (v:22). As no strictly literal interpretation of Scripture can make sense of the whole of it, one must decide when to read it literally and when metaphorically. Hobbes argues, for example, that the idea that God is King of the Universe is metaphorical (xxxi:2), as is every apparent reference to an otherworldly hell (xxxviii:11, 14).[15] Hobbes recommends avoiding passages "as are of obscure or controverted interpretation" and claims that his own interpretations are always "most plain and agreeable to the harmony and scope of the whole Bible" (xliii:24). His preferred hermeneutics principally seeks to render Scripture consistent with materialism (e.g., viii:26; xxxiv:23; xliv:15, 32; xlv:8; App. i:44; n.b. ii:8). He maintains that nothing he writes is "contrary either to the Word of God, or to good manners, or tending to the disturbance of the public tranquillity" (R&C:16). (Observe how these disjunctions suggest that the Word of God taken on its own, *sola scriptura,* may well offend good manners and disturb the peace unless it is deliberately read otherwise.) Never acquiescing in an "implicit faith" (xxxii:2; cf. xxx:6), men should read Scripture in accordance with reason, rendering it consonant with "the articles of the law of nature," which "ought to be" evident to anyone who "pretends but reason enough to govern his private family" (R&C:13). A man need not assent to every point in Hobbes's interpretation in order to embrace the spirit of his approach.

Hobbes reminds the reader that "all the faith required to salvation is declared to be easy" in Scripture (xliii:14), which also "command[s] avoid-

15. Hobbes also says that anyone who denies God's punishments is His enemy (xxxi:2).

ing such disputes" over minute particulars that cause the proliferation of schismatic antagonisms (xlii:25; cf. xxxi:33). He reduces religion to the relief of that part of man's estate that still requires some consolation given our mortality, the insatiability of our appetites, and the incompleteness of our science. "The condition of man in this life shall never be without inconveniences" (xx:18), and men never feel perfectly secure so long as they still die (cf. xi:24–26; xii:5). Hobbes therefore designs religion to allow and encourage people to live the lives of comfort, prosperity, and security that they would be glad to live anyhow, while adding furthermore a sense that God thinks it fine. After all, this befits the nature that He gave to us. If God approves of each man's lifestyle, his personally preferred appetite-satisfactions, then He would disapprove only of one man's disapproval of another's. Hobbes argues that for all the different interpretations of Scripture found among Christians, there is agreement on everything that matters so long as they profess that "Jesus is the Christ" (xxxvi:20; xlii:13, 34; xliii:3, 11–16, 18).[16] All the doctrinal superstructures and institutional orders that men erect on top of that fundamental article are a matter of indifference to God, and as such they should be a matter of indifference to men (xliii:16–18, 22; xliv:33).[17] God is not offended when a man doubts an account of Him offered by any other man (vii:7). He forgives men for their ignorance and the errors that follow from their merely human efforts at meeting the impossible task of trying to understand Him, and so should we all. God gives this forgiveness freely without requiring anyone to repent. Everybody is permitted to think that they understand Him rightly, and nobody needs to apologize for maybe getting Him wrong. Still, every man should be modest regarding the certainty of his understanding.

16. To those whose sirens wail at the slightest tincture of any "exclusivity" in the writings of old-time philosophers, it must look like Hobbes is still "privileging" Christianity. To presuppose that a Hobbesian interpretation of other religions is impossible is, however, to overlook how the nature of man and language make all things endlessly reinterpretable, forget how much adjustment Christianity itself has undergone, and designate the adherents of other revelations as irredeemable madmen, purveyors of misery and perpetuators of war.

17. Believers should decide for themselves issues such as the divinity of Christ (which resembles idolatry [xlv:24]), His resurrection (which Hobbes mysteriously forgets when summarizing Jesus' story according to the Gospel [xliii:12]), and the status of the various Scriptures (xlii:42; cf. xliii:15), such as Paul's awfully judgmental Epistles, or the disconcerting Revelation. The Penitent Thief of Luke 23:40–43 knew nothing of his Lord's forthcoming resurrection and read not a page of the NT, yet he recognized all that was necessary. Hobbes furthermore notices that Scripture itself seems to admit the possibility of the salvation of non-Christians (xliv:25, 32, 34–35). There may be no necessary articles of faith, and Scripture may well render itself immaterial.

There is nothing that any man can do to directly affect the inward disposition of other men's hearts—the domain of God's care and concern.[18] The thoughts of men are free, Hobbes maintains, meaning that "belief and unbelief never follow men's commands" (xlii:11; cf. xxv:2; xxxii:4; xxxvii:13; xl:2; xliii:22). The hearts of men are imperceptible and impenetrable (xl:2; xlii:43, 80), and they stubbornly resist even well-intentioned manipulations. To suppose that one may look into another's heart is tantamount to judging him, and this, of course, is something that one should not do. God is not honored by phony worship, and everybody hates being made to offer it. Nobody should try to make anyone engage in it. As far as anyone knows, all men are orthodox to themselves but heterodox to each other.[19] No man can determine if anyone else has come to share in his faith, even given plentiful outward signs (xlii:19). Men excel at fooling each other (and themselves) regarding what they believe. The subjectivity of language, given the uniqueness of each man's experiences compounded by the diversity of the objects of their passions, means that men may even speak the same words and think that they agree with each other and yet believe different things. Even those who coincidentally believe the same thing will differ as to why they believe it to be believable (xliii:7). We always "conceive the same things differently" given our different preferences, temperaments, and viewpoints (iv:24). Even if two men were ever "conscious" of the same thing (vii:4), they never could know it.

It is contrary to the law of nature to force a man to "hazard his soul" (xlvi:37), as "in every man his own religion" is naturally prior to "civil society" (xiv:31). Given that "the power of the law" cannot reach "to the very thoughts and consciences of men" (xlvi:37), a civil sovereign, like every "teacher of Christian doctrine," should "abandon" his subjects into God's judgment, even when they proceed "obstinately" in a life that he deems "unchristian" (xlii:31). A sovereign who prescribes rituals still knows nothing of his subjects' faith, however obedient they may be, but he may be sure that many will resent him. In turn, it should not matter to a man whether or not his sovereign is an avowed co-religionist or if the laws promote his

18. Given Hobbes's use of materialism to dismantle religious metaphors, his references to men's "hearts" and the ideas hidden within them are problematic (e.g. xxxi:32; xlii:11, 37, 80, 107). The heart is "but a *spring*" (Intro:1), after all. Likewise, when he echoes St. Paul, saying, "faith comes by hearing," it should mean only that sense impressions shape men's thoughts (xxix:8; xliii:8).

19. This idea is made explicit by John Locke in *A Letter Concerning Toleration*, ed. James H. Tully (Indianapolis, Ind.: Hackett, 1983), 23.

faith. He can never know his sovereign's true convictions or intentions. True Christianity is supposed to thrive under persecution anyhow.[20] The upshot of Hobbes's teaching is to strip categories such as *heretic* and *infidel* of political significance. The best way to handle a heretic is "to *give over admonishing him, to let him alone, to set by disputing with him,* as one that is to be convinced only by himself" (xlii:25). After all, "heresy signifies no more than private opinion" (xi:19), which is what all men are stuck with anyway, even when they imagine that others share their views. Under the new nonsectarian civil religion, showing old-fashioned concern for supposed theological heresies would be a big mistake. Technically speaking, only opinions that contradict the civil law and thereby try to justify injustice deserve to be called heretical (xlii:130).

Hobbes is a master of linguistic engineering. He teaches us to emphasize the elusiveness of theological discourse so as to marginalize and defuse it while downplaying the provisional and metaphorical qualities of scientific language so as to ward off public contestation regarding it.[21] Every attempt to convey meaning is inherently problematic, but perhaps never more so than when it comes to communicating ideas that touch on the mysterious. Hobbes never tires of exposing how nonsensical the doctrines of the Roman Church in particular become when one proceeds, as he does, from a materialist ontology. More broadly, he wants to convince all Christians that silence is the appropriate response to the mysterious (App. i:14–15). Whereas blunt force will not change men's minds, ridicule may well embarrass them into silence. A religion is made less formidable to the mind (xii:25) and less agreeable to the stomach (xxxii:3) by any attempt to explain its mysteries, Hobbes argues. What is worse, discussing them begets quarrel, prompting pretenders to religious authority to usurp sovereign right by trying to fix definitions, police meanings, and punish dissenters (App. ii:20). Hobbes

20. James Madison emphasizes this point in *Memorial and Remonstrance Against Religious Assessments* (1785), in *Writings* (New York: Library of America, 1999), 32.

21. On the relationship between politics, rhetoric, and science in Hobbes's thought, and on the technological nature and power of language more generally, see Leo Strauss, *The Political Philosophy of Hobbes: Its Basis and Genesis,* trans. Elsa M. Sinclair (Chicago: University of Chicago Press, 1952); David Johnston, *The Rhetoric of "Leviathan": Thomas Hobbes and the Politics of Cultural Transformation* (Princeton, N.J.: Princeton University Press, 1986); Raia Prokhovnik, *Rhetoric and Philosophy in Hobbes' "Leviathan"* (New York: Garland, 1991), chapter 4; Quentin Skinner, *Reason and Rhetoric in the Philosophy of Hobbes* (Cambridge: Cambridge University Press, 1996); Bryan Garsten, *Saving Persuasion: A Defense of Rhetoric and Judgment* (Cambridge, Mass.: Harvard University Press, 2006), chapter 1; Philip Pettit, *Made with Words: Hobbes on Language, Mind and Politics* (Princeton: Princeton University Press, 2008), chapters 3 and 8.

recommends cultivating self-censorship with respect to religious speech. Individuals would then find themselves increasingly unable to articulate even to themselves what they think they believe. Their beliefs would precipitate into a muddled and mushy sediment of sentiment. The privatization of religion renders every attempt to communicate it awkward and eyebrow-raising. Even harmless expressions of goodwill bearing religious connotations come to be confused with aggressive proselytizing and received as an odious form of harassment. So as not to offend inadvertently, men will learn to brush the dust off their feet preemptively (cf. xlii:44). They will feel no compulsion to spread their intuitive, inchoate apprehension of spiritual matters, as trying avails nothing, or at least nothing good. Every individual is allowed to imagine that God gives him guidance in his own life, but he ought to be "very circumspect and wary in obeying" anyone else who claims to know what God wants of him (xxxvi:19). Hobbes reassures his readers that only those personally appointed to the task by Christ Himself long ago were obliged to preach, and only they were conceivably obliged to suffer death in His defense (xlii:12–14). Therefore, nobody fails in his duties anymore if he keeps his faith to himself. Religious speech and public displays of devotion need not be stamped out if people are raised to be sufficiently apologetic regarding them and uncomfortable with them that they readily qualify, dilute, and discount them in order to accommodate everyone else.

Hobbesian Christianity is as undemanding in practice as it is in its tenets. Active personal charity is replaced with passive indirect charity. Having the mere "*Desire* of good to another" is reckoned as charity (vi:22). Instead of doing good unto others, merely abstaining from wrongdoing is taken as constitutive of virtue (xiv:5; xv:35; xxvi:13). People should just mind their own business. The habits of charity are positively discouraged because men find it "hateful" to be the recipient of another man's charity (xi:7). The artificial entity of the state is entrusted with the responsibility for meting out all charity (xxx:18),[22] making private efforts to care for particular individuals improper and suspicious. According to Hobbes's theory

---

22. Nowadays, many Christians mistake state-administered social programs for a form of charity when they are instead engines of Machiavellian liberality. See Niccolò Machiavelli, *The Prince*, trans. Harvey C. Mansfield (Chicago: University of Chicago Press, 1985), 64. When today's Aarons and Erins sermonize in support of the bovine modern state, preaching that men should be compelled to make greater offerings unto it (much of which may as well be burnt), it attests to Hobbes's genius for enlisting Christian soldiers in decommissioning their own army.

of authorization, whenever the state distributes public charity to some man, he is really only providing for himself. That even mild forms of loving others are curtailed in the Hobbesian scheme is an essential element of the effort to eliminate the "madness" that attends a passionate expression of faith (viii:16, 17, 23). Directed exclusively toward this-worldly objectives, charity is wholly subsumed by justice.[23] It should be dispensed in an impersonal fashion, without appearing to pass judgment on the appetites that particular men prefer to satisfy, so long as they are peaceable and conducive to the preservation of life. Whatever assists a man in successfully satisfying whichever appetites he happens to have or avoiding those things to which he happens to be averse comes to constitute apt charity. With the lack of any basis upon which to guide, alter, or refine any man's appetites, no man should be made to undergo any hardship for his own benefit—excepting perhaps efforts that help him to secure a healthier, safer, and longer life, since a man must stay alive if he is to continue satisfying his appetites. A fair degree of conformity undergirds the rainbow of delights that men so well cared for will enjoy. All men are expected to find their happiness in appetite-satisfaction without reevaluating their personal preferences or caring about those of others. Religion becomes just another object of consumption. A man shall satisfy his craving for meaning and purpose by taking his meals from a spiritual and ideological smorgasbord (or not at all, if he is disinclined), selecting from a variety of pleasantly flavored options, each processed so as to be rid of all contagions and guaranteed to be neither too spicy nor very filling.

Religion and the Laws of Nature

People would rather persist in their own errors than have them challenged, let alone exposed.[24] While men naturally respond to disagreement aggressively, they may learn to insulate and shelter their opinions better

---

23. Locke gives this idea a boost in *Two Treatises of Government,* book 1, §42.

24. Using gloomy assumptions to get cheery results is Hobbes's modus operandi. We can safely assume that nobody likes being corrected. The rare exceptions who do enjoy it are not troublemakers. In contrast, it is unwise to expect and require even some men to like being corrected. Many of them are apt to react badly to the attempt. All of Hobbes's generalizations regarding human nature operate in this fashion. They do not have to be empirically incontestable in order to prove efficacious for the sake of deducing a reliable political science. To complain that they are not necessarily true in all (or even most) cases is to misunderstand his method.

through the practice of forgiveness. Forgiveness carries Christian connotations and credentials convenient for Hobbes's immediate purposes. It also allows the person doing the forgiving to feel proud of himself while leaving his own convictions undisturbed. One problem with forgiveness is that an awareness that one has been forgiven engenders shame and spite (xi:8, 22). If forgiveness were given peremptorily, cultivated as an anticipatory response to differences deemed indifferent without examination, people could be forgiven without suffering the indignity of knowing about it.

Hobbes's sixth through ninth laws of nature are most pertinent to this analysis. The sixth law, on pardon, recommends forgiving those who repent of their past offenses *"upon caution of the future time"* (xv:18). This is a rationally calculated forgiveness, fully compatible with an extensive system of impersonal legal punishments oriented toward deterrence rather than retribution. It is not masochistic forgiveness for those who remain dangerously hostile, and so it sidesteps the ancient criticism of Christianity that its emphasis on forgiveness makes it politically pernicious. Hobbes does not recommend trusting that others will disarm themselves and behave like good neighbors should one exhibit a high-minded refusal to defend oneself. He counsels forgiveness from a position of strength, where one can afford it. Enemies should be forgiven when they give up, or at least where there is more to lose than to gain by pursuing reprisals. Reconciliation is especially sensible when both sides can see that a decisive victory for either side is unforeseeable. As men should not punish old enemies who now only want to live in peace, it is prudent for a sovereign to forgive even rebels, including utopian religious zealots, should they cease in their rebellion (xxi:17; OL-xlvii:29). In any case, a man forgives others for his own sake, not theirs.

On a personal level, once men grasp that the future estate of their own souls is not imperiled should they abstain from concerning themselves with the souls of others, and that attempting to make people recant their faith is pointlessly precarious, hostilities should cease. If others will refrain from using their beliefs as a pretext to injure, men should practice forbearance, forgive differences of opinion, and get along well enough. (They do not have to become friends, and Hobbes would rather they did not.)[25] To seek to make a man "condemn some fact of his own" (vi:34) is to desire revenge, which is

25. Travis D. Smith, "Hobbes on Getting By with Little Help from Friends," in *Friendship and Politics: Essays in Political Thought,* ed. John von Heyking and Richard Avramenko (Notre Dame, Ind.: University of Notre Dame Press, 2008), 214–47.

harmful to the one who feels it—and not simply because acting on it often provokes an adverse response. Like drunkenness or any overly strong passion, the passion of vengeance is naturally self-destructive and "hurteth the organs" (viii:19; cf. xv:34; xxviii:8; xxxi:40). Hobbesian men will be more forgiving, more accepting of others, and generally less passionate about anything, if only for the sake of their own health. Despite the diversity in their opinions and appetites, Hobbesian men share an aversion to everything unhealthy.

The seventh law, against excessive revenge, deals further with determining which offenses to respond to with force and how far. Hobbes argues that you should exact retribution for something without employing cruelty and only to the extent necessary to deter unlawfulness and secure future peace (xv:19; xxvii:8; xxviii:9; xxx:23). This means not trying to do anything that one cannot accomplish, like transform a man's heart. The punishment of an offender should check future behavior, but it ought not to endeavor to correct a man's soul. Those who endeavor to impose their religion on another by force must be arrested, but nothing is gained by impugning their faith directly in the process. Perhaps they will reform themselves, but the real crime is that they were not better educated in the first place.

According to the eighth law of nature, no man should *"declare hatred or contempt of another"* (xv:20). In a perfectly generated and fully developed Hobbesian regime, nobody would hate or be hated (cf. R&C:4). A prohibition against hatred is less demanding than a commandment to love one's enemies. Still, not hating other men is not always easy, even if disagreement is their only offense. Hatred is of particular concern since it is the principal passion that readies men to violate the law unless punishments are certain and severe, and sometimes despite even the starkest deterrents (xxvii:18). The success of Hobbesian toleration depends on persuading (or better, raising) men to forgive the different beliefs of others as understandable, blameless, and negligible "errors and infirmities" (R&C:1). The views of others, prejudged as being faulty in ways that cause no harm and cannot be helped, would be deemed worthy of neither scorn nor serious contemplation. A man could even learn to admire another for sticking to his ridiculous convictions while remaining confident about his own, so long as he assumes that they have no bearing on each other. Engaging in respectful dialogue with those who disagree would be neither necessary nor recommended, as it asks and risks too much. We may leave them for God to sort out while being reasonably confident that He will be equally indifferent and forgiving.

Hobbes says that hatred should not be shown *"by deed, word, countenance, or gesture"* (xv:20). This is the furthermost ideal of a tolerant society. How demanding! The eighth law of nature governs not only our deliberate speech but also our less voluntary responses. To fulfill it people must be so well educated that they never find anyone or anything hateful, so that they will not exhibit any reaction that might give away any thought or feeling that could be construed as hatred by anyone else, however sensitive or oversensitive, by anything as minor as a glance or a twitch. The immensity of this expectation is made apparent by considering that some men and women read closeted hatred into insufficiently enthusiastic expressions of approval. A rare type of person may succeed at pretending never to hate, but Hobbes asks everyone to always avoid betraying any sign of hatred, even unwittingly—knowing that to achieve this would require changing human nature (xxvii:18; cf. xvii:2). Ordinarily, human beings cannot be relied on to be such outstanding actors. Hobbes has no patience for romantic imperatives toward personal authenticity (cf. xxxii:4), but it is always better if men are not too conscious of the fraudulence of their lives. We can see therefore just how far Hobbes's teaching does try to reach into the minds of men, though by a circuitous route. The subjects of a commonwealth need a common education that manages their formative experiences, influences their passions, and steers their desires, preferably in ways that make them promiscuous and nonjudgmental. They should share a basic understanding of what really matters, what counts as an offense and what does not, and they should together decree that God accepts everyone just as they are without having to change one bit.

Just as not everyone who repeatedly hears the Christian teaching becomes a believer (xliii:9), it will prove impossible to regulate every man's life so well that nobody acquires firm beliefs for which they will fight. Leaving parents free to educate their own children (xxi:6) has its downside, but Hobbes knows better than to expect every father and mother to surrender their children to be raised communally (although he would, no doubt, be a big fan of universal daycare). He relies on the state to instruct each new generation through trickle-down education, shaping social norms and therefore parental conduct through laws and institutions, from the universities through the professions (i:5; xxx:14; OL-xlvii:29; R&C:16). So that the reeducation he proposes will work for the most part, science rather than religion should be received as "the *way*" (v:20) to mankind's felicity and salvation, for the continual satisfaction of appetites and to relieve men of suffering (cf. xxxviii:15). Abolish the fear of eternal damnation, effectively universalize confidence in salvation, and keep men relatively comfortable in the here and now, and men should find far fewer reasons to hate (or love) each other. While "the greatest and most active part of mankind has never hitherto been well contented with the present," Hobbes trusts that most men by far may be rendered passive and content (xxx:29; cf. R&C:16).

The ninth law of nature requires each man to acknowledge everyone else as his equal (xv:21). A man becomes thereby disinclined to judge other people adversely in God's sight, since any given man is disinclined to think that God's judgment of him is adverse. The pride that Hobbes objects to is comparative. Although, scientifically speaking, human life has no innate value and there is no objective standard of human worth (x:16), Hobbes allows men to remain proud of themselves. (It is not really something that he could prevent.) Having high "self-esteem," as we would say today, is fine, so long as men learn to esteem everyone else, too. While the principle of equality can be satisfied by assuming that all men are similarly depraved, civilized men will take exception to being portrayed as beasts. Reflecting this double truth about mankind, Hobbes's portrait of man in the state of nature is notoriously unattractive, but he also realizes that socialized men will prefer to believe that people are, for the most part, quite all right and not much to blame—each man himself, especially.

Hobbesian Religious Liberty

The acceptance of difference with indifference means not engaging in moral and religious disputes rather than trying to settle them. Having supposed that there is no civilized way of approaching these debates, it is decided that civilization requires averting our attention from them so that nobody risks getting upset. Skirting these potentially nasty disagreements depends on prearranging a fair amount of agreement. Agreement regarding God's inscrutability and an awareness of the subjectivity of language and experience reduce religion to personal opinion, a product of the imagination against which no standards apply except for the prejudice in favor of peace and comfort. Hobbes treats that prejudice as if it were universal, trusting that it will eventually appear incontrovertible. Also, though we cannot know for a fact that God cares for men and that He is merciful, we should say that He is, ostensibly to honor Him (xxxi:17, 25) but really to flatter ourselves—possibly because nature alone hardly supports the supposition that human life is worth preserving. Hobbes furthermore claims that men are naturally capable of attaining sufficient knowledge of the divine law so as to figure out that God does not recommend violations of the civil law (xxvi:41; xxxi:36)—although he recognizes that men have not, to date, fully discerned this truth and lived accordingly (xliii:1). Men should also learn to agree that harmless behavior should not be made illegal. Moreover, legal behavior should not be called immoral. Outside of the prohibitions of the civil law there are no sins either to condemn or to forgive (xiii:10, 13; xxix:7; xlii:43; xliii:5).

Acknowledging that the one necessary article of faith ("Jesus is the Christ") may have complicated doctrinal implications, Hobbes mentions a few of them but eschews elaborate demonstration. He claims that they may be "deduced from it, with more or less difficulty" (xliii:18), but he also knows that he cannot spell them out in an indisputable fashion. In effect, he lets each reader fill them in for himself according to his own predilections, so long as nothing contravenes the civil laws. It sometimes looks as if Hobbes regards penitence as necessary to salvation in addition to believing that "Jesus is the Christ" (xxxviii:25; xliii:4, 18–21). Inspecting Scripture closely, however, Hobbes finds that repentance is but a "counsel" (xxv:10) or an "invitation" (xlii:45). Penitence is incorporated within the endeavor to obey God (xliii:19–21), which is held indistinguishable from obedience to the civil law. Thus, having no present intention to break the civil law is reckoned as righteousness before God (xliii:4) regardless of past action or desire. God does not demand self-incrimination. Explicit repentance may help some men to live more contentedly or strengthen their resolve, but it is strictly optional, and Hobbesian men will lose the habit of it.[26] To be sure, absolution granted by officeholders in the church carries no weight since no man, however frocked, possesses enough power to compel God to forgive anyone for anything (xlii:19). (Priestly confession was invented for purposes of espionage, Hobbes alleges [xlvii:11].) Penitence, whether sacramental, liturgical, or silent, is humiliating, and the God who demands it becomes

---

26. Hobbes's argument emptying repentance of significance does the same for baptism.

hateful for it. The repentance required of the sixth law of nature is not so much an expression of contrition for wrongs already done but a forward-looking resolution not to repeat them. Hobbes observes that men are sorry only when they get themselves into trouble, and their repentance merely represents an avowal not to gamble on not getting caught again. Nobody needs to repent of their opinions or feelings, as only actions call for punishment or pardon. Subjects who are educated properly, however, will gladly seek to have their antisocial tendencies treated by those agents of the state whose assigned task it is to keep the populace complacent, productive, and well-adjusted, using technologies less controversial than religion, under the more agreeable rubric of health.

When *Leviathan* is first published in 1651, Hobbes argues that the three "knot[s] upon Christian liberty" (dogma established by the assemblies of presbyters; the authority of bishops; and the establishment of the papacy) have been dissolved in England, reverting believers to the condition of the original Christians, whose "consciences were free, and their words and actions subject to none but the civil power" (xlvii:19). Hobbes explains that "we are reduced to the independency of the primitive Christians, to follow Paul, or Cephas, or Apollos, every man as he liketh best. Which, if it be without contention, and without measuring the doctrine of Christ by our affection to the person of his minister . . . is perhaps the best" (xlvii:20; cf. xlii:25, 34–35). It would be best, Hobbes indicates, because "there ought to be no power over the consciences of men but of the Word itself," and "because it is unreasonable . . . to require of a man endued with reason of his own, to follow the reason of any other man, or of the most voices of many other men" (xlvii:20; cf. v:3). What should be authoritative to each man with respect to religion is the interpretation of God's will that he finds reasonable. We know that each man's reason is but an instrument used by him for the satisfaction of his own particular appetites, derivative of his passions and experiences. Thus, each man should be free to conceive of God in the manner that presently pleases him most, wherein God encourages him in the satisfaction of his preferred appetites and does not insist on anything that is not to his taste. Indeed, every man's interpretation of God's will is guaranteed to fluctuate throughout his life given that religion is just another mechanism of appetite-satisfaction and aversion-evasion, and every man's preferences undergo "continual mutation" as his experiences change (vi:6; cf. xv:40). Every man should pick and choose which parts of Scripture he likes, and allow everyone else the same freedom to read Scripture selectively or not at all. All religion is reduced to personal spirituality as every religious tradition and organization is stripped of any authority. All devotion to texts or institutions is exposed as mere devotion to men rather than to God Himself (v:4; vii:5–7; xi:17; xii:24; xxxii:6; xxxiii:21; xliii:6). A man should be free to browse around for spiritual guidance, mixing and matching styles and brands to suit his own inclinations, following no teacher (except Hobbes?) with too much devotion.

If independency is best, it must conduce to civil peace most. That it discourages large congregations of likeminded men is advantageous, to say the least. The caveat that it would be best "if it be without contention" establishes the boundaries around which acceptable independent interpretations of the will of God must be distinguished from the unacceptable. A man may believe what and follow whom he will, but he should shun all public controversy. It is true that Hobbes's explicit approval of independency is dropped in the 1668 Latin version of *Leviathan,* after the reestablishment of the episcopacy in England (cf. OL-xlvii:29). The retraction is of slight philosophical significance, seeing as the ideas and arguments that lead to his recommending independency remain in place. A man need not supply or repeat an explicit *therefore* when his premises remain sufficient to draw out the intended conclusion—although Hobbes enjoys being slippery when it comes to leaving some conclusions unsaid (App. ii:37–38). Also note that Hobbes declares that Christian independency is "perhaps" best. It would be better still if that independency extended beyond the varieties of Christianity to embrace all the religious opinions of men, supposing that they too could be made similarly easygoing.

Official independency is a prudent concession to reality rather than an unrealistic attempt to transform it. The "diversity as there is of private consciences" (xxix:7) needs to be managed since it cannot be prevented. Hobbes observes that "ceremonies so different that those which are used by one man are for the most part ridiculous to another" have followed from "the different fancies, judgments, and passions of several men" (xii:11). Even reading the same texts and attending the same schools and services, different people will have different opinions regarding the nature and will of God. Everyone has different kinds of experiences that they will regard as religiously significant. Even supposing that "sense supernatural" is really real, "God speaketh not in that manner but to particular persons, and to divers men divers things" (xxxi:3). Consequently, there is "occasion of feigning of as many gods as there be men that feign them" (xii:6). A man is free to doubt everyone else's claims regarding their religious experiences (xxvi:40), but he should feel no compulsion to voice his suspicions to them.

Men differ with respect to wit, meaning the levels of swiftness, steadfastness, and creativeness in their thinking (viii:2). Among "the most part of men," Hobbes indicates, "they have the use of reasoning a little way"— and even then, sound reasoning is seldom used "in common life, in which they govern themselves, some better, some worse, according to their differences of experience, quickness in memory, and inclinations to several ends, but specially according to good or evil fortune, and the errors of one another" (v:18). They also differ in the degree to which their thinking is scientific (xiii:2), referring to their ability to discern necessary causes. Men are apt to regard God as the immediate cause of this or that event, both in the world around them and in their own minds, out of an ignorance of natural causes interpreted as a lack of natural causes and therefore evidence of supernatural causes. Hobbes tells us (without much demonstration) that reasoning about natural cause and effect leads men to discover a first cause, which may be called God (xi:25; xii:6; n.b. v:3), but science cannot discover the exact nature and will of God.[27]

Hobbes admits that there is no meaningful difference between "teaching" and "preaching" (xlii:17). Education will not make genuinely scientific men of great wit and sound reasoning out of most people. They may, however, be taught fidelity to science and confidence in their own enlightenment. Men certainly cannot be left entirely "at liberty to take for God's commandments their own dreams and fancies" since they would then "despise the commandments of the commonwealth" (xxvi:41). The sovereign

27. On distinguishing God as first cause from His personal attributes, and the concomitant decoupling of science (natural and civil) from revelation, see George Wright, *Religion, Politics and Thomas Hobbes* (Dordrecht: Springer, 2006), 268–93. Intellectual superiority does not confer an immediate right to rule (xv:21). Thus, religious toleration is to be recommended even if certain answers to the religious questions are scientifically superior. It was detrimental to mankind when religion hindered science (xlvii:20), but even if atheism were scientifically true (cf. v:3; viii:25; xi:17, 23; xxxi:33), no imperative to outlaw religion in the name of truth and justice would follow (cf. xlvi:42). Atheists should still heed the laws of nature and therefore the civil laws, and those among them who think otherwise are fools (cf. xv:4). They should not arrogate unto themselves a presumptuous claim to rule on the basis of their vaunted wisdom. That said, the only conceivable infallible authority is science, and Hobbes maintains that science will in time disgrace and destroy "they that trusting only to the authority of books follow the blind blindly" (v:21).

who has the opportunity to institute official independency would have to take an active role in shaping men's attitudes and prejudices so that they feel welcome to devise innocuous beliefs of their own while remaining indifferent to those of others. Their minds must be disciplined so that they find only assertions of privilege or discrimination objectionable, including those found within themselves.

Hobbes imagines that a tolerant society may be built, or rather, built again. The ancient Romans "made no scruple of tolerating any religion whatsoever in the city of *Rome* itself, unless it had something in it that could not consist with their civil government" (xii:21). They even permitted their most prominent citizens to make public expressions of disbelief in the stories told about their own gods (xii:20). Jews ran afoul of the Roman authorities because they refused "subjection to any mortal king or state" (xii:21). They have, however, long since accommodated themselves to the powers that be. That commonwealths under the sway of the Roman Church in his own time tolerate law-abiding "Jews, Turks, and Gentiles" is commendable, but unfortunately they still hassle Protestants (xliv:9). If only everyone were equally free from persecution, every man's religion could be a "novelty" to himself but the cause of neither "trouble nor disorder in a state" (R&C:14).

Forgiveness Now

It is beyond the scope of this investigation to examine in full Hobbes's theological discourse. To be sure, Hobbes would know that the way to reform a religion is to reinstitute it from within, with the assent of the faithful, rather than come as a conqueror, overtly attacking it from without. I resist passing judgment on the sincerity of his professed faith or his interpretations of Scripture.[28] The theoretical implications and practical consequences of his teaching interest me far more than the personal convictions of the man himself. Admittedly, his exegeses contain much that looks like monkey business. Were his teaching untrue (as in unchristian), God would surely "destroy" his "machinations" in time (xlvii:18)—provided, of course, that He is truly there to do so. Hobbes's arguments point toward a nonsectarian

28. That Hobbes exploits God's Word for strictly human purposes, refer to Paul D. Cooke, *Hobbes and Christianity: Reassessing the Bible in "Leviathan"* (Lanham, Md.: Rowman and Littlefield, 1996), chapter 10.

commonwealth with no established church—or more precisely, a common-wealth with nonsectarianism as the established church (without proclaiming it so plainly). When one considers what happens when attempts are made to generate such a regime, one might be tempted to project back onto Hobbes the intention to undermine religion. Setting Hobbes's own beliefs aside, it is still a fair question whether or not the privatization and outward depoliticization of religion merely tames it or eventually extinguishes it. If the latter, then pious men within societies undergoing this process or in societies not presently committed to it are bound to resist it.[29] The commonwealth with no overtly established religion will encounter problems should its more devout subjects come to feel dominated by officious irreligion. While Hobbes may well think that the various religions of men are all mistaken, he recognizes that religion cannot be abolished among men—at least not without changing human nature (xii:23; cf. xxxvii:11–13). He respects this fact better than the rancorous atheist who would emancipate humanity from religious belief altogether and at a stroke if only he could.

While encouraging toleration as indifference at home,[30] Hobbes does not forget that international affairs are less amenable to management. His call for toleration is not based on high-minded global humanism, which explains why his project is not quite utopian. He provides men with the theoretical principles of the "everlasting" commonwealth (xxx:5), but he hardly imagines that perpetual peace is a sure thing. Domestic order requires constant vigilance, remaining watchful of spies and sleeper agents (R&C:7). As external threats cannot be wished away (cf. xxv:13; OL-xlvii:29; R&C:5), Hobbes recommends strength abroad for the sake of civil defense. We are left with the question of whether or not, in practice, over time, a people accustomed to accepting differences indifferently and practicing anticipatory forgiveness based on a presumption of the other's blamelessness and impotence will be able to remain resolute in the face of external enemies who do not prioritize self-preservation, recognize man's natural liberty, grant equal rights to all men and women, or diminish God's expectations regarding professions of faith, daily ritual, or the application of the divine law to civil

29. Hobbes admits that when the episcopacy was abolished in his own time, so too were "law, religion and honesty," and there was "absolutely no sense of divine justice" (OL-xlvii:29).

30. George Weigel refers to "tolerance as indifference to differences" as being postmodernist. I concur insofar as postmodernism primarily makes explicit ideas that are already implicit in early modern thought. Naturally, tolerance as indifference still needs "to be enforced by coercive state power." George Weigel, "Europe's Two Culture Wars," *Commentary* 121, no. 5 (2006): 34.

codes. Does toleration necessarily engender soft nihilism? Hobbes admires a man who neither hates nor is hated by anyone and yet retains "a courage for the war" in defense of the commonwealth (R&C:4). Even before the reestablishment of the Church of England, he anticipated that the knots on religious liberty could be retied. He worries that the Kingdom of Darkness may return (xlvii:34), and the Roman Church is not alone in daring to make "a claim of divine right" (OL-xlvii:27). That said, as the laws of nature recommend, self-preservation requires pardoning enemies who repent and cease their hostilities when forgiving them does not embolden them. It means avoiding a reputation for cruelty while exacting sufficient vengeance to obviate future threats from existing enemies and those who would emulate them. It means not expressing hatred for those against whom one must defend oneself—certainly not by vilifying their religion. If the sovereign determines that lasting peace cannot be had, he must defend his subjects, sometimes employing preemptive measures. The danger is that his subjects, with the opinions and appetites given to them by their education and experiences, may decide that he does not use his might well. If his actions seem to endanger them more than they protect them, they might contest his judgment to their own detriment.

5

Civil Religion as Political Technology in Bacon's *New Atlantis*

DAVID C. INNES

In the *New Atlantis,* Francis Bacon presents a fictional island civiliza-tion, Bensalem, kept secret from the rest of the world. His purpose in this is to illustrate the unrestricted development of his new science. What is strik-ing in the tale, however, is the prominence of religion on the island. The reader's first impression is that Bacon's rhetorical purpose in advancing this new science is not only to suggest to a skeptical establishment the many at-tractive ways in which life could be improved but also to show the compat-ibility of the new science with the reigning religion, even the godliness of the project. No doubt, this was on his agenda.

A closer look at the religion reveals, however, a questionable orthodoxy at best. This calls into question the sincerity of Bacon's most obvious rhe-torical purpose. When he appears to be making a place for the new science within the land of the old religion he is, in fact, refitting the old religion for its use in the world of the new science. The fact that Bacon introduces his readers to the promise of the new science using the story of a "land," or "kingdom," an identifiable place and polity that is devoted to and founded upon this science, alerts the reader to a still larger issue. What Bacon pres-ents is not simply a more comfortable but otherwise recognizable England. He shows us not a familiar place with an improved science added, but an alien civilization whose strangeness stems from its being founded in every respect upon this new science, this new orientation toward the universe. The scientific project is fundamentally a political project. Essential to its success is a perfected religion that is suited for this perfected, or at least steadily perfecting, world. It is a *civil* religion. It fits men not for their eternal rest but for a more peaceful earth. It is an application of Bacon's political science, a political technology as it were.

Bacon's Religious Island

There is an interpretive tradition which holds that Bacon was a sincere Christian who saw no conflict between the conquest of nature and devotion to God. In this view, Bacon saw his project as an act of Christian charity toward both God and men. This was certainly Bacon's explicit claim. In the preface to *The Great Instauration,* he prays:

I most humbly and fervently pray to God the Father, God the Son *(Deum Verbum),* and God the Holy Ghost, that remembering the sorrows of mankind and the pilgrimage of this our life wherein we wear out days few and evil, they will vouchsafe through my hands to endow the human family with new mercies. This likewise I humbly pray, that things human may not interfere with things divine, and that from the opening of the ways of sense and the increase of natural light there may arise in our minds no incredulity or darkness with regard to the divine mysteries, but rather that the understanding being thereby purified and purged of fancies and vanity, and yet not the less subject and entirely submissive to the divine oracles, may give to faith that which is faith's. Lastly, that knowledge being now discharged of that venom which the serpent infused into it, and which makes the mind of man to swell, we may not be wise above measure and sobriety, but cultivate truth in charity. (*GI* 14–15)[1]

Benjamin Farrington takes Bacon at his word that he is simply exploring the book of God's works and that the fruit of the lessons derived from that study are by Christian obligation to be used for the benefit of mankind.[2]

---

1. All references to Bacon's *The Great Instauration* will appear in the text, abbreviated as *GI,* accompanied by the page reference in *New Atlantis and the Great Instauration,* rev. ed., ed. Jerry Weinberger (Arlington Heights, Ill.: Harlan Davidson, 1989).

2. Fulton Anderson is similarly uncritical of Bacon's pious pronouncements. See *The Philosophy of Francis Bacon* (Chicago: University of Chicago Press, 1948), 53–54, 153 ("This science may appropriately be called 'divine philosophy' since, while natural in respect to its knowledge, it is divine in respect to its object."), 171–72 and 212–14. John C. Briggs, in his contribution to *The Cambridge Companion to Bacon,* ed. Markku Peltonen (Cambridge: Cambridge University Press, 1996), makes his judgment in favor of Bacon's religious sincerity based on the reports of William Rawley, Bacon's personal chaplain and secretary, in his *Life of Bacon* (1657), John Aubrey in his *Brief Lives,* and essayist Thomas Babington Macaulay (1800–1859), as well as on the outward conventionality of Bacon's religious life and writings (197n2). Perez Zagorin in *Francis Bacon* (Princeton: Princeton University Press, 1998), recognizes the theological unorthodoxy of Bacon's goals for science, but

"In Bacon's mind there was no conflict between religion and science." Farrington sees "an intimate connection between his religious beliefs and his scientific ambitions."[3] He is in good company going back as far as Bacon's own day. Farrington points out that Bishop Andrews, the lead scholar in the 1604–11 translation of King James's Authorized Version of the Bible, supported Bacon's endeavors, and that many prominent clergymen of that time were later associated with the Royal Society.[4] Stephen McKnight has recently published a book-length defense of Bacon's Christian sincerity and the Christian character of Bacon's efforts.[5] It is true that Bacon's depiction of a world shaped by the unrestricted development of experimental science in the *New Atlantis* is striking in its many religious features and allusions. The European strangers, who are themselves quite pious, notice the pronounced religious devotion of the island. The narrator exclaims, "we are come here amongst a Christian people" (*NA* 43).[6] Bacon parades the point that not only does Christianity coexist alongside this aggressively pursued science, but both are embraced wholeheartedly. The people cherish the faith, and their charity is impressive. The official who greets the visitors asks, "Are ye Christians?" (*NA* 40). When they assure him that they are, he thanks God. Indeed, God is thanked repeatedly in the story. Oaths are taken in Jesus' name. The governor of the Strangers' House commends his European charges for seeking first the Kingdom of God because that is clearly their occupation in Bensalem (*NA* 47). The kindness of the Bensalemites and the accomplishments of their science are described in religious terms: angelic (*NA* 46), a picture of our salvation in heaven (*NA* 45). The central scientific institution, the College of Six Days' Works, or Salomon's House, recognizes the Creator and the wise king of Israel. It is said to be "dedicated to the study of the Works and Creatures of God . . . for the finding out of the true nature of all things, (whereby God might have the more glory in the workmanship of them, and men the more fruit in

nonetheless claims that, of those scholars who say that Bacon "was secretly irreligious but dissembled his unbelief" from Howard White to Robert Faulkner, "[n]one . . . is able to produce any evidence or proof to support the claim of Bacon's irreligion" (Zagorin, *Francis Bacon*, 46, 49, 243n75).

3. Benjamin Farrington, *Francis Bacon, Philosopher of Industrial Science* (London: Lawrence and Wishart, 1951), 74.

4. Ibid., 73–74.

5. Stephen McKnight, *The Religious Foundations of Francis Bacon's Thought* (Columbia: University of Missouri Press, 2006).

6. All references to Bacon's *New Atlantis* will appear in the text, abbreviated as *NA*, accompanied by the page reference in Weinberger, ed., *New Atlantis and the Great Instauration*.

the use of them)" (*NA* 58). The tale ends with the Father of Salomon's House blessing the narrator and blessing the communication of the secrets of their science and its civilization "for the good of other nations" (*NA* 83).

Bensalem's Ambiguous Religion

Though the reader comes away from an initial reading of the *New Atlantis* with the impression that Bacon is a deeply religious writer who would not dream of a future—scientific or otherwise—that was not robustly Christian, reading with more careful attention to Bacon's masterful arrangement of details discloses an author with a more ambiguous commitment to religion. The text itself indicates a less comfortable relationship between sincere religion and a successfully pursued scientific enterprise than Bacon at first leads the reader to believe. A brilliant thinker and master writer like Sir Francis Bacon should certainly be taken at his word, but the reader must weigh all of his words and study them in their context. Bacon engineers a subtle shift from the historic Christian faith to a religion that bears sufficient resemblance to it so that most readers would not be alarmed. The result of the shift, however, is better suited to the new orientation toward the world he is attempting to establish. In the preface to *Of the Wisdom of the Ancients,* Bacon explains how to introduce new ideas that are sure to be upsetting: "even now if any one wish to let new light on any subject into men's minds, and that without offense or harshness, he must still go the same way and call in the aid of similitudes."[7] Accordingly, he draws upon the old religion in order better to establish the new. The religion that Bacon presents includes significant omissions and departures from what his audience would have considered orthodox.[8] This invites the reader to consider what reason Bacon would have for these literary choices.

Bacon makes a display of religion at the first encounter between the Europeans and the Bensalemite officials. The scroll is stamped by a cross. The official seeks assurance that they are Christians and requires an oath

7. *The Works of Francis Bacon,* ed. James Spedding, Robert Leslie Ellis, and Douglas Denon Heath (Boston: Brown and Taggard, 1861), 13:80. Howard White, in *Peace among the Willows: The Political Philosophy of Francis Bacon* (The Hague: Martinus Nijhoff, 1968), suggests that Bacon has *New Atlantis* in mind with these words (109).

8. Christian orthodoxy in early seventeenth-century England was measured not only by the creeds and councils of the early church (e.g., the Apostles' Creed and the Council of Nicea A.D. 325) but also by *The Book of Homilies* after 1547 and by *The Thirty-nine Articles* after 1563.

in the Savior's name. The cross that they observed earlier gives them peace in affirming this (*NA* 39–40). This is nonetheless a broad, nondenominational Christianity that is indifferent to disagreements concerning church government, worship, the sacraments, and even the way of salvation itself. For their part, the sailors share the same broadly ecumenical assumptions.[9] Given the times, this is odd. On one level, therefore, it is no surprise that there is no institutional church on the island to shepherd this Christian people. There are priests, but no preachers.[10] The only priest that we meet is unemployed as a priest per se. He does not serve a parish, but is the governor of the Strangers' House, an institution that has not seen work in many years. He takes orders from "the state" (*NA* 44). It is "one of the wise men" of Salomon's House, not a representative of a church or temple, who verifies the miracle at Renfusa. The Tirsan serves a priestly and pastoral function within his extended family, but he does so as the patriarch. Furthermore, we see him in this role only at the once-in-a-lifetime Feast of the Family, apparently an uncommon accomplishment among fathers. The head of Salomon's House is a pastoral, even papal, figure. He carries a crosier and a staff, both symbols of ecclesiastical authority, and he dispenses blessings (*NA* 70). Bacon gives him a title of ecclesiastical significance: he is the "Father" of Salomon's House.[11] But he is the head of the powerful scientific research institute, "the very eye of our kingdom." He is occupied with human power over nature, not with Christ's power over sin. Furthermore, the people of Bensalem are Christian, but inhumanly so this side of the Lord's return. They do not seem to need shepherding. It is a "land of angels" (*NA* 46), a picture of heaven (*NA* 45), a "happy land" (*NA* 46, 50; also 45, 56, 63). The repeated reference to the people's happiness suggests beatitude, that is, a realized eschatology. The people of this land are "*full* of piety" (*NA* 43; emphasis added). There does not appear to be any struggle

9. David C. Innes, "Bacon's *New Atlantis:* The Christian Hope and the Modern Hope," *Interpretation* 22, no. 1 (Fall 1994): 15.

10. Bacon was aware of the importance of preaching. He praises the theological insights contained in some of the outstanding sermons of his day, "For I am persuaded, . . . that if the choice and best of those observations upon texts of Scriptures, which have been made dispersedly in Sermons within this your Majesty's island of Britain by the space of these forty years and more, leaving out the largeness of exhortations and applications thereupon, had been set down in a continuance, it had been the best work in divinity which had been written since the Apostles' times" (*The Advancement of Learning* II.xxv.18). Subsequent references to *The Advancement of Learning* will appear in the text, abbreviated *AL,* accompanied by William Aldis Wright's 1868 section and paragraph numbers.

11. McKnight, *Religious Foundations,* 17.

with sin. In the land devoted to the conquest of nature, unlike in the moral stew of Europe, there appears to have been a complete conquest of the sinful human nature. Bensalem is still battling the effects of the fall on the physical level, but on the spiritual level those effects appear to have been eradicated.

Though on the surface Bacon makes a show of heart-warming godliness, he signals the true character of his project in the response of the wise man of Salomon's House to the miracle that brought Christianity to the island. We are told that one night, about the year A.D. 53, twenty years after the ascension of Christ and long before Christianity was accepted in Europe, a pillar of light topped by a bright cross appeared roughly a mile off the coast of the Bensalemite city of Renfusa. One of the wise men of Salomon's House rowed out to observe it and, having done so, publicly certified that it was a miracle. How he could know this merely by observing from a rowboat is a fair question. He prefaces his seemingly pious prayer with this information: "Lord God of heaven and earth, thou hast vouchsafed of thy grace to those of our order, to know thy works of creation, and the secrets of them; and to discern (as far as appertaineth to the generations of men) between divine miracles, works of nature, works of art, and impostures and illusions of all sorts" (NA 48).

While we appear to be given a list of four possibilities to explain the pillar of light, a closer examination of the third and fourth possibilities points to a list of only two with qualified sub-possibilities. Impostures and illusions are in fact works of art, but they are mistaken for either miracles or works of nature. They are works of human artifice intended to deceive. Essentially there is no difference between the third and fourth possibilities except in the mind of the perceiver. The distinction between works of art on the one hand and impostures and illusions on the other hand is the distinction of a true knowledge of the phenomena themselves as opposed to credulous and erroneous opinion. Once an observer understands the true nature of the work of art, he is no longer deceived, and the distinction between the categories disappears, at least for the work of art in question. Hence, number four is a subset of number three.

A suspicious reader would then examine the first two possibilities more carefully to see whether the same relationship is present there. This examination is made even more textually inviting by the fact that the two central terms parallel one another in form. Both are "works of" something.

The other two possibilities are "divine miracles" and "works of nature." The obvious distinction is that God does the first and nature does the second. What distinguishes a miracle is that it appears to violate the laws of nature. According to the world's ordinary way of operating, the miracle cannot happen, and yet it does. The Red Sea parts for the Israelites, who pass through on dry ground, but it swallows the Egyptians. The sun stands still in the sky. The axe head floats. The blind see, the lame walk, the dead are raised to life again (Exod. 14; Josh. 10; 2 Kings 6:1–7; Matt. 9). Of course, there are many acts of nature that are mistakenly, or even intentionally for the sake of deception, called miracles.[12] Some so-called miracles are only illusions of nature, that is, works of nature that have fooled the observer into thinking that they are works of God.[13]

At this point, the parallel between the first two possible explanations for the pillar of light and the second two becomes clear. Just as "impostures and illusions of all sorts" is a subset of the "works of art," so too "divine miracles" is a subset of the "works of nature." As "impostures and illusions" are merely works of art that have deceived the observer, so too Bacon is implicitly stating that what we call "divine miracles" are only works of nature that have deceived the observer. Again, the distinction here is one between, on the one hand, credulous and erroneous opinion and, on the other hand, a true knowledge of the phenomena themselves. Once an observer understands the works of nature as they truly are, he is no longer deceived and the distinction between the first two categories disappears. As the natural science that Bacon is proposing advances, the category of "divine miracles" is gradually emptied. Furthermore, as people come ever increasingly to adopt a scientific view of the world, they will simply stop believing in miracles and expect that every unexplained event has a rational explanation that is yet to be discovered.[14]

12. On July 9, 1984, lightning struck York Minster in what appeared to be an indication of divine displeasure (Job 36:30–31) over the installation of the bishop of Durham just three days earlier, a man who denied the physical resurrection of Christ. (L. Eric Calonius, "Anglicans Debate God's Purpose in Fire at York's Cathedral," *Wall Street Journal,* Aug 21, 1984.) In Mark Twain's *A Connecticut Yankee in King Arthur's Court,* the Yank pretends divine powers through his timed use of an A.D. 528 solar eclipse.

13. Consider the most recent supposed appearances of the Virgin Mary in toast and stumps. "'Virgin Mary' toast fetches $28,000," BBC News, November 23, 2004, http://news.bbc.co.uk/go/pr/fr/-/2/hi/americas/4034787.stm (last accessed June 14, 2006); "Image of Virgin Mary found in backyard," WKYC-TV, June 14, 2006, http://www.wkyc.com/news/news_article.aspx?storyid=53562 (last accessed June 14, 2006).

14. *AL* I.iv.9; Jerry Weinberger, "Science and Rule in Bacon's Utopia," *American Political Sci-*

It is worth asking on what basis the wise man from Salomon's House could have pronounced the pillar of light incident to be "a true Miracle." For him to make this judgment simply by observation, he would have to know the limits of what nature can do on its own and of what man can do with nature to produce an illusion. But that is not a judgment that he could make, neither then nor 1,500 years later when Bensalem was still busily pursuing the limits of human knowledge. This points to either sloppy writing on Bacon's part (and there is no evidence of that elsewhere in the book) or an act of deception on the part of Salomon's House. It is also interesting to observe that among the works of Salomon's House, the Father of Salomon's House lists "all delusions and deceits of the sight." He says that they can "represent all multiplications of light, which we carry to great distance" (*NA* 78, 80). The order in which the four possibilities are listed further supports this understanding. They form a chiasm, an $A:B::B_1:A_1$ structure that is common in the Bible. It is a literary device that indicates precisely the relationship between terms, as Bacon is indicating here in the wise man's prayer.[15] Thus:

> A: divine miracles
> > B: works of nature
> > B_1: works of art
> A_1: impostures and illusions of all sorts

Far from showing the piety of the project, Bacon is subtly signaling both our total dependence on the success of his scientific progress and the amazing possibilities that that progress holds for us. He states this impious cosmology indirectly because it would have been perilous for him to state it overtly. In addition, it would have alienated people who would otherwise have supported his efforts, people from Bishop Andrews, the learned translator of King James's Bible, on down.[16] It is not Bacon's intention to purge

---

ence Review 70 (1976): 876 ("The unstated implication must be that there are no criteria for judging the veracity of miracles and that proper acceptance of miracles is simply indistinguishable from ignorance, superstitious simplicity, and politic toleration.").

15. "*Chiasm* (or chiasmus) is another common structural device in which the word order of a parallel line is the reverse of its predecessor *(a b / b' a')*. . . . We also find examples of *extended chiasm* in the Bible. These are chiastic structures that underlie entire passages and even entire books. Basically, when an extended chiasm occurs, the second half of a text or book corresponds to its first half except in the reverse order. Each corresponding section has parallel content" (William W. Klein, Craig L. Blomberg, and Robert L. Hubbard Jr., *Introduction to Biblical Interpretation* (Dallas: Word Publishing, 1993), 237–38).

16. Benjamin Farrington suggests that Bacon's friendship with Lancelot Andrews, "the leading

religion from the popular mind. Apparently, he considered that to be un-natural, and thus impossible, but also undesirable. This natural impulse can be usefully commanded by being "obeyed." Having established among his discerning readers that religion is not spiritual but merely psychologi-cal, he clears the way for using it for strictly civil purposes.

Bensalem's Civil Religion

Christianity is not a religion that sits well with any political order. It stands over and judges political life. The biblical God is holy, undomesti-cated, and jealous.[17] For that reason, biblical religion is politically problem-atic, at least for the kings of the earth who take their stand in opposition to God's revealed will (Ps. 2), as Hebrew kings from David to Zedekiah could attest (2 Sam. 12; 2 Kings 24:17–25:7; 2 Chron. 36:10–21). The theologico-political problem is the difficult and inescapable relationship that exists be-tween divine and human rule or, in the Christian era, between Christ and Caesar. In the Christian context, the problem is exacerbated by the fact that Christ is not just king of an elect nation, but the king of all kings.[18] Thus, the Christian citizens of any given nation recognize a higher citizen-ship "in heaven" (Phil. 3:20) and, accordingly, can offer only a qualified allegiance. When the demands of human political life contravene the re-quirements of God's revealed will, Christians "ought to obey God rather than men" (Acts 5:29). Given that King Jesus has left behind not only an inscripturated teaching but also an institutional religion with a human gov-ernment, the stage is set for at best clashing understandings of orthodoxy and *orthopraxis,* and at worst a good old-fashioned contest for dominion, riches, and glory. This problem plagued the Middle Ages and was a source

---

figure in the commission of learned men which, between 1604 and 1611, produced the Authorized Version of the Bible," had a natural basis in the "parallel between this effort to provide England with a satisfactory version of the Scriptures and Bacon's project to interpret God's other book, the book of nature." Farrington cites, in addition, "the number of eminent clergy who were later associated with the early work of the Royal Society." (Farrington, *Francis Bacon, Philosopher of Industrial Science,* 73–74.) Bacon had every interest to maintain himself in the good graces of the Church hierarchy.

17. When Israel carried the ark into battle in the hope of extracting a victory from the Lord's hand, they were treating God as a political tool of the nation's earthly ambitions. Of course, they were defeated (1 Sam. 4:3–11). The Philistines captured the ark, thinking that they had captured Israel's God, but they learned, as Israel had just done, that YHWH is captive to no one (1 Sam. 5).

18. For a fuller explanation of the theologico-political problem in its several dimensions, see Douglas Kries, ed., *Piety and Humanity: Essays on Religion and Early Modern Political Philosophy* (Rowman and Littlefield, 1997).

of considerable political instability. From the Christian standpoint, this ongoing and seemingly irresolvable problem points not to a fundamental flaw in Christianity, but rather to a flaw in this fallen world. Between the first and second advents, between the initiation and the consummation of the Kingdom of God, this is still a fallen world with enduring problems that will not find their resolution this side of the *parousia,* but that indeed anticipate it (Rom. 8:19–25). If there were not a theologico-political problem during this inter-adventine period, biblical claims that Christ's kingdom is not of this world and that we eagerly await the return of our heavenly king would have less credibility (John 18:36; Phil. 3:20). From the strictly political perspective, however, any religion that is not a *civil* religion is necessarily a threat to the civil authority and to public order.

Broadly speaking, civil religion is driven either religiously or politically. That is to say, either politics taps into religion or religion asserts itself in politics.[19] In its politically inspired use, it is a set of religious beliefs that draws upon an existing and prevailing religion, but that is trimmed and supplemented to support the political order. It forms the character of the citizenry and binds their hearts to the regime. In Bensalem, as in Bacon's project as a whole, the highest consideration is not "the kingdom of God, and his righteousness" (Matt. 6:33) but rather "the enlarging of the bounds of Human Empire, to the effecting of all things possible" (*NA* 71). Accordingly, the religion we encounter there is a civil, or politically oriented, religion. Civil religion for Bacon is the poetic, popular presentation of the enterprise that binds hearts to the empire of science and to the princes and nations who embrace it. Whereas *The New Organon* presents the method that is to be applied to the study of political life and argues for the project as a whole, the *New Atlantis* is a literary presentation of that application. It is a picture of scientific civilization written for the heart.

The Irrelevance of Traditional Religion

The political orientation of Bensalem's religion is apparent in a comparison between the most obvious functions of religion, whether Christian

19. That is not to say that the legitimate application of divine commands and religious principles to government is civil religion. Rather, civil religion in its religiously driven form is the infusion of political life with religious imagery and practices for the purpose of inclining citizens toward the religion and establishing the religion as paramount in their hearts. It is helpful to remember that civil religion is a form of verbal and non-verbal rhetoric.

or not, and what we see on the island in the context of what we learn else-where about Bacon's expectations for the progress of science. Religion of-fers peace with God through forgiveness of sin, moral guidance by divine precepts, and hope of life in the face of death. God, as Bacon presents him, is not holy and thus cannot be offended by sin. At the time of the miracu-lous evangelism, Bensalem already possessed Solomon's writings on natural philosophy. The nation had not troubled itself, however, to obtain Solo-mon's Wisdom Literature (various psalms, as well as the books of Proverbs, Ecclesiastes, and Song of Solomon) or the books of Moses, that he con-sidered indispensable (1 Kings 4:32–34). When the pillar of light and the ark miraculously appear, a wise man of Salomon's House, along with the curious citizenry, approaches it without any sign of holy fear. There is no evident sense of spiritual poverty or dependence upon grace among this su-perlatively holy people. Where they feel their inadequacy is in their knowl-edge of nature. They are struck with "wonder," which is the beginning of philosophy, rather than with the fear of the Lord, which is the beginning of biblical wisdom (Prov. 9:10). If they were to seek the kingdom of God on earth the way they seek the kingdom of man over nature, there would be widespread and regular public worship and private study of the Scriptures as well as a theological institute to support the study of God's creation. The only sin before this God is "philosophic" sin, willful ignorance or a negli-gent failure to subject an aspect of the universe to rational scrutiny accord-ing to the logic of the new natural science.

As for moral guidance, Bacon makes clear in *The New Organon* that the same approach to knowledge of nature is to be extended to moral questions. Earlier, he characterized the subject of the new science in the broadest terms: truth. "There are and can be only two ways of searching into and discover-ing truth" (*NO* I.19).[20] He refers to the old, fruitless method of understand-ing the world and the way in which it is oriented toward human power over the universe. Moral behavior is simply another sphere of life to be brought under human control (*NO* 1.127). Research by the new method will discov-er not only the proper goals of such behavior but also the best means of at-taining them. Thomas Hobbes, Bacon's first great disciple, shows us where that moral science leads. Despite what Bacon says about "sound reason and

20. The standard translation of Bacon's *New Organon* is still that of James Spedding (*The Works of Francis Bacon,* ed. James Spedding, Robert Leslie Ellis, and Dennis Denon Heath [Bos-ton: Taggard and Thompson, 1863], 59–350). All references to *The New Organon* will appear in the text, abbreviated as *NO,* accompanied by book and section number.

true religion" (*recta ratio et sana religio; NO* I.129) guiding man's use of the power unleashed by this science, given the scope of "the new logic," they are both necessarily defined and delineated by the science they are supposedly to govern. Sound reason is the method itself and is incapable of determining appropriate ends apart from simply discovering them.[21] In other words, the method cannot determine how men ought to behave; it merely discovers how they most consistently do behave.[22] By "true religion," his readers are left to assume the dominant religion of their day, which in Bacon's England was high church Anglicanism. Despite the crucial role of religion in directing the virtuous use of man's soon-to-be achieved dominion over nature, however, Bacon gives no attention to how people will maintain truth in their religion. He never speaks either of the importance of reformation to conform religious practice with the Bible alone, as his Calvinist mother might have advocated, or of renewed research into Church tradition beginning with the Church Fathers. Rather, this reformed religion is tailored to the requirements of the new science, not the reverse. Given that the Christian religion is a particularly theological religion and thus fundamentally dependent upon reasoning for its teaching, *sana religio* as a moral guide for the application of scientific discovery is simply *recta ratio,* or Bacon's new logic, serving as judge in its own case. Thus, the "true religion" that looks to this science for its theological reasoning is a form of civil religion, that is, religion simply in the service of power.

As for death, here Bacon subtly shifts hope from the promises of God in Christ to the promise of properly directed and vigorously pursued scientific research. People's confidence in eternal life, that is, in the one who said, "I am the resurrection and the life: he that believeth in me, though he were dead, yet shall he live" (John 11:25), weakens their motivation to conquer sickness and death by natural means. Thus, in the *New Atlantis,* there is no mention of the immortality of the soul. Bartholomew's ark does not bring good news of salvation from hell for individuals who repent, but saves the nation qua nation from "infidelity" (*NA* 49). The Europeans declare themselves free from the "danger of our utter perdition" upon being received graciously and permanently into the community of Bensalem (*NA* 60). The Feast of the Family, a festival honoring any man who has thirty liv-

21. See David C. Innes, "Francis Bacon, Christianity and the Hope of Modern Science" (Ph.D. dissertation, Boston College, 1992), 56–77, 111–23.

22. Cf. Machiavelli, *The Prince,* chapter 15, "Concerning Things for Which Men, and Especially Princes, Are Praised or Blamed."

ing descendents above the age of three, focuses not on the hope of eternal life in Christ passed from one generation to the next, but on perpetuating one-self through one's offspring in great numbers made possible by healthy life-prolonging technologies (*NA* 60–64). Throughout the account of the activities of Salomon's House, we are given examples of research into diseases and cures, prolongation of life, and reversal of the aging process (*NA* 71–83). Death is simply another challenge for science in its understanding of cause and effect (*NA* 71, *NO* I.3). None of these three functions, therefore, has any relevance in Bacon's new world, leaving only a civil role for religion.

An understanding of what Bacon is doing with religion in the *New Atlantis* must begin with a comparison with the religion of the old Atlantis in Plato's *Critias* and *Timaeus,* to which he makes explicit reference (*NA* 53) and with which, as one would expect, there are striking parallels. Plato tells us that Poseidon, the patron god of Atlantis, established that people on their island and provided them with their natural abundance, specifically "a plain, said to have been the most beauteous of all such plains and very fertile" (*Critias* 113c).[23] He endowed them with rich mines and forests (*Critias* 114d–115c). Critias describes wonderful luxuries that the Atlantians enjoyed, but he locates the source of those good things in the land, and thus in Poseidon, "[A]ll these were produced by that sacred island" (*Critias* 115b). Atlantis was thus largely dependent upon the gods for their wealth and power and for their perpetuation as a people. When they lost their self-control and became too attached to the material goods that they possessed in such great abundance and quality, Zeus intervened to punish them (*Critias* 121b). In the *Timaeus,* we learn that the island sank completely into the sea on account of an earthquake and a flood (25c–d). The lesson of the comparison is that trust in God or in the gods is equivalent to trust in ungoverned nature. Piety and virtue are no guarantee against the destruction of a civilization by natural catastrophe (*Timaeus* 23a–c).[24] The lesson that Bacon draws from this account is that a prudent nation does not trust in gods but rather employs them, like all things, for securing themselves against the catastrophic misfortunes of life. In other words, it is foolish to trust in God's unmediated provision or in nature "free and at large (when she is left to her own course and does her work her own way)" (*GI* 27). It

23. A. E. Taylor trans. in Edith Hamilton and Huntington Cairns, ed., *The Collected Dialogues of Plato* (Princeton: Princeton University Press, 1961).

24. Cf. *Essays* #58, Eccles. 2:12–17, and Weinberger, "Science and Rule," 878.

is wiser to extract those blessings from nature forcibly through the proper method of investigation, that is, from nature "under constraint and vexed . . . squeezed and moulded" (*GI* 28).[25] In Bensalem, therefore, the new Atlantians devote their national energies to bringing such natural phenomena under their dominion, that is, conquering the means by which the gods destroy nations.[26]

But as a consequence of this approach to the world, Bensalem does not reject all recognition of the divine. Their God is, however, fully in agreement with their plans. The God of Bensalem and of Bacon's new civil order makes possible and commands scientific research and thus encourages people to overcome the possibility of what once was thought to be judgment. He does not judge the nation, nor does he provide or redeem. By concealing the secrets of nature and giving men the (far from obvious) means to discover them, he engages his human creatures in what Bacon calls a playful game of "hide and seek." He quotes Solomon, whom he calls "the divine philosopher," from Proverbs 25:2, "The glory of God is to conceal a thing, but the glory of the king is to find it out." Bacon reflects upon this, saying: "Even as though the divine nature took pleasure in the innocent and kindly sport of children playing at hide-and-seek, and vouchsafe of his kindness and goodness to admit the human spirit for his playfellow at that game" (*GI* 16).[27] Thus, he is not then a King and Father, but a playmate. In the religion that accompanies and is specifically designed for a world established upon the new rationality, God has been made "civil."

Another indication of how Bacon is using religion is found in the title he gave to his project as a whole: the Great Instauration. Charles Whitney points out that the Vulgate Bible, Jerome's A.D. 405 translation of the Bible from the original Hebrew and Greek into Latin, uses *instauratio* to indicate restoration as well as a new beginning.[28] Bacon uses the term to apply alternatively to the restoration or repair of Solomon's Temple in Jerusalem and to the restoration of commerce between the mind of man and

25. Cf. Machiavelli, *The Prince,* chapter 25, "How Much Fortune Can Do in Human Affairs, and in What Mode It May Be Opposed."

26. Weinberger, "Science and Rule," 878.

27. *AL* I.vi.11, "as if, according to the innocent play of children, the Divine Majesty took delight to hide his works, to the end to have them found out; and as if kings could not obtain a greater honour than to be God's playfellows in that game; considering the great commandment of wits and means, whereby nothing needeth to be hidden from them."

28. Charles Whitney, *Francis Bacon and Modernity* (New Haven: Yale University Press, 1986), 23.

the nature of things (*commercium istud Mentis et Rerum,* literally "the mind and things" (*GI* 1). The former was the place of communion between man and God, whereas the latter was to be the true meeting point between human understanding and the world in its very nature.[29] Comparing James I to Solomon in his character and accomplishments, Bacon invites the king to make provision that philosophy be "built" on a solid foundation (*GI* 6). As Solomon built the Temple, the center of Israel's national life and the focus of her highest affections (Ps. 137:6, quoted in *New Atlantis* with reference to Bensalem, not Jerusalem), James was to build a comparable edifice of learning that, like Solomon's House, would be the "eye" of his kingdom (*NA* 48).[30] In the Old Testament, re-establishing the temple meant re-establishing true religion. By calling his project an "instauration," Bacon signals that he is re-establishing communion between the mind and things, and thus a contemplative communion with God the Creator. Salomon's House, and thus the new science that it represents, therefore takes the place of the new Temple.[31] It follows from this that the new science is the new religion. The Savior, Jesus Christ, who according to the New Testament is himself the New Temple (John 2:18–22), is rendered superfluous and irrelevant along with his gospel, his religion, and his clergy. Bacon offers us a new salvation and a new priesthood that are more compatible with the new regime.

The National Character of the Civil Religion

There is a distinctly Old Covenant character to Bensalem's religion that implies a critique of New Covenant religion.[32] For example, Bacon presents Bensalem as a divinely chosen nation through biblical allusions drawn largely from the Old Testament. Bensalem receives special evangelistic treatment. Whereas in the New Testament, the Apostle Paul, who describes himself as one "born out of time," is chosen for special apostolic

29. Ibid., 23–24.
30. The Hebrew word for both temple and palace, which is a king's house, is *hekal.* The Hebrew word for house, *bayith,* is used also with reference to the Temple, e.g., "he [Solomon] began to build the house of the Lord" (1 Kings 6:1).
31. McKnight, *Religious Foundations,* 29.
32. For an excellent and much fuller discussion of this critique in Machiavelli, whom Bacon follows, see Ronald Beiner, "Machiavelli, Hobbes, and Rousseau on Civil Religion," *Review of Politics* 55, no. 4 (Fall 1993).

commissioning by a miraculous conversion experience on the road to Damascus, in the *New Atlantis* it is the nation of Bensalem that is chosen for conversion through miraculous means and an extraordinary "apostolic" calling. There the parallel with the Apostle Paul ceases, however. The miraculous pillar of light, topped by an even more luminous cross, appears just off the shore by the city of Renfusa. It disappears to reveal an ark,[33] or cedar chest, that was "not at all wet with water, though it swam." Within it was a book, containing not only the Hebrew Scriptures but also the entire New Testament canon, which was doubly a miracle given that many of the books were yet to be written.[34] The pillar of light alludes to the pillar of fire by night and the pillar of cloud by day that led the Israelites out of Egypt, the land of slavery and spiritual darkness (Exod. 13:20–22). The ark has three parallels in the Old Testament.[35] When God flooded the earth in judgment, he preserved the human race from complete destruction by securing Noah and his family in a large ark, or boat (Gen. 6–8). Baby Moses, who eighty years later would bring the Law down from Mount Sinai, was committed to an ark or floating basket to save him from Pharaoh's infant

33. It is McKnight's view that the ark, "is the prime symbol of the special election of the Bensalemites as God's new chosen people" (McKnight, *Religious Foundations*, 16).

34. McKnight reads this passage as indicating that the ark contained not only the entire biblical canon but also some additional inspired books that were lost to us but in this way made available to Bensalem. In fact, the claim is based on the slight ambiguity of Bacon's wording. The governor of the Strangers' House mentions "all the canonical books of the Old and New Testament, according as you have them, (for we know well what the Churches with you receive)" but adds that "some other books of the New Testament which were not at that time written, were nonetheless in the Book" (*NA* 49). McKnight concludes that Bensalem has "a fuller scriptural base to guide it" (McKnight, *Religious Foundations*, 15). Though he does not argue the point and presents it as though it were uncontroversial, he has supposedly observed the emphasis on Bensalem's knowledge of what Europe has received as canonical as well as the conjunction "and" following the reference to "all the canonical books" and followed by "some other books of the New Testament." But between these statements we also find "and the Apocalypse" or the Book of Revelation, the last book of the New Testament and the last book written, likely just before the end of the first century. This suggests that "some other books of the New Testament which were not at that time written" simply indicates those portions of the New Testament that, like the Apocalypse, were written after the date of this evangelistic miracle. If McKnight is correct, however, it implies that Bacon believes there is a defect in the Bible, and thus in Christianity, with regard to its support for modern science. For Christianity to stand behind scientifically based society such as Bacon describes in *New Atlantis,* it needs to be supplemented. Of course, adding to what is perfect is to take away. For Bacon's goals for science and society to be realized, Christianity must change.

35. Gen. 6:14 (the ark of the flood) and Exod. 2:3 (the ark-basket on the Nile) use the Hebrew work *aron,* meaning chest or coffin. Exod. 25:10 (the ark of the covenant) uses the word *tebah,* meaning boat or vessel. The Authorized Version of 1611 uses the word "ark" to translate both words, however.

genocide (Exod. 1:8–2:6). The tablets of the Law were placed within an ark of a different sort within the Tabernacle (Exod. 25:10–22). It represented God's presence among his chosen covenant people, his holiness, and, specifically with reference to the Mercy Seat between the wings of the Cherubim, the redeeming grace of God. The ability of Bacon's ark to stay dry despite floating in the water parallels the burning bush from whence God spoke and from which Moses received his commission. It burned and yet "was not consumed" (Exod. 3:2). All of this suggests the special relationship of Bensalem to God as a chosen nation.

For what was the nation chosen? Israel was chosen by God to record and preserve the Scriptures (Rom. 3:2), to be a light to the nations by the testimony of their holiness (Isa. 49:6) and to produce the Savior (Gen. 12:3; Rom. 9:5). Under the New Covenant, Israel's calling, partly fulfilled, was broadened to include believers from all nations who were to live the same holy lives and proclaim the Savior to all creation (Matt. 28:19–20). Bensalem's calling is to explicate "the book of God's works" (*AL* I.i.3; natural revelation) and bring that light to the nations (*NA* 83). The benefit, thus, shifts entirely to this world and is given indiscriminately. It is illuminating to observe that the Bible came to Bensalem as a nation, and that as a nation Bensalem embraced it. The letter from Bartholomew that was also in the ark states that on the day the ark lands on their shores, "is come unto them salvation and peace and goodwill, from the Father, and from the Lord Jesus." The governor adds, "And thus was this land saved from infidelity (as the remain of the old world was from water) by an ark, through the apostolical and miraculous evangelism of St. Bartholomew" (*NA* 49). Salvation from a vague "infidelity" is set in explicit contrast to the waters of judgment from which Noah was saved. There is no mention of personal conversion on anyone's part and no call for it. Universal conversion on the basis of such an irrefutable wonder cannot be assumed because previous grand-scale miracles, from the parting of the Red Sea to the resurrection of Christ, did not convert the nation of Israel and ensure their perpetual faithfulness. It is true that, in a sense, God brought salvation to Israel as a nation, that is, to all the descendants of Jacob. Even so, their faith waxed and waned. Some feared the Lord and some did not. Salvation in the strict sense had to be individually appropriated. David was saved from the consequences of his sin; Saul was not: "Blessed is *the man* that walketh not in the counsel of the ungodly. . . . For the Lord knoweth the way of the righteous:

but the way of the ungodly shall perish." (Ps. 1:1, 6; emphasis added). There is no such struggle, no such spiritual diversity in Bensalem. It is remarkably "a land of angels" (*NA* 46). The national character of the religion indicates civil religion, and the specific calling of that nation is, accordingly, suited to the character of the regime.

Under the New Covenant, God no longer selects one nation but offers Christ and the gospel to all nations and establishes a Church-nation that permeates and transcends nations. This is problematic from a political point of view as it divides the loyalty of citizens. Bacon's plan is thus to "reform" Christianity into a more Old Covenant form, but without the troublesome interference and distraction of the Old Covenant God. In the *New Atlantis,* Bensalem is chosen as a nation, but avoids Israel's political problem. The kings of Israel and of Judah continually saw their plans interrupted by prophets of the Lord, each a "troubler of Israel" (1 Kings 18:17), who would prosecute the covenant against them. Essentially, they would hold the political sovereign accountable to a higher law. Bensalem's god is a conveniently *unholy* god, however. He brings no higher law, and his concern does not extend beyond Bensalem's "happiness," and this understood in terms of comfort and security, not one's relationship with God (Ps. 1:2; Matt. 5:3–12). The Father of Salomon's House describes their daily worship: "We have certain hymns and services, which we say daily, of laud and thanks to God for his marvellous works: and forms of prayers, imploring his aid and blessing for the illumination of our labours; and the turning of them into good and holy uses" (*NA* 83). There is no word of sin and repentance and redemption, of the cross and the resurrection and of the life to come. This God does not command righteousness and punish sin, but is satisfied rather when Bensalem does what they love the most and what they do best: discover "the knowledge of Causes, and secret motions of things" (*NA* 71). The Bible presents a religion tailored for a holy God and for a people called to be holy as he is holy (Lev. 11:45; 1 Pet. 1:16). Bacon presents the reverse: a God who is tailored for the rational and thus successful conquest and enjoyment of this world.

Bensalem does not remain an exclusively chosen nation, however. At the end of his account of the activities of Salomon's House, the Father of that institution universalizes the religion, commissioning the narrator: "publish it for the good of other nations" (*NA* 83). Thus, the elect nationhood is similarly universalized, comparable to what God arguably did with Israel under the New Covenant (Gal. 3:29), but without entailing the Christian political problem, that is, setting an authority apart from and above the national authorities. The problem does not arise, partly because the God of that religion is still unholy. It is also because there is no church, that is, no independent ecclesiastical authority to rival the secular powers. Even in Bensalem, there is no conflict between Salomon's House and the "king" of Bensalem. Salomon's House simply represents the science that is also the new faith. For this reason, the head of that institution is presented as an episcopal figure. At the same time, he is shrouded in political authority. He is the union of what church there is and the state. He travels "in state" and sits on a throne that Bacon calls "the state" (*NA* 69, 71). The so-called king, on the other hand, is never seen. We are told that the Jews of Bensalem believe that when the Messiah comes, "the king" (not kings) of Bensalem will sit at his feet in Jerusalem (*NA* 65). This religio-political presentation of the Father of Salomon's House along with a seemingly symbolic representation of a king indicates a state control of science comparable to the state control of religion in episcopal England.

The Naturalistic Character of the Civil Religion

Despite the miraculous evangelization of the island, yet consistent with the earthly hope, Bensalem's religion is largely a natural religion. There is much talk of God as creator, but no substantive interest in Christ the Savior. Despite the occasional image of a cross, God is never pictured as savior for sending his Son to die in order to take away sin and guilt. Even in the miraculous evangelization, the land is "saved from infidelity," not from sin and its consequence, damnation. Indeed, once the Europeans travelers are given permission to stay on the island and to become Bensalemites themselves, the narrator sees himself and his men as being "free men," given that "there was no danger of our utter perdition" (*NA* 60). God is pictured as merciful for the comforts that he makes possible through science. He is savior only in that sense. Solomon is revered exclusively for his work in natural philosophy. The religion legitimates and reinforces people's concern with the betterment of life in this world without the distraction of possibly competing otherworldly concerns.

The naturalistic character of the religion is particularly evident in the religious elements of the Feast of the Family. The narrator calls it "[a] most natural, pious and reverend custom" (*NA* 60). Shortly after this, he says in connection with the authority that the Tirsan exercises within his family, "such reverence and obedience they give to the order of nature" (*NA* 61). As before, he mentions nature and reverence, but obedience takes the place of piety. Somewhat later, in his discussion with Joabin, he says only that it is "a solemnity wherein nature did so much preside" (*NA* 66).[36] Given this narrowing of the narrator's attention down to nature, to the exclusion of piety and reverence, at least by name, and given that "solemnity" is related to piety and reverence and is here governed by what he calls nature, clearly religion is subordinate to and in the service of "nature," which itself is to be obeyed only in order to be commanded (*NO* I.3). The religious worship at the end of the feast centers not on Christ the Redeemer, who is supposedly the greatest legacy a godly man would wish to leave his descendants, but on the most notable agents of generation in the Bible: Adam, Noah, and Abraham. The narrator explains this choice: "the former two peopled the world, and the last was the Father of the Faithful" (*NA* 64). Despite the reference to "the Faithful," Abraham is remembered not for his discipling of Isaac in godliness, but simply for his role as the biological father of the chosen nation. At the end of the worship, Christ comes into focus. It is not the cross and the empty tomb that are celebrated, but the nativity. He identifies this moment in the Savior's life as the source of blessing, and not just for Christians, but for all who are born.[37] What Bacon presents, therefore, is a naturalistic universalism tied loosely to biblical characters, including Christ. As universalism, it frees people to concern themselves entirely with this world. The naturalistic emphasis on descendants attempts to satisfy, at least for most people, the desire for immortality within the horizon of this world.[38] The focus on multiplying descendants is politically useful, and the king recognizes it through the charter he gives the Tirsan, expressing the debt he owes for the subjects added to his kingdom. These presumably become soldiers in the nation's war to conquer nature and, of course, consumers of its fruits.

---

36. Cf. Innes, "Bacon's *New Atlantis*," 20–22.

37. Ibid., 21.

38. Bacon offers other means for satisfying the grander ambitions of the few. See his comments on the "grades of ambition" in *The New Organon* I.129 and the honors that Bensalem bestows upon her "principal inventors" (*NA* 82–83).

The Eschatology of the Civil Religion

There is an eschatological theme in Bacon's presentation of the new science as a grand civilizational undertaking, but, consistent with the naturalism of the religion, one that is entirely of this world. Again it takes a more Old Covenant form while being nonetheless radically Baconian. In Christian theology, eschatology is the doctrine of the last things, that is, of the second coming of Christ, the completion of his redemptive work, the consummation of the Kingdom of God, and the fulfillment of God's ultimate purposes in his creation. A biblical eschatology provides the Christian with meaning in his suffering and thus encourages perseverance. It also sets pleasures in their proper context and thus helps Christians to order their desires properly. Thus Paul writes, "For the grace of God that bringeth salvation hath appeared to all men, teaching us that, denying ungodliness and worldly lusts, we should live soberly, righteously, and godly, in this present world; looking for that blessed hope, and the glorious appearing of the great God and our Saviour Jesus Christ; who gave himself for us, that he might redeem us from all iniquity, and purify unto himself a peculiar people, zealous of good works" (Titus 2:11–14). Christians support their efforts to live self-controlled and godly lives by keeping in mind the return of their Savior and all that that entails. Bacon presents, however, a rival eschatology.

Marc LePain, in an unpublished manuscript, shows that Bacon describes Bensalem in terms evocative of the biblical Promised Land and of the eschatological rest that it anticipates in biblical redemptive history. The spies who returned from the Promised Land brought with them a large cluster of grapes as a token of the land's fruitfulness (Num. 13:23). The first technological marvel that the European travelers encounter in Bensalem is "a fruit of that country . . . with a most excellent odour . . . a preservative against infection" (*NA* 41).[39] As the children of Israel had to wander in the wilderness for forty years before entering the Promised Land, specifically because they doubted God's loving and faithful providence, so Bacon describes the Europeans as being helplessly tossed in a "wilderness of waters" prior to their arrival in Bensalem (*NA* 37). Bacon's European audience will suffer a similar wilderness wandering and never enter into the true escha-

39. Marc A. LePain, "The Fruit of the Land: Biblical and Classical Allusions in Francis Bacon's *New Atlantis*" (unpublished manuscript), 5.

tological rest if they doubt the providential capacities of the new scientific method.[40] The narrator describes the island as "a picture of our salvation in heaven" (*NA* 45). He finds in Bensalem all that Christianity has promised in heaven, only in the future. Christianity is supplanted by a better religion, which offers a more certain hope and which accordingly, like the regime it supports, has a more sure hold on people's hearts.

Civil Religion as Conquest of Fortune

For Bacon, the primary function of civil religion is to provide a remedy for the vicissitudes of political life or, as Machiavelli presents it in chapter 25 of *The Prince,* the conquest of fortune. In *Essays* #58, Bacon identifies "sects" as the greatest problem facing political stability: "The greatest vicissitude of things amongst men, is the vicissitude of sects and religions."[41] He distinguishes "sects and religions," in particular Christianity ("true religion," that is "built upon the rock," quoting Matt. 16:18), from "the rest," that are "tossed upon the waves of time." Nonetheless, he says these things having just cited Machiavelli, who makes no distinction between true and false religion when speaking of what Bacon calls "the jealousy of sects" in obliterating the historical record of previous religions and any cultural accomplishment associated with them.[42] Whereas Machiavelli calls them religions, Bacon, in citing him, calls them "sects" without distinction. If a sect is to establish itself, it must fulfill two conditions: it must supplant or oppose an established authority because this gains it popularity, and it must "give license to pleasures and a voluptuous life." With his new science, Bacon fulfills both of these conditions. In *The New Organon,* he opposes the received logic and the sciences as they stood in his day (I.84). In the *New Atlantis,* he presents the marvelous comforts and pleasures that the new way of thinking about the world will provide. The three means by which he claims new sects are established are miracles, rhetoric, and force of arms. The new science, which is oriented exclusively toward the effectual

40. Ibid., 6.
41. Francis Bacon, *The Essays or Counsels Civil and Moral,* ed. Brian Vickers (Oxford: Oxford University Press, 1999), 129. Lincoln sees the perpetuation of the American republic, its escape from the cycle of the rise and decline of civilizations, as tied to a form of "political religion." ("Address to the Young Men's Lyceum of Springfield, Illinois: On the Perpetuation of Our Political Institutions," January 27, 1838.)
42. Ibid., 128; Machiavelli, *The Discourses,* II.5.

truth,[43] brings its own wonders, *namely,* its useful inventions. Bacon supplies the persuasive speech through his writings, and, as his epistle dedicatory for *The Great Instauration* indicates, he expected James I of England to supply the sword.[44] Bacon is offering this new science, that is, this new orientation not only of the mind but of the heart toward the world, as a new sect to supplant all previous religions and to bring to a close the succession of one sect after another and bring "the vicissitude of things" under human control. The hope of this lies in its foundation upon the solid rock—not of Christ's gospel and Church, but of empirical observation.

Christianity, Science, and Scientism

Our interest in Bacon's adaptation of Christianity for his envisioned brave new world is not based on any suspicion that we might discover an incompatibility between Christianity and science in the very genesis of the relationship. A Christian can be a good scientist and nonetheless faithful to Christ. The study of God's world by the godly presents no problem. All truth is God's truth. There is no contradiction between natural revelation (the creation) and special revelation (the Bible). Biblical religion provides the theological basis for an expectation that the world is fundamentally rational and thus intelligible and operates with predictable regularity. Understanding God's creation with a view to useful inventions is not only possible and permissible for a Christian, it is commanded. In Genesis, Adam and his descendants are commanded to "take dominion" over the earth (1:28). On account of man's fall into sin and God's cursing of the ground, however, God told Adam that his efforts at dominion would come only "by the sweat of your brow"; that is, they would be frustrated (3:19). Thus, until Christ's redemptive work is brought to fulfillment in the New Heavens and the New Earth (Rev. 21–22), there are limits to what we can expect from those efforts at dominion.

What is at issue in its relation to Christianity is not science, one pursuit among many within modern Western civilization, but scientism or scientific civilization, an orientation toward the universe that is directed by the epistemology and goals of the new science for which Bacon is arguing. Within

43. Machiavelli, *The Prince,* chapter 15.
44. For further illuminating discussion of this subject, see Robert K. Faulkner, *Francis Bacon and the Project of Progress* (Lanham, Md.: Rowman and Littlefield, 1993), 78.

that cultural horizon, nothing is recognized except what can be known empirically, that is, what can be measured and broken down into its constituent parts. It is a civilization devoted exclusively to the conquest of nature for the relief of our earthly estate. For Bacon, the scientific project is part of a larger political project, which itself is comprehensive. For this reason, the conquest of nature must be extended ultimately to the conquest of specifically human nature. Though science has a legitimate and even necessary place within the Christian universe, between Christianity (or Judaism or Islam, for that matter) and scientism there is necessarily a "clash of civilizations."

In light of the ultimately hostile relationship that Bacon sees between Christianity and a fruitfully rational approach to the world, it is fair to ask why scientific civilization requires any religion at all. Why should Bacon not expect that the triumphant empire of the mind over all things will result in an overtly atheistic humanity? It appears from the *New Atlantis* that Bacon does not see religion as a prescientific feature of human life that will naturally fall away once the population is taught to be thoroughly rationalistic, but rather something rooted in human nature itself. Thus, Bensalem's civil religion is a technology of sorts. It obeys, that is, follows the hidden operations of, nature—human nature in this case—but only in order to command it better (*NO* I.3). Religion does not supply that power with wisdom for its use, but is instead merely an aspect of the power. It is true that religion has often been subordinated to political goals and used for the effective subjugation of some people by others. Under the regime of this new science, however, religion is used in the context of a larger subordination of all human knowledge to human power over all things, including human beings themselves in every aspect of their being. It is Bacon's subtle teaching that if political life is to be tamed, brought under rational human control by scientific means and directed toward publicly useful ends, religion must also be incorporated into the scientific political project. Religion must become not only civil, as it has often been in the past, but now also technological.

6

Jean-Jacques Rousseau
on Civil Religion

Freedom of the Individual, Toleration,
and the Price of Mass Authenticity

RONALD WEED

It is no accident that Rousseau treated the problem of civil religion as such a central one in his political writings.[1] His apparently strong commitment to freedom of the individual required a level of extreme unity within the state that made the spiritual force of public religion indispensable. The spiritual force of public religion is the one basis for attachment between citizens that rivals the power of the state itself. It is, therefore, the one powerful basis for unity between citizens that, if not incorporated into the power of the state, diminishes the unity available to the state. So, the level of extreme unity called for by Rousseau's strong priority of individual freedom also adds an equally strong motivation for the state to consolidate these resources for unity.

But the fact that Rousseau's political priorities contributed motivations for civil religion did not, in itself, entail civil religion as a practice either then or now. It is true that a political climate where the progress of individual rights is vigorous requires a deep unity of state for the continued progress of those rights. Consequently, this makes civil religion an attractive practice for the state. Rousseau's reason for this is that the state with a politically strong core of unity is made either less united by public religion or more intolerant by it. Religions whose teachings, membership, or activities

1. All references from Jean-Jacques Rousseau will be drawn from *Discourse on Inequality* and *The Social Contract* in *The Essential Rousseau,* trans. L. Blair (New York: Penguin, 1975), and *Emile,* trans. Allan Bloom (New York: Basic Books, 1979).

extend into public life are public religions. And the existence of these public religions in a state with strong political unity will either lead to political
and religious intolerance or undermine the unity of state.[2] If that public religion is separated from the state it will explicitly and implicitly undermine
the unity of the state. If that public religion is not separated from the state,
the added unity it provides for the state will reinforce whatever boundaries
of political impermissibility already exist in the bonds of state. It will also
amplify the exclusivity of that religion, lending its power to the state and
consequently reinforcing its own religious tenets. The existence of public
religion in a state with strong unity can make that state either even more
unified, but intolerant, or less unified by the separation of religion from it.[3]
Civil religion becomes an attractive option for the state under this Rousseauian analysis because it increases the crucial unity of the state, while
still precisely enabling the state power to minimize the intolerance that will
inevitably ensue.

The usefulness of civil religion in Rousseau's thought is motivated by the
restraint of intolerance almost as much as it is by the very important con-
solidation of unity in the state. But the version of civil religion that Rousseau found useful in the restraint of intolerance is not exactly the solution
to intolerance that his contemporary interlocutors ascribe to him. Rousseau
believed that a civil religion guided by an external morality would help
unify the state, while the theological distinctives of revealed religion would
remain entirely private and personal to the individual.[4] Those common fea-

2. By public religions I take Rousseau to be referring to those revealed religions (but not necessarily just revealed religions) with teachings, membership, and activities that involve a set of citizens with shared religious beliefs.

3. Rousseau often appeals to the notion of unity with respect to individual persons, groups,
and organizations, as well as society itself. Rousseau doesn't offer an explicit account of how unity
is constituted in each of these contexts. However, in the case of individual unity, some of his texts
suggest (and part of the next section highlights) a few key features: the positive exercise of self-
sufficiency, the absence of restraint from others (whether physically, psychologically, etc.), and the
avoidance of internal conflict, such as the possible tension that might arise between desire and "artificially" inspired obligations. While the positive exercise of self-sufficiency is a very ideal basis for
unity in his view, the absence of restraint is a more achievable and more basic condition for personal unity. Yet, the absence of internal conflict seems to be the most likely framework for his version
of unity—avoiding aspirations or obligations that would come into conflict with one another and
unhinge the agent driven by them. With respect to unity within and among groups, organizations
and society itself, Rousseau highlights similar notions depending on the group configuration and
goals. But the aim of avoiding factional conflict and interests looms as large in his view of social
unity, though his more ideal grounding of unity is through a more robust social integration and
cohesion based on common goals and priorities.

4. Rousseau, *Social Contract*, 110–12.

tures of revealed religion concerning moral practice that are consistent with the good of the state are collapsed into a common, vigorous, and external morality cultivated under the rubric of state religion. Any other features of revealed religion relating to moral practice would be excised. And the other theological distinctives of revealed religions—especially the most controversial ones—are submerged into the purely private and individual sphere of belief. Rousseau treats this sphere of belief as safe and private, but not a central source of spiritual strength for the state. The spiritual strength of the state is a religiously centered and institutionally endorsed external morality; one that is reinforced by the absence of religious disagreement concerning its precepts.[5] Rousseau argues for the usefulness of this kind of civil religion as a consequence of his highly political project. He does not discuss an authenticity-oriented religion to accommodate these kinds of political priorities, even though he had much to say in his other writings about the value of authenticity—the unhindered embracing of the natural sentiment of self-love (*amour soi*).[6] This is important because if the presence of public religion in states with strong unity threatens either their unity or their tolerance,[7] then an authenticity-oriented religion may seem like an attractive means for reconciling both.

An authenticity-oriented civil religion has two dimensions—cognitive and affective. Its cognitive dimension includes theological affirmation— the most significant of which could be made only by individual believers as their conscience dictates. But the individual must not be internally conflicted by externally imposed religious requirements and one's own deepest religious passions—passions that can be sustained only by following one's own longings rather than the frustration of heteronymous motivation. Accordingly, the measure of religious authenticity is how sincerely one internalizes and expresses the religious affirmations of one's own conscience.

An authenticity-oriented religion emphasizes exactly those interiorized

5. Ibid., 109.
6. For the purposes of this essay I shall refer to a notion of authenticity that is at work in much of Rousseau's writings, though not always referred to explicitly. By Rousseauian "authenticity" I am referring to the unhindered embracing of the natural sentiment of self-love (*amour soi*). It is common for that self-love to be misshaped by the denaturing demands of social convention into a self-love that is misunderstood (a*mour propre*). But an *authentic* individual for Rousseau would maintain (or, possibly, regain) that internally guided, undivided, passion of self-love that might have been characteristic of the individual in the state of nature. These topics are discussed further below. See also note 44.
7. Ibid., 107–8.

distinctives of religion whose interiorization was thought by Rousseau to effectively restrain their controversial character. The recovery of authenticity in Rousseau's less political writings involved a retreat into the interior life—that place free from the denaturing impositions of society. But a response to the tension between intolerance and unity of the state that emphasizes an authenticity-oriented religion actually becomes a greater instrument of intolerance. The pressure in a society that is increasingly intolerant and among individuals in that society who are increasingly authenticity-centered is to interiorize those inevitable sources of intolerance, thereby diluting whatever basis for a common morality might be available. For the inner religious principle of authenticity cannot sincerely coexist with an institutionally endorsed religious morality. Its external demands will compromise the authenticity of citizen responses to those demands. A fully authenticity-driven religion would consider a common morality as still an imposition on the conscience of other citizens.

This essay considers the Rousseauian view that the theoretical motivations that lead to a tension between unity and intolerance reinforce the tendencies in society for various forms of civil religion to reduce that tension. And when the rapid expansion of individual freedoms leads to a tension between unity and tolerance, it is more likely that authenticity-based civil religions will emerge as a response to that tension. But an authenticity-oriented religion becomes a greater instrument of intolerance because its increasingly interiorized solutions to intolerance actually create more dynamic opportunities for intolerance. This is because its more sincere penetration and personalized diffusion directly undermine efforts to ground a common religious morality compatible with the vast range of moral voices thereby authenticated on a mass scale.

Freedom of the Individual and Public Religion: Unity or Intolerance?

The strongest political motivation for civil religion in Rousseau's thought is the unity of state.[8] But the deeper motivation for both that unity itself and the justification of the measures necessary to ensure that unity is Rousseau's understanding of freedom.[9] What is the complexion of human freedom for

8. Ibid., 17, 20, 107–8, 110.
9. See A. Melzer, *The Natural Goodness of Man: On the System of Rousseau's Thought* (Chicago:

Rousseau? And how does its development drive the unification of the state?

For Rousseau, the basis for any human freedom originates in the sort of freedom that characterizes the individual in the state of nature. The individual in the state of nature is free there because he is unified. There are two latent features of this unity in the state of nature. The unity of the person there is manifest in (1) the positive exercise of self-sufficiency and (2) the absence of restraint upon it from others (whether physically, psychologically, etc.). So the person is positively able to exercise his self-sufficiency because his benign solitude in the state of nature limits his desire to the reliable and predictable satisfaction of simple need.[10] Furthermore, the solitude of the individual in the state of nature preserves him from that interaction with other wills that might either (a) move him by force or fraud against his own desires or (b) artificially induce in him false desires and dependencies that exceed his basic needs. In either case, his desires for those objects that would satisfy his simple needs are either frustrated by some external source or altogether divided by it. The limits of his aspirations in the state of nature, Rousseau contends, make him *both* more likely to be self-sufficient *and* less vulnerable to those external sources that would frustrate or distort his desires.

But the overall value of freedom of the individual in the state of nature is ambiguous. The freedom there is absolute by the standard of the state of nature itself. But it is unclear how free the person might become in society. The scale of human interaction available in society may either enable a greater individual freedom than that in the state of nature or greatly undermine it. Whether civil society can protect the most basic level of freedom for the individual, let alone promise a more enhanced version of it, depends on the state. Society may always enslave the individual, but the state need not distribute the chains.

For only the state can effectively organize and implement a collective transformation of the human will. In society, the totality of wills consti-

University of Chicago Press, 1990), 97, 194, 195, 235. For other general discussions on this issue, see Ronald Grimsley, *Rousseau and the Religious Quest* (Oxford: Clarendon Press, 1968), 13, 24, 49, 60, 67; Alesandro Ferrara, *Modernity and Authenticity: A Study in the Social and Ethical Thought of Jean-Jacques Rousseau* (Albany: State University of New York Press, 1993), 60–65; Charles W. Hendel, *Jean-Jacques Rousseau Moralist* (London: Oxford University Press, 1934), 21, 27, 125, 165; Roger D. Masters, *The Political Philosophy of Rousseau* (Princeton, N.J.: Princeton University Press, 1968), 348–50; Judith Shklar, *Men and Citizens* (London: Cambridge University Press, 1968), 18, 55, 84, 176; A. Ripstein, "The General Will," *History of Philosophy Quarterly* 9, no. 1 (January 1992): 58.

10. Rousseau, *Discourse on Inequality*, 154; *Emile*, 213–20; *Social Contract*, 8.

tutes a collective but arbitrary force against the individual. But the state can fashion a collection of wills as massive as society if it does so with unity. The general will provides the ideal organizing structure for the particular wills of individual citizens. For the state unifies the particular wills of individual citizens *as* the general will. The overall freedom of each individual citizen cannot be increased unless each individual forgos his more immediate individual interests. When a citizen submits his particular will to the general will he enhances his long-term freedom as an individual. But why would a citizen—even an extremely civic-spirited one—forgo his immediate interests when those more immediate interests may outweigh the amorphous promise of freedom? It is in the interest of any one citizen to forgo his immediate interests and submit his particular will to the general will only if each and every other citizen also does so.[11] The state is the one agent capable of achieving more freedom for the individual than was possessed in the state of nature.[12] This is because it (the state) is the one agent able to radically unify the particular wills of citizens under the general will. Therefore the unity of the state becomes perhaps the crucial political condition achieving Rousseau's principle of freedom.[13]

This fundamental emphasis on the priority of state unity animates Rousseau's discussion of civil religion. Since, according to Rousseau the serious political commitment to freedom of the individual requires a strong core of unity in the state, then it seems fair to assume that a state committed to a Rousseauian version of freedom of the individual would have to prioritize the unity of the state. The existence of public religion in those societies with a strong fabric of state unity will be subject to a problematic alternative. The presence of public religion in these states will either reduce the unity of state or induce a greater level of intolerance. The presence of public religion in a state with a solid base of unity will reduce that unity when there is a separation of public religion from the state. Rousseau notes that "[i]t was in these circumstances that Jesus came to establish a spiritual kingdom on earth. By separating the theological system from the political system, this destroyed the unity of state, and caused the internal divisions

11. See Rousseau, *Social Contract*, 19; Melzer, *The Natural Goodness of Man,* 96; Ripstein, "The General Will," 47; Joel Schwartz, *The Sexual Politics of Jean-Jacques Rousseau* (Chicago: University of Chicago Press, 1984), 73.
12. Rousseau, *Discourse on Inequality*, 186; *Social Contract,* 16–18, 21.
13. Rousseau, *Social Contract,* 27–30.

that have never ceased to agitate the Christian peoples."[14] The separation of public religion undermines the unity of state explicitly and implicitly.[15] This separation diminishes the unity of state most explicitly by the proliferation of factions. Since a religious body that is separated from the state cannot be considered a division of the state, it must be a sub-political association of interest—religious interest. But it is unlikely that it would be just one association of interest. In matters less controversial and weighty than religion it is almost always the case that a single-interest association fails adequately to embrace the concerns, interpretations, and criticism of the participants in that activity. Religious history has left a long trail of sectarianism of some form or another in nearly every regime, but especially in those ones where there has been a strong emphasis on the separation of church and state.

Rousseau argues that these proliferating associations of interest, especially religious ones, constitute factions.[16] Factions are some of the most forceful agents of disunity in Rousseau's analysis. The members of a faction create a smaller version of the general will organized around the interest of their faction.[17] That it is an interest, and not a principle that can be generalized around the whole good of the polity, disqualifies it from being the general will. The faction is a distorted form of the general will and must always be a distorted form of the general will. But because it performs a role for the members of the faction that imitates the general will on a more limited scale, it always absorbs an increment of social interest that necessarily cannot be integrated into the activity of the state. The faction weakens the unity of the state because it re-channels social interest that would have otherwise been incorporated under *the* general will.

The kind of social force for unity that factions deny the state is the kind most vital for state unity. A faction is a grouping of interest that is organized for more specific purposes than the state can organize. But for Rousseau it is the overlapping of interest that makes society uniquely possible. "For while the creation of societies was made necessary by the clash

14. Rousseau, *Social Contract*, 107.

15. Tim Fuller, "The Theological-Political Tension in Liberalism," *Philosophy and Theology* 4, no. 3 (1990): 268–271; A. Melzer, "The Origin of the Counter-Enlightenment," *American Political Science Review* 90, no. 2 (June, 1996): 348; Melzer, *The Natural Goodness of Man*, 357.

16. Rousseau, *Social Contract*, 27, 47.

17. Fuller, "The Theological-Political Tension in Liberalism," 268–71; Masters, *The Political Philosophy of Rousseau*, 328–30; Ripstein, "The General Will," 61; Shklar, *Men and Citizens*, 176; Schwartz, *The Sexual Politics of Jean-Jacques Rousseau*, 113.

of individual interests, it was made possible by the fact that those same interests also coincide. It is what they have in common that forms the social bond, and if there were no point at which all interests coincided, no society could exist. It is solely on this basis that society should be governed."[18] It is only because people have overlapping interests that they are willing to forgo some of their natural freedoms to gain greater freedoms in civil society. When individuals understand that the interests they forgo are similar to the interests that others must forgo, it is much easier to maintain the unity of will necessary to achieve this greater freedom. But factions are a particularly dangerous challenge to unity of the state because their particular success must borrow from just that motivation for freedom that the state needs to fortify its unity—the common interests of its members. And the more factions there are, the more these factions are a challenge to that unity of state.[19]

According to Rousseau, the separation of public religion from the state is a costly option for the state that hopes to maintain its unity. The separation of public religion from the state fundamentally separates the interests of those inevitable groupings of religion from both the interests of those individuals in competing religious groupings and the interests of the remaining mass of individuals not participating in any religious association. The aims of those public religions may be more or less compatible with the political aims of the state. But the very separation of public religions from the state dilutes the efforts of the state to reinforce the common interests of its citizens. For the participation of some citizens in public religions whose structure is necessarily distinct from the state cultivates interests distinct from the state, even if they are supportive of the state. This inevitable division of interests reduces the overall unity of state. For these reasons Rousseau rejects the separation of public religion from the state.

Intolerant Unity: The Sovereignty of Self-love and the State

Rousseau's rejection of the separation of public religion from the state is not an immediate endorsement of civil religion as a politically salutary alternative. Rousseau prescribes civil religion as a useful form of public religion that is superior to separated public religion because it enhances unity

18. Rousseau, *Social Contract,* 24.
19. Ibid., 18, 110.

and uniquely controls the consequences of that enhanced unity.[20] For the failure to separate public religion from the state will lead to religious and political intolerance. The added spiritual force contributed by public religion from within the state creates an intolerant form of unity.

Anything that breaks social unity is worthless. All institutions that place man in contradiction with himself are worthless. The second is good in that it joins divine worship to love of the law, and by making the fatherland an object of worship for its citizens, teaches them that to serve the state is to serve its tutelary god ... But it is also bad when becoming exclusive and tyrannical it makes a people bloodthirsty and intolerant, so that its members breathe only murder and slaughter, and believe that they commit a holy act when they kill anyone who does not accept their gods.[21]

Rousseau seems to hold both political and philosophical grounds for this view.

Rousseau maintains that the very structure of unity in the person and the state makes the toleration of differences difficult. So any increases of unity, but especially religiously based increases of unity, tend toward intolerance. There are a few crucial features in the moral psychology of the individual and his function within society that fuel this understanding of intolerance. But to understand these features as they function within society they must be understood in their more innocent form prior to society.[22] For Rousseau those aspects of the person that will issue socially into intolerance are already present in a very primitive form—*amour soi*, or self-love.[23] When the happy self-love of the individual in the state of

---

20. See Fuller, "The Theological-Political Tension in Liberalism," 269–70; Grimsley, *Rousseau and the Religious Quest*, 3, 84, 137; J. Maritain, *Three Reformers: Luther, Descartes, Rousseau* (New York: Charles Scribner's Sons, 1940), 357; Melzer, *The Natural Goodness of Man*, 167, 190, 197–98, 235.

21. Rousseau, *Social Contract*, 110. See also Grimsley, *Rousseau and the Religious Quest*, 19, 85; Hendel, *Jean-Jacques Rousseau Moralist*, 236–38, 56–57, 160–61; Shklar, *Men and Citizens*, 114.

22. One of Rousseau's most complete discussions of the person and authenticity is in his work *Emile*. This work is concerned with the education of just one individual, the imagined subject of the work—Emile. Some of Rousseau's most penetrating discussions of authenticity can be found there. But Rousseau does not understand the version of authenticity outlined there to be a blueprint for authenticity within mass society. The built-in social limits of such a lofty version of authenticity as it is discussed in this work is one of the most helpful points of comparisons between it and his much more political treatise, *The Social Contract*.

23. The language of the self as distinct from the individual or the person underscores the psychological character of Rousseau's description of one's bondage to society. The full identity of the individual depends both on society for its development and on society for its alienation. The notion of *self* implies an ambiguity or open-endedness about its social purposes that is more common in Rousseau's less explicitly political writings. For example a self might be many things (mother,

nature is extended into society it becomes subject to the opinions of others, thereby transforming the independence of one's self-love into a state of dependence—*amour propre*, or self-love misunderstood. Even to understand one's self, let alone love that self, one is inextricably dependent on what others take to be valuable. The self in civil society always consults the assortment of opinions constituting society's prejudices to judge what is valuable in others and oneself.

In the state of nature one's self-love is so strong and pure because one's standard for perfect self-love is so easily available and so easily perfectible.[24] That standard is so easily available in the state of nature according to Rousseau's psychology because the best standard for our love is a very familiar one—ourself. Along these lines, there is no one in the state of nature better able to supply this standard for love than ourself. Secondly, self-love is so easily perfected in the state of nature because the fundamental principle that one perfects there is that of self-preservation.[25] One generates self-love by successfully preserving oneself. In a state of simple solitude one's needs are so limited that self-preservation is much easier. And the character of the person we are preserving under our benign absorption in simple need is so primitive that it is automatically perfected whenever it is preserved. So, self-love in the state of nature is strong and pure because the standard for it is so available and perfectible there.

The self-love in the state of nature is also inherently good. It is easier to preserve a self with few attachments, who is easily contented with what is familiar. In this setting, the simple and localized character of our needs sustains the harmony between our self-love and goodness.[26] It is the proliferation of false needs that distorts the natural equilibrium between self-love and goodness, giving rise to *amour propre*.[27] What gives birth to these false needs from a state of rustic contentment according to Rousseau? His answer is other people. To be more accurate it is other people who inspire us to

---

father, brother, ruler, subject, baker, barrister, etc.), and its identity may be so vague or underdescribed that it isn't clear that society has any essential relation to its development or meaning. These kinds of differences are consistent with the fundamental differences in Rousseau's intentions for *Emile* as opposed to *The Social Contract*.

24. Rousseau, *Emile*, 221.

25. Ibid., 223.

26. Ibid., 214; Ferrara, *Modernity and Authenticity*, 79–85; Masters, *The Political Philosophy of Rousseau*, 136–146; Melzer, *The Natural Goodness of Man*, 46–47; Shklar, *Men and Citizens*, 21, 23, 31, 36, 48, 61, 63; Schwartz, *The Sexual Politics of Jean-Jacques Rousseau*, 76–78.

27. Rousseau, *Emile*, 220.

value objects that are not true needs but false needs. These are objects well beyond our basic needs that we do not have and, perhaps, cannot have.[28]

In the state of nature our distance from others, even the absence of awareness of others, preserves the simplicity of our needs. Anything in the external world that helps preserve us, such as a river, a branch, or the sun, must love us as much as we love ourselves.[29] Anything that does not thwart us is at least consistent with our self-love. But we eventually become aware of other wills that inevitably resist our own will. With this change of self comes a new complexion of needs, a fertile imagination, and greater demands upon loving that self.[30] The depth of our attachment to others then depends on the depth of our attachment to ourselves. No one can love as much as we love ourselves. Therefore the most well developed model of human attachment will be the one that enhances our self-love.

How can the Rousseauian person perfectly love themselves *and* love others very well? This can be attempted through the proper formation of the imagination. Even our understanding of others reminds us chiefly of ourself. So if our understanding of another person is always one or another reflection of our self, then the best relationship we can have with another person is one that reflects the most favorable version of our self. The reason that we may even have a range of different reflections of our self inspired by different people is because the imagination provides such an ambiguous image of ourself. The imagination was unformed in the state of nature because we were so content with what was familiar to us, especially ourself. Contact with other people inspires such false needs because the imagination—also inspired by others—gives us easier access to false needs. When we imagine what someone else has it reminds us of what we don't have. The imagination therefore attaches us to others in all kinds of new ways because it attaches us to ourself in so many new ways. But it is un-

28. Ibid., 221.

29. Ibid., 213.

30. "A child is therefore naturally inclined to benevolence, because he sees that everything approaching him is inclined to assist him; and from this observation he gets the habit of a sentiment favorable to his species. But as he extends his relations, his needs, and his active or passive dependencies, the sentiment of his connections with others is awakened and produces the sentiments of duties and preferences. Then the child becomes imperious, jealous, deceitful, and vindictive. If he is bent to obedience, he does not see the utility of what he is ordered, and he attributes it to caprice, to the intention of tormenting him; and he revolts. If he is obeyed, as such as something resists him, he sees in it a rebellion, an intention to resist him. He beats the chair and table for having disobeyed him" (ibid., 213).

clear whether our more expanded attachment to others and more penetrating reattachment to ourself improves or diminishes our self-love. We can be positively attached to people beyond our range of experience because it reminds us of something that we can understand in ourselves. This may be an improvement over the weak goodness that indifference provides in the state of nature. But if that wider imaginative attachment reminds us of something deficient in our self then it may bring harm to both others and ourself. According to Rousseau the worst things in life are inspired by comparisons with others. They produce envy, vanity, greed, and hatred.

Self-love, which regards only ourselves, is contented when our true needs are satisfied. But amour-propre, which makes comparisons, is never content and never could be, because this sentiment, preferring ourselves to others, also demands others to prefer us to themselves, which is impossible. This is how the gentle and affectionate passions are born of self-love, and how the hateful and irascible passions are born of amour-propre. Thus, what makes man essentially good is to have few needs and to compare himself little to others; what makes him essentially wicked is to have many needs and to depend very much upon opinion.[31]

In this sense, the development of the imagination by our contact with others is no improvement over the state of nature.[32] To minimize the destructive expression of *amour propre* in civil society we must develop attachments to others that remind us of the most favorable qualities we possess. Personal authenticity is a matter of fostering bonds with others that draw us to them by drawing us to ourselves.

Intolerance can be so pervasive in society because both the aspiring unity of the individual and the aspiring unity of the state so strongly foster it. Intolerance in society refers to both the psychological basis for it between specific individuals and the related political basis for it in the growing unity of the state vis-à-vis other groups and individuals. Accordingly, it

31. Rousseau, *Emile*, 214.

32. "It follows from this that we are attached to our fellows less by the sentiment of their pleasures than by the sentiment of their pains, for we see far better in the latter the identity of our natures with their and the guarantees of their attachment to us. If our common needs unite us by interest, our common miseries unite us by affection. . . . Imagination puts us in the place of the miserable man rather than in that of the happy man. We feel that one of these conditions touches us more closely than the other. Pity is sweet because in putting ourselves in the place of the one who suffers, we nevertheless feel the pleasure of not suffering as he does. Envy is bitter because the sight of a happy man, far from putting the envious man in his place, makes the envious man regret not being there. It seems that one exempts us from the ills he suffers, and the other takes from us the goods he enjoys" (ibid., 221).

can be said that intolerance is so pervasive in society because self-love is so intolerant. Consider this problem in a society composed of only two individuals. To be unified as an individual I must love myself most of all. And Rousseau also argues that others must love me as much as I love myself if I am to preserve myself and avoid the disunifying force of *amour propre.* For Rousseau's version of self-love only regards ourselves and so is satisfied when our true needs are satisfied. Yet *amour propre* arises precisely when others don't prefer us more than themselves (see previous quotation). That is, person A with strong self-love must also be loved by person B as much as person A loves himself, if person A is to preserve himself and also avoid the disunifying force of *amour propre.* But person B with strong self-love must love person B most of all. Furthermore, person B's continued preservation and immunity to *amour propre*'s disunifying force crucially rests on whether person A loves person B as much as person B loves person B. Of course, person A and person B cannot both preserve his own self-love. His self-love can be maintained only at the cost of the other diminishing his own level of self-love. This is the competitive nature of self-love in Rousseau in a society with only two individuals. Think of how intolerant self-love would be in a larger society, let alone a complex industrial society like our own. So for Rousseau the hegemonic character of our self-love simply is not equipped to tolerate an association where another individual does not love us as much as we love ourself.[33]

The intolerance of groups within society and, especially, the state thrives for parallel reasons. The increasing unity of the state is constrained by limitations similar to that of the individual. The individual's unity demands the very peak of love from both himself and every other individual. Any available resources for unity of the state not already employed for the state deprive the state of the unity required for freedom to be achieved. The general will does not tolerate other collective wills or other particular wills not already subsumed under it. In this sense, it promotes the unity of the state according to the strong constraints parallel to the unity of the individual, whose zero-sum calculus of self-love supplies strong demands upon his own unity. Assume that the individual self-love of every member of the state is submerged as particular wills into the general will. Self-love

33. One option for minimizing this problem is the one elaborated in Rousseau's *Emile.* According to Rousseau the social passion of pity provides a bond that can be shared between individuals without as sharply buckling the tension between one person's self-love and the self-love of another.

can be re-identified in the general will's exercise of collective self-love of the state. This is like the collective self-love of the state, not in the sense that the affections of the individuals are necessarily translated to and exercised under the heading of the group. Nor is it similar in the sense that the motivations of self-love in an individual will be merely expanded to the scale of the group. The part of ourselves that would attach us to someone else is the same part that attaches us to ourselves. When our contact with someone else induces a loyalty to something as much as ourself, it produces an inevitably divisive competition within ourselves. So when the sentiments of the individual are translated to society there is a similarly fixed surplus of loyalty. The unified state in Rousseau's discussion possesses a fixed surplus of loyalty. The character of its unity requires that the other groups or individuals not already subsumed under it be so subsumed if the state is to maintain its unity.

The unity of the individual person requires attachments to others that best foster the individual's self-love. So also, the collective self-love of the state cannot be divided between competing claims upon its corporate loyalty.[34] The preservation of our self-love demands a scale of unity that issues into intolerance. In society any collective exercise of our self-love magnifies the exclusivity of our commitment and collaboration on our own behalf. This is why, for example, two nations that believe in the same god cannot be at war with one another without sacrificing their god or their political unity. The part of their collective will that must be united under god *and* country either replaces the god of their enemy with a new god or finds their loyalty to their god dissolving their patriotism.[35] Just as our self-love cannot bear the loyalty to others that society can cause and that the imagination can heighten, our collective self-love cannot tolerate a division between two masters. The intolerance of the individual in society creates an intolerant society. Intolerance was not a price that the individual in the state of nature had to pay to preserve unity. But it is a price that civil society has to pay if it is to preserve unity since it can never return to the state of nature.

34. On the function of the state as a person see Melzer, *The Natural Goodness of Man*, 160, 164, 184, 188; Ripstein, "The General Will," 52–55.
35. Rousseau, *Social Contract*, 106.

Civil Religion and Tolerant Unity: Catechizing Public Toleration, Enforcing Privacy of Conviction

The deep unity of civil religion produces an intolerance that only civil religion can minimize. What is the structure of Rousseau's civil religion? And how can it channel unity while minimizing intolerance? Rousseau's civil religion brings increased political unity to society with a morality that is common enough to overlap with the precepts of most revealed religions and still compatible with the aims of the state.[36] Those features of external morality common among various public, revealed religions can be fashioned into a single religious morality for the state. But this is ultimately a civil religion that serves the morality of the state by borrowing from the spiritual power of public religion, while avoiding the drag on unity that other more controversial religious distinctives might create. So those controversial distinctives of revealed public religions related to the nature and character of God, the form and context of revelation (as well as its transmission), must be submerged to the level of private belief.[37] Those aspects of religion cannot be disseminated and practiced publicly, since they can cause deep divisions between citizens. And more importantly, they offer corresponding incentives to form factions among those like-minded citizens. Those aspects of religious belief can, thereby, be preserved in their most interiorized form in each separate believer.[38] Those religious beliefs restricted to the private sphere are also restricted from issuing into actions involving other people.

Now it is quite important to the state that each citizen have a religion that will make him love his duties; but the dogmas of that religion concern neither the state nor its members except insofar as those dogmas are related to morality and

36. See Paul Chazan, "Rousseau as Psycho-Social Moralist," *History of Philosophy Quarterly* 10, no. 4 (October 1993): 354; Fuller, "The Theological-Political Tension in Liberalism," 269–70; Grimsley, *Rousseau and the Religious Quest*, 3, 84, 137; Hendel, *Jean-Jacques Rousseau Moralist*, 292–94; Melzer, *The Natural Goodness of Man*, 190; Schwartz, *The Sexual Politics of Jean-Jacques Rousseau*, 44.

37. "There is thus a purely civil creed whose tenets the sovereign is entitled to determine, not precisely as dogmas of religion but as sentiments of sociability, without which it is impossible to be a good citizen or a loyal subject. Though unable to oblige anyone to believe in them, the sovereign can banish from the state anyone who does not; it can banish him not for impiety, but for being antisocial, for being incapable of sincerely loving law and justice and of sacrificing himself to his duty as necessary" (Rousseau, *Social Contract*, 39–40).

38. Fuller, "The Theological-Political Tension in Liberalism," 270–71; Grimsley, *Rousseau and the Religious Quest*, 8, 34; Melzer, *The Natural Goodness of Man*, 190; Shklar, *Men and Citizens*, 39–40.

the duties toward others that are imposed on all who profess the religion. Aside from that, everyone may have whatever opinions he chooses, and the sovereign has no right to know what they are. The sovereign has no jurisdiction in the next world; therefore, whatever may be the subjects' fate in the life to come, it is not the sovereign's affair, as long as they are good citizens in this life.[39]

The crucial limitation upon such private beliefs, which restrains their conversion into action, also has the effect of reinforcing their interior status. And, those other features of revealed religion that might demand action not consistent with the aims of state must be excised. For beliefs that promote actions that undercut the goals of the state could not be permitted even a private religious status since it might, even in this attenuated form, still constitute a passive resistance to areas of public morality.

An important assumption in Rousseau's presentation of civil religion is that the external sphere of morality provides a crucial contribution to state unity. But the private sphere of religious belief is useful only insofar as it limits the emergence of divisive beliefs into the public square. So, this privatization of religious belief does not increase unity. It only keeps disunity in check. The positive use of civil religion is to tap from revealed religion the fullest reservoir of spiritual power available to the state through the tailoring of a vigorous, common, and religiously endorsed external morality, without generating side effects that are markedly disunifying. This is why Rousseau so strongly emphasizes the importance of civil religion in making people more sociable. He does not place emphasis on the cultivation of the interior religious life of the individual. He only mentions the interiorization of religious belief as a necessary concession to religion. The positive power of religion cannot be borrowed for political purposes without incidentally sustaining a body of remaining religious beliefs that cannot be employed for public morality. Those remaining beliefs that are not politically safe are permitted in the internal life of the private citizen as private citizen. But this is only a concession to revealed religion, not a program for the religious authenticity of these individuals.[40]

By controlling the practice of religion in this civil context, intolerance can also be controlled. The tendency in the moral psychology of the individual not to tolerate other wills can be religiously catalyzed in any reli-

39. Rousseau, *Social Contract*, 113.
40. Melzer, *The Natural Goodness of Man*, 30, 147; Melzer, "The Origin of the Counter-Enlightenment," 350, 356–57; Schwartz, *The Sexual Politics of Jean-Jacques Rousseau*, 73.

gion, especially a civil religion. The individual wants others to love him as much as he loves himself. And each and every other person would demand the same for himself. This inevitable clash of wills, based on Rousseau's principle of self-love, is present whether religious authenticity is emphasized or not. This intolerance of others—the natural outgrowth of Rousseauian personal unity—increases in scale when that individual unity is harnessed into state unity. Then their common interests, emboldened by the promise of greater freedoms, further strain the capacity for toleration in society. Toleration becomes easily compromised when the will of emerging religious factions is not subordinated to the general will.

Rousseau argues that the kind of civil religion that he describes in the *Social Contract* can restrain intolerance. An important moral aim of this civil religion is to foster behavior consistent with tolerance. The submersion of theological distinctives into the private sphere controls the emergence of those doctrines whose divisiveness might induce factions between citizens. But Rousseau forcefully argues that those religious beliefs, endorsing intolerance of other religious beliefs, will by no means be tolerated. This is *the* definitive theological maxim to be inculcated in Rousseau's civil religion. "As for negative tenets, I limit them to a single injunction. There should be no intolerance which is part of the religions we have excluded."[41] Since the vice of intolerance is such a prominent byproduct of the extremely unified society discussed by Rousseau, it must be monitored vigilantly. Rousseau says, "If after having publicly acknowledged those tenets, anyone behaves as though he did not believe in them, let him be put to death; he has committed the greatest of all crimes: He has lied before the law."[42] Rousseau's civil religion provides solutions to the problems it creates. The spiritual vitality harnessed by the moral tenets of this civil religion creates a special bond of unity within the state. And it is precisely this spiritual vitality in civil religion that adds a decisive level of force to special commandments such as toleration. In Rousseau's civil religion the special commandment against intolerance is itself a religious maxim that must be obeyed above all. Intolerance is a natural consequence of the extreme unity mastered by civil religion.[43] But of all civil injunctions against deep-seated intolerance,

41. Rousseau, *Social Contract*, 113.
42. Ibid.
43. Rousseau distinguishes religious and political tolerance as terms. But his modification of public religion under his account of civil religion makes even those terminological differences less

an injunction that is religiously centered may be the most promising option for controlling intolerance. Rousseau's civil religion must vigorously forbid intolerance because his system so profoundly nurtures it.

In Rousseau's social contract the state protects the freedom of the individual to which its members have implicitly committed themselves. The state becomes a collective will whose conflict, like that of the individual in the state of nature, cannot accommodate other wills. The state tends toward intolerance of those wills not unified under it. But a civil religion that rallies unity for the state uses its civil religious powers to restrain its own propensities toward intolerance. For Rousseau the right kind of civil religion is necessary for the state to minimize the birth of wills as intolerant as its own.

Civil Religion, Mass Authenticity, and Intolerance

A regime whose protection of individual freedoms energizes an authenticity model of individualism will be less likely to restrain intolerance. The practice of an external rule-based civil religion that is fashioned around common features of morality, yet sharply separated from the private internal sphere of belief, divides the person religiously. And for an authenticity-based civil religion, the failure of the theological content of revealed religion to issue out into actions that can be performed and organized in a public setting even more deeply divides the person into a public and private religious self. This level of dividedness is possible in the civil religion of the *Social Contract* since authenticity—and religious authenticity in particular—is not the path to individual freedom.[44] But when the self-love of the indi-

---

important. This is because any kind of unauthorized intolerance is in his view a threat to a highly unified polity. "Those who distinguish civil intolerance from religious intolerance are mistaken, people who one believes to be damned; to love them would be to hate the God who punishes them; it is imperative that they be either redeemed or tormented" (ibid.).

44. The necessary level of dividedness for long-term freedom in *The Social Contract* is not compatible with religious authenticity (Chazan, "Rousseau as Psycho-Social Moralist," 354; Melzer, *The Natural Goodness of Man*, 30, 147; Melzer, "The Origin of the Counter-Enlightenment," 350, 356–57; Schwartz, *The Sexual Politics of Jean-Jacques Rousseau,* 73). Consider also Rousseau's statement about the anti-social character of the Christian Gospel. "There remains the religion of man or Christianity—not the Christianity of today, but that of the Gospel, which is completely different. By that holy, sublime, and genuine religion, men as children of the same God recognize all others as their brothers, and the society that unites them is not dissolved even by death. But this religion having no specific relation to body politic, leaves the law with only the force that it draws from itself, without adding any other force to it, and hence one of the great bonds of particular society

vidual is not greatly subsumed under the general will and re-identified as a collective solidarity, an authenticity-driven model will emerge. And whatever spiritual force for unity it may provide, it will also aggravate religious fragmentation among those same citizens. Moreover, the internal disunity within mass numbers of individual citizens is the worst pathology possible for an authenticity-centered religious model. The authenticity-based model of civil religion has the effect of generating the sorts of problems it is most concerned with curing. But what is the specific effect on *toleration* from an extreme unity of the state achieved at the expense of greater internal disunity of citizens within an authenticity-based model of civil religion?

The pursuit of Rousseau's principles of religious freedom, while also pursuing personal authenticity—an ideal Rousseau denied could be successfully realized on a mass scale—awakens the problem of intolerance in an even more problematic way. The propensity of the individual toward intolerance is due to the centrality of self-love as the passion that uniquely preserves the individual's freedom. There is an inherent tension between Rousseau's understanding of self-love and the toleration of others. For, if person A's self-love is strong he cannot tolerate those other citizens who fail to love him as much as he loves himself. The full authenticity of the individual requires a kind of socially competitive self-love. This is why Rousseau thought that it would be impossible to realize on a mass scale. But when individual freedoms drive the movement of the state toward unity it is possible that the kind of civil religion that would emerge to restrain the ensuing intolerance would be an authenticity-based one. To the extent that this is so there will be a disunifying gap between, on the one hand, the private religious beliefs of increasingly authentic citizens and, on the other hand, those religious beliefs that can be publicly endorsed.[45]

---

remains ineffective. Still worse, far from attaching the hearts of the citizens to the state, it detaches them from it, as from all earthly things. I know of nothing more contrary to the social spirit" (*Social Contract,* 110). This suggests that the authentic life of the Christian believer is not an element in society that unifies the Rousseauian society. The more inauthentic, rules-based civil religion is the more promising unifier of the Rousseauian society.

45. For example, think of the range of doctrinal disputes that exist across the wide spectrum of North American Protestant Christianity. The range of denominations that have traditionally existed are constantly supplemented or superseded by new ones (i.e., splinter denominations, sub-groups within a denomination, not to mention the ordinary factions and tensions that arise but don't quite lead to the birth of a new church or denomination). Of course this doesn't even include independent churches without official denominational affiliations). Moreover, the scope of religious beliefs that arise even within this cross section of North American religious life is already enormous and proliferating (see Clifford Orwin, "The Unravelling of Christianity in America," *Public Interest* 155

Then, the even more radical submersion of controversial doctrines into the purely private sphere would seem like a plausible corrective to the dangerously proliferating sources of religious intolerance. This sort of corrective would also reinforce the overall unity of the state, since it would more severely attenuate the public contexts for those more sincerely penetrating and widely diffused beliefs. But it is unclear that this would be an effective solution to the problem of internal disunity in citizens; and certainly not, if authenticity is very important. The strong pretense in this more radically interiorized form of religion is that its interiority preserves its authenticity and thereby relocates religious controversy in a place where toleration is not necessary—in the heart of the individual citizen. This displacement of religion into the purely private sphere would guarantee both its existence and spiritual benefits for the state, and would more severely restrict any public context for those beliefs. There is a strong pretense in this more radically interiorized form of religion that the religion is an authentic one. For the person's religion is fully personal and free of those external contexts in which a person might be religiously divided. The wholly interiorized status of this kind of religion spares the individual those inevitable ambiguities concerning moral action between people that can divide the person religiously.

But whether the status of such an authenticity styled civil religion is wholly interiorized is not so much the issue. The crucial point is that the intolerant characteristics of an increasingly unified state create pressures on an authenticity-styled civil religion that make it a more interiorized religion.[46] And such an authenticity-centered model of civil religion generates the intolerance that self-love generates, and reinforces the intolerance that a more unified state produces. But it does not seem able to restrain either

---

(Spring 2004): 20–36). While some of these beliefs may be overlapping, many of them are not. Yet this occurs in a time in which religious authenticity—the sincere internalizing of a set of religious beliefs, whatever they may be—is quite characteristic of the religious trends in a North American culture that is also increasingly therapeutic in its ethos. Therefore, there is an ever greater magnitude of religious beliefs that are disconnected from theological and church traditions and increasingly unique to wider and disparate groups. But these are not beliefs of marginal significance and interest level to those holding them. They are oftentimes beliefs of great significance that are deeply held. But the more these beliefs are removed from a common tradition and are increasingly unique among a sea of sectarian associations, the more they must be privatized, if they are to be sincerely held. But this creates a gap between the private religious beliefs of increasingly "authentic" citizens and those religious beliefs that are commonly held enough to be publicly endorsed.

46. Melzer, *The Natural Goodness of Man,* 280; Melzer, "The Origin of the Counter-Enlightenment," 357.

the scale and species of intolerance that it produces. How can the intolerant self-love of masses of citizens, increasingly authenticated, become even more strongly attached to a common religious maxim of toleration, as well as the other important forms of external morality, when they are increasingly alienated from their fellow citizens (on the most important topics)? It is unlikely that a more interiorized haven for religion is the best answer, even for Rousseau.

This is the location where that murkier and more dangerous form of intolerance can grow, unchastened by any socially attaching religious morality. In this sense, the most private and personal sphere of the person becomes the breeding ground for intolerance. But social pressures inducing intolerance in this supposedly sacred sphere of freedom also make the inner life the perfect retreat for intolerance of this kind. The full submersion of religion into the fully personal and private sphere of the inner life is the natural outgrowth of even an external civil religion attempting to enclose material for religious intolerance in the individual. So the natural response to the more deeply interiorized version of intolerance is to interiorize more deeply just those beliefs, attitudes, or differences that provoke this more passive form of intolerance. But this cycle does not restrain intolerance. It complicates intolerance.[47]

It seems unlikely that religious authenticity can civically or religiously support the political principles Rousseau elaborates in the *Social Contract*. If society accentuates what is harmful in the exclusivity of our self-love and the kinds of human bonds that form as a consequence of our selfishness, then a public religion of any sort can influence this process. It seems that an authenticity-oriented civil religion may actually narrow the range of bonds that can be accommodated under Rousseau's moral psychology. This would be a hope to minimize religious intolerance by in effect increasing religious solitude. But according to Rousseau's moral psychology the benevolent solitude found in the state of nature was so unified because the needs there were so limited. The last vestige of such freedom not achieved by the state and yet still available in the internal habitation of the human heart may in fact be the most alien and least beneficial kind. If the solution to the problems brought about by the straining force of individual intolerance is more internal freedom and solitude, then the individual will be more unsatisfied and more isolated. If religion becomes more diffusely in-

47. Melzer, "The Origin of the Counter-Enlightenment," 356, 358.

teriorized under the natural cultivation of authenticity, it seems like it will actually be a decisive contributor to a more acute caliber of dissatisfaction and solitude. But surely dissatisfaction and solitude do not make people more tolerant. They have always represented the conditions under which intolerance thrives. The psychology of romanticism is one that makes the unification of human beings very difficult without intolerance. A public psychology of romanticism exercised in religious forms will tend implicitly to inculcate intolerance, no matter how strict its laws against it may be.

Rousseau was much more aware of this tension than were his intellectual successors, and his more contemporary interlocutors. Rousseau is considered by many to be the one of the greatest theorists on both the problem of authenticity and the problem of toleration. But Rousseau considered toleration to be very difficult to foster in society and authenticity perhaps even more difficult. Certainly the progress of individual freedoms required a scale of unity that an authenticity-based civil religion could not support. We moderns who have inherited his political legacy can often ignore his analysis of the problems in light of the radical implications of his solutions. But in doing so we may suffer from the very difficulties that his political legacy inspired, while depriving ourselves of perhaps his most helpful contributions. Rousseau recognized a permanent political tension between a society interested on the one hand in the development of individual freedoms and the unity of state it entailed and on the other hand the healthy exercise of public religion. But this tension would become even greater if the trajectory of those individual freedoms cultivated an authenticity-oriented model of religious exercise. The price of those eventual individual freedoms would be a transformed species of religious freedom; one whose increasingly interiorized complexion preserves it authenticity at the cost of its tolerance.

7

Alexis de Tocqueville
on "Civil Religion" and
the Catholic Faith

DOUGLAS KRIES

In 2004, Marcello Pera, philosophy professor at the University of Pisa and president of the Italian Senate, addressed a letter to Joseph Cardinal Ratzinger, now Pope Benedict XVI. In the course of the letter, Pera, generally thought to be a secularist, proposed to Ratzinger the advantages of a civil religion for awakening Europe from its state of moral and spiritual indifference. In his reply, Ratzinger states that Pera's proposal reminded him especially of the view articulated by Alexis de Tocqueville in *Democracy in America,* which he summarized as follows:

During his study of the United States, the French scholar had noticed, to put it briefly, that the unstable and fragmentary system of rules on which, to outward appearances, this democracy is founded, functioned because of the thriving Protestant Christian–inspired combination of religious and moral convictions in American society. No one had prescribed or defined these convictions, but everyone assumed them as the obvious spiritual foundation. The recognition of this basic religious and moral orientation, which went beyond the single denominations and defined the society from within, reinforced the corpus of the law. It defined the limits on individual freedoms from within, thereby creating the conditions for a shared, common freedom.

Ratzinger also reminds Pera of Tocqueville's distinction between the American view of separation of church and state and the French view; the former, he says, is "a separation whose motivation and configuration could not be more different from the conflictual separation of church and state im-

A grant from the Earhart Foundation supported the research for this essay.

167

posed by the French Revolution and the systems that followed it." Indeed, says Ratzinger, "On the basis of the structure of Christianity in the United States, the American Catholic bishops made a unique contribution to the Second Vatican Council. . . . They brought . . . to the Catholic tradition the experience of the non-state church (which had proven to be a condition for protecting the public value of fundamental Christian principles) as a Christian form that emerged from the very nature of the Church." In recent times, Ratzinger suggests, the Protestant denominations have not been able to sustain Tocqueville's vision for religion in America; in his view, it is an alliance between Catholics and Evangelicals that is defending America's "Christian consciousness" and its "civil Christian religion" against the forces of secularization. Ratzinger does not simply endorse the American situation described by Tocqueville, but he does clearly say that it is superior to the situation that generally prevails in Europe, which is still too indebted to the secularizing longings of the French revolution.[1]

In invoking Tocqueville's name in the letter exchange with Pera, Ratzinger is not attempting a detailed academic argument. As a result, his remarks invite new scholarly reflections on Tocqueville's understanding of America's religious orientation and the role that civil religion and the Catholic Church might play within it. The present essay will therefore attempt to answer two questions that come to mind upon pondering Ratzinger's comments: First, to what extent, and in what sense, does Tocqueville advocate civil religion for American democracy? Second, to what extent, and in what sense, does Tocqueville think it is truly possible and desirable for the Catholic faith to participate in such a civil religion?

Before such questions can be addressed directly, however, it is necessary to consider, or reconsider, what Tocqueville says about religion in *Democracy in America*. For roughly two decades now, Tocqueville's thought about religion has been the subject of great interest and much discussion among scholars in the United States.[2] This American conversation has been aug-

1. The entire letter exchange between Ratzinger and Pera has been translated into English by Michael F. Moore and published in a brief collection titled *Without Roots: The West, Relativism, Christianity, and Islam* (New York: Basic Books, 2006), 95–6 and 108–113. In referring to the contributions of the American bishops at the Second Vatican Council, Ratzinger is referring especially to the debate surrounding the conciliar statements on religious liberty and on the church's relationship to the world. The American Jesuit John Courtney Murray played a very visible role in the early stages of that debate.

2. Indeed, even earlier came the publication of Doris Goldstein's *Trial of Faith: Religion and*

mented, moreover, by the publication and then translation of important books written by French Tocqueville scholars, and especially by Pierre Manent.[3] The reading offered here will make free use of insights gleaned from this academic conversation, but it will also offer some fresh insights that arise in reading Tocqueville with an eye toward answering the questions that arise from Ratzinger's comments to Pera.

The expository portion of the essay—its longest section by far—will be divided into four parts, corresponding to the four principal treatments of religion in *Democracy*. The first two of these are in volume 1 (published in 1835): the discussion of the Puritans, or what Tocqueville calls "the point of departure" (1.1.2) and the discussion that begins with the Irish Catholics, or what we may conveniently refer to as "the point of arrival" (1.2.9). The two extended treatments of religion in volume 2 (published in 1840) are not contained so neatly within a single chapter, but they do reach climaxes in single chapters. The first of these discussions, which we may refer to as the discussion of "civil religion," reaches its peak in 2.1.5. The second of these, which we may call, again for the sake of convenience, the "turning souls" discussion, attains its high point in 2.2.15. It will not be possible to analyze in this essay the many letters, notes, and other writings that Tocqueville left behind, but two items must be considered because of the light they cast on our subjects. Thus, after consideration of the point of arrival chapter in volume 1, Tocqueville's notes from his 1835 journey to Ireland will be analyzed, for although they have been largely overlooked in the recent American discussion of Tocqueville's thoughts on religion, they help clarify the crucial question about Catholicism and the separation of church and state. Similarly, after treating the civil religion chapters from volume 2, we will examine Tocqueville's well-known 1831 letter to Kergorlay, which helps to illuminate those particular chapters.

Politics in Tocqueville's Thought (New York: Elseveier, 1975), which seems to be the first of the book-length treatments of Tocqueville's thought on religion.

3. See especially *Tocqueville and the Nature of Democracy,* trans. John Waggoner (Lanham, Md.: Rowman and Littlefield, 1996), originally published as *Tocqueville et la nature de démocratie* (Paris: Juliard, 1982). Also to be mentioned in this regard is Jean-Claude Lamberti's *Tocqueville and the Two Democracies,* trans. Arthur Goldhammer (Cambridge, Mass.: Harvard University Press, 1989), originally published as *Tocqueville et les deux "Démocraties"* (Paris: Presses Universitaires de France, 1983).

Discussion #1: The Puritans and the Point of Departure

Tocqueville's initial discussion of religion is contained in the second chapter of *Democracy in America,* a chapter titled "On the Point of Departure and Its Importance for the Future of the Anglo-Americans." In Tocqueville's view, the "point of departure" for the United States occurred long before the events of 1776 or 1789 and has nothing to do with the events that are usually referred to as the "Founding."[4] Nevertheless, he insists that "[t]hose who read this book will find in the present chapter the seed of what is to follow and the key to almost the whole work" (29).[5] What could the seed of the work or the key to it be? Almost at the end of the chapter, Tocqueville finally says that the point of departure "is the product ... of two perfectly distinct elements that elsewhere have often made war with each other, but which, in America, they have succeeded in incorporating somehow into one another and combining marvelously. I mean to speak of the *spirit of religion* and the *spirit of freedom*" (43).

At first glance, however, this chapter on the point of departure seems to be devoted almost completely to a history lesson. The historical moment that is considered is not revolutionary America but colonial America. Tocqueville quickly divides the colonies into those of the North and those of the South. He is dismissive of the significance of Virginia and the southern colonies; they were originally populated by fortune-seekers, and slavery soon became established there. As a result, they are not part of the point of departure. Among the northern colonies, it soon becomes evident that the only colonies in which Tocqueville is interested are the Puritan colonies of New England. He explains that in describing the Puritans, he is especially following the work of historian Nathaniel Morton, who composed a book called *New England's Memorial;* in fact, Morton's book particularly

4. On Tocqueville's view of America's founding, see Sanford Kessler, "Tocqueville's Puritans: Christianity and the American Founding," *Journal of Politics* 54, no. 3 (1992): 777–79; Aristide Tessitore, "Alexis de Tocqueville on the Natural State of Religion in the Age of Democracy," *Journal of Politics* 64, no. 4 (2002): 1137–43; and Tessitore's "Alexis de Tocqueville on the Incommensurability of America's Founding Principles," in *Democracy and Its Friendly Critics: Tocqueville and Political Life Today,* ed. Peter Augustine Lawler (Lanham, Md.: Lexington Books, 2004), 59–76.

5. The translation of *Democracy in America* used throughout this essay is that of Harvey C. Mansfield and Delba Winthrop (Chicago: University of Chicago Press, 2000). Further references to *Democracy* will be to page numbers in this translation and will be included in parentheses in the text. The abridged translation of Stephen D. Grant (Indianapolis, Ind.: Hackett Publishing, 2000) has also been consulted.

emphasizes Plymouth plantation, and indeed it relies heavily on the reports of long-time Plymouth governor William Bradford. Thus, to find the very "tip" of the point of departure, Tocqueville does not address himself to all of the American colonies, nor to all of the northern colonies, nor to all of the New England colonies, nor really to all of the Puritan colonies, but only to the small subset of Puritans, the Separatist "pilgrims" of the tiny settlement at Plymouth.

Why does he care so much about this sect of Pilgrims—a group that many Puritans, such as those who settled at Massachusetts Bay, sometimes looked askance at? If Tocqueville is interested in Puritans, why emphasize the small Plymouth plantation at the expense of the much larger and more prosperous Massachusetts Bay colony? The historical problem confronting Tocqueville is that the colony of Massachusetts was originally founded by a charter from King Charles I, whereas Plymouth's Pilgrims founded their colony with the compact drawn up on the *Mayflower.* The compact explains that the Pilgrims intend to make their settlement "for the glory of God" and the "advancement of the Christian faith." They are uniting themselves into "a civil body politick" and promise "all due submission and obedience" to the "just and equal" laws that the colony may draw up (35). Fortunately for Tocqueville, the distinction between the Pilgrims and the other Puritans is not so great that he cannot ignore it, and this makes it possible for the tip of the point of departure to be the *Mayflower* compact rather than a royal charter.

When he gives his readers examples of the sort of legislation that marks the point of departure, Tocqueville turns to the laws of Connecticut, which was a "mainstream" Puritan colony settled principally by people from Massachusetts Bay. Tocqueville says that in such legislation the reader will find "the password to the great social enigma that the United States presents to the world in our day" (37). These laws begin, as does the *Mayflower* compact, with reference to God. They say that worshipping any God but the Lord God will merit the death penalty. After such a preamble, the Connecticut laws that follow "are above all preoccupied with the care of maintaining moral order and good mores in society; so they constantly penetrate into the domain of conscience, and there is almost no sin that does not fall subject to the censure of the magistrate" (38). Laziness, drunkenness, and kissing are among the proscribed offences that Tocqueville points out. There is no "religious liberty" in the Connecticut code (39); in fact, says

Tocqueville, several of the laws are borrowed directly from the texts of the Old Testament. The law for establishing schools contains a preamble explaining that "saint seeming deceivers," and indeed the "old deluder," Satan himself, have conspired to keep people from reading the Scriptures, and thus schools must be established and supported. "In America," Tocqueville concludes, "it is religion that leads to enlightenment; it is the observance of divine laws that guides man to freedom" (42).

Tocqueville's historical depiction of the point of departure is, to say the least, most curious. For starters, there are all the items he leaves out. As has already been noted, nothing much is said about the southern colonies, including Virginia. Moreover, hardly a word is said about William Penn's colony or about New York. Our author, a citizen of an historically Catholic nation, says nothing about that church in the text, nor about the colony of Maryland, which was founded with Catholics and other religious dissenters in mind. He does mention anti-Catholicism, but only in his annotations. In one annotation to the text, Tocqueville does say that, in Massachusetts, a Catholic priest who returns to the colony after having been expelled is to be put to death (39n25); in another annotation he records that one of the reasons stated by the Puritans for coming to America was to "raise a bulwark against the kingdom of *antichrist,* which the *Jesuits* labour to rear up in all parts of the world" (687). In the same note, he remarks that a Virginia historian named Beverley "detests his Catholic neighbors of Maryland even more than the English government" (684).

Another way to point out the curiousness of Tocqueville's treatment of the point of departure is to consider the story that American history textbooks used in the United States today typically tell. If they speak of the spirits of religion and freedom, they usually offer a narrative that emphasizes the religious toleration present in Pennsylvania and in Maryland; most especially that narrative features Roger Williams, Anne Hutchinson, and the colony of Rhode Island, where the Puritans sometimes sent their dissidents. Just about the last colonies that would normally be considered the source of America's liberal policy toward religion would be the Puritan colonies of New England.

In a lengthy annotation appended to the chapter, however, Tocqueville explains that in the chapter he has "not claimed to do a history of America." Rather, his "sole aim" in the chapter is to show the reader that "the opinions and mores of the first emigrants" exerted great influence on "the fate of the different colonies and of the Union in general" (683). In the note, Tocqueville provides a sort of annotated bibliography for any historian who might wish to write a more thorough history of colonial America. Even in giving us this bibliography, however, Tocqueville does not mask his enthusiasm for the rather peculiar, if brilliant, Puritan divine Cotton Mather, the author of the *Magnalia Christi Americana,* which is, in Tocqueville's judgment, "the most esteemed and most important document that we possess on the history of New England" (685). He describes Mather's book at much greater length than any of the other books on the subject. He notes that Mather has severe morals and is often intolerant; at the same time, he thinks that Mather's book speaks of freedom and political independence (685–88). In other words, it seems that Mather reflects the features of the point of departure, the combination of the spirits of religion and freedom, the joining of "two perfectly distinct elements" that the Americans "have succeeded in incorporating somehow into one another and combining marvelously."

It is not hard to see in Tocqueville's chapter on the point of departure the heavy influence of Rousseau, who spoke of social contracts establishing primitive democracies guided by severe moral laws. According to Rousseau, these primitive democracies had at the moment of their foundation a legislator who gave them laws that supposedly came from the gods; one of these legislators, according to *The Social Contract,* was Moses.[6] One quickly notes Rousseau's elements in Tocqueville's account: the *Mayflower* compact, the autonomy of the settlers, the austere moral laws of Connecticut, which had their origin in the Mosaic legislation of the Old Testament. Of the New Englanders, Tocqueville says, "One sees them at each instant performing an act of sovereignty; they name their magistrates, make peace and war, establish police regulations, give themselves laws, as if they came under God alone" (37). Even the phrase "social contract" occurs in one of the annotations to Tocqueville's chapter (35n10).

Yet, it is also not hard to see that, in Tocqueville's view, Mather and the Puritans inhabit a world very different from the one Rousseau envisioned. Tocqueville's Puritans are a little schizophrenic. They are dominated by "two tendencies" (43), the two spirits of religion and freedom. In a particularly poetic passage, Tocqueville first speaks of their political freedom and then contrasts it with their religious bondage:

6. *Social Contract,* 2.7.

Before them fall the barriers that imprisoned the society in whose bosom they were born; old opinions that have been directing the world for centuries vanish; an almost boundless course, a field without a horizon, are discovered: the human mind rushes toward them; it traverses them in all directions; but, when it arrives at the limits of the political world, it halts; trembling, it leaves off the use of its most formidable faculties; it abjures doubt; it renounces the need to innovate; it even abstains from sweeping away the veil of the sanctuary; it bows with respect before truths that it accepts without discussion. (43)

What one sees developing within the breast of the individual Puritan is the incipient separation of church and state. Tocqueville will not make that distinction explicit, however, until the chapter on the point of arrival.

Discussion #2: The Point of Arrival

After the chapter on the Puritans and the point of departure, Tocqueville does not return to a sustained reflection on religion until toward the end of the volume. He clearly, however, wants his readers to compare the later chapter (1.2.9) with the earlier one (1.1.2). For one thing, the later chapter explicitly refers to the earlier one and even restates its thesis. "I see the whole destiny of America," says Tocqueville, with a curious allusion to Romans 5, "contained in the first Puritan who landed on its shores, like the whole human race in the first man" (267). The two chapters, moreover, to some extent mirror each other. The earlier chapter is the second of the entire volume, or the post-positive one; the later is the second-to-the-last chapter, or the penultimate one. The earlier chapter was devoted principally to the Puritans; the later chapter begins its discussion of religion by emphasizing the new religious immigrants in America, the Irish Catholics. The earlier chapter contains a speech by John Winthrop; the later chapter a speech by a Catholic priest. The earlier chapter treated the point of departure; the later one treats, in effect, the point of arrival, for it treats the current situation of religion in the United States.

Tocqueville initiates his second reflection on religion in America by noting something that was hardly anticipated by the Puritans, for, as already mentioned, he reports that Catholics have started arriving in America, especially Catholics from Ireland. In fact, not only are Catholics now present in America, but they are prospering and even winning converts to their faith.[7]

---

7. One wonders, of course, whether Tocqueville's rosy description is in fact accurate. In any case, historian Joseph Moody has argued for a strong correlation between Tocqueville's assessment

The Puritans who first landed on American shores would have viewed the Catholics as threats to their experiment, but Tocqueville says that Catholics now form "the most republican and democratic class there is in the United States" (275). He reaches this unexpected conclusion by claiming that, within Catholicism, all are equal but the priest, and thus that Catholicism is favorable to equality of conditions. His argument—that Catholicism is compatible with equality of conditions because within Catholicism everyone below the priest is equal—is strange: except for a major and glaring inequality, he asserts, everyone is equal. Tocqueville hints, however, that perhaps the Catholic support for democracy in America has more prosaic grounds, for he comments that Catholics in America are poor and in the minority, and thus equality of conditions seems attractive to them. In any case, Tocqueville insists that, on the old question of whether democracies love equality or liberty most, the Catholics are in favor of equality; it is the Protestants who prefer liberty.[8]

The main reason that the division of the Catholic faithful into priest and people tends toward a politics of equality, however, is that in America the Catholic priest does not engage in politics. The one major inequality that exists within Catholicism, then, is not transferred to the world of government. Tocqueville claims that he was surprised to learn on his journey to America that neither the Protestant nor the Catholic clergy there fill any "public post" (283). This practice of the clergy voluntarily remaining aloof from government is what he calls "the complete separation of church and state" (283).

This practice has advantages for both the faith and the government. It protects the faith from the vicissitudes of the life of the government, which is very important in all democratic contexts, for democrats have a tendency to change governments often. It is also helpful in aristocratic contexts,

---

of the situation of Catholics in America and the assessment of the Catholic press in France in the 1840s. Particularly interesting in this regard is Henry de Courcy, who originally came to the United States as a representative of a French chemical company but also served from 1845 to 1849 as special correspondent to the French Catholic journal *L'Univers*. Moody notes that de Courcy's comments on American religion and politics, which were superior in analysis to all other such correspondents, often match the view articulated in *Democracy in America*. See "The French Catholic Press of the 1840s on American Catholicism," *Catholic Historical Review* 60, no. 2 (1974): 185–214.

8. For Tocqueville to say that Catholics prefer equality to liberty is a warning that Catholicism is susceptible to despotism, as Cynthia J. Hinckley rightly points out in "Tocqueville on Religion and Modernity: Making Catholicism Safe for Liberal Democracy," *Journal of Church and State* 32, no. 2 (1990): 329–31.

though. Tocqueville is quite insistent that the Catholic Church made a mistake in allying itself with the aristocrats of France; the result of its imprudence was that, when the Old Regime fell, as all governments eventually will, the Church became hated by many simply because of its prior association with it.[9] Since the true basis not only of the Christian faith but of all religion lies in passions that are natural to the soul, and in particular to the longing for immortality, Tocqueville concludes that religion will fare better if it limits itself voluntarily to appealing to these longings and sentiments: "As long as a religion finds its force in the sentiments, instincts, and passions that one sees reproduced in the same manner in all periods of history, it defies the effort of time, or at least it can only be destroyed by another religion. But when religion wishes to be supported by the interests of this world, it becomes as fragile as all the powers on earth" (285). The "complete separation of church and state" also aids government. Once separated from religion, government becomes demoted to a skill or a trade, and thus errors in government are only mistakes and not sins. In America, "there is no more sin in erring in matters of government than in being mistaken about the manner in which one must build a dwelling or plow a furrow" (283). Of course, one can freely experiment in practicing a skill or an art, and thus the separation of church and state opens up the political realm to innovation.

The separation of church and state, then, is in a way the result of the application of the principle of specialization to the Puritan soul. The two spirits of religion and freedom, originally combined in the single person of a Cotton Mather, are now separated into the distinct persons of the priest and the politician. Although what is now a complete separation of church and state was only a partial separation in colonial times, the division was nascent even then. This is what enables Tocqueville to claim that the whole destiny of America was contained in the first Puritan, or that the America that contains Catholics is not so different from Puritan America, or that the point of arrival was already present in the seed that comprised the point of departure.

The other aspect of Tocqueville's thought on the separation of church

9. Tocqueville repeats this claim—that the French Revolution was not inherently anti-Catholic but only incidentally so because of the attachment of the Church to the French aristocracy—in a dramatic way in *The Old Regime and the Revolution*. The second chapter of that work is titled "That the Fundamental and Final Objective of the Revolution Was Not, as Has Been Thought, to Destroy Religion and Weaken the State."

and state has not yet been explained, however, for the mutual incorpora-
tion of the spirits of religion and freedom cannot remain simply at the level
of "separation." Tocqueville asserts that the two spirits are not antagonistic
but that they combine marvelously in America. One way to see how religion and freedom cooperate is to compare the two speeches that he includes within the chapters on the points of departure and arrival. The first
speech is attributed to John Winthrop, who, in the course of defending
himself against accusations of arbitrary behavior as a magistrate, explains
that a distinction must be made between two types of liberty. On the one
hand there is the liberty of "corrupt nature" to do what one wants, but
such a liberty is opposed to all restraint and authority and thus is opposed
to God. On the other hand, there is "a liberty for that only which is just
and good." For this liberty, he says, "you are to stand with the hazard of
your very lives" (42).

The second speech is one that Tocqueville himself attributes to an un-
named Catholic priest. This speech is actually a prayer that the priest delivers at a "political" meeting for raising assistance for the Poles, another
Catholic people. The priest, "in his ecclesiastical habit," advances "to the
edge of the platform meant for orators" (emphasis added) but apparently
observes the principle of separation and remains distinct from it. He says
that God supported the "sacred rights" of the American revolutionaries,
and he now asks God to secure the same rights for the Poles. He prays that
God would remove inequality from the earth, and begs, "Permit us always
to be the most religious people as well as the most free" (277). He also
urges the Poles to take up arms and fight for their rights. Both the Puritan
and the Catholic, then, combine the spirits of religion and freedom, albeit
with different words. One invokes "the liberty for what is just and good,"
the other "rights."

Tocqueville is left, however, with one more important problem to resolve. If the Puritan and the Catholic, the point of departure and the point
of arrival, are so similar, why is the "complete" separation of the two spirits
now required when only a "partial" distinction was sufficient before? The
clear answer to this question is that the spirit of religion has now divided
into at least two smaller parts, the Puritan, or Protestant, and the Catholic.
The way to render this division within the realm of religion innocuous is
to separate it from the realm of freedom and government. But this seems
to make it impossible for religion to guide and limit government, which

Tocqueville had suggested was the primary way that it benefited the political realm. He resolves this problem by distinguishing between dogmas and
morality. Puritans and Catholics each have their own dogmas, and these
are to be separated from the state and to be preached only with their own
churches. Fortunately, however, "all the sects in the United States are within the great Christian unity, and the morality of Christianity is everywhere
the same" (278). Since morality is common, there is no need to separate it
from the realm of politics. Thus, the complete separation of church and
state really means, for Tocqueville, the complete separation of dogma and
state. Morality and state may, nay must, remain marvelously combined
and incorporated. It would seem, though, that once morality is separated
from dogma, it would have no basis or support to ensure that it is followed.
Tocqueville will address this problem in volume 2 of *Democracy*. For now,
he says only that the preservation of morality within society can be done by
the family, and particularly by the American woman, who is the keeper of
mores. Failing that, there is always the pressure of public opinion (278–80).

Interlude: Tocqueville's Journey to Ireland

Volume 1 of *Democracy in America* appeared in January 1835; early in
the same year, Beaumont's *Marie, or Slavery in the United States* was also
published. Relieved of these burdens, the traveling companions decided to
visit England and Ireland during the summer and spent about six weeks in
Ireland during July and August. Afterward, Beaumont published *Ireland:
Social, Political and Religious* in 1839, whereas Tocqueville returned to his
work on America, publishing volume 2 of *Democracy* in 1840. Although
he never published on Ireland, during his journey there Tocqueville kept a
diary in which he preserved records of his observations and conversations.
These notes have been edited and translated, most recently, by Emmet Larkin.[10] An interpreter must be cautious about using Tocqueville's unpublished notes to elucidate his published writing. Nevertheless, what he says
about Catholics in Ireland does seem to illumine what he says in volume 1

10. *Alexis de Tocqueville's Journey in Ireland, July–August, 1835* (Washington, D.C.: The Catholic University of America Press, 1990). Further references to this work will be to page numbers and
will be given in parentheses in the text itself. An earlier translation by George Lawrence and J.-P.
Mayer was published in *Journeys to England and Ireland* (London: Faber and Faber, 1958). Some
background information and commentary on Tocqueville's Ireland trip is offered by Seymour
Drescher in *Tocqueville and England* (Cambridge, Mass.: Harvard University Press, 1964), ch. 6.

of *Democracy* about the Irish Catholics who have come to America. These Irish journals especially help with understanding Tocqueville's view of the separation of church and state.[11]

The Ireland described in Tocqueville's journal entries is not a very happy place. The Protestant aristocracy is quite disconnected from its Catholic peasantry and is often absent. Those who should be governing have a habit of spending in foreign lands the money they extract from their renters. Often land that could be cultivated is not, and thus there are many Irish who are willing to work but are unable to. The lack of responsible government by the aristocracy results in a Catholic population that is poor, even to the point of starvation. Tocqueville's writing skills, of course, were considerable, and sometimes the journal entries wax into moving accounts of Irish poverty. About the only hopeful aspect of his portrayal of Ireland is that a program for national education seems to be gathering Catholic students into classrooms in large numbers.

What is more directly relevant to our subject, however, are the many recorded conversations that Tocqueville engaged in with local clergy, both Protestant and Catholic. The Protestant clergy are supported by the government; they are "established." The Protestant clergy are relatively well educated, but they have very few people to minister to. The Catholic clergy do not receive state support; they rely entirely on voluntary contributions from their laity. The Catholic priests and bishops consequently earn much less than their Protestant counterparts, even though they have many times more parishioners. Tocqueville always asks the Catholic priests he interviews whether they should not be paid by the state as the Protestants are, and they always answer in the negative. The following entry, from July 20, 1835, is not atypical:

There exists an unbelievable union between the Irish clergy and the Catholic population. But that is not only because the clergy are paid by the people, but also because all the upper classes are Protestants and enemies.

The clergy, rebuffed by high society, leans entirely toward the lower classes. They have the same instincts, the same interests, the same passions as the people. A state of affairs altogether particular to Ireland, and which it is necessary

11. On the development of the principle of separation of church and state in Ireland, see Professor Larkin's most recent book, *The Pastoral Role of the Roman Catholic Church in Pre-Famine Ireland, 1750–1850* (Washington, D.C.: The Catholic University of America Press, 2006), 214–15, 263–66.

to examine well when one speaks of the advantages of the system of voluntary remuneration.

In the streets of Carlow, I noticed that the people greeted with great respect all the priests who passed.

I was at dinner today with an archbishop, four bishops, and several Irish parish priests. All were agreed that it was necessary at all costs to avoid being paid by the government. (48–49)

The most intriguing item in Tocqueville's Ireland file is a sort of extended parable or moral story that, even though unfinished, runs to some eighteen pages in Larkin's edition.[12] It is titled "A Catholic Priest and a Protestant Minister in Ireland" and purports to be an account of Tocqueville's encounter with both in a small Irish village and its surrounding lands. In telling this morality story, Tocqueville combines aspects of other journal entries; it seems that he intends this tale to sum up, in a personal narrative, the whole problem Ireland presents. Tocqueville's readers will find allusions to many of Tocqueville's favorite themes in the story: newspapers, education policy, aristocracy, and, of course, religion. The Protestant minister in this tale is supported by and attached to the aristocracy and lives comfortably (128). Tocqueville's depiction of him is very incomplete, but apparently the goal was to paint him as well-mannered and amiable but out of touch with the majority of the Irish people. He compares badly with the Catholic priest, who is the hero of the tale. This man lives simply in a house whose door is always open. He cares deeply for his parishioners, hoping to find work for some of them and schooling for others. He offers Mass in a small, overcrowded church built without state assistance. The priest takes Tocqueville on his rounds, which conclude with a visit to an old man who is dying. The priest seems not to have anything about Catholic dogma to say to the man, but he does tell him that he has good reason for hope in the afterlife. Indeed, the only Catholic doctrine that the priest refers to throughout the story is belief in the afterlife, which the "simple and naïve imaginations" of his followers are easily led to (124, 127).

12. Larkin notes that it is impossible to reconstruct the chronology of this episode, which is item #44 in his collection. He suggests that it is possible "that this episode *actually* never took place in its integrity, but is *really* a montage, or composite 'set-piece' that is morally rather than historically true. In other words, it is really a moral tale or essay based on a series of actual events" (148). What Larkin suggests as a possibility is, in my view, surely the case. One notes that Tocqueville's famous concluding chapter to volume I of *Democracy,* the chapter on the future of the three American races, includes a story that may well be another such moral tale, albeit a much shorter one (1.2.10; 306–7). Both this moral tale and the one on Ireland include young women at a spring or stream.

In an extended conversation with the priest, Tocqueville says that he is indignant because the local Catholics receive no support from the state for the building of their churches or for their clergy. "Do you not think," he asks, "that it is regrettable that the government does not take upon itself the building of churches and endowing the clergy? If that were so, would not religion be more honored, its ministers more respected and independent?" The priest responds adamantly:

It is only the enemies of our Holy Religion ... who hold such language; only those who wish to break the bonds that unite priest and people. You have seen, Sir, how I am looked upon in this village. The people love me, Sir, and they have reason to love me, for I myself love them. ... How does this happen, Sir? It is that the people and I every day have need of each other. The people share liberally with me the fruit of their labors, and I give them my time, my care, my whole soul. I am nothing without them, and without me they would succumb under the weight of their sorrows. ... The day when I should receive money from the government the people would not look upon me as one of their own any longer. On my side, I should perhaps be tempted to believe that I no longer depended on them. Little by little we would become strangers to each other, and then one day perhaps we should consider ourselves as enemies. (126)

Professor Larkin has published, as annotations, the notes that Tocqueville had written to himself in the margins of his draft of this moral tale. The marginal comment that Tocqueville attaches to his draft of this conversation with the priest is "No connection between church and state!" (127).[13]

The entire conversation with the priest about establishment of religion parallels Tocqueville's teaching on the separation of church and state in the chapter on the point of arrival in *Democracy in America*. In fact, Tocqueville says in that chapter of *Democracy* that he had spoken in America with several Catholic priests who offered similar prescriptions for the health of the church as did the priest in the Irish village:

Among us [the French], I had seen the spirit of religion and the spirit of freedom almost always move in contrary directions. Here I found them united intimately with one another: they reigned together on the same soil.

I felt my desire to know the cause of this phenomenon growing daily.

To learn it, I interrogated the faithful of all communions; above all, I sought the society of priests, who keep the depositories of the different beliefs and who

13. Tocqueville's marginalia for the moral tale include two other references to church and state (118, 123) and one connecting liberty and religion (117).

have a personal interest in their duration. The religion that I profess brought me together particularly with the Catholic clergy, and I was not slow to bond in a sort of intimacy with several of its members. To each of them I expressed my astonishment and exposed my doubts: I found that all these men differed among themselves only on details; but all attributed the peaceful dominion that religion exercises in their country principally to the complete separation of church and state. (282–83)

On the basis of volume 1 of *Democracy in America* and Tocqueville's Ireland file, it becomes clear that, at least in Tocqueville's view, the separation of church and state is desirable to the Catholic clergy in both nations. It is also clear that what Tocqueville principally means by the separation of church and state is simply non-establishment. Separatism means that support for religion will not come from government taxation but from voluntary contributions of the laity. It also implies that clergy, as clergy, do not have a reserved political office. It does not imply, however, that morality is separated from politics. Tocqueville does not justify separatism by an appeal to an abstract right to religious liberty, nor to a wall of separation between religion and politics established by philosophical principles. His argument for separatism is utilitarian; it is based on his observations that the effects or consequences of separatism are beneficial to the nations that practice it.

Discussion #3: Civil Religion

In the first volume of his work on America, Tocqueville presents an interpretation of the relationship between religion and democracy that is quite upbeat. The Christian faith of the Americans moderates and guides the government from which it is separated, and the result is a great benefit to all. To be sure, Tocqueville pointed out in volume 1 that his rosy description of America was to be contrasted with the unfortunate relationship existing between the Christian faith and the French democracy, but the French situation was said to be the unnatural or accidental one. France had been poisoned by unique historical factors, and most especially by the French Catholic Church's failure to anticipate the demise of aristocracy and to separate itself from the doomed regime in a timely manner. Presumably the French predicament will be resolved as time passes.

In returning to the subject of religion in volume 2 of *Democracy,* however, Tocqueville begins to change tone. He reveals, more and more, certain doubts he harbors about the American experiment with Christianity, and indeed about the entire relationship between democracy and religion.[14] Scott Yenor has suggested that today Tocqueville's readers fall increasingly into two groups. The first group follows the "popular view that Tocqueville considers America to be a successful example of democratic vices tempered by a genuine religious commitment to Protestantism." The second group, which he characterizes as "a growing consensus" that has emerged around "a more radical reading," emphasizes that Tocqueville recognized that "the corrosive skepticism and worldly hopefulness typical of the American spirit were undermining Christianity" and that "exhausted Christian culture would be leveled in the direction of pantheism, a religious sensibility more consistent with the democratic thirst for unity and equality."[15] Yenor's taxonomy has a certain plausibility if it is understood simply as a general rule of thumb. One suspects, though, that what determines whether one falls into the first camp of interpreters or the second is largely dependent upon which volume of *Democracy* one prefers.

Tocqueville begins to reveal his more ominous thoughts on religion in the opening chapters of volume 2, laying down three important principles for understanding the theologico-political problem in democratic times. First, since all human beings are now thought to be equal, each human being prefers to rely upon his own intellect in order to find truth rather than

14. Catherine Zuckert argues that Tocqueville had, for several reasons, to some extent changed his mind between the two volumes. See "The Role of Religion in Preserving American Liberty—Tocqueville's Analysis 150 Years Later," in *Tocqueville's Defense of Human Liberty: Current Essays,* ed. Peter Augustine Lawler and Joseph Alulis (New York: Garland Publishing, 1993), 224–33. The whole dispute about whether the two volumes of *Democracy* are continuous or discontinuous, not merely with respect to religion but in multiple ways, is summarized well by James T. Schleifer in his epilogue "How Many *Democracies?*" in the 2nd edition of *The Making of Tocqueville's Democracy in America* (Indianapolis, Ind.: Liberty Fund, 2000), 354–68. The interpretation offered in this essay is that Tocqueville's thought in both volumes is consistent, even if different parts of his complete interpretation are offered in various places within the work. In fact, there are certain passages in volume 1 that indicate that Tocqueville is aware that his rosy picture of the health of American religion is not accurate. For example, in one of the lengthy notes appended to the chapter on the Puritans, Tocqueville says that "the Puritan rigor that presided at the birth of the English colonies of America has already been much weakened" (680). He also says that the Puritan "mores have already bent with the movement of time" (682). Another example is Tocqueville's comment on the role that public opinion plays in checking unbelief among democrats in the chapter on the point of arrival (279). Public opinion masks the problems religion faces among democrats, "and one must penetrate to the bottom of their souls to discover the wounds that it has received" (287).

15. Scott Yenor, "Natural Religion and Human Perfectibility: Tocqueville's Account of Religion in Modern Democracy," *Perspectives on Political Science* 33, no. 1 (2004): 11.

to turn to authorities. Moderns do not read Descartes, but they follow his advice to rely on themselves rather than on books (2.1.1). Second, since discovering the truth regarding the highest matters pertaining to human life is extremely difficult, almost all democrats, despite their inclinations, are forced to rely on authorities in that one crucial area. They are forced into adopting dogmatic beliefs from others (2.1.2). But in a democracy, this means adopting the views of public opinion, of the majority. Third, most democrats, having neither the aptitude nor the opportunity to develop detailed knowledge about all the particulars, prefer general religious ideas, for they are easy to grasp and to maintain (2.1.3–4).

Based on these three principles, Tocqueville calls for a sort of civil religion in chapter 5, which is the climax of *Democracy's* third discussion of religion. Since human beings need dogmatic beliefs about the highest things in order to act, he says that "[m]en therefore have an immense interest in making very fixed ideas for themselves about God, their souls, their general duties toward their Creator and those like them" (2.1.5; 417). To have precise knowledge about these matters is very difficult even for philosophers to attain, yet alone busy democrats: "Some fixed ideas about God and human nature are indispensable to the daily practice of their lives, and that practice keeps them from being able to acquire them" (418). The conclusion is easy enough to draw: "General ideas relative to God and human nature are therefore, among all ideas, the ones it is most fitting to shield from the habitual action of individual reason and for which there is most to gain and least to lose in recognizing an authority" (418).

This political need that democratic human beings have for religion finds a correlative solution especially in Christianity. Islam, for example, provides the dogmatic beliefs about the general ideas for which human beings require an authority, but unfortunately it also includes all sorts of superfluous doctrines about politics and laws, and thus there is no separation of the realms of religion and freedom in Islam. The Gospels, on the other hand, "speak only of the general relations of men to God and among themselves. Outside of that they teach nothing to be believed" (419–20). This last statement would strike most Christians as a patently false description of their faith, of course, for Christianity at least seems to require belief in Christ as God incarnate, not to mention the other articles of the Nicene Creed. Tocqueville gives his statement a tiny fig leaf of plausibility by speaking only of the Gospels and remaining silent on Paul, and indeed, the Koran does include many more details about politics and law than the New Testament. But Tocqueville's goal is to explain how Christianity is particularly well suited to serve as a civil religion for democratic times. The title of his chapter is "How, in the United States, Religion Knows How to Make Use of Democratic Instincts," but it turns out that perhaps it should be "How, in the United States, Democratic Instincts Know How to Make Use of Religion." Indeed, Tocqueville concedes as much within the chapter: "One cannot deny that Christianity itself has in some fashion come under the influence exerted over religious beliefs by the social and political state" (420).

Tocqueville wants the Christian faith in general, and Catholicism in particular, to make three accommodations to democracy.[16] First, it is necessary to reduce "the homage due to angels and saints," for "it is . . . particularly in centuries of democracy that it is important not to allow the homage rendered to secondary agents to be confused with the worship that is due only the Creator" (421). Why is this? Within the chapter, Tocqueville gives a brief history of the cult of saints. In antiquity, when Christianity was born, the Roman world was united and the faith restricted itself to general ideas. When the empire disintegrated into the "thousand shards" of the medieval era, each nation wanted "to be able to obtain some separate privilege and . . . particular protectors." Now that a new era has dawned, the situation needs to change back to the pre-medieval posture, for the equality of conditions within democracy renders all human beings in the same position before God, and thus the "almost idolatrous worship" of secondary agents needs to be reduced, if not eliminated entirely (421).

Tocqueville's comments on the saints are curious for a number of reasons. For starters, Christian interest in the saints began early on, within the time of Antiquity itself, when it was especially connected to the martyrs; it was not simply invented in the Middle Ages. One notes as well that Tocqueville is silent about the honor given to Mary, which also began in

16. Ralph Hancock notes that whereas we might have anticipated that Tocqueville would intend "to treat the disease of democracy with a form of Christianity purged of democratic influences," in calling for these accommodations on the part of Catholicism, he seems to do just the opposite. Hancock also perceptively connects our chapter containing Tocqueville's criticism of the cult of saints with a later chapter in the volume (2.1.17) titled "On Some Sources of Poetry in Democratic Nations." See his "The Uses and Hazards of Christianity in Tocqueville's Attempt to Save Democratic Souls," in *Interpreting Tocqueville's Democracy in America,* ed. Ken Masugi (Savage, Md.: Rowman and Littlefield, 1991), 362–68.

Antiquity. Presumably he includes her among the "angels and saints," but presumably he does not think it prudent openly to advocate for the curtailing of her status.[17] Finally, one wonders whether the interest in local saints would not coincide rather than conflict with one of Tocqueville's most precious political teachings, namely, the practice of federalism. It might seem that the cult of saints would offer a sort of religious federalism that would be helpful in democratic times, which aim too much at centralization of power.

In any case, the second accommodation that Tocqueville wants religion to make to democracy is the suppression of the external "forms" or ceremonies of religion.[18] A Catholic reader immediately wonders what Tocqueville thinks should be done with the liturgy of the Eucharist. He seems to reassure such questioners when saying that he knows that some forms are needed but that "one ought to retain only what is absolutely necessary for the perpetuation of the dogma itself, which is the substance of religions, whereas worship is only the form" (422). In a footnote appended to this sentence, Tocqueville says, "In all religions there are ceremonies that are inherent in the very substance of belief and in which one must indeed guard against changing anything. That is seen particularly in Catholicism, in which the form and the foundation are often so tightly united that they are one" (422n1). This seems to imply that Tocqueville recognizes that there are limits to the extent to which Catholicism can become democratic.

Finally, Tocqueville asks that Christianity make some concessions to the love of material well-being that is so common in modern times. In other words, he asks that Christians not emphasize the practice of asceticism. Tocqueville will return to this issue in the section to be taken up below; here he simply urges that Christians not offend public taste when it is not necessary to do so. It would seem to any Catholic reading this chapter, however, that, as Hinckley points out, what Tocqueville wants with these three changes is for Catholics to be more like Protestants.[19]

17. Henry de Courcy (see note 7), in reporting that the American bishops had dedicated the nation to the patronage of Mary at a meeting in Baltimore in 1846, noted that her "cult is currently practiced little among Catholics here." Moody, "The French Catholic Press," 208.

18. De Courcy (see note 7) reports that, unlike most American Catholic churches, which imitate the simplicity of the Protestant churches, the new French church in New York, Saint Vincent de Paul, celebrates "the solemn ceremonies of the great feasts, so little known in America" and alone preserves "the touching poetry so dear to the French, Italian, and Spanish heart." See Moody, "The French Catholic Press," 202.

19. Cynthia J. Hinckley, "Tocqueville on Religious Truth and Political Necessity," *Polity* 23, no. 1 (1990): 48.

What is most striking in Tocqueville's chapter on civil religion is precisely the deference he gives to public opinion. He wants religion to accommodate itself to democracy, for "common opinion appears more and more as the first and most irresistible of powers; there is no support outside of it strong enough to permit long resistance to its blows" (423). If, however, public opinion is to determine religious practice and mores, what chance does religion have for controlling democratic urges such as are present in public opinion? As Ernest Fortin has pointed out about Tocqueville's plan for religion, "The scheme had its drawbacks, not the least obvious of which was that it heightened religion's vulnerability to the single greatest threat to the life of democratic societies, the tyranny of public opinion." Since public opinion has now come to dominate the content of Christian faith, "what the churches were finally able to offer to society is often little more than what they had received from it."[20] Tocqueville anticipated the problem to some degree and tried to ameliorate it. He will take up the issue in the next section of volume 2, but it is first necessary to consider a letter in which Tocqueville addresses the question of Catholicism and civil religion.

Interlude: A Famous Letter to Kergorlay

Tocqueville's first statement on religion in volume 2 of *Democracy* concludes with two short chapters devoted to the progress of Catholicism in the United States (ch. 6) and to the propensity for pantheism among democratic peoples (ch. 7). Tocqueville seems to suggest that these two positions are the two poles of a range of views available to democrats. If they remain religious, like the Americans, democrats at least secretly want a religion that is one and uniform. They have "the taste for and idea of a single social power that is simple and the same for all" (424). Thus Tocqueville predicts that, once Catholicism escapes "from the political hatreds to which it gave birth" (425), it will prosper. The philosophical position of pantheism, however, is in a way even more simple. Democrats have a secret desire for it as well because it destroys even the last distinction, that between material and immaterial, and reduces absolutely everything to a unity, which is the most general of all general ideas. He speaks derisively of the "laziness" of the pantheistic mind and says that all who "remain enamored of the genu-

20. Ernest L. Fortin, "A Tocquevillian Perspective on Religion and the American Regime," in *Ever Ancient, Ever New: Ruminations on the City, the Soul, and the Church*, vol. 4 of *Ernest Fortin: Collected Essays*, ed. Michael P. Foley (Lanham, Md.: Rowman and Littlefield, 2007), 158.

ine greatness of man" should combat it (426). Tocqueville suggests that, in the future, democrats will become either believing Catholics or philosophical pantheists, with not many remaining in between.[21]

A famous letter from Tocqueville to his friend and distant cousin Louis de Kergorlay sheds some light on Tocqueville's comments on Catholicism and pantheism, and indeed on the contents of the first discussion of religion in volume 2 of *Democracy* in general.[22] This fascinating letter was written in the summer of 1831, not long after Tocqueville and Beaumont landed in America. Tocqueville indicates that already he is most intrigued by the picture that American religion presents to him; he notices, in particular, that religious opinions seem to be dispersed along a continuum between two poles. These poles or extremes are not Catholicism and pantheism but Catholicism and deism: "The Catholic faith is the immobile point from which each new sect distances itself a little more, while drawing nearer to pure deism" (49). Protestantisms of all kinds and degrees stand between the two poles, but Tocqueville thinks that they all represent compromises, rather like "a sort of representative monarchy in matters of religion" (40). Such compromises are inherently unstable and will eventually wind up at either extreme. Already, Protestants, particularly if they are poor, are converting to Catholicism, for they tire of living the tension between reason and authority:

It is evident that all the naturally religious minds among the Protestants, serious and complete minds, which the uncertainties of Protestantism tire and which at the same time deeply feel the need for a religion, are abandoning the despair of seeking the truth and are throwing themselves anew under the empire of *authority*. Their reason is a burden that weighs on them and which they sacrifice with joy; they become Catholics. (51)

The other extreme struggling for the Protestant soul Tocqueville has already called "deism," but the deists, not wanting to offend Christian sensibilities, have organized themselves into a group called Unitarians. Their service, which Tocqueville has attended, emphasizes only the existence of

21. On these two chapters and the problems they raise, see especially Peter Augustine Lawler, "Tocqueville on Pantheism, Materialism, and Catholicism," *Perspectives on Political Science* 30.4 (2001): 218–26.
22. The letter has been translated by James Toupin and Roger Boesche in the collection *Selected Letters on Politics and Society* (Berkeley and Los Angeles: University of California Press, 1985), 45–50. Subsequent references to the letter in this section will be given as page numbers in parentheses in the text itself.

God, the immortality of the soul, and moral duty. "This sect," Tocqueville writes, "is gaining proselytes in almost the same proportion as Catholicism, but it recruits in the upper ranks of society" (51).

Tocqueville emphasizes in the letter that his views are still very provisional and subject to revision, so the interpreter must be cautious about making too much of them. Nevertheless, he does say that his question in 1831 has to do with the future of Protestant Christianity, stretched out as it is between two extremes. He poses the matter directly to Kergorlay:

Thus you see: Protestantism, a mixture of authority and reason, is battered at the same time by the two absolute principles of *reason* and *authority*. Anyone who wants to look for it can see this spectacle to some extent everywhere; but here it is quite striking. . . . At a time that does not seem to me very far away, it seems certain that the two extremes will find themselves face to face. What will be the final result then? Here I am absolutely lost in uncertainty, and I no longer see the clear path. Can deism ever be suitable for all classes of a people? Especially for those who have the most need to have the bridle of religion? That is what I cannot convince myself of. I confess that what I see here disposes me more than I ever was before to believing that what is called natural religion could suffice for the superior classes of society, provided that the belief in the two or three great truths that it teaches is real and that something of an external religion mixes and ostensibly unites men in the public profession of these truths. By contrast, the people either will become what they once were and still are in all parts of the world, or they will see in this natural religion only the absence of any belief in the afterlife and they will fall steadily into the single doctrine of self-interest. (52)

During the interval from 1831 to 1840, it seems that the two poles of Catholic faith and deistic philosophy became, for Tocqueville, the two poles of Catholic faith and pantheistic philosophy. The deism, or Unitarianism, of 1831—the natural religion that consists of a sort of stripped-down Christianity emphasizing only the three doctrines of the existence of God, the immortality of the soul, and the moral duties of human beings—is by 1840 replaced by pantheism. What has happened to deism or Unitarianism in Tocqueville's thought? In fact, what we have called the civil religion of volume 2 of *Democracy* looks suspiciously like the earlier deism or Unitarianism of the letter to Kergorlay. Both are a sort of stripped-down Christianity consisting of the bare number of doctrines needed to keep morality in place. With volume 2, then, Unitarian deism has been changed into a sort of Christian civil religion and now occupies a middle position in the continuum, with the extremes of Catholicism and pantheism on either end. In

Tocqueville's eyes, the extreme of Catholicism needs to be nudged toward becoming more like the civil religion, and the other extreme of pantheism needs to be combated and forcibly pushed, it seems, toward the center as well. The Protestantism of 1831, which seemed so unstable to Tocqueville because of its tension between reason and authority, has dissolved into Unitarianism, which is the new compromise between the spirits of religion and freedom, the new civil religion that Tocqueville thinks will work best in modern times. How this compromise can still serve as the "bridle" for those who need it, so that they will not fall simply into the doctrine of self-interest, is the problem that Tocqueville will take up in the second major statement on religion in volume 2 of *Democracy*.

Discussion #4: Turning Souls

The first part of volume 2 of *Democracy* is titled "Influence of Democracy on Intellectual Movement in the United States"; the second part turns to "Influence of Democracy on the Sentiments of Americans." Tocqueville is thus turning from what Americans think to what they love. Just as Christianity must adjust itself in order in support American intellectual movement, so now Tocqueville seeks to explain how Christianity must adjust itself to American desires. In this second part of volume 2, in which Tocqueville's treatment of religion reaches a certain high point in chapter 15, Tocqueville is much more concerned about how to use American religion to control American desire. He especially wants to turn American souls away from their taste for the material. Hence the title of chapter 15: "How Religious Beliefs at Times Turn the Souls of Americans toward Immaterial Enjoyments."

In order to summarize briefly the argument of the famous second part of volume 2, one must begin with the basic principle regarding democratic desire, which is that what democrats love most of all is equality. Indeed, if forced to choose between equality and freedom, they will forsake the latter for the former (2.2.1). But if all human beings are viewed as equal, they also all come to be viewed as the same. If all appear the same to all, then all are equally detached from each other. No one citizen is any more attached to this particular citizen than to that one. In the end, one is by oneself and seeks to live only by oneself, in an isolated, self-sufficient manner. "Individualism," as opposed to egoism, becomes dominant (2.2.2–3). Individualism is a great danger; perhaps it is *the* great danger of democracy, for it would seem to indicate the end of political life altogether, including the political life of democracy. Americans have somehow recognized this danger, and they combat individualism in various ways. One way is through the art of association (2.2.4–7); another is through the doctrine of self-interest well understood (2.2.8).

The doctrine of self-interest well understood is thus an idea—almost a sort of philosophical argument—that Americans have used in order to control their passion for individualism. What this doctrine claims is that, in fact, what is in my own interest coincides with what is also in the interest of others. By helping my neighbors, I help myself; by helping myself, I help my neighbors (2.2.8). Tocqueville is clearly aware that, stated without qualification, the argument has its problems. One of these is the problem presented by death. Perhaps by dying I might promote the interests of the neighbor whom I am defending, but how does such an act promote my own interest? The problem, Tocqueville suggests, can only be resolved by transferring the notion of self-interest into the afterlife. Only if self-sacrificial actions are rewarded in an afterlife does the doctrine of self-interest well understood make sense. Fortunately, this part of the argument is provided by religion, including American Christianity, which preaches that good deeds will be rewarded and bad ones punished by a provident deity.

Tocqueville is amused that the Americans so easily meld the doctrine of self-interest well understood into their religion, but he is unconvinced that all Americans really believe their own argument anyway. In fact, many Christians in America, even while mouthing the doctrine, act according to a nobler, aristocratic motivation. He is aware, however, that the Americans know an even baser version of the argument, which holds that often God will reward good deeds and punish evil ones even in this life (504–5).

In addition to individualism, however, there is another powerful democratic passion that stems from the fundamental love of equality. This other passion is "the taste for material well-being." Because all men are equal, they realize that they can move up and down the economic ladder. They know that, whatever their material conditions at present, they could be better, and they are smitten by the desire to improve their positions. The Americans slowly come to devote themselves wholly to this passion and abandon nobler ones. And of course, since these material goods that are sought are temporalized by the finitude of the human life span, the Americans are always in a hurry to grasp and enjoy these goods while they can. If the taste for material well-being is connected with the inclination to individualism, a truly brutal human future awaits. Indeed, Tocqueville says, one can imagine human beings reduced to brutes, to "brutish indifference" (523).

Just as religion in America seeks to control individualism by supporting the doctrine of self-interest well understood, so American religion seeks to control the taste for material well-being, which can move from a passion to an idea or doctrine very quickly: "Democracy favors the taste for material enjoyments. This taste, if it becomes excessive, soon disposes men to believe that all is nothing but matter" (519). Religion helps democracy, then, by doing combat with the idea of materialism. It combats materialism by preaching that the soul is immortal—indeed, by reminding Americans that they have immortal souls, and thus that their souls need to be turned toward the immortal things. Tocqueville even thinks that it is more important for religion to combat materialism by asserting the immortality of the soul than it is for religion to combat individualism by asserting a doctrine of rewards and punishments: "Belief in an immaterial and immortal principle, united for a time with matter, is so necessary to the greatness of man that it produces beautiful effects even when one does not join to it an opinion in favor of rewards and punishments, and when one is limited to believing that after death the divine principle contained in man is absorbed into God or is going to animate another creature" (520). In the first part of volume 2, Tocqueville suggested that pantheism was one of the extremes opposed to the sort of civil religion that America needed; now, in the second part of volume 2, he suggests that materialism takes pantheism's place as the extreme. Pantheism and materialism, of course, are not necessarily in contradiction to each other, in that pantheism can simply deny the distinction between the material and the immaterial, thus rendering everything material. On the other hand, pantheism at least invites the individual to consider the whole of which one is a small part. Perhaps materialism, in Tocqueville's view, is what results when pantheism is combined with individualism.[23]

In any case, Tocqueville is sure that the idea of materialism is the enemy of human greatness and that it must be combated in all ages, and particularly in democratic ones, for in democracies it combines with passion or taste: "Materialism," he says, "is a dangerous malady of the human mind

23. Cf. Lawler, "Tocqueville on Pantheism, Materialism, and Catholicism," 225.

in all nations; but one must dread it particularly in a democratic people because it combines marvelously with the most familiar vice of the heart in these peoples" (519). Tocqueville's complaint against materialism is not only that it is harmful to political life. In the end, Tocqueville thinks that materialism simply does not correspond to human nature. In fact, human beings often act in ways that reveal that they have souls, or at least they act *as if* they had souls.[24] The soul's longing for immortality is a given, a natural feature of human beings that will tend to reveal itself in unanticipated ways: "Man did not give himself the taste for the infinite and the love of what is immortal. These sublime instincts are not born of a caprice of his will: they have their immovable foundation in his nature; they exist despite his efforts. He can hinder and deform them, but not destroy them" (510). Thus, the Americans are given, Tocqueville says, to spiritual fits and paroxysms. "Religious follies," he reports, "are very common there," and he wonders whether mysticism will not soon break out (520–21). Restlessness and even madness can result (514). Fortunately, American religion has therapeutic ways of dealing with these religious fits. The one Tocqueville emphasizes is the seriousness with which the Sabbath is preserved in America (2.2.15; 517).

Despite his confidence that the human being's taste for the eternal can never be repressed indefinitely, there are also texts in this section of *Democracy in America* in which Tocqueville seems to wonder about the possibility of the opposite, about the possibility of a total eclipse of the human taste for the infinite by the human taste for material well-being. Thus, this section of *Democracy* seems to be the most pessimistic about democracy in all of the work. Indeed, Tocqueville raises the possibility that democrats might sink to a situation in which they would accomplish "nothing great, peaceful, and lasting" (523). How can such a future, such a future without a future, be avoided? Here our author has much less to say than his readers might hope: "If it is easy to see that it is particularly important in times of democracy to make spiritualist opinions reign, it is not easy to say what those who govern democratic peoples ought to do to make them reign" (520). One thing we must *not* do, he emphasizes, is permit clergy to engage in political affairs or to pursue "official philosophies" or "state religions." What he earlier called the separation of church and state must be preserved: "I feel myself so sensitive to the almost inevitable dangers that beliefs risk when their interpreters mix in public affairs, and I am so

24. Cf. ibid., 222.

convinced that one must maintain Christianity within the new democracies at all cost, that I would rather chain priests in the sanctuary than allow
them to leave it" (520, 521). Later, he does say that governments should attempt to "banish chance as much as possible from the political world" and
concomitantly try to give people a "taste for the future" by insisting that
getting ahead in the world is the result of long labors and planning. In this
way, the taste for material well-being could be attached to long-term goals
and, apparently, from long-term goals to eternal ones (524). But this seems
to be a rather anemic response to a major problem, and in the chapter on
turning the American soul, Tocqueville concludes by saying that his only
advice for those who would turn any democratic soul is to lead by example:
"I believe that the only efficacious means governments can use to put the
dogma of the immortality of the soul in honor is to act every day as if they
themselves believed it" (521).

What is needed, then, is a political leader who combines within himself
the taste for material well-being with the taste for the infinite, the democratic longing for equality with the aristocratic longing for rank, the spirit
of liberty with the spirit of religion. This person may seem to be a walking contradiction, but Tocqueville insists in this chapter on turning the
American soul that "[t]he human heart is vaster than one supposes; it can
at once contain a taste for the goods of the earth and a love of those of
Heaven" (520). Indeed, in speaking of the "whole art of the legislator" in
this chapter, Tocqueville says that the legislator in aristocratic times should
try to temper fascination with a higher world by introducing material longings into the souls of the people, whereas in democratic times, the legislator
must try to balance a fascination with this world with a longing for the
spiritual or immaterial (518–19). We return, it seems, to the first Puritan
who washed up on the shores of America, already containing the spirit of
religion and the spirit of freedom within himself—a soul that is not exactly
schizophrenic, but certainly potentially in tension with itself. Ultimately,
Tocqueville's fourth and final major statement on religion in *Democracy
in America* leaves one with very little confidence in the future of either religion or democracy in America, and we realize that Tocqueville, who had
seemed so reassuring about that future earlier in his work, is himself well-
aware of the potential problems that lie ahead.[25]

25. See Ernest L. Fortin, "The Regime of Separatism: Theoretical Considerations on the Separation of Church and State," in *Human Rights, Virtue, and the Common Good: Untimely Meditations*

Tocqueville and the Question of Civil Religion

The first of the questions posed in our introduction, prompted by Cardinal Ratzinger's letter to Marcello Pera, concerned Tocqueville's understanding of civil religion. The phrase "civil religion" is today common within the debates surrounding modern political philosophy primarily because it enters the discussion so spectacularly in the final pages of Rousseau's *Social Contract*.[26] Since Tocqueville was a serious student of Rousseau, it is especially appropriate to approach Tocqueville's position on civil religion by comparing his views with those of Rousseau. To what extent does the teaching on religion contained in *Democracy in America* correspond to the teaching contained in *The Social Contract?* The phrase "civil religion" does not appear in *Democracy in America,* so the question is to what extent and in what sense Tocqueville uses the concept without the name.

The most direct way to approach this question is to compare the dogmas of Rousseau's civil religion with the dogmas that Tocqueville ascribes to America's Christian "civil religion," especially in the third discussion of religion in *Democracy*. In other words, the most direct way to begin is to compare the two "creeds." As Rousseau presents the matter, the dogmas of the civil religion are to be determined by the demands of utility. It is useful—indeed necessary—for each citizen to have a religion that supports morality. Most dogmas are irrelevant to morality and hence should be ignored if not simply suppressed; the creed of the civil religion must therefore be short. The few dogmas of civil religion that are needed include: the existence of a provident deity; the afterlife; rewards and punishments for the just and the wicked; and the sanctity of the laws and of the social contract itself.[27]

The dogmas of Tocqueville's American religion largely coincide with those of Rousseau's civil religion. The two creeds, in fact, are almost identical. What Tocqueville, like Rousseau, wants from civil religion is morality, and particularly a political morality that will support the laws. He, too, ar-

---

on Religion and Politics, vol. 3 of *Ernest L. Fortin: Collected Essays,* ed. J. Brian Benestad (Lanham, Md.: Rowman and Littlefield, 1996), 6–7.

26. *Social Contract* IV.8.

27. My views on Rousseau's civil religion and indeed his religious teachings generally are explained in much greater detail in "Rousseau and the Problem of Religious Toleration," in *Piety and Humanity: Essays on Religion and Early Modern Political Philosophy,* ed. Douglas Kries (Lanham, Md.: Rowman and Littlefield, 1997), 259–86.

gues for a civil religion that includes as few dogmas as possible. The number of dogmas can be minimized by confining most of them to the interior of churches and permitting only those essential for promoting morality to have a public life. The short list of dogmas that Tocqueville uses to describe American religion largely corresponds to Rousseau's list. Tocqueville insists only on the existence of God, the immortality of the soul, the duties of morality, and rewards and punishments in the afterlife. As we have seen, Tocqueville emphasizes the importance of the immortality of the soul even above the others. Tocqueville does not exactly include a dogma that renders the social contract and the law sacred, as does Rousseau, but he does say that morals determine the laws, and morals are articulated within his Christian civil religion.

A second way to compare Rousseau and Tocqueville on the question of civil religion is to note that both authors use civil religion as a way to criticize Enlightenment philosophy, especially as it was advocated by thinkers such as Voltaire. Rousseau became famous almost overnight for having the audacity to attack the irreligious posture of the *philosophes*. He did not disagree with their criticisms of religion, however, but with the Enlightenment idea of making such criticisms public. Rousseau insisted that it was helpful and even necessary for the many to accept belief and hence they should be shielded from the truth about religion. The philosophers may discuss their criticisms behind closed doors, but at the very least they should not publish their conclusions. The citizens of democracies in particular must give themselves laws, but because of their passion for freedom they will not accept laws unless they appear to be divine in origin. The Enlightenment philosophers should have recognized this and kept their criticisms of religion to themselves.

As has become clear, Tocqueville is critical of Enlightenment philosophy for reasons similar to those of Rousseau. Volume 2 of *Democracy* begins with a justification for civil religion that argues that democrats in particular need civil religion. Like everyone, they need some precise knowledge about the highest things, but they are especially indisposed toward accepting authority due to their commitment to equality. What they most need they are least in a position to acquire. Enlightenment philosophers are politically imprudent because they publicize their views and thus destroy religion within the souls of those whom they are attempting to enlighten. The stubborn refusal of the Americans to read books turns out to be their protection from the acids of Enlightenment philosophy, which would dissolve the dogmas they need in order to live well.

Indeed, Tocqueville returned to the problem of Enlightenment philosophy in the last work he published, the first volume of *The Old Regime and the Revolution*. He begins the third book of that work with a chapter explaining how Enlightenment authors in France were imprudent and naïve in publishing their views without taking into account the political effects such publication would have. They practiced what he terms "abstract and literary politics." Tocqueville, it must be remembered, was a practicing politician when not writing books, and he recognized that literary politics can be disastrous: "What is merit in a writer is sometimes vice in a statesman, and the same things which have often made lovely books can lead to great revolutions."[28] Like Rousseau, then, Tocqueville thought that the Enlightenment authors should have been more politically savvy in the use of their pens. Indeed, one wonders whether Tocqueville does not think that Rousseau made the same mistake as the Enlightenment authors he criticizes. After all, while it was imprudent for Voltaire to attack religion openly, it was also imprudent for Rousseau to say openly that a civil religion should be invented in order to defend against Voltaire's mistake. In other words, openly advocating civil religion would seem to be as politically naïve as openly attacking religion. Thus, Tocqueville does not use Rousseau's term "civil religion," and he is considerably more circumspect in his criticism of Christianity than was Rousseau.

In sum, then, there is much to be said for interpreting Tocqueville's thought on American religion along the lines of *The Social Contract*'s civil religion. Both Tocqueville and Rousseau think similarly with respect to the creeds or dogmas of those religions, and both want such religions as bulwarks against Enlightenment philosophy. Within the recent American discussion on Tocqueville's thought on religion, referred to in the introduction, the two authors who emphasize the similarity between Rousseau and Tocqueville are John Koritansky and Sanford Kessler, who have not been reserved in simply ascribing the term "civil religion" to Tocqueville's thought. Hence, their published works include "Civil Religion in Tocqueville's *Democracy in America*" and *Tocqueville's Civil Religion*, respectively.[29]

28. *The Old Regime and the Revolution*, 1.3.1; trans. Alan S. Kahan (Chicago: University of Chicago Press, 1998), 195, 199.
29. John C. Koritansky, "Civil Religion in Tocqueville's *Democracy in America*," *Interpretation*

Yet, despite all these basic similarities between Rousseau and Tocqueville in the matter of civil religion, there are several important differences that reveal that Tocqueville is far more moderate than Rousseau on this question. In the chapter on civil religion in *The Social Contract,* Rousseau had insisted that the civil religion must also contain one "negative" doctrine, a doctrine that proscribed intolerance. This proscription of intolerance, moreover, extended not simply to civil intolerance, but to theological intolerance as well. What Rousseau meant by this is that one not only must grant political liberty to another with whom one disagrees, but one must not even think that what another holds is wrong. Civil toleration, then, would be the sort of toleration practiced by a Catholic who thinks that Muslims should have full political and legal rights; theological toleration would be the sort of tolerance practiced by a Catholic who thinks that Muslims can be saved by practicing their own faith. Taken to its logical extreme, by insisting that theological toleration is mandatory for the civil religion, Rousseau is insisting that everyone belonging to the social contract must think that no religion is superior to any other, which would seem to undermine the rationale for practicing any particular religion except the civil religion.

Tocqueville surely agrees with Rousseau about the need for civil toleration, and in asking the various Christian sects to keep their discussion of dogmas within the confines of their own churches, he demotes the importance of dogmas and thereby opens the door to a sort of theological tolerance or at least theological indifference. Nevertheless, at one point in the chapter on the point of arrival, Tocqueville clearly distances himself from Rousseau's position. "American priests," he says, "pronounce themselves in a general manner to be in favor of civil freedom without excepting even those who do not accept religious freedom" (1.2.9; 278).[30] In America, it seems, the civilly tolerant are willing to tolerate even the theologically intolerant. The Americans are willing to engage in political life with people, some of whose religious views they reject or even find abhorrent. Tocqueville will be satisfied if citizens can agree on the dogmas needed to sup-

---

17, no. 3 (1990): 389–400; Sanford Kessler, *Tocqueville's Civil Religion: American Christianity and the Prospects for Freedom* (Albany: SUNY Press, 1994). See also Koritansky's *Alexis de Tocqueville and the New Science of Politics* (Durham, N.C.: Carolina Academic Press, 1986).

30. In this passage, by "priests," Tocqueville means clergy in general. Stephen Grant translates the passage thus: "American clergy pronounce themselves in a general manner in favor of civil liberty, without excepting even those among them who do not accept freedom of religion" (132).

port morality. Superfluous doctrines, confined to the interiors of churches, can be left to themselves.

An even more dramatic way in which Tocqueville departs from Rousseau's teaching on civil religion is with respect to the separation of church and state. In the famous chapter on civil religion in *The Social Contract,* Rousseau insists that Christianity, in particular, is politically destructive, and that this destructiveness has its origins in the teachings of Jesus himself, for he destroyed political unity by "separating the theological system from the political system." The result of Jesus' teaching was that religion became separated from the sovereign, and the two authorities, the political and the religious, were always engaged in disputes and conflicts. Such a divided arrangement, Rousseau says, is "worthless."[31]

Tocqueville, of course, sees no need to attack Christianity, especially in its Protestant versions, and he is not afraid of separating church and state. The problem of divided sovereignty that troubled Rousseau is precisely democracy's salvation in Tocqueville's account. As becomes clear in studying the chapters on turning souls, Tocqueville does not find it remarkable that the human soul would be in tension with itself, would struggle against itself, would be forced to live with certain contradictory loves and impulses. He is not committed to reducing the soul to a unity, and hence he advocates keeping separate what Rousseau wants to unite. Rousseau admits that a unified soul is ultimately impossible in civil society but laments the loss of unity. Tocqueville insists on the advantages of preserving tension and division. Another way to explain this point is to note that, in his chapter on civil religion, Rousseau praises Mohammad as a great legislator because he preserved the unity of religion and politics within his government. Tocqueville, in his chapters on civil religion, criticizes Islam, and for precisely the same features noted by Rousseau (419).

A third major argument between Rousseau and Tocqueville concerns the role of the family. In a footnote to his chapter on civil religion, Rousseau argues that the principal way through which Christian clergy preserve the division of political sovereignty and prevent the regime from being unified is through their insistence that marriage is a sacred matter rather

---

31. *Social Contract,* IV, 8; trans. Judith R. Bush, Roger D. Masters, and Christopher Kelly, in *The Collected Writings of Rousseau* (Hanover, N.H.: University Press of New England, 1994), 4:218–19.

than a civil contract. The priest cannot be permitted to say whose children are legitimate and whose are not, for these children are also prospective citizens. The laws concerning marriage must therefore come under the regulation of the civil laws established by the social contract, and once the regulation of marriage is taken away from the church, Rousseau predicts that its power will dissipate. Tocqueville, however, looks at marriage quite differently. Having separated church and state, he needs to be able to show how Christianity can still be influential in politics, how it can serve as a civil religion. The family, he argues, is the locus of morality and the school of mores. The woman is the keeper and bearer of morality, for she is the one who accepts or rejects marriage proposals. It is most necessary then, for Tocqueville's program to work, that the woman be religious, for within the separation of church and state, the family needs to be on the side of the church. The woman, as it were, gives the mores their muscle and the civil religion its teeth.

Tocqueville and the Question of Catholicism as Civil Religion

Rousseau's hostility toward the Catholic faith is boundless in the chapter on civil religion in *The Social Contract.* His hostility is more serene but equally severe in his subsequent *Letter to Beaumont,* which was addressed to the archbishop of Paris, if not to the entire Catholic world. Rousseau does indicate in the *Letters Written from the Mountain* that perhaps Protestant Christianity could be thoroughly transformed so that it became the civil religion, but he has nothing redeeming to say about Catholicism. Tocqueville, as we have seen in his chapter on the point of arrival, says that it is not only possible, but indeed an empirical fact, that Catholicism can participate in the common Christian religion of America and thereby serve, alongside the Protestant sects, as a component in the American version of civil religion. What Catholics can contribute specifically to this project is not a true love of liberty but rather a true love of equality.

It was clear to Tocqueville that if the France of his time were to have a political future, Catholicism would somehow have to play a role in it. One is therefore not surprised to see him frequently insisting on the need for reconciliation between modern liberalism and the Catholic faith. The outlines of his solution, the regime of separatism, are by now clear enough. The Catholic sacraments and the theological doctrines that support them may be practiced, but they must remain strictly within the confines of the sanctuary. The conclusions that follow from the speculative theological dogmas, the moral implications of Catholic faith, are fortunately not different from the morality that is advocated by Protestant Christianity, or at least the differences can be glossed over for the minds of busy democrats. This common, and supposedly uncontroversial, Christian morality, along with a handful of doctrines such as the existence of God, the immortality of the soul, judgment in the afterlife, and duty to God and neighbor, can suffice for the American civil religion. This civil religion, in Tocqueville's view, refers only to those doctrines that all Christians hold in common. Civil religion is thus a subset of Catholic faith, as well as a subset of the Protestant faith. Philosophers, who think with precision, who practice abstract and literary politics, can anticipate multiple theoretical problems with the solution offered by the regime of separatism, but democrats are unlikely to notice them. And thus, the Catholic Church can participate in the regime of separatism almost as well as other Christian sects. Besides, as Tocqueville frequently points out, it is not as though the Catholic Church, or any other Christian church, any longer has much choice in the matter.

Tocqueville's concern with Catholicism, however, runs much deeper than immediate political interests. That is, while he wants Catholicism to participate in the American civil religion, and while he thinks that in fact it can and does do so, he also wants Catholicism in particular to play an important part in turning souls. As became clear in his fourth and final discussion of the problem of religion in America, the modern democrats need something of the old aristocratic religion to keep them from turning themselves over completely to the taste for material well-being. While Tocqueville advocates that Catholicism make concessions to democratic times, he does not want Catholicism to lose its distinct capacity for recalling the democratic soul to its senses, for reminding the democrat that he has a soul.

In addition to studying Rousseau, Tocqueville was also a serious student of Pascal, and indeed it seems that Tocqueville generally accepts Pascal's understanding of the Catholic faith as definitive.[32] American Toc-

32. Pascal is today often understood as holding a somewhat fideistic position on the central question of the relationship between faith and reason. As such, his position contrasts starkly with the more typical Catholic position articulated by, among others, Thomas Aquinas. Tocqueville's *Democracy* is "Pascalian" in that it generally views philosophy and Catholic faith as enemies. Toc-

queville scholars are therefore greatly indebted to Peter Lawler's book for making clear the pervasive influence of Pascal's restless faith within Tocqueville's thought.[33] Pascal's Catholic faith has a fundamental argument to make with Rousseau and modern democracy. Catholicism says to democracy that its passion for equality is exaggerated, for there are distinctions of rank within the cosmos that must be respected. Chief among these is the distinction between Creator and creature, a distinction overlooked by pantheism and its companion, materialism. Tocqueville thus recognizes that the central feature of Catholicism is, as it were, aristocratic, and hence that Catholicism is irreducible to a purely democratic civil religion.

Nowhere does the influence of Pascal on *Democracy* come more to the fore than in the final discussion of religion on turning souls. It is in these pages especially that Tocqueville acknowledges that Catholicism constitutes an aristocratic inheritance that is antithetical to certain democratic extremes. Catholicism's gift to democracy, then, is not only to participate in the common Christian civil religion available through the separation of church and state, but also to be the antidote to extreme democracy, or to bring democrats back to their own souls and their natural longings for the infinite. Beyond the reconciliation between the spirit of religion and the spirit of freedom that the regime of separatism makes possible, there is an irreducible tension, a dialectical relationship, between religion and liberty that the regime of separatism must preserve.

These reflections bring us back to the remarks of Cardinal Ratzinger, now Pope Benedict XVI, with which this essay began. Tocqueville would certainly agree that the American version of Christian civil religion should be advocated over the French version of secularized civil religion. As a political strategy, then, Ratzinger's invoking the name of Tocqueville in support of a Christian civil religion for both Europe and America is unassailable. One worries, though, whether the Catholic Church is not in danger of becoming more Tocquevillian than Tocqueville, or whether the Church is

---

queville is silent on Thomism, which views philosophy and Catholic faith as ultimately harmonious. Since it seems unlikely that Tocqueville is ignorant of the Thomistic tradition of Catholic philosophy, one is inclined to conclude that his silence indicates a rejection of Thomism in favor of Pascal. Aristide Tessitore also thinks that Tocqueville views the relationship between faith and reason as one of conflict rather than harmony, but he adds that Tocqueville also views the conflict as salutary for politics. See his "Tocqueville and Gobineau on the Nature of Modern Politics," *Review of Politics* 67.4 (2005): 649–54.

33. Peter Augustine Lawler, *The Restless Mind: Alexis de Tocqueville on the Origin and Perpetuation of Human Liberty* (Lanham, Md.: Rowman and Littlefield, 1993).

reading Tocqueville carefully enough so that it grasps the Pascalian element within Tocqueville's thought. One reads, for example, in Benedict's first encyclical, *Deus Caritas Est,* that "Fundamental to Christianity . . . is the distinction between Church and State, or as the Second Vatican Council put it, the autonomy of the temporal sphere."[34] We will not stop to consider whether Tocqueville is to be interpreted as implying that the separation of church and state is "fundamental to Christianity" rather than simply a politically prudent course of action, particularly in democratic times.[35] One must point out, however, that, from a Tocquevillian point of view, the phrase "autonomy of the temporal sphere," which does not originate with Benedict, is most unfortunate, for Tocqueville insisted that the laws were a reflection of mores, and mores were established principally by religion. The Catholic Church cannot possibly mean, and in fact does not really hold, that government is autonomous;[36] the Church's view is that government is bound by, if nothing else, the natural law, which has its ultimate foundations in God.

Hence, the Church must avoid becoming so accepting of the Tocquevillian teaching on the separation of church and state that it glosses over the Tocquevillian teaching on the need to remind democrats that they have souls with longings for the immortal. Even while accepting the Enlightenment dictate denying political authority to the Church, the Church must maintain its dialectical relationship to the Enlightenment. It must preach the Gospel, which has certain aristocratic elements within it, to those democrats who have succumbed to the taste for material well-being. It must remind humanity of its nature, which includes a taste for the infinite as well. Pierre Manent has stated the point clearly and recognized its implications, and so we will permit the conclusion of one of his essays to serve as the conclusion to this one as well:

The political submission of the church to democracy is, perhaps, finally, a fortunate one. The church willy-nilly conformed itself to all of democracy's demands.

34. *Deus Caritas Est,* #28.

35. In any case, during the pontificate of John Paul II, in which Ratzinger played an important role, the Church was quite rigorous in refusing to permit clergy to serve in political positions, even if they were elected through voting—a strategy Tocqueville would have thought most prudent.

36. Consider the remarks of Pierre Manent in commenting on the implications of the Enlightenment: "If there is a God, the human will cannot be 'autonomous,' or 'sovereign': to affirm this 'autonomy' or 'sovereignty' is to deny the existence of God." "Christianity and Democracy," in *Modern Liberty and Its Discontents,* trans. Daniel J. Mahoney and Paul Seaton (Lanham, Md.: Rowman and Littlefield, 1998), 99.

Democracy no longer, in good faith, has any essential reproach to make against the church. From now on it can hear the question the church poses, the question that it alone poses, the question *Quid sit homo*—What is man? But democracy neither wants to nor can respond to this question in any manner or form. On democracy's side of the scale, we are left with political sovereignty and dialectical impotence. On the church's side, we are left with political submission and dialectical advantage. The relation unleashed by the Enlightenment is today reversed. No one knows what will happen when democracy and the church become aware of this reversal.[37]

37. "Christianity and Democracy," 115.

Two

The Enduring Relevance
of Civil Religion in
North America

8

Rational Theology

Thomas Jefferson and the Foundation
of America's Civil Religion

JEFFREY SIKKENGA

I can never join Calvin in addressing his god. . . .
The being described in his five points is not the God whom
you and I acknolege [*sic*] and adore, the Creator and
benevolent governor of the world.
—Thomas Jefferson to John Adams, April 11, 1823

I know in my heart that man is good
That what is right will always eventually triumph
And there is purpose and worth to each and every life
—Gravestone of Ronald Reagan

Thomas Jefferson's "Bill for Establishing Religious Freedom"
and the Theological Cornerstone of American Civil Religion

Americans commonly believe that the United States was founded on the idea of religious liberty. Did not the early European settlers come to America in order to worship God as they saw fit? Do not the very first clauses of the First Amendment protect religious freedom? To the American mind (and perhaps the modern mind more generally), the free and equal way of life of democracy is impossible without this most fundamental of freedoms; the presence of religious liberty, we might say, ultimately defines whether a country is free. While acknowledging that America has been by no means historically free from religious prejudice against non-Christians (and non-Protestants), Americans take special pride in the country's basic commitment to the idea that everyone should be able to believe what he or she wants in religious matters and practice that belief without coercion or interference from government or fellow citizens. If there is a modern demo-cratic civil religion (especially in America), its theological cornerstone is the opinion that every person has a fundamental, natural right to freedom of religion that cannot be taken away or infringed.

Of course, such belief in freedom of conscience was not always domi-nant, even in America. For generations before and during the Founding period, Americans generally embraced the idea of freedom of religion, but they believed that such freedom entailed only limited toleration for dissent-ers from the legally established view of Christianity or permitted govern-ment to require citizens to support Christian clergy. For them, freedom of religion was an important right, but for the sake of both healthy reli-gion and politics, government could legally establish a church or least en-courage religious practice and set the outer bounds of permissible religious opinion.[1]

Perhaps the most philosophically dramatic and politically influential public break from this view began with the Virginia Declaration of Rights in 1776 and culminated in the decade-long struggle to disestablish the An-glican Church in Virginia.[2] While pushed by religious dissenters such as Presbyterians and Baptists, the fight was led philosophically by statesmen such as George Mason, James Madison, and Thomas Jefferson.[3] Jefferson's

---

1. According to Mark McGarvie, "[t]he symbiotic relationship between church and the civil order that had existed in Europe persisted throughout English America in the colonial era. . . . In 1774 nine of the thirteen colonies had legally established churches. De facto establishments existed in three of the others. All people within establishment colonies were taxed for the support of a church building and the salary of a clergyman. In those colonies in which law did not specifically provide for the legal toleration of dissenters, only the established church could incorporate or per-form authorized civil functions such as marriage ceremonies" (Mark McGarvie, *One Nation under Law: America's Early National Struggles to Separate Church and State* (DeKalb: Northern Illinois University Press, 2004), 22, 41).

2. We should not neglect the importance of George Mason's draft of Virginia's Declaration of Rights as a forerunner to Jefferson's bill. Robert Rutland argues that "[w]ords, phrases, and sen-tences copied from the committee draft of May 27, 1776, may be found in every Declaration of Rights adopted in America since May 1776, and in most of the other such declarations adopted elsewhere in the world," including the French Declaration of Rights of 1789 (Robert Rutland, *George Mason: Reluctant Statesman* (Baton Rouge: Louisiana State University Press, 1961), 67). He concludes that the document is "the grandfather of *all* the bills of rights. Not only is it one of the great state papers of the American Revolution, it is a milestone in the development of the world-wide Enlightenment" (ibid., 90).

3. For discussion of the political maneuverings of Mason, Jefferson, and Madison, and the shifting political alliances of various economic, regional, and religious groups, see Thomas E. Buckley, S.J., *Church and State in Revolutionary Virginia, 1776–1787* (Charlottesville: University of Virginia Press, 1977); Buckley, "The Religious Rhetoric of Thomas Jefferson," in *The Founders on*

contribution is especially well known, and he has been invoked time and time again as one of the great founders (if not *the* greatest) of the idea of religious freedom in America.[4] Whatever historical truth exists for Jefferson as the founder of religious liberty in America, he certainly regarded his contribution to that cause as one of his greatest lasting achievements. He famously insisted that only three accomplishments be put on his tombstone: "Author of the Declaration of American Independence, of the Statute of Virginia for religious freedom, and Father of the University of Virginia." Chronologically, and perhaps in importance, securing religious freedom was, in his own mind, Jefferson's central achievement. As his tombstone suggests, nowhere did he think that he articulated his views more clearly than in the Virginia Statute for Religious Liberty—or as Jefferson's 1779 draft was known, the Bill for Establishing Religious Freedom.[5]

The debate over Jefferson's arguments in the bill actually began in May 1776 at the Virginia Assembly. Nearly all revolutionaries at the Assembly (which had turned itself into a kind of constitutional convention) supported article XVI of George Mason's Declaration of Rights, which said (in its final version) "That Religion . . . can be directed only by reason and conviction, not by force or violence; and therefore, all men are entitled to the free exercise of religion, according to the dictates of conscience; and that it

<hr />

God and Government, ed. Daniel Dreisbach et al. (Lanham, Md.: Rowman and Littlefield, 2004); Daniel Dreisbach, *Thomas Jefferson and the Wall of Separation between Church and State* (New York: New York University Press, 2002); Hamilton James Eckenrode, *Separation of Church and State in Virginia: A Study in the Development of the Revolution* (Richmond, Va.: Davis Bottom, 1910).

4. Besides the well-known example of *Everson v. Board of Education* (1947), consider also the Supreme Court's unanimous decision in *Reynolds v. US* (1878), which referred to Jefferson's understanding of the religious liberty protected by the First Amendment as "almost authoritative."

5. Jefferson drafted the bill in 1777, but it was not printed until it was introduced in 1779 (in *The Portable Thomas Jefferson*, ed. Merrill Peterson [New York: Viking Press, 1975]). According to Thomas Buckley, Jefferson's understanding of religious liberty was developed by 1776 and remained constant throughout his life: Jefferson's notes "[i]n support of his resolutions [at the 1776 Virginia constitutional convention] for complete religious freedom and disestablishment . . . provide proof positive that the thoughts embodied in the Bill for Establishing Religious Freedom . . . were already fully developed in 1776." These also "bear a marked resemblance to another product of his facile pen . . . his *Notes on the State of Virginia*. . . . We can take these three texts together as essentially expressing his convictions on religious freedom" (Buckley, *Church and State in Revolutionary Virginia, 1776–1787*, 61). Jefferson's later theological reflections are not different in their fundamental principles from those of the 1770s and 1780s—he simply developed them more fully later because his "chief occupations" until 1809 were "in the practical business of life," and he could not "abstract" his "mind from public affairs" (to John Adams, October 12, 1813; to Benjamin Rush, April 21, 1803). Unless otherwise noted, all citations of letters and papers of Jefferson are taken from *The Papers of Thomas Jefferson*, 29 vols., ed. Julian P. Boyd (Princeton, N.J.: Princeton University Press, 1950–).

is the mutual duty of all to practice Christian forbearance, love, and charity, towards each other."[6] But when Jefferson spoke later at the October 1776 Assembly in favor of disestablishing the state church and removing government support for *all* religions, he was opposed by many of his fellow Whigs such as Robert Carter Nicholas and Edmund Pendleton, who, "[w]hile embracing the Declaration of Independence, with its essentially Lockean political philosophy . . . could not accept Jefferson's argument that natural rights included complete freedom of religious belief and practice, required the disestablishment of the state church, and mandated equality of all religious groups."[7]

Jefferson tried again in June 1779, when his Bill for Establishing Religious Freedom was presented as part of "the general revision of the laws ordered by the legislature in 1776."[8] Though defeated at the Assembly in 1776 in his call for full religious liberty and disestablishment, Jefferson had been named part of a legislative committee charged with legal reform and, according to Thomas Buckley, "dominated the revision from the beginning. His fertile mind envisioned a sweeping reform of the Virginia legal system to remove from it the last vestige of aristocracy and bring it into conformity with republican principles and spirit."[9] For Jefferson, addressing the legal reform of the religious establishment was a central part of the task, which became even more important in 1779, when it looked like the generally unpopular Anglican establishment—which had fallen on legal and political hard times during the Revolution because of lack of money during the war, Virginia's repeal of acts of Parliament (including state salaries for clergy), and the church's identification with Britain—might be replaced by a more popular law defining and establishing (Protestant) Christianity as the official religion of Virginia and enacting a "general assessment . . . on every one, to the support of the pastor of his choice."[10] It was the possibil-

---

6. The final version reads as it does because Madison substituted "full and free exercise" of religion for Mason's original wording: "the fullest toleration in the exercise of religion." See Buckley, *Church and State in Revolutionary Virginia, 1776–1787,* 210–12.

7. Buckley, *Church and State in Revolutionary Virginia, 1776–1787,* 62. Jefferson called Pendleton and Nicholas "honest men, but zealous churchmen," and he described his "desperate contests" against them and their allies as "the severest contests in which I have ever been engaged" ("Autobiography," in *Thomas Jefferson: Writings,* ed. Merrill Peterson [New York: Library of America, 1984 (1821)], 34).

8. Buckley, *Church and State in Revolutionary Virginia, 1776–1787,* 46.

9. Ibid.

10. Jefferson, "Autobiography," 35. According to Jefferson, "the principles" of his bill "had,

ity of the assessment bill's passing that gave Jefferson even more urgency in pushing his Bill for Establishing Religious Freedom.[11]

Jefferson's bill had three one-paragraph sections: preamble, legal enactment, and conclusion. The legal section was fairly short, declaring:

that no man shall be compelled to frequent or support any relig[i]ous Worship place or Ministry whatsoever, nor shall be enforced, restrained, molested, or burthened in his body or goods, nor shall otherwise suffer on account of his religious opinions or belief, but that all men shall be free to profess, and by argument to maintain their opinions in matters of religion, and that the same shall in no wise diminish, enlarge, or affect their civil capacities.

"[T]he preamble to the bill was much longer," as Buckley notes, and "[i]n sweeping phrases, it presented Jefferson's philosophical justification for the measure and reiterated the arguments which he had developed in the committee meetings of the Assembly in 1776."[12] The long preamble shows that the bill was meant to be more than merely one law in a long series of legal revisions: it was to be, as Jefferson said, the philosophical and theological foundation for abolishing "spiritual tyranny" in Virginia.[13]

It is the argument of this chapter that Jefferson went further politically than many of his fellow Virginia revolutionaries in pressing for total dises-

---

to a certain degree, been enacted before" in December 1776 when the legislature voted "to repeal the laws which rendered criminal the maintenance of any religious opinions, the forbearance of repairing to church, or the exercise of any mode of worship: and further, to exempt dissenters from contributions to the support of the established church; and to suspend, only until the next session levies on the members of that church for the salaries of their own incumbents" (ibid.). But this action "prevailed only so far" and was not the disestablishment that Jefferson sought; his "opponents carried . . . a declaration that religious assemblies ought to be regulated, and that provision ought to be made for continuing the succession of the clergy, and superintending their conduct" (ibid.).

11. Buckley, *Church and State in Revolutionary Virginia, 1776–1787*, 56–7. Jefferson worried that a general assessment, which was "debated at every session from 76 to 79," might pass because "some of our dissenting allies, having now secured their particular object [of freedom from an assessment for the Anglican church], [were] going over to the advocates of a general assessment" ("Autobiography," 35). Jefferson's own bill was offered on June 12, 1779, by John Harvie (Jefferson had been elected governor by the legislature on June 1, 1779) in response to a request from the House "to bring in a bill 'concerning religious freedom'" (Buckley, *Church and State in Revolutionary Virginia, 1776–1787*, 47). On the place of Bill 82 in the overall revision of Virginia's legal code, see ibid.; Dreisbach, "Thomas Jefferson and Bills Number 82–86 of the Revision of the Laws of Virginia, 1776–1786: New Light on the Jeffersonian Model of Church-State Relations," *North Carolina Law Review* 69 (1990): 159–211; and Dreisbach, "A New Perspective on Jefferson's Views on Church-State Relations: The Virginia Statute for Establishing Religious Freedom in Its Legislative Context," *American Journal of Legal History* 35 (1991): 172–204.

12. Buckley, *Church and State in Revolutionary Virginia, 1776–1787*, 47.

13. Jefferson, "Autobiography," 34.

tablishment because he went further than them theologically.[14] It has long been recognized that while Jefferson insisted that "*I* am a *real Christian, that is to say, a disciple of the doctrines of Jesus,*" he embraced a theology that was very unorthodox for his day, earning the calumny of "infidel" from his political enemies and from what he called "the Platonists . . . who draw all their characteristic dogmas from what [Jesus] neither said nor [his disciples] saw" (to Charles Thomson, January 9, 1816—emphasis original). Jefferson attributed the attacks from clergy (some of whom, especially in New England, excoriated him viciously during the election of 1800) in large part to his authorship of the bill, declaring that "[t]he priests indeed have heretofore thought proper to ascribe to me religious, or rather antireligious sentiments, of their own fabric, but such as soothed their resentments against the act of Virginia for establishing religious freedom. They wished him to be thought atheist, deist, or devil, who could advocate freedom from their religious distractions" (to Mrs. Samuel H. Smith, August 6, 1816).

Relying on evidence from Jefferson himself, scholars should rightly reject the claim that he was an atheist or that he banished theology from his political philosophy. Indeed, as this chapter will try to show, Jefferson's argument for religious liberty rests on a political philosophy of natural rights that depends on a certain theology. Unfortunately, very few scholars have traced the theoretical connection between Jefferson's unorthodox theology and his radically liberal views on religious liberty and church-state relations: as Charles Sanford laments, "[e]ven scholars who are familiar with Jefferson's deism, Unitarianism, and enthusiasm for Bible study do not seem to appreciate the importance of his religious beliefs to his political philosophy and career."[15]

It is important to outline Jefferson's understanding of this connection

14. Buckley notes that "[i]n the theological foundation Jefferson laid for religious freedom and its universal application, he surpassed the thought of his generation" (Buckley, "The Religious Rhetoric of Thomas Jefferson," 63). He does not say, however, exactly what Jefferson's theology was. This is because he thinks that Jefferson's theological "outlook was normal for his time and place" and therefore not in need of great attention (ibid., 55).

15. Charles B. Sanford, *The Religious Life of Thomas Jefferson* (Charlotteville: University of Virginia Press, 1984), "Preface." For some more recent treatments of this theme, see Garrett Ward Sheldon, *The Political Philosophy of Thomas Jefferson* (Baltimore, Md.: Johns Hopkins University Press, 1991), and Aristide Tessitore, "Legitimate Government, Religion, and Education: The Political Philosophy of Thomas Jefferson," in *History of American Political Thought,* eds. Bryan-Paul Frost and Jeffrey Sikkenga (Lanham, Md.: Lexington Press, 2003).

because a number of scholars have argued—not without some reason—
that the idea of freedom of conscience in America grew out of traditionally
orthodox, especially Reformed, theology.[16] Jefferson, however, completely
rejected this argument and believed that to defeat establishments and secure full religious liberty, "orthodox" theology had to be seriously modi-
fied.[17] But because such theology could not be attacked too vigorously in
public, it had to be subterraneously altered by another theology—a true
theology—that could come alongside and effect "a quiet euthanasia of the
heresies of bigotry and fanaticism which have so long triumphed over human reason" (to William Short, October 31, 1819). In particular, this theology must "humble" Calvinism—"this haughtiest of all religious sects" (to
Thomas Cooper, November 2, 1822)—by substituting the science of the

16. Some like David Little, for example, argue that "many a good Calvinist Baptist during
Jefferson's time saw no problem in arguing for the restraint of civil coercion in religious affairs
precisely in order to allow God to exercise his sovereign dominion over conscience" (Little, "Religion and Civil Virtue in America: Jefferson's Statute Reconsidered," in *The Virginia Statute for
Religious Freedom: Its Evolution and Consequence in American History,* ed. Merrill Peterson and
Robert Vaughan [New York: Cambridge University Press, 1988], 247). Little goes on to say that
these Baptists were not unique: "Christian tradition itself, especially certain parts of it, transmit-
ted doctrines of freedom of conscience, natural rights, and a secular civil order that were later
elaborated and institutionalized by the writings and efforts of Jefferson and Madison in the 1780s"
(ibid.). In particular, he says, Jefferson's view of conscience has its "strongest connection . . . to the
'free church' strand of the tradition, represented most characteristically by Roger Williams" (ibid.).
While Jefferson may have been familiar with the separationist views of Separate or free church
Baptists, Edwin Gaustad states that "[n]o evidence survives of Jefferson's or Madison's having read
Roger Williams" (Gaustad, *Sworn on the Altar of God: A Religious Biography of Thomas Jefferson*
(Grand Rapids, Mich.: Eerdmans Publishing, 1990), 72). Indeed, J. G. A. Pocock rejects the at-
tempt to "derive the Virginia Statute's philosophy of religious freedom from such giants of the
American past as Roger Williams" because to Pocock "it seems clear . . . that the freedom of the
Spirit [Williams's concern] is one thing and the freedom of opinion [Jefferson's priority] is another,
and that although there are ways of seeing the latter as a historical mutation of the former, there are
just as many of seeing it as a strategic means of reducing and minimizing the power of the Spirit to
disturb the civil order" ("Religious Freedom and the Desacralization of Politics: From the English
Civil Wars to the Virginia Statute," in Peterson and Robert, eds., *The Virginia Statute for Religious
Freedom: Its Evolution and Consequence in American History,* 70).

17. Jefferson claims that what passed for orthodox theology in his day had "compounded from
the heathen mysteries a system beyond the comprehension of man, of which the great reformer
of the vicious ethics and deism of the Jews, were he to return on earth, would not recognize one
feature" (to Charles Thomson, January 9, 1816). His own theology, he argues, is orthodox because
it comports with the real theology of Jesus: as he famously said to Benjamin Rush, "To the corruptions of Christianity I am indeed opposed; but not to the genuine precepts of Jesus himself. I am a
Christian, in the only sense he wished any one to be; ascribing to himself every *human* excellence;
& believing he never claimed any other" (to Benjamin Rush, April 21, 1803). "Our God," he said to
John Adams, is "the God of Jesus" (to John Adams, April 11, 1823). In this chapter, however, we will
use "orthodox" to designate the traditional Christian theology Jefferson rejected.

mind for dogmas of sin, Nature for revelation, the reasonable goodness of God for the indecipherable holiness of God, and a republican morality based on the natural rights of man for a religious moral code built on the need to revere publicly the Christian God. Jefferson believed that the theology articulated in the Bill for Establishing Religious Freedom was such a theology, and that it finally restored justice to God and man. In laying out his theology, this chapter hopes to shed some light not only on the crucial political debate in Virginia over disestablishment but also on the theological underpinnings of one of the most important and influential articulations of American civil religion from the Founding era.[18]

Why the Mind Is Free: Jefferson's Theology of Religious Liberty as Revealed in the "Mutilations" of the Bill's Preamble

According to Jefferson, the bill "finally passed" in 1786 as part of the "main body of work [that] was not entered on by the legislature until after the general peace, in 1785[,] when by the unwearied exertions of Mr. Madison, in opposition to the endless quibbles, chicaneries, perversions, vexations, and delays of lawyers and demi-lawyers, most of the bills were passed by the legislature, with little alteration."[19] However, the bill's passage was not a foregone conclusion, despite the collapse of the Anglican establishment during the Revolution. In 1784, Patrick Henry had drafted a more ecumenical bill creating an assessment for "Establishing a Provision for Teachers of the Christian Religion," which had occasioned James Madison's famous "Memorial and Remonstrance" in 1785. Madison then maneuvered to get Bill Number 82 of the revisal—Jefferson's Bill for Establishing Religious Freedom—considered by the assembly. There it "still met with opposition,"

---

18. According to Buckley, the "Virginia Statute for Religious Freedom offers the preeminent statement of the American faith as Jefferson defined it: a belief in God-given natural rights, the most important being freedom of thought and its expression, and the precedence of this right over any other claims of civil government to control or influence it" (Buckley, "The Religious Rhetoric of Thomas Jefferson," 65). Merrill Peterson adds that "the celebrated statute became a powerful directive for the unique relationship between church and state in America, and, by its bold assertion that the opinions of men are beyond the reach of civil authority, one of the great charters of the free mind as well" (Peterson, "Introduction" in *The Portable Thomas Jefferson*, xx). Because of the bill's importance, Buckley concludes that "Jefferson bears conspicuous responsibility for the development of an American civil religion" (Buckley, "The Religious Rhetoric of Thomas Jefferson," 74).

19. Jefferson, "Autobiography," 40.

especially in the Senate, from those who believed that government should promote "the general diffusion of Christian knowledge," as the preamble to Henry's bill puts it. Finally, in January 1786 it passed the House of Delegates but, as Jefferson noted, only after "some mutilations in the preamble."[20] Those "mutilations" are especially important to understand because, in Jefferson's view, the original bill was "drawn with all the latitude of reason & right": it embodied the full set of arguments that Jefferson believed necessary for finally recognizing religious freedom not as a grant of toleration or a right limited to believers, but as one of "the natural rights of mankind" (as the bill's concluding paragraph puts it).[21] The pieces of the preamble cut from the bill, then, reveal Jefferson's deeper and more comprehensive theology, a theology rooted in an understanding of "natural right" (the last words of the bill) that gives primacy to human reason and to the goodness of man and God.

The Science of the Mind versus Dogmas of Sin

Four significant phrases of the bill were deleted by legislative amendment. The first is the opening line of Jefferson's draft: "Well aware that the opinions and belief of men depend not on their own will, but follow involuntarily the evidence proposed to their minds." In this phrase we find the first important principle of Jefferson's theology: religion is a matter of the *mind,* not the heart, soul, or especially will. Penalties might terrify the heart, distress the soul, or force the will, but they cannot change the mind. According to Jefferson, attempting to use civil penalties to change people's minds simply does not understand how the mind works in matters of reli-

---

20. Ibid.

21. Ibid. Buckley claims that of the four, "the first two were relatively minor deletions from the preamble, primarily relating to sentences considered too rationalistic or deistic in tone. The third amendment [concerning government jurisdiction over opinions] . . . however, struck . . . a key tenet of the proponents of the bill" (Buckley, *Church and State in Revolutionary Virginia, 1776–1787,* 163). (Buckley does not discuss the fourth.) It is the argument of this chapter, however, that all four deletions are very important because they reveal Jefferson's theology and because Jefferson himself believed that every word in (or not in) the bill had political and theological implications for the future. Consider, for example, his statement about the importance of the failed legislative attempt to insert "Jesus Christ" into the bill's text: "Where the preamble declares that coercion is a departure from the plan of the holy author of our religion, an amendment was proposed, by inserting the word 'Jesus Christ,' so that it should read 'a departure from the plan of Jesus Christ, the holy author of our religion.' The insertion was rejected by a great majority, in proof that they meant to comprehend, within the mantle of it's protection, the Jew and the Gentile, the Christian and the Mahometan, the Hindoo, and infidel of every denomination" ("Autobiography," 40).

gion (and in all other matters): it receives "evidence" from its senses (e.g., the author of the book of Joshua says that Joshua made the sun stand still); considers the meaning of the evidence (e.g., Joshua performed a "miracle"); rationally forms an opinion about whether the assertion is true by using the "law of probabilities" to weigh the evidence (including the credibility of the author) against what the mind knows of reality (e.g., given that the earth is in constant rotation around the sun, could the author be right that the sun stood still?); and then converts that opinion into "belief"—that is, an opinion that a person calls his own (e.g., I do/do not believe that Joshua miraculously made the sun stand still) (to Peter Carr, August 10, 1787). If the mind comes to the conclusion that the evidence for a theological opinion is true, it necessarily embraces that opinion. People are, in effect, "hard-wired" for truth because the mind is independent of the will; people can choose to investigate a theological opinion, and they can choose whether to act on the beliefs formed as part of that investigation; but no one chooses his beliefs—and no one can truly believe what he thinks to be false.[22] Because no one chooses his beliefs, it does not make sense to say that someone can be forced to abandon them and adopt others.[23] Force can only "beget habits of hypocrisy and meanness," as the bill says.

Jefferson begins the bill with this first deleted phrase because he believed that arguments in favor of religious establishment or assessment in Virginia persisted in part due to a philosophical error about how the mind works. The revolution begun by John Locke in understanding the mind had not yet transformed the thinking of the commonwealth's statesmen and clergy (much less the common people): as he wrote in 1781, sympathy for some

22. Jefferson is aware that passions like self-love can affect the mind: as he says, "all men who have attended to the workings of the human mind . . . have seen the false colours under which passion sometimes dresses the actions and motives of others" (to John Adams, October 12, 1823). Yet if passion colors theological opinion, it is *after* the mind has formed an opinion. Then people love their own opinion because it is their own. But to the end of his life Jefferson believed—though with greater or lesser confidence depending on the issue and the times—that opinions could be changed through enlightenment because all those who study the mind "have seen also these passions subsiding with time and reflection, dissipating, like mists before the rising sun, and restoring to us the sight of all things in their true shape and colours" (to John Adams, October 12, 1823). In his last known letter he famously proclaims that notwithstanding centuries of "monkish ignorance and superstition," "[a]ll eyes are opened, or opening, to the rights of man" through "the general spread of the light of science" (to Roger Weightman, June 24, 1826).

23. If men cannot choose their theological beliefs, how can God punish or reward them for the correctness of those beliefs? Jefferson did not believe that God does: as he says to Peter Carr, sincerity (how you believe) is more important than orthodoxy (what you believe): "you are answerable not for the rightness but for the uprightness of the decision" (to Peter Carr, August 10, 1787).

kind of establishment persisted because "[t]the error seems not sufficiently eradicated that the operations of the mind" can be coerced by the law.[24] To defenders of government promotion of religion, however, their sympathy was rooted in a clear-sighted view of the real liberty of the mind. The mind is free, they argued, in that it was originally in uncoerced submission to God through the conscience. But the mind became enslaved to sinful passions as a result of the Fall, giving humans thoughts and imaginations (not to mention desires) at odds with their conscience.[25] The Calvinists in Virginia added that the Fall also shows the will to be depraved—because of its pride, the will wants (and even believes it has the right) to be its own governor; hence, human beings not only desire but choose to rebel against their conscience and its deepest desire to submit to the truth (*Virginia Gazette*, August 14, 1779, in O'Malley 2006, 76). Sinful people believe it is naturally right to decide for themselves what is true and to obey only their own decision. They deny the sovereignty of God over the conscience, even though the core of true piety consists in recognizing the need to submit to God's authority and obeying His call by embracing true Christian articles of faith and striving to live a life of moral holiness. A political community based on these insights could certainly promote obedience to true religion; in doing so, the law would not be violating the operation of the mind but merely correcting the influence of sinful passions on the mind and the will. True to this principle, Virginia—like all colonies and states during the Revolutionary era—had anti-blasphemy laws and—like many colonies and states—imposed legal and political penalties on dissenters or non-Christians.[26] Even when Virginia effectively eliminated such penalties during the Revolution, the idea of government promotion of religious obedience remained strong.

24. Thomas Jefferson, *Notes on the State of Virginia*, "Query XVII," in *The Portable Thomas Jefferson*. Jefferson clearly attributed the idea behind the first deleted phrase to Locke, whom he praised as one of "the three greatest men that ever lived, without any exception" for laying the philosophical foundation for "the Moral sciences" (to John Trumbull, February 15, 1789). In talking to Peter Carr about religion, Jefferson says that "[t]hese questions [of inspiration] are examined in the books I have mentioned to you under the head of religion." The first of these books is "Locke's Conduct of the Mind" (to Peter Carr, August 10, 1787).

25. *Virginia Gazette*, November 1, 1776, in Deborah Ann O'Malley, *"The Dictates of Conscience": The Debate over Religious Liberty in Revolutionary Virginia* (Ashland, Ohio: Ashbrook Center, 2006), 73; available at http://www.ashbrook.org/publicat/thesis/. Hereafter in text as O'Malley 2006.

26. Buckley, *Church and State in Revolutionary Virginia, 1776–1787*, 5–6.

Nature, Not Revelation, as the Source of Theological Truth

The critics of Jefferson had a powerful theological position—powerful enough, it seems, to get the first phrase deleted. Jefferson was familiar with the argument, however, and he included a second claim—subsequently cut—that provided a response. The deleted portion came after the statement (preserved in the statute as its opening line) that "Almighty God hath created the mind free." The second phrase said God "manifested his supreme will that free it shall remain by making it altogether insusceptible of restraint." It is not the will of God, argues Jefferson, that human beings can be coerced into choosing obedience because the mind is His creation and we know that it cannot be restrained. To attempt to do so is an "impious presumption" of "fallible and uninspired men" simply trying to assume "dominion over the faith of others," as the bill goes on to say.

To the bill's critics, however, it is "folly and absurdity" to say that we know God's will by looking at how the mind works (*Virginia Gazette,* August 14, 1779, in O'Malley 2006, 78). To be understood correctly, the "facts" of the physical and human worlds must be looked at through the lens of supernatural revelation, whether in the form of the Scriptures, church teaching, or the direct inspiration of the Holy Spirit. These revelations provide the "evidence" that shows the fundamental character of God and man; after all, the central doctrines of traditional Christianity (e.g., the Fall, original sin, the Trinity, the Virgin Birth, the Resurrection) are available only through revealed sources. And revelation tells us that the mind is not "altogether insusceptible of restraint" because it is not free nor does it want to be "altogether" free: on the one hand, it is enslaved to sin; on the other hand, it longs to free itself from sin by giving itself over completely to God (*Virginia Gazette,* September 18, 1779, in O'Malley 2006, 81). When the law commands us to respect true religion or support what we believe to be true religion, it is helping to liberate us from bondage to our sinful passions or will. Such law is therefore in accord with "natural right" understood as what revelation shows us about our nature before the Fall. After the Fall, there is no "imaginary state of uncorrupted nature," and hence Nature is no longer the only or even best standard of truth in theology, morality, or politics (*Virginia Gazette,* August 14, 1779, in O'Malley 2006, 78).

According to Jefferson, the orthodox reasoning is backward: we can infer God's will that the mind be free from the epistemological fact that it is naturally subject only to its own faculties because Nature, not revelation, is the standard of right in both theology and politics. Nature is the way God rules us, including our minds. If that were not true, there could be no "laws of Nature and of Nature's God," as they have been discovered by the great minds, because the principles we know would be only patterns of appearance, not facts of Nature. But there are discoveries of Nature that give us "all the certainties we can have or need," and if another revelation contradicts the facts of Nature, then either we do not know all the facts or the supposed revelation is not true (to John Adams, August 15, 1820; to Peter Carr, August 10, 1787). Yet Jefferson admits that the argument from scientific laws is not simply conclusive because while "Nature" means the totality of "matter and motion," "the materialist" has a difficult time trying to "explain the process by which matter exercises the faculty of thinking" (to John Adams, August 15, 1820). There must be "Nature's God"—a power distinct from Nature that organizes matter with its particular "mode of action" (to John Adams, August 15, 1820).

Thus, there must be an even more important idea than science for Jefferson's argument that human beings start with Nature rather than revelation as the source of religious truth. That idea is, for Jefferson, the idea of justice. According to Jefferson, calling revelation before the bar of Nature is not an unjust act of "infidelity" against "the religion of your country" (to Benjamin Waterhouse, June 26, 1822; to Peter Carr, August 10, 1787).[27]

27. Buckley contends that Jefferson's "religious rhetoric" cannot be seen as a rebellion against the conventional Christianity of his "time and place" because Jefferson had no need to make such a rebellion: his theological views, Buckley claims, were within the theological mainstream for Virginia Anglicans, who were not terribly concerned about doctrinal orthodoxy: "Throughout his life he [Jefferson] would equate religion with morality rather than doctrine. That outlook was normal for his time and place. Morality, not creed, was the key to Virginian Anglicanism. Controversies over theological doctrines and devotional practices were to be avoided at all costs, lest they fragment colonial society, as had occurred in England, most notably during the English Civil War. . . . Eighteenth-century enlightened, rational Anglicanism did not require a confessional belief, but rather a mode of worship. . . . The church did not command one how or what to think about God, and Jefferson made full use of that latitude. . . . But like most Americans of his and succeeding generations, he grew up and moved within a religious framework" (Buckley, *Church and State in Revolutionary Virginia, 1776–1787*, 55–57). However, the fact that Jefferson had a "religious outlook" and made "full use" of the latitude provided by rationalist Anglicanism to develop his own theological views does not mean that he shared the particular doctrines or theology of any branch of Anglicanism. He does say that his views on Christianity "ought to displease neither the rational Christian nor Deists," but even Latitudinarian Anglicanism did not go as far as Jefferson in denying the central idea of revealed doctrines (to Benjamin Rush, September 23, 1800). Nor does

The reason for his "defections from the Platonic Christianity of the priests" is theological: it originates in the theology of God's goodness (to Law, June 13, 1814). All theology, in Jefferson's view, must embrace—even start from—the idea that if God exists, He is "all perfect" (to Benjamin Waterhouse, June 26, 1822). He cannot be the "malignant daemon" into which Calvin twists Him, wrathfully demanding obedience from men who cannot possibly please Him with their obedience because they are sinful and He is holy (to John Adams, April 11, 1823). That would be unjust, and God cannot be unjust because if He is "all perfect," then He must be good. And if He is good and created Nature, then Nature is good, including human nature.[28] It will not do to say that our nature is stained by original sin so that what makes us happy is not always (or ever) good: this would imply that God was a "bungling artist" Who made a being that could deform its nature to the point of constantly pursuing its unhappiness (to Thomas Law, June 13, 1814). Why would He do that if He is good? It would not be, as the orthodox maintain, so that He could send His Son to redeem us, thereby showing us the full depth of His love for us and enthusing us to glorify Him for that love and redemption.[29] Why would God use us to get glory for Himself? Does He need or want such glory? How could He, since He is "all perfect"? The orthodox doctrines of original sin and the holiness of God are, like so much of their theology, "absolutely incomprehensible" (to John Adams, April 11, 1823), and Jesus himself "would disclaim them

---

Buckley grapple with the importance of the fact that, as Aristide Tessitore notes, Jefferson was "[k]eenly aware of the differences separating his own views concerning religion from those of the majority of his countrymen" and so "reserved the candid expression of his ideas to private conversation and correspondence" (Tessitore, "Legitimate Government, Religion, and Education," 138).

28. So how do we know what are gifts of Nature and what are corruptions? Whatever makes us truly happy is a gift, according to Jefferson, since God is good and therefore must want "the happiness of man," which is the greatest comprehensible good (to Benjamin Waterhouse, June 26, 1822). A true understanding of happiness, however, is found not in the teachings of Jesus but in "the well-regulated indulgences of Epicurus" (to William Short, October 31, 1819). "Epictetus and Epicurus give laws for governing ourselves," Jefferson says, while Jesus provides "a supplement of the duties and charities we owe to others" (to William Short, October 31, 1819). "Our master Epicurus" teaches us that by Nature, happiness is found in the delights of the body (health, vitality, food, drink), the delights of the heart (love, family, home, doing good to others), and the delights of the mind (learning, discovering, inventing, administering); pain can be avoided or minimized by having virtuous habits (i.e., practicing courage, wisdom, moderation, and justice) (to William Short, October 31, 1819). Above all, Epicurus teaches, "In-do-lence is the absence of pain, the true felicity" (to William Short, October 31, 1819).

29. According to Calvinist orthodoxy, glorification of God, while knowing one's sinfulness, is the greatest happiness: "What is the chief end of man? To glorify God and to enjoy Him forever" (*Westminster Shorter Catechism*, Question 1).

with the indignation which their caricatures of his religion so justly excite" (to William Short, October 31, 1819). Thus, it is not sinful rebelliousness that "drives thinking men into infidelity"—it is orthodox theology's injustice against man and its "blasphemies" against the goodness of God (to Benjamin Waterhouse, June 26, 1822).

What we can justly say is that if God is good, He is good *to us*—that is, He benefits us in a way that we can comprehend (or how could we call Him good?). At the same time, however, we cannot define His Nature: it is a subject like "the summum bonum and finis bonorum . . . the knolege [*sic*] of which is withheld from man" (to John Adams, Oct. 12, 1813). Yet orthodox theology denies this truth, claiming, for example, that we will be damned unless we give our minds over to the "incomprehensible" proposition that "there are three Gods" in One (to Benjamin Waterhouse, June 26, 1822). According to Jefferson, it is impossible to assent to such a proposition because there is no innate idea of such a God (or we would not need revelation), no known faculty of mind for receiving such irrational revelations, and nothing in our nature that supports the orthodox argument that people (whether believers now or prophets in the past) have "inspiration"—that is, a personal experience of the Divine that teaches a truth about God or man not otherwise accessible to the mind through Nature.[30] He argues that the claim for inspiration—and hence prophecy—rests on a warped understanding of the moral experience of God. No matter how "rational" their theology, the orthodox explicitly or implicitly believe that all people have a sense that there is something more than Nature (or Nature's God) in the world to guide us. There are moments of the uncanny sublime or, more importantly, of overwhelming beauty that proclaim the presence of the Christian God, whose Reality moves human beings when they sense the "beauty of His Holiness" as the Psalmist says (Psalm 27:4)—whether (depending on the denomination) that beauty is found in the Scriptures, the sacraments, church tradition, rituals of worship, common prayer, or the Inner Light. All

---

30. Even Jesus—the teacher of a "system of morals . . . which, if filled up in the true style and spirit of the rich fragments he left us, would be the most perfect and sublime that has ever been taught by man"—was not inspired (to Benjamin Rush, April 21, 1803). The difficulty of Jesus' mission to reform "the religion of the Jews" meant that he "had to walk on the perilous confines of reason and religion" that did not allow him "a step to the right or left" (to William Short, August 4, 1820). Jesus therefore might have had to pretend to inspiration to effect the reforms; or, "[e]levated by the enthusiasm of a warm and pure heart, conscious of the high strains of eloquence which had not been taught him, he might readily mistake the coruscations of his own fine genius for inspirations of an higher order" (to William Short, August 4, 1820).

of these are forms of the "testimony of the Holy Spirit," Whose presence satisfies, if only for a moment, our soul's deepest longing to be reunited with the true God. It sparks the "love of God" that the orthodox claim is the foundation of morality and piety (to Thomas Law, June 13, 1814).

In Jefferson's view, this sentiment is "enthusiasm," and the notion that the moral experience of "enthusiasm" bespeaks "inspiration" is false and ultimately rooted in Plato's view of *to kalon,* or longing for beauty, which crept into Christianity sometime after the rise of "the Platonising successors" to "the primitive Christians" (to John Adams, October 12, 1813). Jefferson admits that "[w]e have indeed an innate sense of what we call beautiful"; but, he says, it is "a faculty *entirely* distinct from the moral one" (to Thomas Law, June 13, 1814—emphasis added). The beautiful "is not even a branch of morality" because our innate sense of beauty "is exercised chiefly in subjects addressed to the fancy, whether through the eye in visible forms, as landscape, animal figure, dress, drapery, architecture, the composition of color, etc. or to the imagination directly, as imagery, style, or measure in prose or poetry, or whatever else constitutes the domain of criticism or taste" (to Thomas Law, June 13, 1814). Because a sense of beauty does not move us to God, the moral experience of God ("the love of God") cannot be rooted in longing for the beautiful. In the Christian context, this means that the true experience of the Divine is not found in the supposed beauty of recognizing the ugliness of one's sin and in giving oneself over in total subjection to a Holy God Who purifies the soul through the noble sacrifice of His Son. According to Jefferson, that interpretation of the experience of "enthusiasm" rests on the false dogma of original sin, one of many such doctrines that have so thoroughly corrupted orthodoxy that he calls for a "euthanasia for Platonic Christianity" in order to get the religion of Jesus back to "the primitive simplicity of it's [sic] founder" (to Adam, Oct. 12, 1813).[31]

31. In reality, Jesus came only for a "reformation" of the religion of the Jews: "1. He corrected the Deism of the Jews" by "giving them juster notions of his attributes and government"; "2. His moral doctrines, relating to kindred and friends, "greatly" "more pure and perfect . . . than those of the Jews; and they went far beyond both [the teachings of the ancient philosophers and the Jews] in inculcating universal philanthropy . . . to all mankind"; "3. "The precepts of philosophy & of the Hebrew code, laid hold of actions only. He pushed his scrutinies into the heart of man; erected his tribunal in the region of his thoughts, and purified the waters at the fountain head"; "4. He taught emphatically, the doctrines of a future state, which was either doubted, or disbelieved by the Jews; and wielded it with efficacy, as an important incentive, supplementary to the other motives to moral conduct" (to Benjamin Rush, Apr. 21, 1803; see also to Joseph Priestly, Apr. 9, 1803). Because his mission was merely the reformation of Judaism, "the pure doctrines of Jesus" were very straightforward and simple: "1. That there is one only God, and He is perfect, 2. That there is a future state of

Because Jefferson believed that true reformation would lead to an end of claims of unnatural, mystical revelations, he was cool, almost sarcastic, when claims of such quasi-erotic experience were made by "our Platonizing Christians" (to Benjamin Waterhouse, June 26, 1822). For example, he scornfully wrote of the Presbyterian-led revivals "in our Richmond" in 1822: "there is much fanaticism, but chiefly among the women. They have their nightly meetings and praying parties, where, attended by their priests, and sometimes by a hen-pecked husband, they pour forth the effusions of their love to Jesus, in terms as amatory and carnal, as their modesty would permit them to use to a mere earthly lover" (to Thomas Cooper, November 2, 1822). Those moments of beautiful ecstasy are not piety but "fanaticism," as he says, because there is nothing in Nature or human nature to support the idea of a human connection to the Divine that can reveal doctrines that transcend or contradict what the mind apprehends. For example, no amount of ecstatic experience can establish the truth of the doctrine that "God, from the beginning, elected certain individuals to be saved, and certain others to be damned, and that no crimes of the former can damn them; no virtues of the latter save" (to Benjamin Waterhouse, June 26, 1822). Such doctrines are simply too contrary to the idea of justice—to our natural understanding of God's goodness and justice—to be true; if they are widely professed, it is only because of fraud or the fact that they cannot be questioned without fear of harm (to Benjamin Waterhouse, June 26, 1822).[32] Because the mind has no innate idea of God or supernatural fac-

---

rewards and punishments, 3. That to love God with all thy heart and thy neighbor as thyself, is the sum of religion" (to John Adams, May 5, 1817).

32. Despite his confidence that Calvinism's "demoralizing dogmas" would be defeated, "the growth of Presbyterianism" aroused Jefferson's great consternation, even anger (to Thomas Cooper, November 2, 1822). This was partly because in the 1770s and 1780s, he believed that the Presbyterians in Virginia petitioned for religious liberty not based on principles of "right and reason" but based on their own animosity against the Anglican Church (Buckley 1977, 167). Later, according to Jefferson, that same concern for their own influence showed itself in Presbyterian opposition to his plan for the University of Virginia: the Presbyterians' "ambition and tyranny would tolerate no rival if they had power. Systematical at grasping at an ascendancy over all other sects, they aim, like the Jesuits, at engrossing the education of the country, are hostile to every institution which they do not direct, and jealous at seeing others begin to attend at all to that object" (to Thomas Cooper, November 2, 1822). He traces their desire for dominion to their theology: they seek complete power because "the impossibility of defending" the "blasphemy and absurdity of the five points of Calvin" renders "their advocates impatient of reasoning, irritable, and prone to denunciation" (to Thomas Cooper, November 2, 1822). Jefferson's repudiation of Calvin is total: "Calvin . . . was indeed an Atheist; which I can never be; or rather his religion was Daemonism. If ever a man worshipped a false god, he did. . . . It would be more pardonable to believe in no god at all than to blaspheme him by the atrocious attributes of Calvin" (to John Adams, April 11, 1823).

ulty to receive or experience revelation, including ecstatic inspiration, all it has left is Nature. For Jefferson, then, the implication of the second deleted phrase is that religious liberty rests on rejecting the idea that God communicates the most important religious truths to man through revelation rather than Nature.

What Does Nature Tell Us? Rational Theology and the Character of God

If Nature is the source of theological truth, then the question is what Nature tells us theologically. But how do we know that? For Jefferson, the answer is found very clearly in the third phrase deleted from his bill: that God chose "to extend it ["our religion"] by its influence on reason alone." This phrase clearly rules out the possibility that true religion was spread by miracles or inspiration, an idea central to traditional Christianity. Like the rest of "[t]he long preamble," said one critic in the press, it reflected "the principles of a deist," and so it had to be cut.[33] Instead, the final statute simply explains that "the holy author of our religion" did not use coercion to spread that religion, despite "being lord both of body and mind." This leaves open orthodox interpretations of His means; and, indeed, the bill calls religion a matter of "faith," leaving the source of faith unspecified.

The deletion removed Jefferson's boldest attempt to make explicit the implications of his theology recognized by his critics in the press and Assembly: "our religion," which is the theological framework for the bill's defense of religious freedom, is not Christianity traditionally understood. Like the orthodox, Jefferson believes that religion is faith (or "belief"); but he understands faith not to be the experience of "the reality of Christ's presence"[34] but as "persuasion" to a certain "opinion" (a word he uses twelve times in the bill). A person's opinions are his theology; a person's persuasion (his state of being persuaded that these opinions are true) is his faith. Religion is the combination of theology (opinion) and faith (persuasion). Religion, then, exists in "the field of opinion," and since opinion is generated by reason, religion must lie in the realm of reason.[35] Jefferson's con-

---

33. *Virginia Gazette,* September 11, 1779, in O'Malley 2006, 76; see also Buckley, *Church and State in Revolutionary Virginia, 1776–1787,* 163.

34. Pocock, "Religious Freedom and the Desacralization of Politics," 69.

35. As he says to Peter Carr about evaluating the claims of revelation: "In the first place divest yourself of all bias in favour of novelty & singularity of opinion. Indulge them in any other subject rather than that of religion. It is too important, & the consequences of error may be too

clusion is that true religion, "our religion," must be a religion of rational theology.[36] That is, it must offer an understanding of God and His relation to human beings that uses Nature as its standard of right and reason as its "oracle," as he told his nephew Peter Carr.[37]

This rational theology, while it cannot define God, can tell us much about Him. As we saw earlier, reason deduces from the idea of justice that *if* God exists, He is good to us. Jefferson adds that reason deduces from Nature that God does exist—that there is a First Cause and orderer of the universe. Jefferson is aware that some rationalists like "the disciples of Ocellus, Timaeus, Spinoza, Diderot, and D'Holbach" believe in "the eternal pre-existence of the world" and thus deny a Creator God; but he says: "On the contrary, I hold (without appeal to revelation) that when we take a view of the Universe, in it's [*sic*] parts general or particular, it is impossible for the human mind not to perceive and *feel a conviction* of design, consummate skill, and indefinite power in every action of it's [*sic*] composition" (to Adams, April 11, 1823—emphasis added). This opinion of a First Cause is not an abstract formalism—it produces a sense of sure persuasion (i.e., a feeling of "conviction") that is a kind of religious sentiment. But because it is a conviction based on reason, it is open to discussion, debate, and criti-

---

serious. On the other hand shake off the fears & servile prejudices under which weak minds are servilely crouched. Fix reason firmly in her seat, and call to her tribunal every fact, every opinion. . . . Your own reason is the only oracle given you by heaven, and . . . if there be one [a God], he *must* more approve of the homage of reason, than that of blindfolded fear" (to Peter Carr, August 10, 1787—emphasis added). Jefferson makes this implication clearer when he explains to Peter Carr how to study the Bible: "Read the Bible then, as you would read Livy or Tacitus. . . . Examine upon what evidence his pretensions ["to inspiration from God"] are founded, and whether that evidence is so strong that its falsehood would be more improbable than a change in the laws of nature in the case he relates. The pretension is entitled to your inquiry, because millions believe it. On the other hand, . . . keep you reason firmly on the watch" (to Peter Carr, August 10, 1787).

36. Jefferson claims that the Bible itself, when properly interpreted, supports his rational theology. For example, John 1 talks about *logos,* which "has been perverted by modern Christians to build up a second person of their tritheism" (to John Adams, April 11, 1823). While Jefferson admits that "word" is "one of it's [*sic*] legitimate meanings," he argues that the translation of *logos* as "word" in the context of John 1 "makes an unmeaning jargon: while the other meaning 'reason', equally legitimate, explains rationally the eternal preexistence of God, and his creation of the world" (to John Adams, April 11, 1823). "When truly translated," therefore, John 1 should read: "'In the beginning God existed, and reason (or mind) was with God, and that mind was God'" (to John Adams, April 11, 1823).

37. While the two may hold similar opinions in the end, Jefferson's use of "oracle" to describe the importance of reason goes beyond the description offered by his hero Locke, who said that reason is our "only Star and compass" (*First Treatise,* sec. 58). "Star and compass" suggests that reason is what we "steer by" in evaluating the claims of revelation (*First Treatise,* sec. 58); "oracle" implies that reason *is* the source of revelation (i.e., the only way in which God speaks to us).

cism, confident in its truth and not needing to attack, suppress, or convert its opponents (to Thomas Cooper, November 2, 1822).[38]

Rational theology produces another religious sentiment as well: adoration. Because God must be good as well as having "Almighty power," His order must not only be consummately skillful in a technical sense but also beneficial for the created order, including human beings. As evidence of God's care, Jefferson points to "the movements of the heavenly bodies . . . the structure of the earth itself . . . the mineral substances"—from these "it is impossible, I say, for the human mind not to believe that there is, in all this, design, cause and effect, up to an ultimate cause, a fabricator of all things from matter and motion, their preserver and regulator while permitted to exist in their present forms, and their regenerator into new and other forms" (to John Adams, April 11, 1823). More than just Creator, God is "a superintending power to maintain the Universe in it's [sic] course and order"; in this respect, He is a "benevolent" governor of the world, including man. Since the greatest benefit for man is happiness, reason tells us that God cares for "the happiness of man" (to Benjamin Waterhouse, June 26, 1822). Rationally comprehending that God cares for human beings' happiness, according to Jefferson, evokes the warm-hearted adoration of true theology, which stands in stark contrast to either the crazed longing or servile fear, irascible anger, and desire for dominion created by orthodox theology, especially Calvinism (to Thomas Cooper, November 2, 1822; to John Adams April 11, 1823).

However warm-hearted, though, adoration is not the "enthusiasm" characteristic of orthodox (i.e., Platonic) Christianity. This is because rational theology understands that God renews, sustains, and governs the physical and human worlds through the "course of Nature" (to Peter Carr, August 10, 1787). He does not intervene directly to cure our diseases or save our souls. He is not personal in that sense. Rather, God works through the "law of Nature and of Nature's God" whose fundamentals have been discovered by "Bacon, Locke, and Newton," whom Jefferson considered "as the three greatest men that have ever lived, without any exception" for "having laid the foundation of those superstructures which have been raised in the Physical and Moral sciences" (to John Trumbull, February 15,

---

38. Jefferson claimed to embody these traits: "I never told my own religion, nor scrutinized that of another. I never attempted to make a convert, nor wished to change another's creed" (to Mrs. Samuel H. Smith, August 6, 1816).

1789). Each of these three thinkers—far above "the herd of other great men"—made a distinct contribution: Bacon taught us the proper way to conduct natural science; Newton taught us the physical properties of matter (like gravity); and Locke taught us about how the mind works and about the purposes of political society (to John Trumbull, Feb. 15, 1789; see also to Peter Carr, August 10, 1787). Starting with the foundation laid by these thinkers, rational theology can use the growing discoveries of natural and moral philosophy to add to its system, although—as we said—it can never hope to define God fully. The best it can do is to say what God must be at a minimum if He is God, and to say what God cannot be. Therefore, it cannot offer hope of an experience of direct knowledge of God of the kind claimed by the enthusiasts. It must consider such claims to be "superstition" (to Peter Carr, August 10, 1787) or "the *deliria* of crazy imaginations" (to Benjamin Waterhouse, June 26, 1822).[39] But it does offer spiritual sustenance—a moral experience of gratitude to God for His Creation and Government of the world through Nature that is the foundation of a reasonable sense of the sacred—of "the holy mantle which shall cover within its charitable circumstance all who believe in one God, and who love their neighbor" (to Benjamin Waterhouse, June 26, 1822). Moreover, it has a great religious advantage over "every Christian sect," especially Calvinism; unlike them, it does not give "a great handle to Atheism by their general dogma that, without a revelation, there would not be sufficient proof of the being of a god" (to John Adams, Apr. 11, 1823). It leads "thinking men" to God, not away (to Benjamin Waterhouse, June 26, 1822). According to Jefferson, this will be increasingly important as America and the world become more enlightened as the "happy influence of reason and

39. Does Jefferson's theology give us hope for life after death? He emphatically argues that one of Jesus' greatest reforms of Judaism was to teach the certainty of rewards and punishments in the life to come, which can be a great incentive to virtue, especially for those lacking in the development of their moral sense (to Peter Carr, August 10, 1787). He also wrote to John Adams that "I join you cordially, and await his [God's] time and will with more readiness than reluctance. May we meet there again, in Congress, with our antient Colleagues, and receive with them the seal of approbation: 'Well done, good and faithful servants'" (to John Adams, April 11, 1823). Yet Charles Sanford notes that it is not clear that Jefferson himself believed in such a state. Sanford concludes that Jefferson hoped it might be true but was not convinced (Sanford, *The Religious Life of Thomas Jefferson*, 170–71). This conclusion seems apt given that Jefferson avowed a "creed of materialism" that rejected "all organs of information . . . but my senses" (to John Adams, August 15, 1820). While he admitted that God had the power to re-constitute and re-enliven dead bodies, it is also true that his rejection of inspiration suggests that for him, God works only through the laws of nature, none of which seem to support a belief in animate life after death (to John Adams, August 15, 1820).

liberty" spreads "over the face of the earth" ("Response to the Citizens of Albemarle," Feb. 12. 1790). Indeed, as the "light of science" shines brighter (to Roger Weightman, June 24, 1825), Jefferson has "no doubt" that only a rational theology like Unitarianism is likely to survive (to Thomas Cooper, November 2, 1822).[40]

The Happiness of Man on Earth: Creating and Sustaining a Republic of Natural Rights

It is one thing, of course, for Jefferson's theology to tell us that God cares about man's happiness on earth. What provision has He made for realizing it? This issue goes to the heart of the fourth phrase deleted from Jefferson's bill: "that the opinions of men are not the object of civil government, nor under its jurisdiction." The immediate implication of the deleted phrase is that government has no business establishing a denomination or levying an assessment to support religion because it has no reason or even power to take notice of citizens' religious views. "[G]overnments are instituted among men," Jefferson wrote in the Declaration, "to secure these rights," "among which are life, liberty, and the pursuit of happiness." Politically, this means—he says in the bill—that government's power is limited to intervening against "overt acts against peace and good order."

Theologically, the larger implication of the deleted phrase is that God cares for man's happiness on earth by giving him natural rights that can be secured by the creation of a political society (and civil government) in which truth will be free to prevail by "free argument and debate," as Jefferson puts it at the end of the preamble. While the Whigs in Virginia who defended government promotion of religion generally agreed that political society exists to protect man's fundamental rights, they also believed that government could and should be concerned with citizens' opinions, including (indeed, especially) religious opinions. Political society protects "civil rights" (i.e., the interests that deserve protection by civil society), but these interests include morality, which human beings bring with them into civil society just as they bring their lives, liberties, and properties (*Virginia Ga-*

40. Writing to John Adams, Jefferson declares that "the day will come when the mystical generation of Jesus, by the supreme being as his father in the womb of a virgin will be classed with the fable of the generation of Minerva in the brain of Jupiter. . . . But we may hope that the dawn of reason and freedom of thought in these United States will do away with all this artificial scaffolding, and restore to us the primitive and genuine doctrines of this most venerated reformer of human errors" (to John Adams, April 11, 1823).

zette, August 14, 1779, in O'Malley 2006, 78). While church and government have distinct functions (and, in that sense, separate realms), political society is more than a collection of individuals united to protect their bodies or estates. It is a moral *community* united for the "general good," which government secures by having laws that are an authoritative statement about what the citizens believe together to be true and false, right and wrong, noble and base. In a Christian community, such a shared notion of justice or morality based on protecting people's rights implies shared religious principles because those rights come from God, and God is the God of Christian revelation.[41] Hence, the commonwealth should affirm "what a majority shall determine to be for the common good" in religion, especially by supporting the denomination of the majority of Christians in the society or at least the essentials of the Christian religion (*Virginia Gazette,* August 14, 1779, in O'Malley 2006, 78). Contrary to what the bill says in this respect, religious opinions are decisively different from "opinions in physics or geometry." Political society is not a community of physicists or geometers; but it is a religious community, at least to the extent that citizens as citizens must share some common religious principles in order to share a common political understanding of justice and rights.

Moreover, defenders of establishment argued, the lack of such principles causes moral and political chaos in a republic. Religions (or denominations) that are fundamentally opposed to each other theologically will inevitably fight using all the resources available (including political power). An establishment removes doctrinal conflict as a source of political struggle and promotes "social tranquility"—and even friendship—among citizens (*Virginia Gazette,* August 14, 1779, in O'Malley 2006, 79). Moreover, wicked actions are encouraged and even produced by wicked ideas, and false religion is necessarily the greatest breeder of bad ideas. Republican liberty and self-government require moral and civic virtue among citizens, the defenders argued, and virtue requires religion because human beings are naturally selfish and so neglect the common good or even violate others' rights in order to get what they want. True religion has a "natural tendency to correct the morals of men, restrain their vices, and preserve the peace of society" by inculcating a capacity to overcome wicked desires by strengthening both men's natural (but too often neglected) sense of nobility and their

41. Buckley, *Church and State in Revolutionary Virginia, 1776–1787,* 180–81.

fear of punishment.[42] A realm of complete religious freedom is a place of "inevitable confusion" where 1000 different voices offer "1000 different systems of religion" (as Jefferson put it) and all religious truths can be questioned, which implies that those truths are not sacred nor held with the kind of reverence that does not dishonor their authority by demanding to know why they should be respected (*Virginia Gazette,* August 14, 1779, in O'Malley 2006, 80). For political society to say officially that religion is "a concern purely between our God and our consciences," as Jefferson puts it, is to imply that other people *as citizens* have no reason to care about a person's views, which suggests that religion is only a private matter (to Mrs. Samuel H. Smith, August 6, 1816). If it is so private, then it must be subjective and particular to the person—a matter of personal opinion, not *truth.* But Christianity is true, and so should be held or approached in reverent awe, or at least not publicly dishonored (*Virginia Gazette,* August 14, 1779, in O'Malley 2006, 80). Penalties for dissent or assessments to support one's own denomination uphold the sacred quality of true religion and thereby restrain the spread of seductive doctrines and licentious disregard for truth that undermines the morality necessary for republican government. Paying taxes to support clergy promotes reverence by honoring those clergy and giving them a more authoritative voice with which to exhort the citizens to virtue. These measures reflect the fact that, for Jefferson's opponents, "the fabric of society and the survival of the republican experiment depended on something more than the pure light of reason."[43] A society that knows the true religion yet imposes no penalties on unbelievers (or at least makes no authoritative statement of the true religion) either will leave this spiritual side of man unfulfilled, or will deify individual "license" *as* the common religion.

According to Jefferson, these defenses of establishment on moral and political grounds are based on a wrong understanding of the true character and bonds of political society. Political society is based on "natural right" (the concluding words of the bill). To understand "natural right," we need to start with the fact, according to Jefferson, that Nature has given human beings a moral sense, which "is as much a part of his nature as the sense of hearing, seeing, feeling; it is the true foundation of morality, & not the

42. Patrick Henry, "A Bill Establishing a Provision for Teachers of the Christian Religion," in Buckley, *Church and State in Revolutionary Virginia, 1776–1787,* 188.

43. Buckley, *Church and State in Revolutionary Virginia, 1776–1787,* 182.

to kalon, truth, &c. as fanciful writers have imagined" (to Peter Carr, August 10, 1787). We know about this "moral instinct" ("the brightest gem with which the human character is studded") because we see that human beings—even atheists—have a "love of others, a sense of duty to them … which prompts us irresistibly to feel and to succor their distresses" (to Thomas Law, June 13, 1814). Hence, we know that there is a "Moral law of our nature … to which Man has been subjected by his creator, & of which his feelings, or Conscience as it is sometimes called, are the evidence with which his creator has furnished him" ("Opinion on the French Treaties to George Washington," April 28, 1793). "For the reality of these principles," Jefferson says, "I appeal to the true foundation of evidence, the head & heart of every rational and honest man. It is there Nature has written her moral laws, & where every man may read them for himself" ("Opinion on the French Treaties to George Washington," April 28, 1793).

   In its operation, however, the moral sense by itself is not sufficient to support a republican society. The moral sense generates "moral feeling" (e.g., outrage) when moral "data" (e.g., that man just stole one's property) are filtered through moral principles received from the conscience (e.g., it is wrong to steal). Moral feeling is necessary in order for us to leave the state of nature and live happily in society, for which we have been ordained by our needs (to Thomas Law, June 13, 1814). To preserve a sense of morality, people need only to be kept from bad habits and exposure to successful examples of outrageous vice when young, not to be "led astray by artificial rules" in philosophy, and to be shielded from "contamination" by bad ideas gathered from an injudicious reading of the Bible when "their judgments are not sufficiently matured for religious inquiries" (to Peter Carr, August 10, 1787; to Thomas Law, June 13, 1814; *Notes on the State of Virginia,* "Query XIV"). The moral sense alone, however, does not support a republican society because the moral sense is relative to the society in which a person lives: "nature," Jefferson says, "has constituted utility to man the standard best of virtue. Men living in different countries, under different circumstances, different habits and regimens, have different utilities: the same act, therefore, may be useful, and consequently virtuous in one country which is injurious and vicious in another differently circumstanced" (to Thomas Law, June 13, 1814). This means that the moral sense does not on its own provide the principles of right and wrong that establish sentiments of pity and duty proper to republican morality.

According to Jefferson, however, such a morality does not require a religious establishment because it can be produced by reason, specifically liberal political philosophy and rational theology. A person's moral principles come not from the moral sense but from our minds, which hold the religious and moral opinions generated by our reason through education and—in the best case—reflection on Nature, including human nature (to Mrs. Samuel H. Smith, August 6, 1816). In a republic, the moral sense has to be infused with a republican conscience—that is, a knowledge of natural rights and a theological persuasion that those rights are endowments from a benevolent Creator. Together, these will produce a "pure love of liberty" that will make men "determined to make every sacrifice, and to meet every danger" in defending others' rights as well as their own (*Notes on the State of Virginia*, "Query XIII"). Americans had such a sense, Jefferson argued in 1774, because they knew that they were "a free people claiming their rights as derived from the laws of nature and not as the gift of their Chief Magistrate" (*A Summary View of the Rights of British North America*, final paragraph). Jefferson worried, however, that "from the conclusion of this war we shall be going down hill" because the love of liberty kindled by the Revolution will be "forgotten" by the people, who will be lost "in the sole faculty of making money, and will never think of uniting to effect a due respect for their rights" in religion (*Notes on the State of Virginia*, "Query XVII"). For that reason, he felt an urgent need in 1781 to fix religious freedom "on a legal basis . . . while our rulers are honest, and ourselves united" (*Notes on the State of Virginia*, "Query XVII").

Yet Jefferson remained optimistic about overthrowing religious establishments of all kinds (including their Platonic/Calvinist theology) because of the comprehensibility of natural rights. As with the moral sense, Nature gives each person the "Instinctive Impulses" to preserve himself and pursue his happiness (to Thomas Law, June 13, 1814); because these impulses are by Nature irresistible, reason concludes that they are rights—the natural (thus God-given) rights of life, liberty, and pursuit of happiness (and property). If Nature gives men innate impulses, how can it forbid them from acting to fulfill them? Jefferson illustrates this point by talking about when it is naturally just to break contracts, which human beings sense are obligatory: "Reason . . . gives this right of self-liberation from a contract in certain cases [when self-preservation is threatened by keeping the contract]" ("Opinion on the French Treaties to George Washington," April 28, 1793).

To require human beings to keep a treaty that destroys them is to forbid them from acting on "the law of self-preservation," which "overrules the laws of obligation to others" ibid.). Jefferson calls self-preservation a "law" because it is—like the pursuit of happiness—an irresistible impulse of Nature that compels us to act. To forbid human beings from acting on their natural compulsion would be unreasonable, even cruel. That would make Nature, and thus God (the Creator of Nature), cruel. But, as Jefferson says, God must be good if He is God; and He must be good in a way that is rationally understandable to human beings. Therefore, men must be authorized to preserve themselves and pursue their happiness. This authorization is the "natural right" of which Jefferson speaks at the end of the bill.[44] The "rights of mankind" to life, liberty, and property are derived from this "natural right," and are the means that God has given to "all men" (as the Declaration says) by which they can pursue their preservation and happiness.

Here, Jefferson believes, we can discern the true political relation between God and man. God provides for man not by making him naturally subject to a divinely ordained government that directs his life toward the true religion but by authorizing men to assert boldly "the sufficiency of human reason for the care of human affairs" ("Response to the Citizens of Albemarle," February 12, 1790). Human beings in turn provide for their own happiness by exercising their natural liberty to form a political society that protects their natural rights. Jefferson believes that human beings can be bold in their assertion of republican self-government because "natural right" is based on a rational (even scientific) understanding of human beings; thus, he is convinced that while reason will advance and change our understanding of the world and the laws of nature, it will not change the moral fact of natural rights: "Nothing then is unchangeable," he declares, "but the inherent and unalienable rights of man" (to Major John Cartwright, June 5, 1824). And because these rights are generated from "natural right" by only a simple and rationally accessible theology of God, republican morality can be sustained among the people without a religious establishment, religious

---

44. Jefferson uses the phrase "natural right" in the same way in his famous 1785 description of the concentration of property in France "in a very few hands": "Whenever there are in any country uncultivated lands and unemployed poor, it is clear that the laws of property have been so far extended as to violate natural right" (to James Madison, October 28, 1785). "Natural right" here refers to the liberty of every person to preserve themselves in accord with the impulse for preservation given them by Nature.

assessments, or even belief in traditional revelation. The people need only to understand "the lessons we have learned together" from rational reflection on Nature and experience: that God is the Creator and "benevolent governor" of the world, and that man is good enough and reasonable enough "to enjoy in peace and concord the blessings of self-government" ("Response to the Citizens of Albemarle," February 12, 1790).[45] It is, then, the rationally grounded character of the bill's understanding of natural rights and God that underlies Jefferson's conviction at the end of the preamble that government need not concern itself with men's opinions as long as "free argument and debate" are allowed to undercover the truth. Conversely, a true understanding of natural right cannot be sustained with a theology like Calvinism, which demands obedience to irrational doctrines and contends that natural, irresistible human impulses are evil or tainted by sin.

Conclusion: "I Have Sworn upon the Altar of God"

While it is important to understand the social, economic, and political aspects of the fight over Jefferson's bill, he recognized that the struggle in Virginia was, at its deepest, a *theological* dispute between very different understandings of God and the human condition. For its part, Jefferson's theology was not simply a dogmatic assertion of Enlightenment rationalism; rather, it was based on an understanding of "natural right" derived from a critique of the justice of "orthodox" theology, especially as exemplified by Calvinism. From Jefferson's point of view, his theological understanding advanced during the Revolution as a result of the political advance of natural rights philosophy, which he believed necessarily entailed a movement away from orthodoxy.

But the persistence of support for government promotion of religion in the 1780s showed Jefferson that his fellow revolutionaries remained bounded by orthodox Christian understandings of God as a holy Being demanding obedience in the form of moral perfection and embrace of true doctrine, and man as a being needing but rejecting obedience because his passions, will, and even mind are corrupted by sin. While they generally accepted re-

45. After the election of 1800, Jefferson compared his views to "those of the leaders on the other side, who have discountenanced all advances in sciences as dangerous innovations, have endeavored to render philosophy and republicanism terms of reproach, to persuade us that man cannot be governed but by the rod, & etc. I shall have the happiness of living and dying in the contrary hope" (to John Dickinson, March 6, 1801).

ligious liberty, they did not understand that the natural right to freedom of religion had to mean embracing the idea that human beings could be left to find religious truth without being compelled by the law, even for the sake of public virtue. They had to come to see that any God worthy of the name not only must have endowed men with rights of life, liberty, and property but also must have created the mind wholly free and left for its direction to the moral sense and "the reason of man," which—as he wrote to James Madison upon hearing of the adoption of the statute—Virginia had finally recognized "may be trusted with the formation of his own opinions." Because of the "mutilations" in the preamble, however, Virginia's recognition of the full theological ground of religious liberty was incomplete. But it was, for Jefferson and his ally Madison, a great step forward.

Still, the deletions must have been a source of real disappointment for Jefferson, for whom no concession could in principle be made to what he regarded as any unjust religious institution or theology. Because religious liberty requires a theological as well as a political foundation, establishing religious liberty in Virginia had to mean not only an open political confrontation with the entrenched Anglican establishment but also a greater, riskier, and necessarily more covert theological struggle against the traditional (especially Calvinist) view of God and man that could threaten the conscience. Passage of the bill was a great political victory against the establishment, but the "mutilations" cost Jefferson the utterly decisive theological triumph he had hoped for. But as subsequent events have shown, even those "mutilations" have not stopped the Bill for Establishing Religious Freedom from being his greatest weapon in his long campaign "against every form of tyranny over the mind of man."

9

Unsettling Faith

The Radicalization of the First
Amendment and Its Consequences

THOMAS F. POWERS

Struck by America's thriving religious life, Alexis de Tocqueville noted the explanation for it offered by clergymen. "[A]ll thought that the main reason for the quiet sway of religion over their country was the complete separation of church and state. I have no hesitation in stating that throughout my stay in America I met nobody, lay or cleric, who did not agree about that."[1] Writing in the 1890s James Bryce also concluded, "It is accepted as an axiom by all Americans that the civil power ought to be not only neutral and impartial as between different forms of faith, but ought to leave these matters entirely on one side."[2] Even as late as 1955, sociologist Will Herberg described American religion in terms of its relation to liberal principle: Americans were "quite obviously secularist at the very time that they exhibit every sign of a widespread religious revival." The American religion question was framed by him in terms of "this secularism of a religious people, this religiousness in a secular framework."[3]

Today things are different. Leading First Amendment scholar Michael McConnell characterizes religious Americans as thinking that "the First Amendment works against them"; Stephen Carter is not surprised when believers feel that "the nation is actively at war against them."[4] The same

1. Alexis de Tocqueville, *Democracy in America,* trans. George Lawrence (Garden City, NY: Doubleday, 1969), 295.

2. James Bryce, *The American Commonwealth,* rev. ed., vol. 2 (New York: Macmillan, 1911), 766.

3. Will Herberg, *Protestant-Catholic-Jew: An Essay in American Religious Sociology* (Garden City, N.Y.: Doubleday, 1955), 3.

4. Michael W. McConnell, "Equal Treatment and Religious Discrimination," in *Equal Treat-*

pastor of the First Baptist Church of Dallas (the Southern Baptist Convention's largest congregation) who held in 1960 that "church and state must be, in this nation, forever separate and free," would by 1984 say that "the separation of church and state was the figment of some infidel's imagination."[5] Today "religion" as such, and not as in the past the claims or clashes of particular denominations, is politicized in unprecedented ways. The "religious right," feeling itself to be "marginalized" by much of American law and culture, increasingly abandons the framework of liberty in favor of one centered on equality, borrowing heavily from the civil rights movement and the framework of identity politics. In turn, the response to this development has been partly the lamenting of religion in politics, partly the launching of a fledgling "religious left." New policy responses—voucher programs in education and social services, the "faith-based initiative" of the Bush administration (embraced in general terms by Democrats as well)—work to break down the wall between church and state especially when it comes to spending public money. A new pattern of religious politics seems to be emerging, one that is not obviously connected to America's liberal past and that indeed takes shape against it.

Religion and the politics of religion have long been controversial in American life, but only recently has the First Amendment itself been the centerpiece of conflict and debate. What happened? Why did the liberal solution, which had worked so well, suddenly come apart? This is certainly not what the vaunted "secularization thesis" would predict for America. Under the many powerful influences of modernity (science, technology, commerce, democracy and liberal ideology), religion was supposed to fade into the end of history. Are we now in need of a "collapse of secularism" thesis?

I will take up these questions by examining the contributions of the United States Supreme Court to this puzzling drama. Many trace the rise of the religious right and the recent politicization of religion in America to a broad set of developments included under the heading of the "culture wars." Traditional religion, pressured by challenges arising in the 1950s and 1960s

---

ment of Religion in a Pluralist Society, ed. Stephen V. Monsma and J. Christopher Soper (Grand Rapids, Mich.: William B. Eerdmans, 1998), 38; Stephen Carter, *God's Name in Vain: The Wrongs and Rights of Religion in Politics* (New York: Basic Books, 2000), 2.

5. These statements, made by the Reverend W. A. Criswell, are quoted in John C. Jeffries and James E. Ryan, "A Political History of the Establishment Clause," *Michigan Law Review* 100, no. 2 (2001): 327.

to law and order, authority, patriotism, and especially traditional family and sexual mores, is attempting to stem the tide of modern life through direct political engagement. Such an explanation is perfectly consistent with the secularization thesis, suggesting only that modernity pressed religion too quickly and too forcefully for a time, thus provoking a cultural reaction.

The story of the U.S. Supreme Court's involvement paints a different picture. To be sure, the Court has played a role in every important battle of the culture wars (*Roe v. Wade* and the Court's denial of tax-exempt status to Bob Jones University are often cited as key moments in the rise of the religious right). But this is not the Court's most important role in the story. For one very important source of worry for religious conservatives is the radicalization by the Court of the very principles enshrined in the religion clauses of the First Amendment. For 150 years the First Amendment reigned unquestioned from on high, almost never directly invoked but effective and well-supported by all nonetheless. Without warning, and without immediate provocation by any development in American religious life, the Supreme Court began in the 1940s to use the First Amendment to lay down a new law for religion, radicalizing both religious freedom for non-mainstream denominations and the idea of the separation of church and state.

What has been the result of this effort? Certainly not what its original advocates intended or hoped. First, the secularist or separationist radicalization of the First Amendment provoked an "accommodationist" response from conservative defenders of mainstream American religion.[6] As of yet, neither side has clearly won in this struggle, though conservatives have been much more successful at pushing back than is usually recognized. Second, the ensuing legal battles revealed a political dividing line between secularists and accommodationists that heretofore had only been implicit in American public life (earlier lines being drawn primarily among religious groups). Third, First Amendment law itself has become a minefield of competing doctrines, tests, and legal principles, none of which has been able to sustain a majority of the Court for long. It is very hard for any-

6. I will use these somewhat crude but necessary labels, secularist/separationist and accommodationist, to denote progressives and conservatives in religion (especially Establishment clause) debates. Secularists/separationists are more committed to keeping church and state separate; accommodationists are more willing to accommodate religion in American life by allowing greater state recognition of and aid to religion. But accommodationists, like separationists, are committed to religious liberty and endorse some notion of the separation of church and state.

one studying First Amendment jurisprudence not to begin to jump to the "political" conclusions of legal realism. Indeed, legal realist accounts have begun to take hold. The most disturbing result of the political conflict and turmoil and the legal incoherence and confusion associated with the First Amendment is the emergence of a series of radical theoretical critiques of the very idea of religious freedom.

This story is not, then, the one predicted by the secularization thesis. The First Amendment eruption of the decades following World War II had little to do with the gradual impact of liberalism and modernity *on religion* and everything to do with a strangely zealous application of the liberal ideal itself. The culture wars may explain some things, but it was the Court's moralistic insistence upon secularism that provoked an open feud between religion and the First Amendment. Explaining that original impulse must be an important part of this inquiry. On Robert Bellah's view, the American civil religion was always a mixture of general and vague invocations of divine support coupled with appeals to liberal moral principle. But Bellah also maintained that "[t]he American civil religion was never . . . militantly secular."[7] At the very least, the separationist turn of the Supreme Court seems to have revealed a tension at the heart of the American civil religion. But it may also reveal something about liberal principle itself: if the religion clauses of the First Amendment are at the heart of America's "constitutional faith," it would seem that they proved capable of inspiring a zealous intransigence and heedlessness more commonly associated with religious fervor.

Principle under Pressure: The Radicalization of the Religion Clauses

From 1940 until about 1980, both the idea of the separation of church and state and the idea of religious liberty for members of minority sects were taken more seriously and pushed farther by the Court in a radical departure from the past. Prior to this time, very little attention at all had been paid to the First Amendment's two clauses, the Court having taken up almost no "Establishment" clause cases (such cases deal, roughly, with the question of the separation of church and state), and just a handful of "Free Exercise" clause cases (generally dealing with the question of exemption from legal limitations upon religious practices, typically those of religious

7. Robert Bellah, "Civil Religion in America," *Daedalus* 96, no. 1 (1967): 13.

minorities). It was not until 1940 and 1947 that the First Amendment's two clauses were "incorporated" and held by the Court to apply beyond federal law to reach state and local government.[8]

The radical character of the position taken by the Court in its sudden interest in the First Amendment was signaled immediately by the tone and language of its first mid-century decisions. In a 1943 case upholding the right of Seventh-day Adventist students not to salute the flag (a free speech case involving a prior Free Exercise clause decision), the Court staked out a bold declaration of the extent of its commitment to liberty. "Freedom to differ is not limited to things that do not matter much. That would be a mere shadow of freedom. The test of its substance is the right to differ as to things that touch the heart of the existing order."[9]

But it was especially in the 1947 case *Everson v. Board of Education* that the Court signaled the tenor of what was to come. *Everson* addressed the question of whether students of private religious schools should be permitted to ride to school on public school buses. While the Court's five-to-four majority permitted the students access to this public good, Justice Black's opinion, which relied extensively on the thought of Madison and Jefferson, contained the following oft-to-be-repeated passage:

The "establishment of religion" clause of the First Amendment means at least this: Neither a state nor the Federal Government can set up a church. Neither can pass laws which aid one religion, aid all religions, or prefer one religion over another. . . . No tax in any amount, large or small, can be levied to support any religious activities or institutions, whatever they may be called, or whatever form they may adopt to teach or practice religion. . . . In the words of Jefferson, the clause against establishment of religion by law was intended to erect "a wall of separation between Church and State."[10]

Black's embrace of the "wall of separation" metaphor, as well as his characterization of its meaning, signaled the birth of what came to be termed "strict separationism." Not only was this somewhat extreme formulation boldly stated, but it was the unanimous view of the Court (the four dissenters, vying with Black to provide an adequately separationist rendering of Madison and Jefferson, disagreed only in the case's outcome; they would have denied the students access to the public school buses).

8. *Cantwell v. Connecticut* 310 U.S. 296 (1940); *Everson v. Board of Education* 330 U.S. 1 (1947).
9. *West Virginia Board of Education v. Barnette* 319 U.S. 624, 642 (1943).
10. *Everson v. Board of Education*, 15–16.

Over the next three decades, the logic of *Everson* would be extended and applied in a number of controversial decisions. Most notably, in 1962, 1963, and 1964 the Court struck down prayer and Bible readings in public schools.[11] Writing in 1967, Sidney Hook went so far as to say that these cases "produced possibly the greatest outcry against the Supreme Court since the days of the Dred Scott decision." The decisions of the Court "created a national issue where one did not exist before."[12] In 1968, the Court went on to declare unconstitutional a state law restricting the teaching of evolution.[13] The Court also staked out in these years a position hostile to the public funding of religious schools.

In the course of the struggle over aid to religious education, the Court enunciated a major "test" for Establishment clause cases. Under the three "prongs" of the ubiquitous *Lemon* test (after *Lemon v. Kurtzman,* a 1973 decision), laws must have not only a secular purpose, but also a secular effect, and they must avoid any undue "entanglement" between church and state.[14] No clearer statement of the requirements of "strict separation" could be imagined. As in *Everson,* the Court here unanimously accepted as uncontroversial this fairly radical articulation of the standard of separation. In the years since, no other related doctrinal position has carried the same weight. Even though the test is increasingly under fire (and could conceivably be repudiated in the future), it is still for many an obvious starting point for thinking about the Establishment clause.

The Free Exercise clause revolution started later and has perhaps already ended, but its ambition was in a way even more dramatic. Since 1879, when the Court denied Mormons a religious exemption from federal laws prohibiting polygamy, the crux of Free Exercise clause jurisprudence had been the distinction between belief (which the state may in no way regulate) and religiously inspired action (which may be regulated, as may be all actions, by the law). The act/belief doctrine, taken by the Court from Jefferson, is a simple, clear, and practically effective guide and provides the essential starting point for Free Exercise clause analysis. But, because it insists upon the law as a basic limit to religiously inspired action, it is also a stingy standard from any perspective that wishes to take seriously "the right to

11. *Engel v. Vitale* 370 U.S. 421 (1962); *Abington Township School District v. Schempp* 374 U.S. 203 (1963); *Chamberlain v. Public Instruction Board* 377 U.S. 402 (1964).

12. Sidney Hook, *Religion in a Free Society* (Lincoln: University of Nebraska Press, 1967), 78.

13. *Epperson v. Arkansas* 393 U.S. 97 (1968).

14. *Lemon v. Kurtzman* 403 U.S. 602 (1971).

differ as to things that touch the heart of the existing order." The Court's polygamy cases, for example, are not framed in any very culturally sensitive way ("Polygamy has always been odious among the northern and western nations of Europe"; "To call their advocacy a tenet of religion is to offend the common sense of mankind").[15]

In 1963, the Court marked out a new effort to extend the promise of religious free exercise beyond belief to include action as well. In *Sherbert v. Verner,* the Court decided that any law regulating or restricting religiously inspired behavior must pass the highest level of constitutional scrutiny (any such policy must be justified by a "compelling" governmental interest and must be "narrowly tailored" to that end).[16] Such "strict scrutiny" is extended to only a few other highly sensitive areas of constitutional protection, and in such cases there are in turn few governmental interests that the Court will admit to be "compelling" enough to override the constitutional protection invoked.

Explaining the Religion Clause Revolution: Liberal Zeal(otry)?

Why did this burst of principled idealism on the Court occur during this period? There was no obvious cause for concern arising out of the politics of religion itself. Discrimination against, and several outright vigilante attacks on, Jehovah's Witnesses (important in early 1940s cases) by itself was only a spark, not the main source of the fire.[17] The Court's Establishment clause decisions proved to be extremely unpopular with a significant number of religious Americans, who now for the first time began to see the Supreme Court and the First Amendment as threats to religion.

Several converging trends and events help to explain the Court's abrupt break with the past. To some extent the reinterpretation of the religion clauses was part of a much broader shift in the self-understanding of the Court as an institution. Taking religious liberty and the separation of church and state more seriously went together with similar developments of the same period. In its treatment of free speech, due process (criminal procedure), and civil rights, the Court likewise undertook an ambitious effort to extend

15. *Reynolds v. United States* 98 U.S. 145, 165 (1879); *Davis v. Beason* 133 U.S. 333, 341–42 (1890).
16. *Sherbert v. Verner* 374 U.S. 398 (1963).
17. Thomas C. Berg, "Minority Religions and the Religion Clauses," *Washington University Law Quarterly* 82, no. 3 (2004): 934–35.

and radicalize its understanding of the Constitution's moral commitments. After the collapse of various legal doctrines (concerning property and federalism) during the New Deal era, so the story goes, the Court was looking for a new role in American political life and found it in policing civil liberties and civil rights instead.[18]

More generally, secularization on the Court was also to some extent a reflection of broader cultural changes in the early twentieth century. The astonishing technological feats of modern science lent to science an authority rivaling and sometimes challenging that of religion. Newly prominent sciences of economics, psychology, anthropology, and sociology offered to explain how human beings live, singly and collectively, and perhaps to provide guidance on how they ought to live. A new breed of non-religious or anti-religious intellectuals—Darwin, Marx, Durkheim, Weber, Freud—gained the allegiance of many educated Americans. It was precisely these intellectuals and their followers who developed the "secularization hypothesis," predicting the inevitable decline of religion in the face of modernity. This cultural drift also had a more assertive public face, most notable in the 1925 Scopes "monkey trial" and the drafting in 1933 of a "Humanist Manifesto" (signed by John Dewey and several other prominent intellectuals). The manifesto held not only that "the nature of the universe depicted by modern science makes unacceptable any supernatural or cosmic guarantees of human values," but also that "humanism will take the path of social and mental hygiene and discourage sentimental and unreal hopes and wishful thinking."[19]

Realist students of the Court will also insist that one look beneath the layers of legal doctrine and moral argumentation to the actual interests affected on the ground. Especially on the question of state aid to religious schools, the turn begun in *Everson* reflected "in some measure the sanitized residue of nativism and anti-Catholic animosity."[20] Protestant America, fearing to lose previously unchallenged control of American cul-

18. Richard L. Pacelle, *The Transformation of the Supreme Court's Agenda: From the New Deal to the Reagan Administration* (Boulder, Colo.: Westview Press, 1991).

19. See Frederick Mark Gedicks, *The Rhetoric of Church and State: A Critical Analysis of Religion Clause Jurisprudence* (Durham, N.C.: Duke University Press, 1995), 18–19; Richard P. McBrien, *Caesar's Coin: Religion and Politics in America* (New York: Macmillan, 1987), 177–80; Paul Kurtz, *Humanist Manifestos* (Buffalo, N.Y.: Prometheus Books, 1973), 8–9.

20. Jeffries and Ryan, "Political History," 291. Throughout this paragraph, I am indebted to Jeffries and Ryan's analysis; see Philip Hamburger, *Separation of Church and State* (Cambridge, Mass.: Harvard University Press, 2002).

tural and political life to an immigrant population beholden to a church whose leaders disavowed the liberal democratic approach to religion, reacted most forcefully on the question of education. From this perspective, *Everson* might be viewed only as an attempt to negotiate a not-so-hidden battle between Catholics and Protestants that had gained force by the 1940s and that continued until the emergence of the religious right in the late 1970s changed the politico-religious landscape.

The influence of various religious minorities must also be taken into account. To repeat, the struggles of Jehovah's Witnesses in the 1940s helped to launch the Court's effort. American Jews, energized by the horrors of the Holocaust, helped to shape the Court's agenda in important ways. "Led by the American Jewish Congress—and imitating civil rights agencies like the ACLU and NAACP—the Jewish bodies initiated and financed 'planned, strategic litigation' to challenge religious programs in public schools and other government actions that pressured Jews as a religious minority."[21] Leo Pfeffer, general counsel of the American Jewish Congress, argued more religion cases (including *Lemon*) before the Supreme Court than any one else in American history.

But if combustible material was at hand, pressure and a catalyst were still needed to turn these trends into the unprecedented and revolutionary campaign undertaken by the Court. These were provided above all by the moral pressures of World War II, the Holocaust, the Cold War, and the civil rights movement. World War II was clearly a pivotal event. More than one quarter of the Court's Free Exercise clause decisions (many dealing with Jehovah's Witnesses) were handed down between 1940 and 1945. Justice Roberts, writing in the 1940 case in which the Free Exercise clause was incorporated, indicates that the Nazi persecution of Jews loomed large in the Court's thinking about the meaning and extent of liberal principle: "The danger in these times from the coercive activities of those who in the delusion of racial or religious conceit would incite violence and breaches of the peace in order to deprive others of their equal rights to the exercise of their liberties, is emphasized by events familiar to all."[22] The Cold War, like World War II, called forth a specifically liberal moral idealism in response to such a stark challenge to liberalism's place in the world. These

21. Berg, "Minority Religions and the Religion Clauses," 936; see also Naomi Cohen, *Jews in Christian America: The Pursuit of Religious Equality* (New York: Oxford University Press, 1992).
22. *Cantwell v. Connecticut*, 310.

same moral impulses were then sustained and extended by the domestic moral drama of the civil rights movement. By 1963, the *Sherbert* revolution was launched precisely as a way to turn the Free Exercise clause into yet another tool by which to protect vulnerable minorities, especially religious ones.

Out of these pressures, a heightened moral commitment to the ideals of religious liberty and the separation of church and state seemed obvious to the Court. It is important to insist on the reality of the moral dimension in this development. An interpretation emphasizing only the political history of the clash between Protestants and Catholics in America or the struggles of various religious minorities does not explain how radical separationism would extend itself to the point where (not so long after *Everson*) many religious people (uniting Protestants and Catholics) began to feel threatened by it. The idealistic and moralistic radicalization of the First Amendment's principles by justices who took them seriously must form a central part of any "realistic" explanation of the Court's separationist tack.

The Conservative/Accommodationist Reaction

Writing in 1976, Walter Berns characterized the Court of the day as "incorporating Jefferson's metaphorical wall into the Constitution and raising it to a height it was not intended to reach."[23] But a generation later, the wall is crumbling if not fallen; one must agree with Jeffrey Rosen that "the era of strict separation is over."[24] The revolution did not succeed in establishing a broad consensus (either legal or cultural) supporting secularism or strict separation. Instead, the main achievement of the Court was to make the First Amendment itself, for the first time in American history, a central battleground in political struggles over religion. When secularization became not only implicit in the law but also the law's explicit *credo,* defenders of religion on and off the Court began to respond with vigor and, increasingly, with success. This effort has not yet simply won out, but it is very close to affecting a thoroughgoing repudiation of the secularists' main achievements.

Most successful has been the effort in Free Exercise clause jurisprudence

23. Walter Berns, *The First Amendment and the Future of American Democracy* (New York: Basic Books, 1976), 77.
24. Jeffrey Rosen, "Is Nothing Secular?" *New York Times Magazine,* January 30, 2000, 40–45.

to roll back the *Sherbert* revolution. In practice, the *Sherbert* test proved too high a standard. It turned out that in most cases where it was applied, the Court did *not* take the side of exempting religious "actions" from the strictures of the law. Eventually, in 1990, the *Sherbert* test was seemingly cast aside as "a constitutional anomaly" (though it was not strictly speaking overturned) in Justice Scalia's extremely contentious opinion in *Employment Division v. Smith* (a case denying a religious exemption for ceremonial drug use).[25] In fact, *Smith* did not go beyond earlier cases that had backed away from the *Sherbert* standard, but Scalia's provocative opinion succeeded in provoking. The unpopularity of *Smith* among scholars and many religious groups, and hence politicians, means that the issue may not be entirely settled. As constitutional scholar Kenneth Karst, put it, for many *Smith* amounted to a "radical contraction of free exercise doctrine" triggering a "large body of overwhelmingly hostile commentary."[26] Congress, registering seemingly widespread concern, attempted to restore the *Sherbert* standard in the Religious Freedom Restoration Act (RFRA) and succeeded at least in making it a rule for federal (but not state and local) government.[27]

The conservatives' Establishment clause counterrevolution has been less overtly or obviously successful. However much abused, *Lemon* has never been overturned, and there are several members of the Court—and many more law professors—who continue to use the *Lemon* test as an essential guide to thinking about religion. Indeed, in a number of high-profile cases something like strict separation still seems to prevail, and commentators who assume that the secularization of America proceeds apace at the hands of the Court have some important evidence on their side. Apparently committed to continuing resistance against any form of prayer in the public schools, the Court ruled out moments of silence (in 1985), nondenominational prayer at a high school graduation ceremony (in 1992), and a student-led prayer before a high school football game (2000).[28] Other high-profile cases involving public displays of religious symbols (Christmas decorations,

---

25. *Employment Division, Dept. of Human Resources of Oregon v. Smith* 494 U.S. 872, 886 (1990).

26. Kenneth L. Karst, "Religious Freedom and Equal Citizenship: Reflections on *Lukumi*," *Tulane Law Review* 6 (December 1994): 339.

27. The Court struck down RFRA as it applies to state and local government in *City of Boerne v. Flores* 521 U.S. 507 (1997) but has accepted its standard with reference to federal law (see *Gonzales v. O Centro Espírita* 546 U.S. 418 (2006)).

28. *Wallace v. Jaffree* 472 U.S. 38 (1985); *Lee v. Weisman* 505 U.S. 577 (1992); *Santa Fe Independent School District v. Doe* 530 U.S. 290 (2000).

the Ten Commandments) and the teaching of evolution have also gone the separationists' way.[29]

But these noteworthy and much-debated decisions exaggerate the strength of strict separation on the Court. In fact, since the 1980s, conservatives have mounted a series of legal counter-assaults on the *Lemon* test's strict separationist line, offering a variety of alternative doctrines and legal standards of their own. Generally speaking, the position of the Court's conservatives is termed an "accommodationist" stance, one that appeals, in effect, to the basic ideal of the Free Exercise clause on behalf of the Christian majority against the strict separationist interpretation of the Establishment clause.[30]

As a matter of Supreme Court doctrine, a general appeal to the idea of accommodating religion does not connect as usefully with traditional liberal principles of government as does the *Lemon* test's simple evocation of the inescapably liberal idea of the separation of church and state. As a result, an array of other more precisely drawn doctrines advance the position of the Court's accommodationist conservatives. First is the ideal of non-coercion. This is made an accommodationist stance by holding that the state, so long as it does not coerce religious action, worship, or belief, may *otherwise* aid or advance religion in American life.[31] Likewise, the principle of "individual private choice" has been used by conservatives since the 1980s to permit aid from the state to religious schools or organizations so long as it issues not from the state directly but from individual recipients of vouchers or other forms of aid.[32] Third, again beginning in the early 1980s and borrowing from eminently liberal free speech jurisprudence, conservatives on the Court have countered separationist limitations upon religion (and especially limitations on *access* to public schools and other facilities) by deeming such restrictions forms of "content discrimination" or "viewpoint discrimination."[33] Finally, and most important, conservatives advance an ideal of "neutrality" as a more accommodating standard for judging the

29. *County of Allegheny v ACLU* 492 U.S. 573 (1989); *Stone v Graham* 449 U.S. 39 (1980); *McCreary County v. ACLU* 545 U.S. 844 (2005); *Edwards v. Aguilard* 482 U.S. 578 (1987).

30. See *Wallace v. Jaffree,* 57n45, 79.

31. See, e.g., *Abington Township v. Schempp,* 316; *Wallace v. Jaffree,* 90. See also the debate over the non-coercion standard in *Lee v. Weisman.*

32. *Mueller v. Allen* 463 U.S. 388 (1983); *Witters v. Washington Dept. of Services for the Blind* 474 U.S. 481 (1986); *Zelman v. Simmons-Harris* 536 U.S. 639 (2002).

33. See, e.g., *Widmar v. Vincent* 454 U.S. 263 (1981); *Rosenberger v. Rector and Visitors of the University of Virginia* 515 U.S. 819 (1995).

permissibility of laws that seem to advance or aid religion. So long as laws are general or neutral (for example, laws funding education), so the conservative argument goes, these laws are valid even if they incidentally benefit religious groups. The new conservative interpretation of neutrality, often working in tandem with other conservative tests and standards, has become the main doctrinal alternative to the concept of "separation."

Leaving doctrine aside, as a practical matter, the Court's conservatives have been very successful in cases where the question of aid to religion is at issue. *Lemon* itself was a case involving state aid to religious education, and between the time it was decided (in 1973) and 1985, the Court struck down more programs that benefited religion (typically education bills) than it upheld. But since 1986, the separationists have not won a single aid-to-religion case.[34] Indeed, in decisions in 1997 and 2000, the Court *overturned* four earlier precedents denying aid to religious groups.[35] A far-reaching decision in 2002 upheld the use of government funding of religious schools through the mechanism of "vouchers," given to individuals, and opened the door to government funding of a wide variety of services provided by religious organizations in addition to education.[36]

In other areas of policy the conservatives have made gains as well. The Court's content/viewpoint discrimination cases have entrenched a principle of "equal access" for religious groups to schools and other public facilities. Following the Court's lead, Congress passed in 1984 an "Equal Access Act" that guaranteed the same. Even in prayer cases, the conservatives do have at least one "win," in a 1983 case upholding the use of chaplains in the Nebraska state legislature.[37] Similarly, religious symbols have been permitted by the Court where they are found to be in a context that minimizes their religious significance.[38]

34. See *Witters v. Washington Dept. of Services for the Blind; Bowen v. Kendrick* 487 U.S. 589 (1988); *Zobrest v. Catalina Foothills Sch. Dist.* 509 U.S. 1 (1993); *Rosenberger v. Rector; Agostini v. Felton* 521 U.S. 203 (1997); *Mitchell v. Helms* 530 U.S. 793 (2000); *Zelman v. Simmons-Harris.* The only possible exception is *Locke v. Davey* 540 U.S. 712 (2004), but there the Court merely upheld a state law restricting scholarship aid to ministerial students.

35. *Agostini v. Felton* overturned *Aguilar v. Felton* 473 U.S. 402 (1985) and *Grand Rapids School District v. Ball* 473 U.S. 373 (1985); *Mitchell v. Helms* overturned *Meek v. Pittenger* 421 U.S. 349 (1975) and *Wolman v. Walter* 433 U.S. 229 (1977).

36. *Zelman v. Simmons-Harris; Freedom from Religion Foundation, Inc. v. McCallum* 324 F.3d 880 (7th Cir. 2003).

37. *Marsh v. Chambers* 463 U.S. 783 (1983).

38. *Lynch v. Donnelly* 465 U.S. 668 (1984); *County of Allegheny v. ACLU; Van Orden v. Perry* 545 U.S. 677 (2005).

Overall, the conservative counterrevolution's impact has not been suffi-ciently recognized. Regardless of whether conservatives dominate the Court in the future, it seems likely that the shift on the questions of aid to reli-gion will be an enduring legacy. Even the 2004 Democratic Party platform promised to "strengthen the role of faith-based organizations in meeting challenges like homelessness, youth violence, and other social problems."[39]

The First Amendment as "Mess"?

If the first result of the separationist revolution was to provoke a conser-vative counterstroke, the second was to create at least the appearance of ex-treme legal flux. The standard view of the Court's religion clause jurispru-dence is summarized by Frederick Mark Gedicks: "The Court's decisions in this area have been described as 'ad hoc,' 'eccentric,' misleading and dis-torting,' 'historically unjustified and textually incoherent,' and—finally—'riven by contradiction and bogged down in slogans and metaphors.'"[40] One may add that they are also viewed as being "confused and confusing," "notoriously incoherent," "in hopeless disarray," "plagued by multiple in-consistencies and contradictions," a "muddle," a "mess," an "impossible-to-understand mess," and a "disaster."[41] With so much doctrinal fluctuation in such a short period of time, it is not surprising that participants and ob-servers (of all doctrinal stripes) find the First Amendment a frustrating area of the law. The overall result is an array of competing tests and standards that apply differently in different situations.

The conservatives have fought back, and in some areas they have won, but the broader battle continues, and neither side can claim a general vic-

39. "Strong at Home, Respected in the World: The 2004 Democratic National Platform for America," 2004 Democratic National Convention, 39; available at http://www.democrats.org/pdfs/2004platform.pdf.

40. Gedicks, *Rhetoric of Church and State,* 1.

41. Erik Owens, "Taking the 'Public' Out of Our Schools," *Journal of Church and State* 44, no. 4 (Autumn 2002); Marylin Perrin, "Note, *Lee v. Weisman:* Unanswered Prayers," *Pepperdine Law Review* 21 (1993): 252; L. Scott Smith, "From Typology to Synthesis: Recasting the Jurispru-dence of Religion," *Capital University Law Review* 34 (2005): 51; Michael W. McConnell, "The Religion Clauses of the First Amendment: Where Is the Supreme Court Heading?" in *1990 First Amendment Law Handbook,* ed. James L. Swanson and Christian L. Castle (St. Paul, Minn.: West Group Publishing, 1990), 269; Rich Lowry, "Thou Shalt Make No Sense: Commandments and Confused Jurisprudence," *National Review Online* (March 4, 2005), http://www.nationalreview.com/script/printpage.p?ref=/lowry/lowry200503040741.asp (accessed June 7, 2009); Vincent Phil-lip Muñoz, "Establishing Free Exercise," *First Things* 138 (2003): 14.

tory that might settle doctrine into something recognizably clear and co-herent. None of the conservative alternatives has become a unifying flag for the Court or even for all of the Court's conservatives. Worse yet, both sides co-opt the other's tests, only to alter their inner logic so as to subvert their original meaning. Even if we can say that the *Lemon* test is still in effect, what is or is not a "secular purpose" or "secular effect," for exam-ple, is far from clear. The conservatives' non-coercion standard has been stretched by the progressives and by Justice Kennedy to include what Jus-tice Scalia disparagingly refers to as "psycho-coercion" (as including subtler forms of coercion, like peer pressure).[42] And one must add still other lesser known tests, like the standard of *Marsh v. Chambers,* justifying the state's endorsement of religion (prayer in a legislative assembly) in the name of a seemingly sweeping anti-separationist argument from nothing more than longstanding historical practice. So too one must add alternative tests and various ancillary sub-tests proffered by centrist Justice O'Connor, such as her "endorsement" and "reasonable observer" tests or the so-called acknowl-edgement and ceremonial deism tests (permissible as something short of endorsement of particular faiths).[43] If one important test of the law is its predictability, one could say that the Court's religion jurisprudence leaves something to be desired.

Perhaps more troubling than the simple complexity and messiness of the law is the lack of any obvious higher standard by which it might be sorted out. Appeals to the original intent of the framers, or the founding generation, or all of American history, only fan the flames and settle noth-ing. Likewise, conservatives and progressives may appeal to different moral terms, but all principles in the debate are firmly fixed in the liberal demo-cratic firmament. Is the progressive stance—the separation of church and state taken seriously and pushed far—more or less liberal than the con-servatives' non-coercion, individual private choice, free speech principle, or neutrality standards? It is hard to see how one could answer such a ques-tion; on the Court's presentation of the issues, liberalism seems simply to be at odds with itself.

Such an interpretation is not without some basis, but it is also impor-tant not to exaggerate the complexity or confusion of the Court's position.

42. *Lee v. Weisman.*

43. *Marsh v. Chambers;* for the "reasonable observer" test, see O'Connor's concurrence in *Cap-itol Square Review Board v. Pinette* 515 U.S. 753 (1995); for "acknowledgment" and "ceremonial de-ism," see her concurrence in *Elk Grove Unified School District v. Newdow* 542 U.S. 1 (2004).

First Amendment scholar Carl Esbeck is fundamentally correct when he insists that the post-*Smith* Court "is not at all in chaos" when it comes to Free Exercise clause jurisprudence.[44] In Establishment clause cases, much of the complexity on the conservatives' side arose from Justice O'Connor's reluctance to go all the way down the accommodationist path, and her departure alone will likely simplify things.

But a more forceful answer to the charge of the messiness of the contemporary meaning of the First Amendment would be to insist upon a *political* analysis of the outlines of doctrinal debate, at which point the whole thing becomes extremely simple, with fairly easily identified separationist and accommodationist and in-between camps. The law itself here seems to cry out for a legal realist analysis: stop looking for coherent doctrines and count the votes, and then most of these cases are not in fact so hard to predict. But if an emphatically political approach to the First Amendment's religion clauses serves usefully to simplify and clarify what is going on legally, it does not for that reason reassure. The normal effects of the legal realist attitude—cynicism or, at best, a tendency to despair of the law's ability to reach moral principle—have begun to be felt even here, in connection with the Court's religion jurisprudence. To say that law is reducible to politics is always to question the language—general, moral—that the law wishes to speak.

The First Amendment in Question

That such an important area of law is confused in a way that everyone must admit has not gone unnoticed. The most striking result of the radicalization of the First Amendment that began in the 1940s has been the emergence, a half-century later, of a fairly extensive critique not just of the law, but of the moral and theoretical underpinnings of the idea of religious freedom as such. For a very long time, in the face of Marxist critiques of property, New Deal critiques of federalism, civil rights critiques of the public/private divide and freedom of speech, postmodernist critiques of the reason and universalism underlying liberal principle, the one thing in liberalism that seemed to stand above criticism was its foundational ideal of religious liberty. But the invitation to criticism engendered by the Court's

44. Carl H. Esbeck, "A Restatement of the Supreme Court's Law of Religious Freedom: Coherence, Conflict, or Chaos?" *Notre Dame Law Review* 70 (1995): 613.

disagreements and conflicting principles has given rise to a variety of often radical and harsh attacks on the basic building blocks of the liberal religion teaching. Something moving in the direction of serious dialectical encounter or refutation has begun to emerge as perhaps the most important consequence of enduring political and legal conflict over the question of religion in America.

Criticism of the basic underpinnings of Free Exercise clause jurisprudence has been especially pronounced since Scalia's provocative opinion in *Smith*. The beginnings of a critique of the foundational act/belief doctrine are not only visible in the musings of academics, but issue from the pen of Justice O'Connor as well. "[A] law that prohibits certain conduct . . . manifestly does prohibit that person's free exercise of his religion. A person who is barred from engaging in religiously motivated conduct is barred from freely exercising his religion."[45] Law professor Marci Hamilton goes so far as to say that it is "patently ridiculous" to say that "regulation which affects religious conduct does not affect belief."[46] "The question remains why the Court would choose to remain true to a distinction that is so at odds with religious reality wherein religious conduct is permeated with religious belief and highly important to the religious life."[47] If the act/opinion doctrine is false, if the regulation of action serves in effect to regulate opinion, then the liberal religion teaching would serve to transform religion while claiming to protect it.

Stephen Carter helps to illuminate all that is at stake in the critique of the act/belief distinction in his prominent book *The Culture of Disbelief.* The beliefs of religion and politics (or the state) have something very important in common when it comes to *moral* claims, but "even today, more than two centuries after the Enlightenment, we have no settled rules by which to determine their truth."[48] The problem with contemporary jurisprudence is that "religious ways of knowing are relegated to inferior status in the justification of moral and factual claims."[49] Above all, by not giving

45. *Employment Division v. Smith*, 893.

46. Marci Hamilton, "The Belief/Conduct Paradigm in the Supreme Court's Free Exercise Jurisprudence," *Ohio State Law Journal* 54 (1993): 759.

47. Ibid., 771–72; see also 765–66. She has since changed her mind; see also Marci Hamilton, *God vs. the Gavel: Religion and the Rule of Law* (New York: Cambridge University Press, 2005).

48. Stephen L. Carter, *The Culture of Disbelief: How American Law and Politics Trivialize Religious Devotion* (New York: Harper, 1993), 214–15.

49. Ibid., 213.

the claim to *moral* knowledge of religion due weight, the liberal secular state in effect must "treat it as false."[50] To insist on the primacy of the (necessarily moral) authority of the state in its conflicts with religious moral belief "is to trivialize the idea that faith matters to people."[51]

If the act/belief doctrine is false, and if it trivializes religion, what *is* the theoretical ground of the liberal state's authority when it must deny to religion its claims, especially its moral claims? The answer cannot be "neutrality." Neutrality is an idea employed (though understood differently) by separationists and accommodationists alike in the Court's Establishment clause as well as its Free Exercise clause cases. Perhaps as a result, critiques of neutrality are by now legion. Carter, for example, wrote an essay in 1987 seeking "to expose the contradictions at the heart of the liberal theory of neutrality toward religion."[52] But Steven D. Smith's exhaustive treatment makes the point most forcefully. Every account of neutrality begins from some perspective that is not, and indeed cannot be, neutral in its judgments: "there is no neutral vantage point that can permit the theorist or judge to transcend these competing perspectives."[53] Smith goes further, extending this analysis to the very ideal of religious freedom itself: "The function of a theory of religious freedom is to mediate among a variety of competing religious and secular positions and interests, or to explain how government ought to deal with these competing positions and interests. To perform that function, however, the theory will tacitly but inevitably privilege, or prefer in advance, one of those positions while rejecting or discounting others."[54]

The main line of attack of the Court's Establishment clause thinking is to question the public/private divide that undergirds it. Critiques of the public/private divide are familiar from New Deal battles over the private business sector and from recent feminist theory, but those earlier criticisms were tailored to the political battles being waged at the moment. Now it is conservatives who insist, with Frederick Mark Gedicks, that the public/private divide merely "reflects an experience of the world filtered through

50. Ibid., 220.

51. Ibid., 37–38.

52. Stephen Carter, "Evolutionism, Creationism, and Treating Religion as a Hobby," *Duke Law Journal* (1987): 978.

53. Steven D. Smith, *Foreordained Failure: The Quest for a Constitutional Principle of Religious Freedom* (New York: Oxford University Press, 1995), 97.

54. Ibid., 63.

secular individualist discourse, not the disinterested discovery of essential meaning or preinterpretive reality."[55] Borrowing again from progressives, Gedicks and others insist that the demarcation of religion as "private" brings about the marginalization or exclusion of religious groups. "The privatization of religion by secular individualist discourse is an act of power that can plausibly be defended as religiously neutral only if religion is presented as a 'naturally' private activity, excluded from public life."[56] In other words, the separation of church and state amounts to discrimination against religion—and "[f]ew indictments of government policy are more powerful in the contemporary United States than a demonstration that policy discriminates unfairly."[57]

Most of the critics so far mentioned are ultimately defenders of some version of the First Amendment. But Gedicks introduces another dimension of critique since he argues explicitly from a postmodernist perspective, pointing to a more radical plane of engagement altogether. Through postmodernism, the critique of the First Amendment begins to become entangled with a much broader attack on the universalistic accounts of human reason and human nature upon which liberalism rests. Judd Owen's masterful account of the encounter between postmodernism and contemporary liberals such as John Rawls on the question of religion does not inspire confidence in liberalism's ability to stand up to such criticism.[58] Moreover, the tendency of religion's defenders to embrace postmodernism against the perceived hostility of modern liberal rationalism may reflect an unsettling broader trend. Wilfred McClay notes a "fascinating convergence of what might very loosely be called 'fundamentalist' and 'postmodern' perspectives, each very hostile to secularism, in the emergence of 'postliberal' Christian theologies."[59]

55. Gedicks, *Rhetoric of Church and State,* 32.

56. Ibid., 43.

57. Ibid.; see Carl H. Esbeck, "A Constitutional Case for Governmental Cooperation with Faith-Based Social Service Providers," *Emory Law Journal* 46 (1997): 21–22; Stanley Fish, "Mission Impossible: Settling the Just Bounds between Church and State," *Columbia Law Review* 97 (1997): 2279–83; Ira C. Lupu, "The Lingering Death of Separationism," *George Washington Law Review* 62 (1994): 258–59; Michael McConnell, "'God Is Dead and We Have Killed Him!': Freedom of Religion in the Post-modern Age," *Brigham Young University Law Review* (1993): 183–84.

58. In discussing postmodernism and religion I rely generally on J. Judd Owen, *Religion and the Demise of Liberal Rationalism* (Chicago: University of Chicago Press, 2001).

59. Wilfred M. McClay, "Two Concepts of Secularism," in *Religion Returns to the Public Square: Faith and Policy in America,* eds. Hugh Heclo and Wilfred M. McClay (Baltimore: Johns Hopkins University Press, 2003), 39.

Postmodernists raise the stakes in the controversy over the First Amendment to the level of the ultimate ground of liberalism's claim to contain and limit the place of religion in political life. American liberalism of any stripe rests on a theoretical foundation that does not trace its fundamental insights to any revealed religion. What is the basis of this momentous step? Stanley Fish brings the broader question to bear on the question of the separation of church and state in an essay appropriately entitled, "Mission Impossible: Settling the Just Bounds between Church and State." Fish begins by harvesting the critiques that arose more narrowly, out of the frustrations of legal conflict and confusion; he makes use of the work of Hamilton, Carter, and Smith and an array of others, but is dissatisfied with their half-heartedness: "For all the radical talk, what we have here is liberalism all over again."[60] His object is to radicalize such critical insights into a broader assault on the basic ideas undergirding liberalism and its rationalism altogether. Every argument in the language of an apparently neutral liberal rationalism for confining faith within certain bounds rejects the religious perspective. "There are no reasons you can give to the devout, not because they are the kind of people who don't listen to reason, but because the reasons you might give can never be reasons for them unless they convert to your faith or you convert to theirs."[61] For Fish, the real ground of liberalism's bounding in of religion is that of a brute "political" contestation in which appeals to general principle are ubiquitous but always exaggerations—or false. Fish is also of course famous for saying that "liberalism doesn't exist."[62] The critique of the First Amendment culminates, then, in the view that liberal secularism is merely one political imposition among many, no better and no worse than, say, theocratic impositions. Fish himself does not of course take the final step to advocate the overthrow of liberalism in the name of religion (according to Fish, no "conclusions" ever "follow" from antifoundationalist insight).[63] But other postmodernists in the grips of religion (or vice versa) will not necessarily be so restrained, as in the argument of Alistair McGrath's *The Twilight of Atheism:* "Yet there is a second part to the Greek myth, studiously overlooked by the apologists

60. Fish, "Mission Impossible," 2329.

61. Ibid., 2300.

62. Stanley Fish, *There's No Such Thing as Free Speech* (New York: Oxford University Press, 1994), 138.

63. Fish, "Mission Impossible," 2332–33.

of the Enlightenment. The gods retaliated when Prometheus stole their fire and gave it to humanity."[64]

The Limits of Originalism

The Court's attempt to involve itself in the legal and political struggles of religion in America has sullied and diminished the First Amendment. Can the Founders help? Their settling of the question certainly succeeded much better, for a long time and from almost every conceivable perspective, than did the radical secularist Court's fateful tinkering. The Founders have also been from the very beginning the authoritative source for the Court, and both secularists and accommodationists sift their writings and actions to vindicate their respective causes. The writings of Jefferson and Madison in particular stand very clearly at the origins of both the Court's Free Exercise and Establishment clause cases.[65] But there are very important limitations to any effort to try to find in the American Founders' perspective answers to our problems. The Founders did not contemplate the Supreme Court acting as a moral censor to enforce rigidly the provisions of the Bill of Rights throughout the land. Certainly none of the American Founders' statements about religious freedom pretends to offer a one-size-fits-all "solution" to the complex practical questions the Court has attempted to settle. Attempts to find support in the views of the Founders are further complicated by competing historical interpretations marshaled by separationists and accommodationists alike.[66] Since both sides appeal to an array of different principles, all of which are liberal, it would not be surprising if earlier analogues of all of them were readily available in some or another pronouncement or policy of some of the American Founders.

Conservatives would object that beginning from Jefferson and Madison, in particular, stacks the deck in favor of the separationists. Though their successful effort to disestablish the Anglican Church in Virginia is

---

64. Alister McGrath, *The Twilight of Atheism* (New York: Doubleday, 2004), 234–35.

65. See *Reynolds v. United States* and *Everson v. Board of Education*.

66. See, e.g., Robert S. Alley, *The Supreme Court on Church and State* (New York: Oxford University Press, 1988); Berns, *First Amendment;* Leonard W. Levy, *The Establishment Clause* (New York: Macmillan, 1986); Hamburger, *Separation of Church and State;* Isaac Kramnick and R. Lawrence Moore, *The Godless Constitution: The Case against Religious Correctness* (New York: W. W. Norton, 1996); Michael McConnell, "The Origins and Historical Understanding of Free Exercise of Religion," *Harvard Law Review* 103 (1990).

idea of a Supreme Being, governor, rewarder, and avenger."[76] Locke goes so far as to say that "the true ground of morality . . . can *only* be the will and law of a God, who sees in the dark, has in his hand rewards and punishments, and power enough to call to account the proudest offender."[77] Benjamin Franklin's profession of faith in the *Autobiography* is a compendium of these widely embraced views of the Enlightenment.[78] Even Rousseau, who disagreed with so many other aspects of the early modern program, insisted that a healthy society must have an official civil religion, the dogmas of which ought to include "the existence of a powerful God, intelligent, benevolent, foreseeing and providential, the life to come, the happiness of the just, the punishment of the wicked, the sanctity of the social contract and the laws."[79] One could extend this list as well to figures as diverse as Spinoza, Montesquieu, Kant, and, with some qualification, Adam Smith.[80] The claim of George Washington in his "Farewell Address" that "reason and experience both forbid us to expect that national morality can prevail in exclusion of religious principles" does not mark any doubt of the teachings of Enlightenment but is only another instance of its influence.[81]

This question of the connection between religion and politics by way of morality has never been an important part of the Court's thinking. Even conservatives seem to concede that the law must always serve a "secular purpose"; to suggest that the state needs divine support for its efforts is simply out of bounds. Seeming exceptions are justified by the Court tepidly, either from an argument from mere historical usage (Burger's defense of

76. Voltaire, "Atheist, Atheism, first section," in *Philosophical Dictionary,* vol. 1, trans. Peter Gay (New York: Basic Books, 1962), 103.

77. John Locke, *Essay Concerning Human Understanding,* vol. 1, ed. Alexander Campbell Fraser (New York: Dover Publications, 1959), 70, emphasis added; see also 475.

78. Benjamin Franklin, *The Autobiography of Benjamin Franklin* (New York: Random House, 1950), 91.

79. Jean Jacques Rousseau, "On the Social Contract," in *On the Social Contract, with Geneva Manuscript and Political Economy,* trans. Judith R. Masters, ed. Roger D. Masters (New York: St. Martin's Press, 1978), 131.

80. Benedict Spinoza, *A Theologico-Political Treatise,* trans. R. H. M. Elwes (New York: Dover Publications, Inc., 1951), 186–87; Montesquieu, *The Spirit of the Laws,* ed. and trans. Anne Cohler, Basia Miller, and Harold Stone (New York: Cambridge University Press, 1989), 465–81; Immanuel Kant, *Critique of Pure Reason,* ed. and trans. Paul Guyer and Allen W. Wood (New York: Cambridge University Press, 1998), 680; Adam Smith, *The Theory of Moral Sentiments* (Indianapolis: Liberty Classics, 1969), 269–82; Thomas L. Pangle, "Respondent, The Tanner Lecture," University of Toronto (October 1996).

81. George Washington, "Farewell Address," in *Writings,* ed. John Rhodehamel (New York: Library of America, 1997), 971.

legislative prayer) or from precisely the *harmlessness* of "ceremonial Deism" (O'Connor's view of "under God" in the pledge of allegiance).[82] Recognition of this dimension of the relation between religion and politics would not lead to any precise rules to settle every legal dispute, but it would at the very least suggest in general terms the doubtfulness and insobriety of a zealous insistence upon a principle of strict separation. Classical liberalism saw more clearly its own limits and prudently accommodated them.

But if the deepest stratum of early modern liberal thought might be used to question the reasonableness of the separationists on the American Court, is there not some way in which the achievement of the former helped to make possible and even perhaps likely the strivings of the latter? To be sure, the early modern effort to tame Christianity (whether one understands that to be merely a means or its end) was careful, appealing to religion directly, and always considerate of its dignity, where the separationist Court proved itself clumsy, impassioned, and unyieldingly principled. Early modern liberalism sought to influence Christianity through a variety of indirect means (historical biblical criticism, theological argumentation, and the new authorities of modern science, technology, commerce, democracy, and natural right) in addition to the doctrine of religious liberty. The early modern religion teaching did its most powerful work subtly: the exclusion of religion from direct legal or political authority (most clearly visible in the United States in the act/belief doctrine of Free Exercise clause jurisprudence) is presented precisely as a way of protecting religions from one another and from political domination—as religious "liberty."

But is it any surprise that in time the subtle and indirect taming (above all, the liberalizing) of religion led to a situation in which the party of liberty forgot religion's moral, social, and political importance and felt so bold as to draw certain conclusions in an indelicate way? Did the Founders never foresee the day when liberal moralism itself would attempt to rule unchecked by religion? If the Court's intervention suggests the inability of liberalism to fly on auto-pilot, is that not a problem for its more thoughtful originators? As Michael Zuckert observes, the Lockean project is fraught with tension, taking the "difficult position both of affirming the necessity of a civil religion and thus the continued dominance of a 'religious attitude,' no matter how transformed or reinterpreted, and of purveying ideas that undermine the possibility of the religious attitude and thus of civil

82. *Marsh v. Chambers; Elk Grove Unified School District v. Newdow.*

religion."[83] The early modern liberals were less dogmatic and more sensible on the question of religion and politics, and their effort was extraordinarily successful in the United States prior to the Supreme Court's meddling, but it is not clear how their resolution of things provides any simple solution to the questions that have now emerged.

Perhaps one could say that the principles underlying the First Amendment in the settlement of the religious question prior to the 1940s were always defined by a tension. The Supreme Court merely made that tension painfully obvious to everyone. Certainly it seems to have been the case that once the genie was out of the bottle, once secularism itself became the explicit principle of the Court, aggressively applied, there was no easy way to put it back. Clarence Thomas's radical (or fantastical) suggestion that we literally "go back" to the situation prior to 1947, where the Establishment clause did not apply to state and local government, has a certain appeal, but it underestimates the changes wrought by the Court over the past sixty years (it is also not embraced by other justices).[84] Perhaps in the end one is compelled to agree with Sanford Levinson and to say that America's *real* civil religion is its "constitutional faith," its adherence to the moral teachings of liberal ideology.[85] As the high priests of *this* civil religion, the separationists on the Court acted in the spirit of true believers, but the god of liberalism has not yet seen fit to reward their virtue.

83. Michael P. Zuckert, *Launching Liberalism: On Lockean Political Philosophy* (Lawrence: University Press of Kansas, 2002), 165.

84. See Thomas's concurrence in *Cutter v. Wilkinson* 544 U.S. 709, 726 (2005).

85. Sanford Levinson, *Constitutional Faith* (Princeton, N.J.: Princeton University Press, 1988).

10

The Personal (Is Not?) the Political

The Role of Religion in the
Presidency of George W. Bush

JOSEPH M. KNIPPENBERG

It is impossible to discuss the presidency of George W. Bush without taking into account the role that his religion plays in it. Pollsters have consistently found a "God gap" in the electorate, with frequent church-goers (who tend to be traditionalist) overwhelmingly approving of him and voting for him and those who rarely if ever darken the door of a sanctuary almost equally overwhelmingly opposed.[1] There is a perception, in other words, that religious traditionalists have "one of their own" in the White House. Commentators—especially those critical of the president—see untoward religious influence in a wide range of policies, from efforts to limit government support of stem cell research and to involve faith-based organizations in the provision of social services to a "moralistic" and "universalistic" approach to foreign policy that seems to focus a great deal of attention on lands traditionally associated with the Bible.[2] Others accuse President

An earlier version of this chapter appeared as "A President, Not a Preacher," *Claremont Review of Books* (Fall 2004).

1. A characteristic study is John C. Green et al., "The American Religious Landscape and the 2004 Presidential Vote: Increased Polarization," available at http://pewforum.org/publications/surveys/postelection.pdf. This study distinguishes between "traditionalist," "centrist," and "modernist" adherents of major Christian faith traditions (evangelical and mainline Protestants, and Roman Catholics), finding that Bush did extremely well among traditionalists, reasonably well among centrists, and poorly among modernists, not to mention those who are secular.

Some have argued that this gap is closing as the 2008 election nears. See, e.g., "Is the 'God Gap' Closing?" a transcript of a conversation with Amy Sullivan and E. J. Dionne Jr., available at http://pewforum.org/events/?EventID=171.

2. Kevin Phillips' *American Theocracy* (New York: Viking, 2006) is a case in point here. Other works that take a similar tack are Esther Kaplan, *With God On Their Side* (New York: New Press,

Bush of speaking in a sort of "code," using religiously inflected words and phrases that are intelligible only to the evangelical elect.[3]

In this chapter I explore the personal and political dimensions of George W. Bush's religiosity, showing both how he manages to distinguish the two and how his faith—so central to his character and self-understanding—cannot help but influence his political speeches and deeds. I do not mean hereby to argue that Bush is a "theocrat" who illegitimately imposes his religious views on an unwilling populace, but rather only that his presidency cannot be understood without taking into account the spiritual resources upon which he draws. I shall also argue that his understanding of religion in politics and the rhetoric he uses to express it are squarely within the tradition of American civil religion.

I will proceed largely by examining what President Bush has to say about the policies he pursues and his reasons for pursuing them, defending this focus on speeches for three reasons. First, those who demand that political leaders and other advocates offer "public reasons" for the policies they favor—assuming thereby that anything explicitly or implicitly religious is "private" and hence inadmissible in public debate and discussion—must in the first instance fairly examine the reasons offered. If they are "rational" and hence in principle accessible to the unaided reason of any human being, then they have passed an important test. One can argue with them and find them wanting, but they are not inadmissible or impermissible on the argument—now revealed as faulty—that they are not "public." As I shall demonstrate, President Bush's "religious" statements pass this test. As I put it in another context, he understands himself to be "a president, not a preacher."[4] Whether this is an appropriate test is a question I do not need to answer for the purposes of this discussion.[5]

2004), and Michelle Goldberg, *Kingdom Coming: The Rise of Christian Nationalism* (New York: W. W. Norton, 2006). In *The Theocons: Secular America under Siege* (New York: Doubleday, 2006), Damon Linker makes a similar argument. For a comprehensive and critical review of this body of argumentation, see Ross Douthat, "Theocracy! Theocracy! Theocracy!" *First Things* 165 (August/September 2006), 23–30. I have written about these matters in "Beltway Bigot," *American Enterprise* 17 (July/August 2006): 7; "Kevin Phillips's American Demagoguery," http://www.ashbrook .org/publicat/oped/knippenberg/06/phillips.html (April 28, 2006); and "Exile on Peachtree Road: 'Disenlightenment' and Theocracy in the New South," *American Enterprise Online,* available at http://www.taemag.com/issues/articleID.19143/article_detail.asp (April 19, 2006).

3. See, for example, Bruce Lincoln, "Words Matter: How Bush Speaks in Religious Code," *Boston Globe* (September 12, 2004), available at http://www.boston.com/news/globe/editorial_opinion/ oped/articles/2004/09/12/words_matter/.

4. See the note to the title of this paper.

5. I have dealt with this issue in "Religion and the Limits of Liberal Pluralism," in *Democracy*

Second, presidents often call upon our tradition of civic religion when they speak, especially on ceremonial occasions. In this connection, it is possible to demonstrate that President Bush, on occasions that might invite him to "preach," stays very close to the mainstream of presidential oratory.[6] Furthermore, by his speeches and deeds on these occasions he has sought to be inclusive, acknowledging, for example, Hanukkah and Ramadan, as well as the more traditional American occasions, like Thanksgiving and Christmas.

My third reason is connected with the first. Very frequently, President Bush's critics employ a "hermeneutic of suspicion," assuming that, whatever the "public" reasons offered, the *real* reasons are impermissibly religious.[7] Aside from the fact that this line of argument contradicts the premise underlying the "public reason" argument—that whatever other reasons a person might have, he or she must *also* be able to offer "public reasons"—it is essentially impossible to prove. We do not have immediate access to what a person believes in his or her heart. We might be able to compare speeches and deeds, and raise questions about the adequacy or directness of the connection, but that, at most, proves a confusion, and in any event requires, first of all, that we take the speeches seriously and understand them. In sum, the beginning of any effort to come to grips with the role of religion in the Bush administration begins with what President Bush has to say. That is where I shall begin.

Bush's Spiritual Journey

Much of Bush's spiritual biography is typical in the contemporary world of evangelical Protestantism. Throughout his life, he was "churched"

and Its Friendly Critics: Tocqueville and Political Life Today, ed. Peter A. Lawler (Lanham, Md.: Lexington Books, 2004), 111–24.

6. I have discussed this sort of presidential invocation of civil religion in the context of Thanksgiving proclamations. It can easily be shown that President Bush's proclamations are within the mainstream of those offered by all the inhabitants of the Oval Office. See my "Thanksgiving and Our Civic Religion," *American Enterprise Online* (November 23, 2005), "The Political Theology of Thanksgiving," www.ashbrook.org (November 23, 2005), and "Presidential Proclamations of Thanks," *American Spectator Online* (November 22, 2006).

7. For an excellent discussion of the deployment of this sort of argument in the abortion debate, see Ramesh Ponnuru, *The Party of Death* (Washington, D.C.: Regnery, 2006). I discussed the book in "Ramesh Ponnuru and the Discourse of Death," *American Enterprise Online,* available at http://www.taemag.com/issues/articleID.19167/article_detail.asp (May 10, 2006). See also notes 22 and 23 below.

in a variety of mainline denominations. As biographer Stephen Mansfield puts it:

He was baptized in a New Haven Episcopal church, trained for a decade in the First Presbyterian Church of Midland, and made to feel "stirrings of faith" in Saint Martin's Episcopal Church of Houston. During his Andover years, he was required to be in a Congregationalist-style chapel five times a week, which meant he spent as much time in church in those three years as a normal attender does in ten.[8]

Once he met Laura, he joined the Methodist church and was a dutiful pillar of First Methodist in Midland. But his faith was not deep and did not give him a direction in life.

What happened over the course of a few years in the mid-eighties, however, did. A series of encounters with evangelists, most notably Arthur Blessitt and Billy Graham, together with his serious engagement in one of the ubiquitous "small group" Bible studies, utterly transformed him.[9] By 1988, he was Bush senior's point man with the evangelical community, "talking to religious leaders in a language they understood."[10] Furthermore, over the course of those years he gained enough discipline and direction to eschew "the charms of Bacchus" and be freed to "live out those [Christian] truths far more powerfully than he must originally have imagined possible."[11]

This is not to say that Bush's newly deepened faith turned him into a profound theologian. As he told a Houston reporter in 1994, "I'm sure there is some kind of heavy doctrinal difference [between the Episcopal and Methodist churches], which I'm not sophisticated enough to explain to you."[12] His "spiritual" biographers are at pains to explain that Bush's faith is particularistic and experiential; it does not come from or result in a systematic engagement in doctrinal, ecclesiological, or theological questions. According to Mansfield, Bush "eschews the theoretical and prefers

8. Stephen Mansfield, *The Faith of George W. Bush* (New York: Jeremy Tarcher/Penguin, 2004), 59–60.
9. Paul Kengor notes that Bush is "uncomfortable using" the expression "born-again." See Paul Kengor, *God and George W. Bush: A Spiritual Life* (New York: Regan Books, 2004), 23.
10. Mansfield, *The Faith of George W. Bush*, 84.
11. David Aikman, *A Man of Faith: The Spiritual Journey of George W. Bush* (Nashville, Tenn.: W Publishing Group, 2004), 79, 80. On the effect of his faith on his drinking, see Kengor, *God and George W. Bush*, 25. It would not be misleading to attribute Bush's interest in the faith-based initiative, especially in dealing with matters of personal transformation, as at least in part an outgrowth of his own experience with overcoming his drinking problem.
12. Mansfield, *The Faith of George W. Bush*, 54.

the simple expressions that lead to action rather than complex theories that he thinks will lead to perpetual debate. . . . He has not grown in his faith by pondering theological problems or meditating on mystical abstractions. He has grown by watching his heroes, listening to stories and learning of the heavenly through earthly example."[13] David Aikman says that "[i]t is probable that he finds himself far more comfortable with a fluid, generic interpretation of the Christian faith than with a sharply stamped version of it."[14] Mansfield and Aikman both call him, in effect, a "mere Christian."[15] Kengor cites a Texas political associate who calls him "a New Testament kind of Christian," "a Sermon on the Mount type. He is not fire and brimstone."[16]

Of course, as noted above, George W. Bush's "mere Christianity," or "self-help Methodism" as one uncharitable critic put it,[17] does not in and of itself distinguish him from perhaps millions of other American evangelicals who talk the talk about walking the walk. Like many of his peers, Bush's newly deepened faith enabled him to focus on the trajectory of his life and find the discipline to live up to his responsibilities; without anything else, it would probably be hard to distinguish him from one of Bill McCarthy's Promise Keepers, whose sense of calling is above all reflected in their approach to their "faith, family, and friends."[18]

Of course, if one happens to be a politician, or if politics happens to be the family business, this approach to one's calling can be highly significant. In *A Charge to Keep*,[19] his 2000 campaign biography, Bush wrote that "[m]y faith frees me. Frees me to put the problem of the moment in proper perspective. Frees me to make decisions that others might not like. Frees me to do the right thing, even though it may not poll well. Frees me to enjoy life and not worry about what comes next."[20] As a (political) man of faith,

13. Ibid., 145, 155.
14. Aikman, *A Man of Faith*, 198.
15. Mansfield, *The Faith of George W. Bush*, 155; Aikman, *A Man of Faith*, 198.
16. Kengor, *God and George W. Bush*, 30. See also Kengor, 35: "It has been said that he mixes a Wesleyan theology of personal transformation and personal relationship with God with a Calvinist understanding of a God who has laid out a 'divine plan.'"
17. This is Jim Wallis's characterization in "Dangerous Religion: George W. Bush's Theology of Empire," *Sojourners Magazine* (September–October 2003). For a response to a related argument, see Kengor, *God and George W. Bush*, 27–28.
18. Aikman (*A Man of Faith*, 15–16) emphasizes the importance of this threesome for several generations of Bushes. See, for example, George W. Bush, *A Charge to Keep: My Journey to the White House* (New York: Harper Collins, 1999), 6.
19. See note 18 above.
20. Bush, *A Charge to Keep*, 6.

his principal constituent would seem to be God. In another passage from *A Charge to Keep*, Bush wrote that "I could not be governor if I did not believe in a divine plan that supersedes all human plans. . . . I've certainly never plotted the various steps of my life, certainly never campaigned for one office to try to position myself for the next."[21]

Taken together with the famous story of his sense that he was called to seek the presidency,[22] this attitude might seem unsettling, indeed downright scary, to some secularists. Here is an officeholder who understands himself as answering above all to God, who seems to have come to believe that he was put on earth to be president, perhaps even during a time of grave crisis. Might not George W. Bush as president be rigid, self-righteously moralistic, and inclined to trust his own intuitions above the advice of experts and the suggestions of allies? Might he not be tempted to use the presidential "bully pulpit" as a literal pulpit from behind which he could bully dissenters?

Religion in the Bush Administration

While some of President Bush's critics display a propensity to attribute virtually every decision of which they disapprove to his (impermissible) religious motives,[23] he has been quite careful in his public expressions.[24] When speaking about his own faith, for example, he has stressed the way in which it humbles him. As he said in his first address to the Presidential

21. Ibid., 6.

22. See the slightly different accounts in Aikman, *A Man of Faith,* 109–10, and Mansfield, *The Faith of George W. Bush,* 107–8. Of course, President Bush is not alone in his "vocational" approach to public office, as an account of Rep. Denise Majette's decision in 2004 to seek the Democratic nomination for the U.S. Senate seat from Georgia demonstrates. See Ben Smith, "Majette's Quantum Leap of Faith," *Atlanta Journal-Constitution* (July 11, 2004).

23. See, for example, University of Chicago Law Professor Geoffrey Stone's characterization of President Bush's veto of stem cell legislation as based upon "simply his own, sectarian religious belief," despite the fact that the president's veto message made no mention of religion. The president's veto message is available at http://article.nationalreview.com/?q=ODVlZWQwYzViMWV VhMTRkODhiOTI4NmUrYzJlNmVlNmU=; Stone's blog comments, entitled "Religious Rights and Wrongs," are available at http://uchicagolaw.typepad.com/faculty/2006/07/religious_right.html#more.

24. The speechwriter who seems to have exercised the greatest influence over President Bush's public expressions is Michael Gerson, profiled by Carl M. Cannon, "Soul of a Conservative," *National Journal* (May 14, 2005), available at http://www.religionandsocialpolicy.org/news/article_print.cfm?id=2753, and Jeffrey Goldberg, "The Believer," *New Yorker* (February 13/20, 2006), available at http://www.newyorker.com/fact/content/articles/060213fa_fact1. A transcript of a conversation between Gerson and a number of journalists, at an event hosted by the Pew Forum on Religion and Public Life on December 6, 2004, can be found at http://pewforum.org/events/index.php?EventID=67.

Prayer Breakfast on February 1, 2001, "Faith teaches humility . . . [a] recognition that we are small in God's universe yet precious in His sight."[25] On the same occasion the next year, he asserted that "[f]aith teaches humility, and with it, tolerance. Once we have recognized God's image in ourselves, we must recognize it in every human being."[26] Biographer Paul Kengor glosses this statement in the following way: "Because every person is made in the image of God . . . believer and non-believer alike are all due respect and dignity by those who believe in God."[27] He also notes the manner in which Bush has been ecumenical in his approach to acknowledging faith in the White House—celebrating Christian, Jewish, and Muslim holidays, among others.[28]

On yet another occasion (May 1, 2003), he said, "Prayer teaches humility. We find that the plan of the Creator is sometimes very different from our own. Yet, we learn to depend on His loving will, bowing to purposes we don't always understand."[29] "We cannot," he says, "presume to know every design of our Creator, or to assert a special claim on His favor."[30] President Bush does not regard himself as in control of his own destiny, let alone the destiny of the nation as a whole. He does not simply trust either his reason or his instincts, but reminds himself constantly, through prayer,[31] of his fallibility and that of all human beings.

25. Thomas M. Freiling, ed., *George W. Bush on God and Country* (Fairfax, Va.: Allegiance Press, 2004), 197.

26. Ibid., 36. Kengor (*God and George W. Bush,* 62–63) quotes a telling passage from a 1999 interview with *U.S. News and World Report:*

> It's really important for someone in my position to live the word, in this case, but also understand that people communicate with God and reach God in different ways. It just doesn't have to be my way. And I think it's really important if you're trying to unite a nation that is as diverse as ours to spend more time living the example I've learned of Christ as opposed to lecturing. And I really mean that. . . . And I am mindful of what Billy Graham one time told me: try not to figure out—try to pick and choose who gets into heaven. . . . It is very important for people to not be haughty in their religion. And there's all kinds of admonitions in the Bible; haughtiness, rightfulness is a sin in itself. . . . Billy Graham said, "Don't play God." I don't get to determine who goes to heaven and who goes to hell.

See also Bush's 2000 Republican National Convention speech, quoted by Kengor (72): "I believe in tolerance, not in spite of my faith, but because of it. I believe in a God who calls us not to judge our neighbors, but to love them."

27. Kengor, *God and George W. Bush,* 106.

28. Ibid., 108–10; cf. also 136–45.

29. Freiling, *George W. Bush on God and Country,* 70.

30. Ibid., 117.

31. On President Bush's prayer and devotional life, see Mansfield, *The Faith of George W. Bush,* 119–21, Aikman, *A Man of Faith,* 158, and an interview with a number of Christian journalists and

President Bush's constant reflection on human weakness and finitude might be taken by some as a counsel of despair, but he quite regularly connects these themes with hope: "The promise of faith is not the absence of suffering; it is the presence of grace. And at every step we are secure in knowing that suffering produces perseverance, and perseverance produces character, and character produces hope—and hope does not disappoint."[32] On the occasion of the *Challenger* disaster, he said, "We can also be confident of the ways of Providence, even when they are far from our understanding. Events aren't moved by blind change and chance. Behind all of life and all of history, there's a dedication and purpose, set by the hand of a just and faithful God. And that hope will never be shaken."[33] Divine Providence gives us the hope that, within limits, events and people are intelligible to us and that, within limits, we can act effectively on behalf of the good and the right.[34]

But, one might object, President Bush's speeches reflect an essentially Christian worldview, one that does not resonate with, and perhaps even

---

intellectuals (May 28, 2004), posted at http://www.christianitytoday.com/global/printer.html?/ct/2004/121/51.0.html.

32. Freiling, *George W. Bush on God and Country*, 37.

33. Ibid., 77. See also the Pew transcript, where Gerson says: "The first category in which we use [religious language] is *comfort in grief and mourning,* and we've had too many of those opportunities: in the space shuttle disaster, 9/11, other things where people are faced with completely unfair suffering. And in that circumstance, a president generally can't say that death is final, and separation is endless, and the universe is an echoing, empty void."

34. See James W. Ceaser, "Providence and the President: George W. Bush's Theory of History," *Weekly Standard* (March 10, 2003), available at http://www.weeklystandard.com/Content/Public/Articles/000/000/002/315mmrvy.asp:

> One of [the] central themes [of Providence] is that the course of history, from a human standpoint, is unfathomable: "The Almighty has His own purposes." One conviction, however, remains supreme: While the path of events before us can never be fully known, and while there will always be difficulty and pain, Providence offers a basis for hope and a ground for avoiding despair. Yet it disclaims any pretension to know the future and offers no assurance of divine reward for our action in this world. At the practical level of human affairs, the focus remains on human responsibility and choice.

In the Pew transcript, Gerson says:

> The fifth category is a *reference to providence,* which some of the other examples have touched on. This is actually a longstanding tenet of American civil religion. It is one of the central themes of Lincoln's second inaugural. It's a recurring theme of Martin Luther King—"the arc of the moral universe is long, but it bends toward justice;" "we do not know what the future holds, but we know Who holds the future."
>
> The important theological principle here, I believe, is to avoid identifying the purposes of an individual or a nation with the purposes of God. That seems presumption to me, and we've done our best to avoid the temptation.

marginalizes or alienates, non-Christians at home and abroad.[35] As Mansfield notes, however, Bush's response to the events of 9/11 showed him as "president of a democracy rather than the 'preacher in chief' his critics thought him to be—and some on the Right wanted him to be."[36] Throughout his presidency, he has been careful to acknowledge his responsibility as the leader of a religiously pluralistic nation, addressing audiences at home and abroad who do not necessarily share his personal faith. "We welcome," he has said, "all religions in America, all religions. We honor diversity in this country. We respect people's deep convictions."[37] While he acknowledges that he has "a fantastic opportunity to let the light shine," he "will do so as a secular politician." His job, he says, "is not to promote a religion but to promote the ability of people to worship as they see fit."[38] He has dealt with America's (and the world's) religious pluralism by emphasizing the practical moral common ground that, he believes, all can share. Human beings can be good without faith, yet faith is a source of goodness for many.[39] Indeed, "faith without works is dead."[40] There is, he says, "a universal call, and that main universal call is to love your neighbor. It extends throughout all faith."[41] For Bush, the practical essence of all religion is "peace and love and compassion."[42] In another context, a sermon he preached as governor of Texas (March 6, 1999), he expressed his ecumenical vision in this way: "We must teach our children bedrock values—not the values of one religious denomination over another, but Judeo-Christian values that have stood the test of time. The importance of family. There are obligations to love your neighbor, give an honest day's work for an honest day's wages. Don't lie, do not cheat, do not steal. Respect others. Respect their opinions,

---

35. For an example of this criticism, see Jane Eisner, "President Bush's religious language may be heartfelt—but what if it's also exclusionary," *Philadelphia Inquirer* (February 11, 2003).

36. Mansfield, The Faith of George W. Bush, 142.

37. Freiling, *George W. Bush on God and Country*, 95.

38. See the interview cited above in note 31, as well as Freiling, *George W. Bush on God and Country*, 131: "Religious freedom is the cornerstone of our Republic, a core principle of our Constitution, and a fundamental human right." In a Beliefnet interview during the 2000 campaign, President Bush characterized his political responsibility in the following way: "[T]he president of the United States's job is to set an example, to make sound decisions, to respect religion, and, if asked, to herald religion," but "not to try to convert people to religion." Excerpts from this and other campaign 2000 interviews are posted at http://www.beliefnet.com/story/33/story_3345.html.

39. See Freiling, *George W. Bush on God and Country*, 82, 95.

40. Ibid., 82, 96.

41. Quoted in Aikman, *A Man of Faith*, 166; see also Freiling, *George W. Bush on God and Country*, 121.

42. See the interview cited above in note 31.

and remember, it's you who is [*sic*] responsible for the decisions you make in life."[43] One can call these affirmations an expression of natural law, common grace, or public reason. They are certainly, as he acknowledges, not specific to one cultural or religious tradition.[44] And they are, just as certainly, characteristic expressions of an *American* civic religion.[45]

Bush's famous invocation of the distinction between good and evil in the aftermath of 9/11 has, as noted above, also drawn the fire of critics.[46] Much of what he has had to say on the subject does not depart substantially from the tenor of Abraham Lincoln's condemnation of slavery: "if slavery is not wrong, nothing is wrong."[47] "Some worry," Bush said on June 1, 2002, "that it is somehow undiplomatic or impolite to speak the language of right and wrong. I disagree. Different circumstances require different methods, but not different moralities. Moral truth is the same in every culture, in every time, and in every place. Targeting innocent civilians for murder is always and everywhere wrong. Brutality against women is always and everywhere wrong. There can be no neutrality between justice and cruelty,

---

43. The speech is reprinted in Aikman, *A Man of Faith*, 205–13; the passage quoted comes from p. 211. In addition, as president, even before 9/11, Bush included mosques as part of America's religious mix. See Freiling, *George W. Bush on God and Country*, 191.

44. In the Pew transcript, Gerson puts it this way:

> We've tried to apply a principled pluralism; we have set out to welcome all religions, not favoring any religions in a sectarian way. I think that the president is the first president to mention mosques and Islam in his inaugural address. The president has consistently urged tolerance and respect for other faiths and traditions, and has received some criticism for it.
>
> We often in our presentations make specific reference to people who are not religious; we've done that right from the beginning. In our first prayer breakfast in February of 2001, we said an American president serves people of every faith and serves some of no faith at all. And there are plenty of other examples.

In Carl M. Cannon's judgment (also recorded in the Pew transcript), "George W. Bush has been by any standard more inclusive and less overtly religious than his predecessors. He is the most ecumenical of presidents—probably the most ecumenical president we've ever had." See also Carl M. Cannon, "Bush and God," *National Journal* (January 3, 2004), 12–18, available at http://nationaljournal.com/reprints/011504pew_cannon.pdf.

45. For a larger argument about the role of moral (and moralistic) rhetoric in the "Anglo-Saxon" world, see Walter Russell Mead, *God and Gold: Britain, America, and the Making of the Modern World* (New York: Alfred A. Knopf, 2007).

46. See, for example, Peter Singer, *The President of Good and Evil: The Ethics of George W. Bush* (New York: Dutton, 2004). For an alternative view defending the President's use of moral language, see James W. Ceaser, "Bush vs. Nietzsche: The Politics of Evil," *Weekly Standard* (April 1, 2002), available at http://weeklystandard.com/Content/Public/Articles/000/000/001/048vhwqw.asp. President Bush's speechwriter Michael Gerson also defends this language in his *Heroic Conservatism* (New York: Harper Collins, 2007), ch. 3.

47. Abraham Lincoln, Letter to A. G. Hodges, April 4, 1864.

between the innocent and the guilty. We are in a conflict between good and evil, and America will call evil by its name."[48]

While few other than the most abject and depraved apologists for terrorism can disagree with part of what Bush says here—the evils he identifies are real[49]—some might wonder about the other part of the dualism, which seems to abandon the humility that seems otherwise to characterize Bush's faith. Is America as good as terrorism is evil? Are we not at the very least all sinners in the sight of God, worthy of condemnation and in need of God's grace? Can we not identify and resist evil without calling ourselves unalloyedly good?[50]

In the immediate aftermath of 9/11, Bush went a step further, speaking of "our responsibility to history," which is "to answer these attacks and *rid the world of evil*."[51] Even if we are (relatively) good, as sinners go, to assert that we can actually rid the world of evil is to assert a superhuman power—the very antithesis of humility. Perhaps we could forgive President Bush and his speechwriters for misspeaking (and miswriting) in the heat of the moment, but he made a similar point in his West Point commencement address (June 1, 2002), where he promised to "lift this dark threat from our country and from the world."[52] It would seem to have been more in tune with the general tenor of his stance to speak of our responsibility to identify and resist evil wherever it appears, recognizing that it is part and parcel of our fallen human condition. Indeed, even in the September 14, 2001, speech he said that in "every generation, the world has produced enemies of human freedom,"[53] which suggests that the struggle against evil is ongoing.

But perhaps the President's hyperbole is, on one level, defensible. In his post-9/11 speeches, President Bush has developed what could almost be called a theology of history, beginning from the proposition that "[l]iberty is . . . the plan of Heaven for humanity," "the right and capacity of man-

---

48. Freiling, *George W. Bush on God and Country,* 263.

49. As Bush speechwriter Michael Gerson observes, "The use of the word *evil* had the virtue of being plainly accurate. The terrorists' worship of death, exhilaration at innocent suffering, and ambitions of genocide left them in a different category from 'political activist': more in the realm of 'serial killer.'" Gerson, *Heroic Conservatism,* 91.

50. To be sure, the President has admitted that "we don't own the ideals of freedom and human dignity, and sometimes we haven't always [*sic*] lived up to them" (Freiling, *George W. Bush on God and Country,* 76).

51. Ibid., 112; emphasis mine.   52. Ibid., 262.
53. Ibid., 114.

kind."[54] America was attacked because "we are freedom's home and defender."[55] "America has no empire to extend or utopia to establish. We wish for others only what we wish for ourselves—safety from violence, the rewards of liberty, and the hope for a better life."[56] We will prevail in our battle for freedom because, variously, "[t]he current of history runs strongly toward freedom," "our cause is just," we have the finest military, people the world over "want their liberty pure and whole," and, finally, "the author of freedom is not indifferent to the fate of freedom."[57] If indeed "the calling of our time" is "the advance of freedom," and if America is "freedom's home and defender," with a "special calling to promote justice and defend the weak and suffering of the world," then it is perhaps easy to understand how President Bush can speak so confidently of a conflict between good and evil.[58] But to act on behalf of the good is a burden and responsibility, rather than a description of everything we do.[59]

Furthermore, this identification of the United States with the cause of freedom around the world is by no means unique to President Bush; one need only recall President Kennedy's promise to "pay any price" and "bear any burden" to "assure the survival and success of liberty."[60] That Bush expresses this commitment in religious language emphasizes, above all, the

---

54. Ibid., 141, 151.

55. Ibid., 114.

56. Ibid., 260.

57. Ibid., 143, 152, 207, 214.

58. Ibid., 151, 255.

59. Consider, in this connection, Abraham Lincoln's words in his Second Inaugural (available at http://www.presidency.ucsb.edu/ws/index.php?pid=25819):

Both read the same Bible and pray to the same God, and each invokes His aid against the other. It may seem strange that any men should dare to ask a just God's assistance in wringing their bread from the sweat of other men's faces, but let us judge not, that we be not judged. The prayers of both could not be answered. That of neither has been answered fully. The Almighty has His own purposes. "Woe unto the world because of offenses; for it must needs be that offenses come, but woe to that man by whom the offense cometh." If we shall suppose that American slavery is one of those offenses which, in the providence of God, must needs come, but which, having continued through His appointed time, He now wills to remove, and that He gives to both North and South this terrible war as the woe due to those by whom the offense came, shall we discern therein any departure from those divine attributes which the believers in a living God always ascribe to Him? Fondly do we hope, fervently do we pray, that this mighty scourge of war may speedily pass away. Yet, if God wills that it continue until all the wealth piled by the bondsman's two hundred and fifty years of unrequited toil shall be sunk, and until every drop of blood drawn with the lash shall be paid by another drawn with the sword, as was said three thousand years ago, so still it must be said "the judgments of the Lord are true and righteous altogether."

60. The phrases are taken from President Kennedy's Inaugural Address, available at http://www.presidency.ucsb.edu/ws/index.php?pid=8032.

way in which it is part of our national heritage, going back to the Declaration of Independence.[61] In addition, by stressing liberty and consistently pointing to religious liberty, President Bush makes it impossible to identify his public invocations of religion with any particular denominational tradition.

President Bush's Second Inaugural

President Bush treated these themes comprehensively in his Second Inaugural Address.[62] There he identified America's cause with the cause of freedom:

America's vital interests and our deepest beliefs are now one. From the day of our Founding, we have proclaimed that every man and woman on this earth has rights, and dignity, and matchless value, because they bear the image of the Maker of Heaven and earth. Across the generations we have proclaimed the imperative of self-government, because no one is fit to be a master, and no one deserves to be a slave. Advancing these ideals is the mission that created our Nation. It is the honorable achievement of our fathers. Now it is the urgent requirement of our nation's security, and the calling of our time.

While he uses "theistic"—though not specifically Christian—language to describe the source of that freedom, he does so in a manner squarely within the tradition initiated by the Declaration of Independence. And while he speaks in terms of "mission" and "calling," both of which obviously have religious resonance, he does not depart much from similar language used by John F. Kennedy in his Inaugural Address:

And yet the same revolutionary beliefs for which our forebears fought are still at issue around the globe—the belief that the rights of man come not from the generosity of the state but from the hand of God.

We dare not forget today that we are the heirs of that first revolution. Let the word go forth from this time and place, to friend and foe alike, that the torch has been passed to a new generation of Americans—born in this century, tempered by war, disciplined by a hard and bitter peace, proud of our ancient heritage—and unwilling to witness or permit the slow undoing of those human

---

61. See Gerson, *Heroic Conservatism*, 106–7.

62. Delivered on January 20, 2005 and posted at http://www.whitehouse.gov/news/releases/2005/01/20050120-1.html. I discussed it in "Bush's Second Inaugural Address and Its (Dis)Contents," posted at http://www.ashbrook.org/publicat/oped/knippenberg/05/inaugural.html.

rights to which this nation has always been committed, and to which we are committed today at home and around the world.

Let every nation know, whether it wishes us well or ill, that we shall pay any price, bear any burden, meet any hardship, support any friend, oppose any foe to assure the survival and the success of liberty. This much we pledge—and more.[63]

Furthermore, President Bush recognizes that the calling is not one that is easily accomplished:

The great objective of ending tyranny is the concentrated work of generations. The difficulty of the task is no excuse for avoiding it. *America's influence is not unlimited,* but fortunately for the oppressed, America's influence is considerable, and we will use it confidently in freedom's cause.[64]

The confidence to which he refers seems to come from two sources. The first is anthropological: "Eventually," he says, "the call of freedom comes to every mind and every soul." The longing for freedom is sewn into human nature. While it can be repressed or effaced for a time, perhaps even a long time, nature will eventually reassert itself.[65] The second source of confidence is expressed in a passage quoted from Abraham Lincoln: "Those who deny freedom to others deserve it not for themselves; and, under the rule of a just God, cannot long retain it."[66] Our attachment to freedom is connected with a conception of justice. To adhere to principles of justice is to believe in a world that ultimately upholds these principles. While it is possible to make a claim of "justice" while self-consciously regarding it as absurd and utterly unsupported, there is a certain self-contradiction there. Justice implies mutual obligations, which in turn implies a capacity on the part of others to recognize and accept those obligations. A claim of justice, in other words, implies a conception of nature receptive to that claim.

63. See above, note 60. Gerson expresses his appreciation for this language and its role in his drafting of Bush's Second Inaugural Address on p. 224.

64. Emphasis mine.

65. See Gerson, *Heroic Conservatism,* 225.

66. Letter to Henry L. Pierce and others, April 6, 1859. The context of this letter is interesting, as it is written in response to an invitation to celebrate a festival in honor of the birthday of Thomas Jefferson. Lincoln discusses how some seek to deny and overturn "the principles of Jefferson," which are "the definitions and axioms of a free society." Despotism is a thing of the past, but it can be reestablished. Still, we should be grateful to Jefferson, who "had the coolness, forecast, and capacity to introduce into a merely revolutionary document, an abstract truth, applicable to all men and all times, and so to embalm it there, that to-day, and in all coming days, it shall be a rebuke and a stumbling-block to the very harbingers of re-appearing tyranny and oppression."

Tying justice to God adds another element to this understanding of a nature capable of being transformed by human effort. Rather than, for example, regarding nature as simply capable of receiving the impress of perhaps infinite human power, this line of argument suggests a finite human power cooperating with and working within the bounds of (a divinely created) nature. Justice is not whatever powerful human beings—individually or collectively—happen to say it is. It makes claims upon us because it is woven into the world by the Creator. In other words, a theistic conception of justice is the only conception that can consistently be connected to an understanding of human finitude. George W. Bush's—and Abraham Lincoln's—theism serves as the ground of a concern with justice that is neither absurd nor self-delusional, on the one hand, nor overweening, on the other.

Promoting freedom within a framework of justice requires both self-sacrifice and self-restraint. While the charms of freedom might appeal naturally, as it were, self-sacrifice and self-restraint have to be cultivated.[67] This leads to the domestic element of Bush's Second Inaugural, which continues a focus he has maintained since he was governor of Texas. He put it this way in a sermon he preached in 1999:

My dream is to usher in what I call the "responsibility era"—an era in which each and every Texan understands that we're responsible for the decisions we make in life; that each of us is responsible for making sure our families come first; that we're responsible for loving our neighbors as we'd like to be loved ourselves; and that we're responsible for the communities in which we live.[68]

He understood then and understands now that presidential leadership and government altogether are limited in what they can do to cultivate the re-

67. "The Bush agenda relies on a certain anthropology. It assumes that human flourishing, whether at home or abroad, is possible only when two conditions are met: first, the political and social freedom to choose one's own pursuits; and second, laws and social institutions to encourage individuals to choose *well*, that is, to live responsibly within self-imposed moral limits. Thus, full self-government is not possible under the yoke of a political or religious tyranny. But neither is it possible in a society in which the formation of character is left completely to chance, or when government policies sever the link between a person's actions and their consequences." Wilfred M. McClay, "Bush's Calling," *Commentary* (June 2005), 51. The text of McClay's lecture on "American Culture and the Presidency," on which this article is based, is available at http://www.eppc.org/conferences/pubID.2271,eventID.90/transcript.asp. I discussed the lecture in "George W. Bush's Conservatism," *American Enterprise Online* (November 2, 2005), available at http://www.taemag.com/issues/articleID.18813/article_detail.asp.

68. Aikman, *A Man of Faith*, 210.

sponsible use of liberty. As he said in his Second Inaugural, that task belongs, above all, to a healthy civil society:

In America's ideal of freedom, the public interest depends on private character— on integrity, and tolerance toward others, and the rule of conscience in our own lives. Self-government relies, in the end, on the governing of the self. That edifice of character is built in families, supported by communities with standards, and sustained in our national life by the truths of Sinai, the Sermon on the Mount, the words of the Koran, and the varied faiths of our people. Americans move forward in every generation by reaffirming all that is good and true that came before—ideals of justice and conduct that are the same yesterday, today, and forever.

The president can celebrate and call our attention to individual sacrifices.[69] He can offer praise and support for the institutions that cultivate character.[70] And he can single out, as he does quite frequently, those "values" that he believes all decent people, regardless of their religion (or irreligion), share:

[I]n our society strong values are shared by good people of different faiths, and good people who have no faith at all. These are universal values, values we share in all our diversity: Respect, tolerance, responsibility, honesty, self-restraint, family commitment, civic duty, fairness and compassion. These are the moral landmarks that guide a successful life.[71]

Thus he makes use of the resources of our various sacred and secular traditions to call us to sacrifice, to engage fully in our community.

But in his Second Inaugural, President Bush does not leave it at virtues conducive to self-reliance, on the one hand, and mutual toleration, on the other. There are also the virtues that constitute and maintain our community:

69. See, for example, his speech on Memorial Day 2006, given at Arlington National Cemetery, and posted at http://www.whitehouse.gov/news/releases/2006/05/20060529-1.html: "All who are buried here understood their duty. They saw a dark shadow on the horizon, and went to meet it. They understood that tyranny must be met with resolve, and that liberty is always the achievement of courage. . . . Here, in the presence of veterans they fought with and loved ones whose pictures they carried, the fallen give silent witness to the price of our liberty—and our nation honors them, this day and every day."

70. See, for example, President Bush's remarks to the White House Conference on Character and Community (June 19, 2002), available at http://www.whitehouse.gov/infocus/character/character-community-conf.pdf.

71. President Bush's remarks to the White House Conference on Character and Community, Proceedings, 5.

In America's ideal of freedom, the exercise of rights is ennobled by service, and mercy, and a heart for the weak. Liberty for all does not mean independence from one another. Our nation relies on men and women who look after a neighbor and surround the lost with love. Americans, at our best, value the life we see in one another, and must always remember that even the unwanted have worth.

While religious people and religious institutions surely do not have a monopoly on "service," "mercy," having "a heart for the weak," "surround[ing] the lost with love," and "remember[ing] that even the unwanted have worth," these concerns are central to the Judeo-Christian tradition.[72]

Still, rather than explicitly call upon us to study our Bibles and remember what we have been taught in our churches and temples, President Bush simply evokes those lessons in language that is intelligible and accessible to all. He draws upon a heritage that many share and that all who would be part of our community can (and, I would argue, must) appreciate. His language is not exclusive or marginalizing, but rather inclusive and hospitable.

Conclusion: George W. Bush and Civil Religion

From these considerations, it should be clear, first of all, that George W. Bush understands and presents himself as a flawed, fallible man of faith. This is certainly the source of some part of his attraction to those evangelical Christian voters who voted overwhelmingly for him. But as president, he has been careful not to speak in exclusively Christian terms. He affects, as it were, a "mere religiosity," calling upon principles and understandings that are certainly at home in the Christian tradition, but also arguably common to a wide range of other traditions. He certainly occasionally makes use of Christian language, but not in a devotional or exclusionary way. His purpose is, rather, to call upon cultural references common to a substantial portion of his audience. As speechwriter Michael Gerson explains,

A fourth category [of the president's employment of religious language] are *literary allusions to hymns and scripture.* In our first inaugural, we had "when we see that wounded traveler on the road to Jericho, we will not pass to the other side;"

72. See, for example, Deuteronomy 10:18 (God "executes justice for the fatherless and the widow, and loves the sojourner, giving him food and clothing."); Psalm 9:18 ("For the needy shall not always be forgotten, and the hope of the poor shall not perish forever."); and James 1:27 ("Religion that is pure and undefiled before God, the Father, is this: to visit orphans and widows in their affliction.")

or "there is power, wonder-working power in the goodness and idealism and faith of the American people" in the State of the Union.

I've actually had, in the past, reporters call me up on a variety of speeches and ask me where are the code words. I try to explain that they're not code words; they're literary references understood by millions of Americans. They're not code words; they're our culture. It's not a code word when I put a reference to T. S. Eliot's *Choruses From the Rock* in our Whitehall speech; it's a literary reference. And just because some don't get it doesn't mean it's a plot or a secret.[73]

I would argue that the most important function of the president's public theism is its capacity to qualify exclusive devotion to the nation and humble any overweening sense of human or national power. While he has on occasion been accused of apotheosizing the nation and attributing omnipotence to it,[74] the principal effect of his invocation of a deity is humbly to remind us that we are not simply masters of our own destiny and that we are to be judged by measures of which we are not the authors. The nation and its leaders may be called to a mission and be encouraged to elevated aspirations, but this mission and these aspirations are not presented as matters of arbitrary choice or national fiat. We the people can fall short and be held blameworthy for so doing.

73. See the transcript cited at note 24, as well as the similar discussion in Gerson, *Heroic Conservatism*, 100–106.

74. See Wallis, "Dangerous Religion"; for a more measured version of this criticism, see Peggy Noonan, "Way Too Much God," *Wall Street Journal* (January 21, 2005), available at http://www .opinionjournal.com/columnists/pnoonan/?id=110006184. McClay ("Bush's Calling," 53) also sounds a cautionary note: "There is a reason why the Christian tradition distinguishes between hope, which is considered a theological virtue, and optimism, which is not. Conservatism will be like the salt that has lost its savor if it abandons its mission to remind us of what Thomas Sowell has called 'the constrained vision' of human existence—the vision that sees life as a struggle full of unintended consequences and tragic dilemmas, involving people whose noblest efforts often fail, sometimes miserably so."

II

Sacred Words, Fighting Words

The Bible and National Meaning
in Canada, 1860–1900

PRESTON JONES

In 1839 Thomas Fowell Buxton argued that Britain needed to "atone" for the historic role it had played in the expansion of slavery. Around the same time John Williams, a British missionary in the South Pacific, said that Britons should plant a "tree of life" in the Pacific islands, around which civilization and commerce could entwine their tendrils. Meanwhile, Sir Charles Trevelyan wrote that teaching English to India's Hindus and Muslims amounted to a "sacred duty."[1]

These examples reveal some of the ways the language of the Bible, and ideas derived from it, was employed to different ends. In some cases these ends were manifestly noble—as in the call to atone for the sin of slavery. In other cases they were less obviously upright—as in arguments for the expansion of British commerce into the South Pacific and for English education in India. The simple point is that the conceptual world of Britain's nineteenth-century empire, which included Canada, was infused with the language of the Bible. What is also clear is that the Bible was put to ends its original authors never could have imagined for it.

Though many of them did not recognize it at the time, French- and English-speaking Canadians, or at least the intellectuals and public figures who spoke for them, drew from the same source when they sought words

A more extensive treatment of the topics raised in this chapter can be found in Preston Jones, *A Highly Favored Nation: The Bible and Canadian Meaning, 1860–1900* (Lanham, Md.: University Press of America, 2008).

1. See the documents in Jane Samson, *The British Empire* (Oxford: Oxford University Press, 2001), 127, 131 and 133.

to define themselves. That source was the Bible. For Protestants, generally speaking, the Bible was a text read privately at home and corporately at church. The Bible was meant to be available to everyone. Protestant Canadian identity revolved around "an open Bible" and its handmaidens, private judgment and a "free and full Gospel."[2] For Protestants, free, unobstructed access to the Bible was as much a mark of progress as railroads, steamships, and printing presses.[3]

For most of Canada's French-speaking Catholics, the Bible was a text read by the priest at Mass and illustrated in stained glass windows, architecture, statuary, and iconography. At the time of the Confederation of Canada in 1867, only about half of French-Quebec's population was literate. That percentage would rise considerably through the nineteenth century,[4] but by 1901 some 22 percent of Quebecers of school age and higher were still unable to read.[5] Yet references and allusions to biblical passages and stories were everywhere. Sculptures of Saints Peter and Paul, with sacred texts in hand, emphasized their status as men of the Book.[6] And statues of prominent clerics such as Abbé Pierre-Marie Mignault, missionary to the Micmacs in Halifax and curé in Chambly, Quebec, pointed to the centrality of sacred texts in Quebec's history; statuary often depicted a minister engaged in reading and explaining, if not the Bible itself, then a religious work dependent on the Bible.[7]

2. Jonathan Shortt, *The Gospel Banner! A Sermon Preached to the Loyal Orange Lodges, Assembled in St. John's Church, Port Hope, July 12th, 1853* (Montreal: Wilsons and Noland, 1853), 2.

3. In *The Seat of Empire* (Boston: Fields, Osgood, 1870), Charles Carleton Coffin wrote: "Railroads, steamships, school-houses, printing-presses, free platforms and pulpits, an open Bible, are the propelling forces of the nineteenth century" (231–32). Coffin was an American, but the words could easily have been written by a Protestant Canadian.

4. One reason for this in the first few decades of the century was that, generally speaking, the clergy themselves were poorly educated. As the decade wore on, however, priests played a greater role in promoting education. In his observations on life in the parish of Saint-Irénée, written in 1861–62, Gauldrée-Boilleau noted that "L'éducation n'est pas aussi avancée à Saint-Irénée qu'on serait en droit de le souhaiter. Il n'y a guère que les adolescents qui sachent lire et écrire." But "[g]râce au zèle des curés, on a réussi à fonder dans la commune de Saint-Irénée trois-écoles: deux sont élémentaires; la troisième est une école-modèle dont la création date de l'an dernier. Ces établissements sont fréquentés par les deux tiers des enfants appartenant à la paroisse. On y apprend à lire, à écrire et à calculer, de même qu'en France dans les écoles primaires." In Pierre Savard, ed., *Aspects de la civilisation canadienne-française* (Ottawa: Editions de l'Université d'Ottawa, 1983), 25–26.

5. A. I. Silver, *The French Canadian Idea of Confederation, 1864–1900* (Toronto: University of Toronto Press, 1982), 29.

6. See Musée du Québec, *L'Art du Québec au lendemain de la Conquête, 1760–1790* (Quebec: Musée du Quebec, 197), 45.

7. See Bruno Hébert, *Monuments et patrie: Une réflexion philosophique sur un fait historique: La célébration commémorative au Québec de 1881 à 1929* (Québec: Les éditions pleins bords, 1980), 356.

The iconography in Ottawa's Notre-Dame Cathedral cannot be taken as representative for all of French-speaking Canada's Catholic churches, though in the late nineteenth century, when the cathedral was completed, comparable places of worship were built in Quebec.[8] Ottawa's cathedral, built and expanded between 1839 and 1885, does provide some insight into the extent to which an illiterate layman could be exposed to Bible stories.[9] In addition to the sculptures one would expect to see of the Virgin Mary, of the baby Jesus surrounded by shepherds and angels, and of the crucifixion the resurrected Christ, the cathedral offered images of John the Baptist, Peter, Paul, Luke, John the evangelist, Mark, and the apostle James. There is a sculpture of Abel, offering a sacrifice to God; of Abraham with a walking staff, marching to the promised land; of Isaac carrying the sticks Abraham, his father, would use to start a sacrificial fire; of Joseph, carrying in one arm the grain that saved Israel's forefathers from starvation; of Moses, holding the law of God written on two stone tablets.[10] Explanations of these images would provide a parishioner, literate or not, with a wealth of biblical knowledge. For Catholics, images such as these were the "books of the illiterate."[11]

At the time, many Protestants viewed this communal, image-based approach to the Bible as the abnegation of the Bible. The Bible is a *book,* the historian hears them say, it ought to be read. And since it was not widely read in Catholic Quebec, Protestants considered the province a Bible-free zone. But they were wrong: Catholic Quebecers' cultural identity, like the Protestants', was shaped by biblical language and themes.[12]

Even if the number of people who put personal faith in the Bible was diminishing as the nineteenth century slipped into the twentieth—partly as a result of Darwinism and biblical criticism[13]—it would be difficult to over-

8. For example, the cathedral of the Immaculate Conception in Trois-Rivières (1858), the church of Saint-François-Xavier in Batiscan (1863), and Sainte-Anne-de-la-Pérade (1869).

9. Norman Pagé, *La cathédrale Notre-Dame d'Ottawa: Histoire, architecture, iconographie* (Ottawa: Les presses de l'Université d'Ottawa, 1988), 153–57.

10. Ibid., 118–23.

11. Christopher Hill, *The Bible and the Seventeenth-Century Revolution* (New York: Penguin, 1993), 14. What Hill writes of seventeenth-century English men and women can be said of nineteenth-century French Quebec: "Men and women who had never opened a Bible would be well acquainted with many of its best stories, with the commandments and the beatitudes, and with moral exhortations based on the Bible" (39).

12. See Preston Jones, "Protestants, Catholics and the Bible in Late-Nineteenth-Century Quebec," *Fides et Historia* 33, no. 2 (Summer/Fall 2001), 31–38.

13. See A. B. McKillop, *A Disciplined Intelligence: Critical Inquiry and Canadian Thought in the Victorian Era* (Montreal-Kingston: McGill-Queen's University Press, 2001).

state the Bible's cultural presence among Canadians. The daily outlook one experienced among, say, Protestants in Halifax and Catholics in Rimouski would have seemed strikingly different. But a foundational source of these outlooks—the Bible—was the same. The extent to which Canada's Protestants and Catholics believed what the Bible said—and the ways in which they believed in it—cannot be stated here and, in any event, is probably unknowable. The Bible's presence as a basic cultural source, however, seems clear.

The Bible was the first book many Canadians knew well; it provided their first exposure to poetry, history, grammar, and, of course, theology.[14] In 1870, nearly 4,000 of Ontario's 4,566 schools reported that pupils read the Bible during school hours,[15] and portions of the Bible were printed in grammar books.[16] The textbook *Lessons on the Truth of Christianity* was used in Ontario's public schools.[17] And in a widely circulated speech given

14. Terrence Murphy and Roberto Perin, eds., *A Concise History of Christianity in Canada* (Toronto: Oxford University Press, 1996), 144, 159. Also see John S. Moir, "The Upper Canadian Religious Tradition," in *Profiles of a Province: Studies in the History of Ontario,* ed. Ontario Historical Society (Toronto: Ontario Historical Society, 1967), 193. On the secularization of Ontario's public schools see R. D. Gidney and W. P. J. Millar, *Inventing Secondary Education: The Rise of the High School in Nineteenth-Century Ontario* (Montreal-Kingston: McGill-Queen's University Press, 1990), 92–93. Given the detail of Gidney and Millar's text, it is somewhat surprising that they never take up a discussion of the Bible in Ontario's schools. Given their attention to the thought of Egerton Ryerson, who wrote forthrightly on the Bible in the schools, this omission is all the more perplexing.

15. Egerton Ryerson, *Annual Report of the Normal, Grammar and Common Schools in Ontario for the Year 1870* (Toronto: Hunter, Rose, 1871), 8.

16. In his *Introduction to the Analytical and Practical Grammar of the English Language* (Toronto: Adam Miller, 1865) the Rev. Peter Bullions provides exercises, often drawing on the Bible, though he does not cite his biblical sources. In one place, for example, he gives the sentence "Remember the Sabbath day, to keep it" (Exodus 20:8). The Beatitudes found in the Gospel of Matthew are excerpted (60). Also see, for example, p. 76 ("Cain wickedly slew his brother"—Genesis 4:8) and p. 89 ("The fear of the Lord is the beginning of wisdom"—Proverbs 1:7). Biblical passages appear frequently in J. D. Morell's *Series of Graduated Exercises* (London: Longman's, Green, 1857). See, for instance, p. 24: "Except ye repent ye shall all likewise perish" (Luke 13:3) appears. Also see Council of Public Instruction for Ontario, *The Spelling Book: Companion to Readers* (Toronto: James Campbell and Son, 1868), 33 and 37; and G. Brown, *The Institutes of English Grammar* (New York: Samuel S. and William Wood, 1861), 125, 143, 173, 181. See sections 1 through 5 (pp. 13–24) in Council of Public Instruction for Upper Canada, *Second Book of Lessons: For the Use of Schools* (Toronto: Robert McPhail, 1864), where the biblical stories of creation, Adam and Eve, Cain and Abel and the flood are recounted. One history text which drew heavily on the Bible was the Religious Tract Society's *British North America* (London: Religious Tract Society), the introduction of which begins with the sentence, "The chief end of man is to glorify God" (1), and then relates a scriptural account of Christian salvation history.

17. Direction of the Commissioners of National Education, *Lessons on the Truth of Christianity, Being an Appendix to the Fourth Book of Lessons, For the Use of Schools* (Dublin: Armour and Ramsay, 1846).

in 1867 titled "The Mental Outlook of the New Dominion," the parliamentarian Thomas D'Arcy McGee praised the "Book of books," as "the rarest and most unequaled [book] as to matter."[18] The same year a Montreal newspaper praised the Bible as "the schoolboy's spelling book, and the learned man's masterpiece; it contains a choice grammar for a novice, and profound treatise for a sage; it is the ignorant man's dictionary, and the wise man's directory. It affords knowledge of witty inventions for the ingenious, and dark sayings for the grave; and it is its own interpreter."[19] In 1893 Ontario's education minister observed that Canada wanted virtuous men who took the Bible as their charter of faith.[20] And when, twenty-six years earlier, Lord Charles Stanley Monck took his oath of loyalty to Queen Victoria as the Dominion of Canada's first governor general, his left hand lay on a Bible.[21] The new country took its motto, "A mari usque ad mare," from a passage in Psalm 72: "And he shall have dominion from sea to sea and from the river even unto the ends of the earth."

In Quebec the Bible's presence was less verbal but no less public. Many of its towns are named after saints, and statues of the crucified Christ were, and remain, seemingly everywhere.[22] Quebec's grammar books also included scriptural passages designed to teach reading, writing, morals, and the rudiments of Catholic theology.[23]

Identity

The day after the Confederation of Canada in July of 1867, the *Halifax Express* rejoiced that the British American provinces, "speaking the same language, [and] animated by the same feelings" had united and joined the

18. Thomas D'Arcy McGee, "The Mental Outfit of the New Dominion," printed in the *Montreal Gazette,* November 5, 1867.

19. The *Presbyterian* (Halifax) (August 1867), 256.

20. George W. Ross, *Patriotic Recitations and Arbor Day Exercises* (Toronto: Warwick Brothers and Rutter, 1893), 109.

21. Reported in the *Unionist* (Halifax), July 12, 1867, 2.

22. Savard, *Aspects de la civilization canadienne-française,* 161.

23. See for example, n.a., *Le livre des enfans* [sic]; *nouvel alphabet français* (Quebec: Imprimerie de Edward S. Pooler, 1850), 37–39; and Jean Palairet, *Nouvelle methode pour apprendre a bien lire* (Quebec: William Cowan et fils, 1847), 77–78, 85–93. In his memoirs Charles Chiniquy recalled: "Avant de quitter le séminaire de Québec, mon père avait reçu du supérieur, comme marque d'estime, une très belle Bible française et latine. Cette Bible fut le premier livre, apres l'A B C, dans lequel ma mère me fit lire. Elle choisissait les chapitres qu'elle croyait les plus propres a m'intéresser, et je les lisais avec une attention et un plaisir incroyables." See *Chiniquy* (Québec: Editions Beauport, 1989).

ranks of nations.[24] One could already detect disunity in the newspaper's optimism. The French- and Gaelic-speakers of Cape Breton and Nova Scotia would steadily dwindle in number over time, but the French of Quebec would not. And while the division of Canada into "English" and "French" is simplistic, at the level of generality (and for the purposes of this chapter) the division holds. To be a French-speaking Canadian was to be different from an English-speaking Canadian.

The difference was not merely one of language. When Quebec's French intellectuals and provincial public figures wondered what French Canadians were *for*—when they wondered what the French Canadian's place in the world was—they arrived at answers quite different from those offered by English-speaking writers and speakers. But—to stick with the simple division—both sides relied on the Bible. Both sides knew they were special— more special than the other. They knew this because the Bible told them so.

English-speaking and Franco-Canadians were chosen peoples. The former were chosen because they were part and parcel of the British Empire, which, "like that mighty tree described by the Prophet," had spread godly roots around the globe.[25] The latter were special because they had picked up where ancient Israel (the chosen nation of old) had left off.[26] Protestant Canadians were special, some said, because they honored the Sabbath and the family more than any other people on earth.[27] French-Canadian Catholics were special because Quebec was "the instrument chosen by Providence to evangelize the American continent, to instruct the ignorant, help the poor, care for the sick, [and] guide children on the right path of life."[28]

The fact that assertions such as these prove nothing and that they strike the twenty-first-century reader as quaint nonsense should not prevent us from seeing that the claims were meaningful to those who made them. The ubiquity of such professions in public statements about the meaning of Canada suggests that Canadians took them seriously as metaphors if not always as literal truths.

24. Article in the *Halifax Express* republished in the Pictou, Nova Scotia, *Colonial Standard*, July 2, 1867, 2.

25. *Evening Express*, July 3, 1867. See Ezekiel 31:3–9.

26. Louis François Laflèche, *Quelque considérations sur le rapports de la société avec la religion et la famille* (1866), excerpted in *French Canadian Nationalism: An Anthology,* ed. Ramsay Cook, (Toronto: Macmillan of Canada, 1969), 102.

27. See Henry Withrow's speech "The Spirit of Canadian Patriotism" in Ross, *Patriotic Recitations and Arbor Day Exercises,* 209.

28. *La Revue Canadienne* (1870) quoted in Silver, *The French Canadian Idea of Confederation,* 234.

And so it went. Catholic Quebec offered "salvation" to wayward Americans wise enough to see it,[29] and the laws of British and Protestant Canada were "justly celebrated throughout the world" because they were founded on the Bible.[30] Quebec's glorious martyrs who gave their lives in defense of the Holy See in Rome against Italian nationalists (1868–70) set a pious example for humankind to behold—they were like the ancient Hebrews who had defended ancient Israel's "national cause" against aggressors[31]— and Ontario's Loyalist settlers had been able to endure the "unparalleled suffering and privations" foisted on them by the American revolutionaries because of their "ardent love for the Bible."[32] Looking back one hundred years after the Loyalists' arrival it seemed, to one commentator, "as if the voice of Christ was heard by them, as he spake to his disciples upon that last day at Jerusalem, 'Arise! let us go hence!' And the ten commandments . . . were set up anew in the rude churches which they built to the worship of God in Canada."[33]

Protestant Canada's greatness was assured because the Bible was its foundation;[34] French Catholic Quebec's greatness could be seen in the ways its history paralleled that of the ancient Israel.[35] Quebec had been entrusted with a "social priesthood"; its inhabitants were "messengers of the spirit of religion."[36] Canada's Protestants were more thoughtful and intelligent than others because they read the Bible,[37] and Canada's Natives benefited from "the civilization resulting from the gospel of the Nazarene," the "superior system of the Carpenter's Son," the "principles found in the gospel of the man of Nazareth," and the "words of the Great Teacher."[38]

Rather obviously, while French- and English-speaking Canadians drew

29. Adolphe-Basile Routhier, *Causeries du Dimanche* (Montreal: C. O. Beauchemin and Valois, 1871), 85.

30. *Christian Guardian,* September 18, 1861.

31. Gustave Bourassa, *Conférences et discours* (Montreal: C. O. Beauchemin et fils, 1899), 107–8.

32. A Loyalist quoted in Norman Knowles, *Inventing the Loyalists: The Ontario Loyalist Tradition and the Creation of Usable Pasts* (Toronto: University of Toronto Press, 1997), 97.

33. The nationalist William Kirby in *The Centennial of the Settlement of Upper Canada by the United Empire Loyalists, 1784–1884* (Toronto: Rose, 1885), 110–11.

34. *Protestant and Evangelical Witness,* March 14, 1863.

35. See Laflèche, *Quelque considerations,* passim.

36. L. A. Paquet, "Sermon on the Vocation of the French Race in America," excerpted in Cook, *French Canadian Nationalism,* 152–54.

37. Egerton Ryerson, *First Lessons in Christian Morals for Canadian Families and Schools* (Toronto: Copp, Clark, 1871), 82.

38. John McLean, *The Indians of Canada: Their Manners and Customs* (London, England: Charles H. Kelly, 1892), 25, 111, 128, and 325.

from the Bible to define themselves and their place in the world, they arrived at very different conclusions. A basic barrier between them was their approach to the Bible itself. Protestants saw that Quebec's Catholics were kept in the dark by medieval clerics who forbade them to read the Bible. Thus Protestants read stories about Catholic priests burning Bibles and about Catholic women trembling with fright as they dared to touch the Scriptures unsupervised.[39] French Canadian Catholics, meantime, saw the Protestant's individualistic approach to the Bible as a precursor to rebellion and anarchy.

The Protestant claim that the clergy in Quebec actively discouraged parishioners from reading the Scriptures was much overstated; in the middle decades of the nineteenth century translations of the New Testament in French were prepared specifically for French Canadians.[40] But Quebec's bishops did object to what they called "false Bibles"—Bibles that did not include the Apocrypha and sanctioned annotations.[41] (Protestants who claimed that Quebec's Catholics were not allowed to read the Bible would have been right had they said that French Canadians were prohibited from reading *Protestant* Bibles.) And Quebec's Catholic bishops warned against the seeming piety of Bible salesmen who peddled truncated tomes and handled the Bible as if it were just another piece of merchandise.[42]

A crusade against laissez-faire Bible reading and Protestant Bibles was waged by Quebec's Catholic bishops through the nineteenth century, along with the promotion of a proper biblical ethic and theologically sound knowledge of the Bible.[43] All the while, Protestants launched campaigns to get the Bible into every French Canadian's hand.

39. R.-P. Duclos, *Histoire du protestantisme au Canada et aux Etats-Unis* (Montréal: Librairie Evangelique, n.d.), 131–37; and Chiniquy, *Chiniquy,* 15–16. Catholic clergy did in fact burn some unauthorized Bibles.

40. See, for example, *Le Nouveau Testament de notre-seigneur Jésus-Christ, traduit de la vulgate en français avec des notes explicatives, morales et dogmatiques, pour en faciliter l'intelligence* (Québec: Atelier Typographique de Léger Brousseau, 1865).

41. In contrast to a requirement that Catholic translations be accompanied with annotations, the scholars responsible for the Authorized (King James) Version of the Bible were commanded to include no marginal notes at all, save "only for the explanation of the Hebrew and Greek words which cannot without some circumlocution so briefly and fitly be expressed in the text." See Stephen Prickett, *Origins of Narrative: The Romantic Appropriation of the Bible* (Cambridge: Cambridge University Press, 1996), 84.

42. See Murphy and Perin, *A Concise History of Christianity in Canada,* 192–93.

43. See *Mandements,* 1:49 and 50; 2:116 and 468; and "Ciculaire au clergé," no. 112, in *Mandements, lettres pastorales et circulaires des évêques de Québec* (Québec: Imprimerie Générale, 1890), 321–22. In 1934 Mgr. Louis-Adolphe Paquet urged French Canada's "faithful" to keep "good books"

The point is that the Bible was always central; the differences between Protestants and Catholic French Canadians could be found in how they thought about and approached the Bible. The ultramontane lawyer Adolphe-Basile Routhier was correct when he claimed that Anglo- and Franco-Canadians had a very important thing in common, namely, their mutual reliance on the Bible—"the Book of books."[44]

Americans

English- and French-speaking Canadians defined themselves in comparison to one another. They also defined themselves in relation to Americans. In the late nineteenth century, the American Civil War provided superior Canadians with an obvious opportunity to celebrate their own society. As one would expect, when they did this, they drew from the Bible.

Canadians condemned Northerners for not keeping the Sabbath (no wonder they had lost the first battle at Bull Run), and President Lincoln's wife was rebuked for going to dancing parties.[45] But most critical commentary was directed at Southerners, a "nominally Christian people" of "covenant breakers" who were "without natural affection" and under the influence of a "titanic demon."[46] Southern slaveholders were likened to "modern Pharaohs," and the Civil War reminded one writer of the plagues inflicted on ancient Egypt.[47] Slavery itself was the "practical impeachment of the Son of God for remembering Africa on Calvary."[48] The very existence of slavery proved Southern infidelity to the Bible.

---

in their homes to be read to families especially on Sundays and saints' days. For an overview of the efforts of Catholic clergy in the United States to protect their flocks from unauthorized Bibles see the first two chapters of Gerald P. Fogarty's *American Catholic Biblical Scholarship* (San Francisco: Harper and Row, 1989).

44. Adolphe-Basile Routhier, *Conférences et discours* (Montreal: Librairie Beauchemin, 1904), 117.

45. *Christian Guardian,* July 31, 1861, and March 19, 1862.

46. *Provincial Wesleyan,* March 6, 1861, September 11, 1861, and April 26, 1865.

47. Ibid., October 29, 1861.

48. *Christian Guardian,* May 29, 1861, 2. Also see the *Canada Christian Advocate,* August 14, 1861. On January 22, 1862, the *Advocate* surmised that in the plan of providence blacks had been brought to America to learn Christianity so that they might to go back to Africa and spread the faith there. To be sure, the blacks had suffered in America, the *Advocate* observed, and "Thus God, in the hot furnace of affliction, and in defiance of all human wrong, prepares his materials for the regeneration of Africa. Thousands thus fitted, may now return to the land of their fathers, to teach and exemplify a pure christianity . . . to inclose within the arms of civilization and christianity tribe after tribe in the interior, and by these several means, to extinguish most effectively slavery and the slave trade. . . . The Bible is the only lever that can raise Africa. Give it room, and it will

All this highlighted the Canadians' exalted place in the world. The negative American example showed Canadians how *not* to be, which in turn led to reflection on how to make good lives in Canada. "A truly Christian nation would be one in which the Word of God was universally read, believed, and understood," the *Christian Guardian* noted in 1861. A nation whose people embraced the Bible would enjoy the leadership of political leaders who feared God; its legislators would be wise and faithful, its judges upright, its public servants incorruptible. The ministers of such a Bible-centered nation would be "burning and shining lights"; its churches would be "Zions, where light, and glory, and salvation from God would be enjoyed in abundance."[49] This was a righteous Canada's future.

Like the Civil War, the Fenian raids on Ontario and Quebec, launched from the United States in the years following the war, presented an occasion to consider the differences between Canadians and Americans. One minister asked his congregation if anyone would be "bold enough to deny that in the ranks of Canada's gallant defenders of the present day, there are many who are both good soldiers of Britain's Queen, and good soldiers of Jesus Christ." The answer to the rhetorical question was obvious, and the preacher acknowledged that the grand design of the Gospel was to produce peace on earth. But the fact remained that "even the Lord Jesus himself, the Righteous Governor, is represented in the New Testament record as 'in righteousness judging and making war.'" Abraham, Joshua, David, Jonathan, and other Old Testament figures had all been men of war.[50] In this context, resistance to the Fenians could be construed as holy war.

For French Canadians, the greater American problem was emigration. In the second half of the nineteenth century perhaps as many as 500,000 French Canadians left Quebec to work and live in the U.S.[51] Many of Quebec's French-speaking Catholics left Canada for the U.S. simply because they could make a better living there, particularly in New England's fac-

---

surely raise the dark continent from the depths of its debasement, and place it alongside the nations which God is pleased to favor . . . the idea is a pleasing one, that the descendants of Ham, emancipated, enlightened, and christianized by their enslavers, may go back to be the happy instruments of reclaiming, enlightening, and christianizing their own native Africa."

49. *Christian Guardian*, July 17, 1861.

50. William Stewart, *The Country's Trouble and the Christian's Consolation* (Brantford, 1866), 7.

51. In 1890 the United States census showed that there were 302,496 Canadians of French origin residing in the U.S., and some students of this question maintain that as many as 500,000 French Canadians emigrated to the U.S. between 1851 and 1901. See Silver, *The French Canadian Idea of Confederation*, 14.

tories. This was problematic because Quebec's Catholics had been trained since childhood to shun worldliness and greed and a thirst for despoiling mammon.

Trois-Rivières Bishop Louis-François Laflèche said that the primary cause of emigration from Quebec was simple faithlessness to the Christian gospel. Jesus had taught his disciples to be content with little, after all, and if Christians were content they would be blessed. But emigration suggested discontent, and this in turn pointed to a lack of Christian seriousness. The emigrants had abandoned hearth and home, language and religion, to pursue earthly contentment. The Bible taught that a man's living should be drawn from the sweat of his brow,[52] but Quebec's emigrants sought a life of ease; they hoped to find in the States bread for which they needed not toil.[53] As the nationalist Henri Bourassa put it early in the twentieth century, Quebec's emigrants had chosen to put America's "golden calf culture" before their own Catholic one.[54] Or, as Laflèche, Bourassa, and Louis-Antoine Paquet agreed—with the biblical account of Jacob and Esau in mind—Quebec's emigrants had sold their Franco-Catholic heritage for a mess of pottage;[55] they had turned their backs on Quebec's providential mission.

Some, looking on what they hoped was a bright side, surmised that Quebec's emigrants were cultural shock troops on the front lines of a spiritual battle that would eventually lead to the annexation of Catholicized parts of New England to Quebec. Even Bishop Laflèche entertained such a vision for a while.[56] But gradual French Canadian assimilation into American culture ensured that this theory's life was short.[57] For some emigrants, connections with the old country remained strong for a few generations,

52. The allusion is to Gen. 3:17–19.

53. In H. J. J. B. Chouinard, ed., *Fête nationale des canadiens-français célébrée à Québec en 1880* (Québec: L'imprimerie A. Côté, 1881), 326–30. As usual Laflèche cited numerous Scripture passages in support of his lecture, including a reference to the godly, "strong woman" ("femme forte") described in Proverb 31. Surely no French Canadian women who was truly devoted to her faith, family, and nation would wish to emigrate to the United States, Laflèche maintained (331).

54. On the golden calf see Exod. 32.

55. "Our language received no divine promise of preservation, except the one that God made to all the peoples and men who have enough heart and energy to defend their soul, their body, and their national and family heritage," Bourassa said in 1912. "[B]ut this promise holds nothing for those whose hearts are so base that they would swap their birthright for a mess of pottage." See Cook, *French Canadian Nationalism,* 141. On the biblical mess of pottage see Gen. 25:29–34.

56. Mason Wade, *The French Canadians,* vol. 2 (Toronto: Macmillan, 1975), 433.

57. I discuss this concern in "Civil War, Culture War: French Quebec and the American War between the States," *Catholic Historical Review* 87, no. 1 (January 2001), 55–70.

but once they were settled in the U.S. not many French Canadians returned to live in Quebec, where devout poverty was sometimes preached as a virtue. Those who stayed home could comfort themselves with the knowledge that they were not like the "errant lambs," who had gone to live "without temples and without pastors" in the Land of the Free.[58]

Sometimes trouble in the U.S. spurred Canadians to search their own consciences. During the Civil War some wondered about the extent to which the sort of political and moral libertinism that had led to the conflict had taken root in Canada West, or Nova Scotia, or Prince Edward Island. To what extent did the provinces that would soon merge into Canada resemble the increasingly unchristian United States? Journalists wrote that crime rates seemed to be going up in the 1860s; alcoholic intemperance was supposedly rife in Canada West; and novels and other fictional literature were wreaking moral destruction. *"Canada was once the most moral country on the globe,"* one newspaper remembered, "but it is fast losing the right to comfort itself by comparisons with other parts of the world."[59] If the United States had been pushed to the verge of destruction for its selfishness, pride, and forgetfulness of God, Canadians could not expect something different if they too transgressed.[60] "Political expediency" was not confined to the United States; "[t]he evil too often reveals itself among ourselves, and Christian principle is also sacrificed to it, in our midst."[61]

Possessing the Land

In the late nineteenth-century, one way a nation could prove its spiritual worth—one way it could show that it had not forgotten God—was by "possessing the land." The phrase is taken from the Old Testament, where the chosen people of Israel take possession of the land of the Canaanites,[62] and it is omnipresent in the nationalist literature of all the western countries. In Quebec, Bishop Laflèche and Adolphe-Basile Routhier, for example, encouraged their French Canadian compatriots to reflect upon the holy way in which their ancestors had "taken possession" of New France and to see how wonderfully Quebec's history resembled that of the Old

---

58. *Mandements, lettres pastorales, circulaires et autres documents,* vol. 8 (Montreal, 1887), 81–82.
59. *Christian Guardian,* February 19, 1862. Italics added.
60. *Presbyterian Witness* cited in *Canada Christian Advocate,* September 11, 1861.
61. *Provincial Wesleyan,* March 6, 1862.
62. See, for instance, Deut. 31.

Testament's holy nation.[63] What Christian, asked Laflèche, "believing in the dogma of an all-wise Providence controlling every event on earth could fail to be struck by the resemblance between Abraham's behaviour when he took possession of the land God promised his descendents, and that of Jacques Cartier as he took possession of this Canadian territory to which, through his king's mandate, the same Providence had guided his foot-steps?"[64]

Elsewhere in Quebec, a nationalist priest appeared at first to be remind-ing his audience of God's decision to rescue Israel from Egyptian servitude, only to suggest a few moments later that it was neither ancient Israel nor Egypt that he had in mind, for God had "fit de la femme juive une femme canadienne"—and part of the French Canadians' mission was to possess (to control and populate) their new "terre promise."[65] When France had sent colonists to what would become New France in the sixteenth century, Curé Labelle explained in 1883, its goal to was to establish a race that was not only virile and vigorous but eminently Christian.[66] Before long, French Canadians themselves came to see that Labelle himself was something like Moses, one in a long line of French and French Canadian prophets who could see that the *patrie* they possessed was a promised land of milk and honey.[67]

Quebec's colonization movement focused on French Canadian settle-ment in, among other regions, the Ottawa Valley, and the land around the Eastern Townships of Quebec (which became predominantly francophone in the late nineteenth century), but *le nord*—an abstract idea that some-times referred to territory only within Quebec, sometimes to the prairie provinces—also attracted colonizers.[68] And however it was defined by

63. Adolphe-Basile Routhier, "Le role de la race française en Amérique," in *Fête nationale des canadiens-français célébrée à Québec en 1880* (Quebec: L'imprimerie A. Cote et Cie, 1881), 289.
64. *Quelques Considerations* in Cook, *French Canadian Nationalism*, 102.
65. Labelle cited in Gabriel Dussault, *Le Curé Labelle: Messianisme, utopie et colonisation au Québec, 1850–1900* (Montreal: Hurtubise, 1982), 91.
66. Antoine Labelle, *La Mission de la race canadienne-française en Canada* (Montreal: E Séné-cal et fils, 1883), 6. Also see Jean-Baptiste Proulx, *Le Canada, le Curé Labelle, et la colonisation* (1885; reprint Saint-Jacques, P.Q.: Editions du pot de fer, 1992), 10. In June 1912 Henri Bourassa encour-aged the first Congrès de la Langue Française au Canada to "take pleasure in thinking" that Joan of Arc's heart had "crossed the Atlantic and come to Canadian soil, where the cross of Christ and the French way of thinking were the first to push back the barbarians, where the French spirit cast the first seeds of Christian civilization." See Cook, *French Canadian Nationalism*, 146.
67. Three decades before, Adolphe-Basile Routhier had referred to New France's Bishop Laval as "le Moïse du Canada." See Chouinard, *Fête nationale des canadiens-français*, 283.
68. See Christian Morissonneau, *La Terre promise: Le mythe du Nord québécois* (Quebec: Hur-

individual nationalists, the north was a promised land in a biblical sense: wherever the French Canadian colonist set his foot he brought with him his faith and religious virtues; everywhere the French Canadian went he "revealed himself as a member of a chosen race who is called to continue on this American soil the providential mission of [Catholic] France."[69] The language of possession was hardly different among English-speaking nationalists and settlers. "Who shall guide us but the great Master of Life, in whose hands are the destinies of nations and men?" one asked; "God has given to us a blessed heritage in that western country, with its vast areas of excellent land.... This is God's heritage for our children, and *we must go up and possess the land* for our Lord and Christ."[70]

Over and again, the biblical example of Joshua leading Israel into Canaan to possess the Promised Land was put to nationalist and expansionist use in speeches and sermons, in exhortations and newspaper columns. In ancient times God commanded Moses's successor, Joshua, to rout the Canaanites, to stamp out their religion, and to prosper in the new land they had possessed. Now it was the Anglo-Saxon's duty to carry true religion and culture around the globe. "Joshua, the servant of the Lord, was the first man who received a portion of the Holy Scripture to be his guide," one preacher said;

[Joshua] ... always referred to the book of the law of the Lord. That shews the estimation in which the Holy Scriptures should be held. And it is to our glory that we [Canadians] profess to make that sacred book our rule and guide. Joshua conquered his enemies, led by God's law. May not we, led also by teaching, achieve a greater victory—the civilization and christianizing [*sic*] of the ignorant, the heathen, the ungodly? And if so what a glorious mission is ours.[71]

In the language of the day, to possess the land (the Canadian West)—to labor in that glorious mission field—was to prepare it for "Commercial

tubise, 1978), 126–46. Morissonneau observes that "the north" tended to be thought of by some French Canadians as the Canadian north, by others as the north of Quebec, and by still others as the land just north of Montreal (128). For Captain J. E. Bernier the "north" extended to the north pole. Morissonneau reprints a letter to Bernier from a priest eager to be the first to celebrate Mass on the pole. "Si, comme Canadien, vous ambitionnez d'arriver le premier au Pôle; moi, comme prêtre, je veux être le premier à y planter la Croix, l'étendard de Notre Roi," the priest wrote in 1899. "Vous planterez la croix et sous son ombre, je célébrerai le Saint-Sacrifice; consacrant par un acte solennel de possession divine ce point de notre globe qui n'a jamais été vu du ciel & qui désormais appartiendra à Dieu ... et à nous" (138).

69. Ibid., 96.
70. McLean, *The Indians of Canada*, 319–20. Italics added.
71. R. W. Norman, *Our Duties and Opportunities* (Montreal: Gazette Printing House, 1877), 8.

enterprise, mental culture, and moral influence"; it was to bring the "The Fairyland of the Rockies! [and] The Wonderland of the West!" into submission to the dictates of the Bible.[72]

For Protestants, this meant getting the Bible into the hands of Canada's Natives, and this, in turn, meant translating the Bible into Native languages and using it as a textbook in Native schools.[73] It also meant a quest for Native conversion to Christianity sometimes expressed in militaristic language.[74] One writer suggested the example of the "Nazarene [who] was destined to conquer and win the red man for Himself."[75] Bishop Laflèche also observed that the displacement of Native peoples and cultures had biblical precedent. Just as in Canaan before the arrival of the Israelites, so it was in Canada before the arrival of the French: the land was infested with a sinful, guilty, and stiff-necked race destined for extermination. But God in his mercy wanted to give the Natives a chance to repent, so he sent them Jacques Cartier, "a heavenly messenger." Predictably, the same fate that came to the ancient Canaanites who failed to turn from evil also befell the natives who hardened their own hearts.[76] The fertile land of the Canaanites had been handed over to the descendents of Abraham, and the great St. Lawrence River valley had been taken from the rebels who inhabited it and providentially given to the *Canadiens* as their rightful heritage. The parallels in the histories of Israel and French Canada were, Quebecers were told, remarkable.

72. Ibid., 189 and 210.

73. McLean's *Indians of Canada* includes frequent comments on efforts to put the Bible in Native tongues. See pp. 143, 158, 243, 244–45, 248, 250, 253, 295, 296, 332, 336, 340, and 343. Also see Edward Carruther Woodley, *The Bible in Canada* (Toronto: Dent, 1953), 306. For further commentary see John Webster Grant, *Moon of Wintertime: Missionaries and the Indians of Canada in Encounter since 1534* (Toronto: University of Toronto Press, 1984), 111; Murphy and Perin, *A Concise History of Christianity in Canada;* and Neil Semple, *The Lord's Dominion: The History of Canadian Methodism* (Montreal-Kingston: McGill-Queen's University Press, 1996), 173–78, 294–7. Also see Marjorie Beaucage and Emma LaRoque, "Two Faces of the New Jerusalem: Indian—Metis Reaction to the Missionary," in *Visions of the New Jerusalem: Religious Settlement on the Prairies,* ed. Benjamin G. Smillie (Edmonton: NeWest Press, 1983), 29.

74. The rhetoric of missions as soldiers' work was not of course unique to Protestants. See Robert Choquette, *The Oblate Assault on Canada's Northwest* (Ottawa: University of Ottawa Press, 1995), which itself is organized around military metaphors.

75. McLean, *The Indians of Canada,* 349. Again: "The Master's marching orders are obeyed year after year by hundreds of devoted men and women, who go out into the desert places of the earth to teach the despised races of men the way of life" (291).

76. Laflèche, *Quelques considerations,* 54 and 60.

Meaning

Southern slaveholders as Egyptian pharaohs; prominent French Canadians as Moses, Jacques Cartier as Abraham; Anglo- and Franco-Canadians as chosen peoples, the West or the "north" as promised lands—these are metaphors, figures of speech. But as unmoving as they are to twenty-first-century readers, it would be a mistake to see them as nothing more than figures of speech. They expressed compelling ideas, and the ideas were expressed in the language of the Canadians' most important book. But, despite what the Canadians themselves might have thought or felt, the ideas do not really seem theological.[77]

Since the Protestant Reformation, biblical tropes had been ubiquitous among non-Catholics. We know that they were also common among nineteenth-century Quebec's Catholic clergy and intellectuals. As Stephen Prickett points out, when England's James I railed against tobacco smoking, "it seemed entirely natural to compare the perverted lusts of smokers to the Children of Israel 'lusting in the wilderness after quails'"; and we have seen that the account of the Israelites' invasion of Canaan was used among Canadians to spur western settlement and colonization. Oliver Cromwell relied on the same biblical texts from the book of Joshua to endorse his raising of the sword against Ireland's Catholics.[78] Abraham Lincoln's Second Inaugural speech is full of biblical language, and before the First World War a German nationalist quoted Jesus—"Greater love hath no man than this: that he giveth his life for his friend"—to support self-sacrifice in glorious battle.[79] And hints of the Puritan John Winthrop's famous sermon aboard the *Arbella* in 1630 were heard in President Ronald Reagan's frequent references to the United States as a "city on a hill" as well as in President Bill Clinton's advocacy of a political "New Covenant."[80]

In late nineteenth-century Canada, some quoted the Bible to prove that the United Empire Loyalists were morally superior to American republicans. Louis Riel and his followers did the same to convince the Métis that

77. Meaning, for example, that their nationalist claims had nothing to do with the essence of Christianity as expressed in the Apostles Creed.

78. Prickett, *Origins of Narrative,* 64.

79. On the German nationalist, see Marvin Perry, *Sources of the Western Tradition,* vol. 2 (Boston: Houghton Mifflin, 2006), 170.

80. For commentary see David Lyle Jeffrey, *People of the Book: Christian Identity and Literary Culture* (Grand Rapids, Mich.: Eerdmans, 1996), 327–28 and 340.

Manitoba was to be the new seat of a new Vatican.[81] The New Israel rhetoric of Puritans, English-speaking Canadians, French Canadians, Mormons (yet another chosen people), and Métis is similar—and none of it accords very well with the self-effacing mandate of the Sermon on the Mount.

This presents a conundrum. On the one hand, Canada's nationalists and cultural interpreters spoke about the Bible with apparent reverence. They said that its holiness, wisdom, and just commandments were unrivaled. They said that the nation—or, perhaps better to say, their nations—would thrive only to the extent that they adhered to the Bible or to a biblical scheme of things. A people must submit themselves to the message of the Bible, they said.

But then the historian sees that English- and French-speaking Canadians twisted the meanings of the Scriptures as they put them to political, cultural, and nationalistic uses. The historian sees that Canadian intellectuals and opinion shapers wrenched Bible verses out of context and arrived at implausible and not very careful parallels between biblical history and their own. They waged rhetorical war against others with the words of the Bible. The Bible was used to inspire and promote opposing visions of the Canadian nation. One historian's claim that during the War of 1812 the sermons of Upper Canadian Anglicans "became progressively less humble and more patriotic in content" rings a familiar bell.[82]

What, then, does the fact that biblical language pervaded late-nineteenth century Canada's public sphere mean? It means that, in the late nineteenth century, most Canadians were still familiar with the Bible, either as a result of their own reading or as a result of cultural transferal. It means that this common knowledge lent the Bible a certain amount of prestige as a cultural currency. It means that the Canadians' vocabulary was enriched by biblical tropes that have, by the early twenty-first century, been mostly forgotten.

But the Bible-based language employed by Canadians when they were speaking about their nation does *not* mean what the Canadians themselves suggested it meant, namely, that they were especially pious and divinely chosen for unique work in the world. There was hardly anything less rare among industrialized western peoples in the late nineteenth century than exclamations of special national favor in the eyes of God. To one extent or

81. See Thomas Flanagan, *Louis "David" Riel: "Prophet of the New World"* (Toronto: University of Toronto Press, 1979), 175.

82. In A. B. McKillop and Paul Romney, eds., *God's Peculiar Peoples: Essays on Political Culture in Nineteenth Century Canada* (Ottawa: Carleton University Press, 1993), 33.

another, the Bible was familiar to all—to some because they strove for genuine piety, to others simply because its metaphors were the stuff of public
culture. But familiarity bred a kind of unwitting contempt: the wrenching
of biblical passages from anything that was remotely related to their original context; the imposition onto Bible passages of apparently irresponsible
interpretations.

"Nothing," writes one biographer of G. F. Handel, "is more difficult
to determine than the real force of conviction with which a creed is actually and individually held."[83] The context of the quote is a discussion of
the eighteenth-century composer's "sacred" oratorios. But, the biographer
asserts, Handel's oratorios—*Messiah, Esther, Solomon,* and so on—were sacred only in the sense that they drew from the Bible. The Holy Book offered Handel themes, but they were not really religious themes.[84]

In the late nineteenth century Canada's nationalists spoke of the wonders and unrivaled glories of the Bible. But they were engaged in a kind
of game they were not aware of. The game involved making a god of the
nation, the ethnic group, the political cause, the cultural project, and then
finding a way to justify having done so.[85]

83. Paul Henry Lang, *George Frideric Handel* (Mineola, N.Y.: Dover Publications, 1966), 383.
84. Ibid., 382.
85. This chapter aligns itself with the general point of view expressed in David B. Marshall,
Secularizing the Faith: Canadian Protestant Clergy and the Crisis of Belief, 1850–1940 (Toronto: University of Toronto Press, 1992). Marshall contends that by the late nineteenth century much of
Canada's public Protestant discourse had largely been reduced to sentimental clichés. He is correct.
If, through their sheer ubiquity, the Bible's words could be construed to mean almost anything,
then one could plausibly conclude that they must in fact not mean not much at all. A different
view is taken by Nancy Christie and Michael Gauvreau in *A Full-Orbed Christianity: The Protestant
Churches and Social Welfare in Canada, 1900–1940* (Montreal-Kingston: McGill-Queen's University
Press, 1990).

12

Civil Religion and
Associational Life under Canada's
"Ephemeral Monster"

Canada's Multi-Headed Constitution

JOHN VON HEYKING

> A constitution that was republican at the head and
> ultramonarchical in all other parts has always seemed to me an
> ephemeral monster. The vices of those who govern and the imbecility
> of the governed would not be slow to bring it to ruin; and the people,
> tired of their representatives and of themselves, would create freer
> institutions or soon return to lying at the feet of a single master.[1]

Canada's Democratic Faith

Canadian evocations of civil religion receive less attention than those of their southern neighbor because they appear to us more as phenomena associated with an earlier historical epoch in the nation's history or as symbols of specific regions, rather than as evocations of a pan-Canadian identity. For instance, in the nineteenth century, Anglican Bishop John Strachan invoked the British Empire as a providential and civilizing force to justify Anglo dominance in what was then Upper Canada (now Ontario), while Québecois Catholics often characterized Québec as a latter-day Promised

Previous drafts of this essay were presented at the Centre for Cultural Renewal's conference on Law and Religion in Lourdes, France, in April 2001; the "Keeping the Faith" conference at Trinity Western University in May 2002; and the Eric Voegelin Society in September 2006. Calvin Townsend, Geoffrey Hale, Ian Brodie, Rainer Knopff, Thomas Heilke, and my religion and politics students helped me to clarify various points and theoretical issues. Errors, omissions, and ambiguities are of course due to me alone.

    1. Alexis de Tocqueville, *Democracy in America,* trans. Harvey Mansfield, Jr. and Delba Winthrop (Chicago: University of Chicago Press, 2000), 2.4.6. Hereinafter *DA.*

Land of a latter-day Chosen People (which still persists among Québec separatists in its quasi-Hegelian secular form).[2] Canadian constitutionalism in the nineteenth century drew from religious mores to sustain liberal democratic practices, but simultaneously shaped Protestantism in Ontario and Catholicism in Québec for its own purposes.[3] However, the lack of a common national bond has prevented evocations of a pan-Canadian civil religion because of the absence of a pan-Canadian myth whose stories and rituals could be regarded as sacred. The first part of the twentieth century saw some attempts to articulate a civil religion, consisting of the Social Gospel movement and Prime Minister Mackenzie King's attempt to wed Christian theology to political economy as a way of overcoming regionalism and of greeting modernity.[4] The much-noted decline of Canadian churches since the 1950s also lessens the likelihood of people evoking sacred symbols to express the Canadian nation. Indeed, most treatments of civil religion in Canada either deny its existence or conflate it with notions of culture, relegating the "sacred" component down to "deeply held beliefs."[5]

The most recent attempt to evoke civil religion is found in the myth that the Charter of Rights and Freedoms represents the progressive historical unfolding of human potentiality, freedom, and equality; this myth is meant to unify a society fractured along regional and cultural lines. Instead of drawing its sacred symbols from historical Christianity, it draws

2. The Right Rev. John Strachan, "On Church Establishment," in *Canadian Political Thought*, ed. H. D. Forbes (Oxford: Oxford University Press, 1984), 10–17; "The Programme Catholique: The Next Elections" and "Pastoral Letter of the Bishops of the Ecclesiastical Province of Quebec," in ibid., 93–106; Barry Cooper, "Quebec Nationalism and Canadian Politics in Light of Voegelin's *Political Religions*," in *Politics, Order, and History: Essays on the Work of Eric Voegelin*, ed. Glenn Hughes et al. (Sheffield: Sheffield Academic Press, 2001), 208–32. See also Filippo Sabetti, "Covenantal Language in Canada: Continuity and Change in Political Discourse," in *The Covenant Connection: From Federal Theology to Modern Federalism*, ed. Daniel J. Elazar and John Kincaid (Lanham, Md.: Lexington Books, 2000), 259–83.

3. Frederick Vaughan, *The Canadian Federalist Experiment: From Defiant Monarchy to Reluctant Republic* (Montréal-Kingston: McGill-Queens University Press, 2003), 134–51; Janet Ajzenstat, *The Political Thought of Lord Durham* (Montréal-Kingston: McGill-Queens University Press, 1988), 35–41.

4. Ramsay Cook, *The Regenerators* (Toronto: University of Toronto Press, 1985); William Lyon Mackenzie King, *Industry and Humanity*, ed. David Bercuson (Toronto: University of Toronto Press, 1973).

5. Andrew E. Kim, "The Absence of Pan-Canadian Civil Religion: Plurality, Duality, and Conflict in Symbols of Canadian Culture," *Sociology of Religion*, 54, no. 3 (1993): 257–75; William Stahl, "Symbols of Canada: Civil Religion, Nationality, and the Search for Meaning" (Ph.D. thesis, Graduate Theological Union, Berkeley, California, 1981); Robert Blumstock, "Canadian Civil Religion," in *The Sociology of Religion: A Canadian Focus*, ed. W. E. Hewitt (Toronto: Butterworths, 1993), 171–94.

its symbols from the "democratic faith" of pluralism, tolerance, cosmopolitanism, autonomy, and equality. Patrick Deneen summarizes "democratic faith" in the following manner:

If faith is a belief in that which is unseen, then it may be that democracy is as justifiably an object of faith as a distant and silent God. This is particularly the case for those who perceive a radical gulf between that system of government that we now call democracy—rife with apathy, cynicism, corruption, inattention, and dominated by massive yet nearly unperceivable powers that belie claims of popular control—and the vision of democracy as apotheosis of human freedom, self-creation, and even paradisiacal universal political and social equality that coexists seamlessly with individual self-realization and uniqueness. In absence of such a faith, ambitions might wither amid cruel facts and hopes dissipate in the face of relentless reality.[6]

This myth most frequently finds its home in the Supreme Court. Former prime minister Paul Martin appealed to this constituency when, in the 2006 election campaign, he promised to withdraw the federal government's ability to use section 33 of the Charter of Rights and Freedoms to override Supreme Court decisions, a move that would transform the constitutional order from one of supposed balance between Supreme Court and Parliament to one with Court sovereignty. Both critics and defenders of the Supreme Court have noted how it has taken over the role, from churches among others, as the "conscience of the nation," which corresponds to the function of the Charter as a force for secularization in Canadian society.[7] Yet, while Canada can no longer be characterized as a regime of, in John Moir's words, "legally disestablished religiosity," neither can it be understood as a fully "secularized" society, nor even a unitary one.[8]

6. Patrick J. Deneen, *Democratic Faith,* (Princeton, N.J.: Princeton University Press, 2004), xvi. This future-oriented democratic faith is also subject to critique in Janet Ajzenstat, *The Once and Future Canadian Democracy* (Montréal-Kingston: McGill-Queens University Press, 2003).

7. George Egerton, "Trudeau, God, and the Canadian Constitution: Religion, Human Rights, and Government Authority in the Making of the 1982 Constitution," in *Rethinking Church, State, and Modernity: Canada between Europe and America,* ed. David Lyon and Marguerite Van Die (Toronto: University of Toronto Press, 2000), 108.

8. John S. Moir, *Church and State in Canada: 1627–1867: Basic Documents* (Toronto: McClelland and Stewart, 1967), xiii; Egerton, "Trudeau, God, and the Canadian Constitution"; Douglas Farrow, "Of Secularity and Civil Religion," in *Recognizing Religion in a Secular Society: Essays in Pluralism, Religion, and Public Policy,* ed. Douglas Farrow (Montréal-Kingston: McGill-Queens University Press, 2004), 140–82; Iain T. Benson, "Considering Secularism," in ibid., 83–98, and "Notes toward a (Re)Definition of the 'Secular,'" *University of British Columbia Law Review* 33, special edition (2000): 519–50; John von Heyking, "Harmonization of Heaven and Earth?: Reli-

The Charter myth is meant to overcome a twofold ambiguity that Canada's constitutional order is neither (1) fully secularized (nor fully not-secularized) nor (2) fully pan-Canadian (nor so decentralized so as to justify dissolving the federation). Pierre Trudeau thought the Charter (with the Supreme Court) could heal both sources of the legitimacy crisis (which he helped to create) and legitimate his founding.[9] The peculiar piety various members of society, including political, academic, legal, and academic elites, display toward the Charter and the Supreme Court expresses the attempt to resolve this crisis of legitimacy. For instance, former Justice Minister Irwin Cotler proclaimed "human rights has emerged as the new secular religion of our time."[10] Editorialist Jeffrey Simpson states with some irony, "The Charter of Rights and Freedoms is the closest thing Canadians have to a canon these days with the Supreme Court justices as legal cardinals."[11] One finds more serious references to the "nation's new secular religion" in legal literature.[12] Pollster Allan Gregg criticizes secular liberals for avoiding moral and political philosophy to discuss major cultural issues. They instead hide behind procedure and sovereign commands by the Supreme Court, in a manner consistent with what Thomas Hobbes refers to the sovereign as a "mortal god."[13] For Gregg, their "secular fundamentalism" is no less "fundamentalist" than those who resort to divine commands found in Scripture.[14] Among Charter-skeptics and critics of the Court, Robert Ivan Martin refers to the Supreme Court as a theocracy of relativism "in the grip of a secular state religion," with the Supreme Court as its rulers.[15]

gion, Politics, and Law in Canada," ibid.: 663–98; Peter Emberley, *Divine Hunger: Canadians on Spiritual Walkabout* (Toronto: HarperCollins Canada, 2002).

9. As a student of Machiavelli, Trudeau knew about Machiavelli's admiration of Numa Pompilius, who established Rome's civil religion to legitimate Romulus's founding. That Trudeau had to double-cross then Quebec premier René Levesque during the negotiations is but a more polite echo of the fratricide Romulus committed against Remus (*Discourses on Livy*, I.11; Guy Laforest, *Trudeau and the End of a Canadian Dream* (McGill-Queens University Press, 1995).)

10. Irwin Cotler, Speech to Parliament of Canada, *Hansard,* (37th Parliament, 2nd session) October 28, 2002, available at http://www.parl.gc.ca/37/2/parlbus/chambus/house/debates/016_2002-10-28/han016_1355-E.htm.

11. Jeffrey Simpson, "Leave the Prayerbook at Home, Stockwell," *Toronto Globe and Mail,* March 31, 2000, A15.

12. Bruce Ryder, "State Neutrality and Freedom of Conscience and Religion," *Supreme Court Law Review,* 29(2d) (2005): 175.

13. Thomas Hobbes, *Leviathan,* ch. 17.

14. Allan Gregg, "The Christian Comeback," *Saturday Night Magazine,* November 2005, 22. A scholarly analysis of "secular fundamentalism" can be found in Paul F. Campos, "Secular Fundamentalism," *Columbia Law Review* 94 (1994): 1814–27.

15. Robert Ivan Martin, *The Most Dangerous Branch: How the Supreme Court of Canada Has*

Many comparisons of the Supreme Court as a "theocracy" or as "high priests" are polemical, though have a grain of truth insofar as the Charter, the Court, and its decisions are considered sacred and beyond contestation. Part of this reverence is par for the course in a constitutional democracy in which the Supreme Court is regarded as the final arbiter of rights and freedoms that must be protected from majority power. However, the Charter myth moves discourse beyond merely respecting rights. Chief Justice Beverley McLachlin expresses this added piety when she describes the Charter as the authoritative statement of the "hypergoods" to which Canadian society subscribes, and views the Supreme Court as the primary arbiter between the "total claim" the law makes upon citizens and the "total claim" religion makes on its believers. Whether either law or religion makes a total claim upon individuals can be seriously questioned.[16]

While McLachlin follows Charles Taylor in distinguishing "hypergoods" from their linguistic instantiation, what is important is that they are consented to and not that they are rooted in an ethical order that takes priority over the commands of the sovereign, as found, for instance, in the philosophy of natural rights originating in the canonists of the Middle Ages and moving through the liberal philosophers such as John Locke. Instead, "hypergoods," including our rights, are rooted in consensus. But said consensus must be constructed, and the Supreme Court is the key institution in this nation-building process. Rainer Knopff elucidates the "theocratic temptation" found in the conflation of rights and "consensus": "Although rights were originally conceived as being rooted in nature, they are more often defended nowadays as expressing the most fundamental consensus of the constituent people. Rights, in effect, are an expression of the oneness of the people, an agreement by that people as to what is shared by all, and is thus so fundamental as to constitute the horizon, rather than the

Undermined Our Law and Our Democracy (Montréal-Kingston: McGill-Queens University Press, 2003), 1.

16. The Right Honorable Beverley McLachlin, P.C., "Freedom of Religion and the Rule of Law: A Canadian Perspective," in *Recognizing Religion in a Secular Society*, 12–34. That the Supreme Court is a political organ that adjudicates both "total claims" necessarily means the "total claim" made by law is a little more "total." Jean Bethke Elshtain, in her rebuttal to McLachlin in the same volume, argues instead that neither law nor religion makes a "total claim." Referring to the Gospels of Luke and Mark in which Jesus says, "Render unto Caesar what is Caesar's; unto God what is God's," she observes that both law and religion make partial, not total, claims upon the self, and that practical, not legal, judgment is the appropriate manner to negotiate the two claims (Elshtain, "A Response to Chief Justice McLachlin," 35–40).

subject, of politics."[17] Yet, this "consensus" is more imagined or anticipated than actual. The Supreme Court, not Parliament, expresses this imagined or anticipated consensus because the consensus exists as only something that exists *as if* citizens conformed to the true principles of the democratic faith. Supreme Court justices perform their role as this "as if" consensus when they emphasize the "purposive" reading of the Charter, or the "living tree" metaphor that points to the imagined community at the end-point of the historical progression we are currently undergoing. If "consensus" is harnessed to a notion of history that is becoming progressively secular, we are left not with a civil religion rooted in the traditional gods of the ancient civil religions, but with the "democratic faith" in the perfect future.[18]

The legitimating action these actors impute to the Charter begins with its role in guarding and advancing the regime of tolerance in Canada. Following the Charter, the Court attempts to ensure that individuals and religious associations are free to think and act as they please unless they harm someone else. This is the negative version of the "Golden Rule" found in nearly all expressions of political liberalism.[19] However, in recent years the Supreme Court has moved its understanding of "harm" to include it to mean the failure to have one's identity "recognized."[20]

This expanded notion of "harm" requires the state to change the beliefs and customs of its citizens, and so requires an expansive state taking a paternal or maternal tutelary role over its citizens in protecting them. This is

17. Rainer Knopff, "Populism and the Politics of Rights: The Dual Attack on Representative Democracy," *Canadian Journal of Political Science* 31, no. 4 (December 1998): 699; see also Alan C. Cairns, *Reconfigurations: Canadian Citizenship and Constitutional Change* (Toronto: McClelland and Stewart, 1995), 197. Brayton Polka argues that the preamble of the Charter indicates how rights get expressed as according to nature (and revelation) instead of consensus: "the founding principles of Canada, which recognize the supremacy of God and the rule of law, are precisely those which acknowledge the truth of all gods and the rule of all laws, insofar as those gods and those laws are compatible with the absolutes of conscience, religion, thought, communication, peaceful assembly, and association" ("The Supremacy of God and the Rule of Law in the Canadian Charter of Rights and Freedoms: A Theologico-Political Analysis," *McGill Law Journal,* 32, no. 4 [1987]: 862.)

18. It should be noted that the "divinity" to which Jean-Jacques Rousseau refers as the basis of his civil religion need not be a transcendent god in the traditional sense. It could be immanent, as in the later Marxian notion of history or in Rousseau's own sense of divinized humanity (Jean-Jacques Rousseau, *Social Contract,* 4:8; Deneen, *Democratic Faith,* 140–65; Farrow, "Of Secularity and Civil Religion," 140–82.)

19. Thomas Hobbes, *Leviathan,* ch. 14 (second Law of Nature); John Locke, *Second Treatise on Government,* ch. 2; John Stuart Mill, *On Liberty and Other Essays,* ed. John Gray (Oxford: Oxford University Press, 1998), 83–103.

20. For details, see Rainer Knopff and F. L. Morton, *The Charter Revolution and the Court Party* (Peterborough, Ont.: Broadview Press, 2000).

where the notion of civil religion enters. A "procedural fundamentalism" (Allan Gregg's term) is needed, but its purpose is one in which "historical injustices," which are by definition indefinite if not infinite, require state intervention to rectify. The state must redeem the past in order to ensure a "progressive" future. State action takes on the character of a permanent revolution because "historic injustices" are infinite and perfect equality impossible fully to achieve, which leads to an infinite spiral of perpetual demands for material compensation and "recognition" that can never be fulfilled.[21] The substance of this politics is postmodern in the sense that its sacred symbols are not found in traditional Christianity, but its style is inherently puritanical. Numerous scholars have referred to this as the "quest for cosmic justice," the new "secular theocracy," and the "myth of the sacred," because, in its own terms, the process points to the indefinite (corrupted past) and the redeemed future as its source of legitimation.[22] In Deneen's terms, the state as defender of "democratic faith," must take corrupted humans as they are and transform them into a democratic people required by such faith; proponents of "democratic faith" are unhappy with "people as they are" but have faith in what "they shall be," which helps to explain the authority of the Court over partisan Parliament in this civil religion.

However, the more seriously the state takes its task in protecting the "dignity" of its citizen-subjects, the less seriously it can take (1) the claims to dignity individuals make for themselves and (2) the moral basis upon which individuals associate with one another in society, for instance in civ-

21. For the classic statement on the impossibility of equality, see Aristophanes, *Assembly-women*. Aristophanes observes that perfect equality would require coerced mating of "ugly" and "beautiful," whose practice, even if successful, is hardly consistent with freedom. For the impact of "beauty" on economic status, see Daniel S. Hamermesh and Jeff E. Biddle, "Beauty and the Labor Market," *American Economic Review* 84, no. 5 (December 1994): 1174–94. See also Tocqueville, *DA* 1.2.5. For a critique of the notion of the state as having to redeem or master the past, see Eric Voegelin, *Hitler and the Germans,* trans. Detlev Clemens and Brendan Purcell (Columbia: University of Missouri Press, 2003), 70–75.

22. Paul Gottfried, *Multiculturalism and the Politics of Guilt: Toward a Secular Theocracy* (Columbia: University of Missouri Press, 2004). Thomas Sowell analyzes this indefinite and futile process of rectifying "historic injustices" in *The Quest for Cosmic Justice* (New York: Free Press, 1999). For a similar analysis that focuses on the indefiniteness of this process in Canada, but without explicitly identifying it in terms of civil religion, see Rainer Knopff, *Human Rights and Social Technology: The New War on Discrimination* (Ottawa: Carleton University Press, 1990); Knopff and Morton, *The Charter Revolution and the Court Party;* Patrick James, Donald Abelson, and Michael Lusztig, eds., *The Myth of the Sacred: The Charter, The Courts, and the Politics of the Constitution in Canada* (Montréal-Kingston: McGill-Queens University Press, 2002).

il and religious associations that the state does not organize. The more the state needs to defend recognition, the more rights depend on the state and the less able individuals and associations are to assert their rights on a basis independent of the state. They must claim their rights on the basis of a state-organized "consensus," and not in nature or conscience, whose origins may lay beyond the state: Rousseau's *non salus extra res publicam,* instead of the *non salus extra ecclesiam* of Christendom.[23] This process is a byproduct of the very function of the Charter as a nation-building device. Not only was it meant to create a pan-Canadian nation of rights-bearing individuals, it was intended to bring about a modern republican form of regime, a shift away from the monarchal model upon which Canada was founded.[24] However, the regime also requires state institutions, or "technocratic pluralism," to enable individuals to exercise those rights. The Charter thus reinforces and strengthens the "top-down" authority of the sovereign, which, as David E. Smith demonstrates, remains in the administrative structure formally known as the Crown.[25] This use of monarchal power for republican ends, which ultimately undermines self-rule, is the primary danger Alexis de Tocqueville thought modern democracies face: their individualism would lead them to a frivolous, childlike state and they would submit themselves to a paternalistic state, an "ephemeral monster" (*DA* 2.4.6).

This essay demonstrates the extent to which this "civil religion" makes a "total claim" (CJ McLachlin's term) upon Canadians, and serves as an attempt to refound the Canadian regime on a vision of citizenship that is at once secular and pan-Canadian. In the next section, Alexis de Tocqueville's account of the pathologies of "individualism" is explained to show why de-

23. Farrow, "Of Secularity and Civil Religion," 140–82.

24. As evidenced in the titles of these works: Vaughan, *The Canadian Federalist Experiment: Defiant Monarchy to Reluctant Republic,* and David J. Bercuson and Barry Cooper, "From Constitutional Monarchy to Quasi-Republic: The Evolution of Liberal Democracy in Canada," in *Canadian Constitutionalism: 1791–1991,* ed. Janet Ajzenstat (Ottawa: Canadian Study of Parliament Group, 1991). David E. Smith illuminates the obstacles preventing the completion of this process, and casts doubt on its historic inevitability (*The Republican Option in Canada* [Toronto: University of Toronto Press, 1999]). General treatments of modern republicanism include Thomas L. Pangle, *The Spirit of Modern Republicanism: The Moral Vision of the American Founders and the Philosophy of Locke* (Chicago: University of Chicago Press, 1988); Paul A. Rahe, *Republics Ancient and Modern: Classical Republicanism and the American Revolution* (Chapel Hill: University of North Carolina Press, 1992); Ellis Sandoz, *A Government of Laws: Political Theory, Religion, and the American Founding* (Columbia: University of Missouri Press, 2002).

25. See Pauline Côté, "From Status Politics to Technocratic Pluralism: Toleration of Religious Minorities in Canada," *Social Justice Research* 12, no. 4 (1999): 253–82; David E. Smith, *The Invisible Crown: The First Principle of Canadian Government* (Toronto: University of Toronto Press, 1995).

mocracy's commitment to equality can result in the rise of a paternalistic and "divine" state that ultimately undermines freedom and equality. It establishes the theoretical framework to show why civil associations, and especially religious associations, are especially needed as counter-pressures on individualism and its effects. The diversity and robustness of associational life, and not just diversity of opinion, is a measure of the power of this civil religion.[26] The third section considers the question of this independence in the area of Canadian law where actors make the strongest claims against the sovereign's "hypergoods": the rights of religious associations whose traditions precede, both historically and ontologically, the moral claims of the state. Minimal freedom for religious associations to conduct their own affairs, and to articulate a moral position that may contravene the morality of the wider society, signifies a strong civil religion; conversely, a high degree of freedom signifies a weak or nonexistent civil religion. These cases involving freedom of religious associations indicate the limits a civil religion can, with Rousseau, proclaim, *"non salus extra res publicam."* The final section considers the broader discussion of Canadian identity, as well as the problematic of using the Charter and the state in general as "top-down" mechanisms to create democratic citizenship.

Pathologies of Homogenization in Democracy: Tocqueville's Analysis

Canada adopted a quasi-republican form of regime in adopting the Charter of Rights and Freedoms in 1982, and so explicitly set about constituting the type of democracy that Alexis de Tocqueville described and criticized in his celebrated *Democracy in America,* written in the 1830s. The book is useful for Canadians because, as its title suggests, the topic of the book is the logic of democracy, and not so much 1830s Jacksonian United States.[27] While an admirer of the fruits of equality and the basic decency

26. On the importance of pre-political religious communities for pluralism, see David Novak, "Human Dignity and the Social Contract," in *Recognizing Religion in a Secular Society,* 51–68.
27. As Canada's former Minister of Intergovernmental Affairs, Stéphane Dion has published scholarly articles and given numerous speeches on Tocqueville and Canadian nationhood. See Stéphane Dion, "Tocqueville, le Canada français et la question nationale," *Revue Française de Science Politique* 40, no. 4 (1990): 501–20; "Tocqueville and the Civic Virtues of Nationalism," Notes for an address by the President of the Privy Council and Minister of Intergovernmental, Canadian Political Science Association, Quebec, Quebec, July 29, 2000, available at http://www.pco-bcp

that accompanies the democratic state form, Tocqueville criticized and illuminated vices characteristic of democratic societies, and specifically directed his attention to the fragility of religious liberty, and the freedom
that religious groups and organizations in particular have to carve out their
own space within the broader society. In fact, he regarded the difficulty of
establishing and maintaining "associations" as the central problem that liberal democrats face because they provide essential schooling in democratic
self-rule and because they are uniquely positioned to offer countercultural,
including nondemocratic, ways of life that resist homogenization. He went
so far as to regard the art or "mother science" of establishing and maintaining associations as the "holy enterprise" and perhaps the one that holds the
key to ensuring the moderation and basic decency that liberal democracy
endures.[28] Tocqueville shows Canadians how the logic of equality can become a statist "democratic faith" hostile to all other forms of faith.

Tocqueville saw equality as the great engine of democracy that elimi-
nates injustices among classes and brings about a more decent regime than
premodern societies. It is the goal of democracy, but it is not an unprob-
lematic good because it is an object of a peculiar faith: "One can imagine
an extreme point at which freedom and equality touch each other and in-
termingle. . . . Then with none differing from those like him, no one will
be able to exercise a tyrannical power men will be perfectly free because
they will all be entirely equal; and they will all be perfectly equal because
they will be entirely free. This is the ideal toward which democratic people
tend" (*DA* 2.2.1). The ideal of equality is the result of people's self-interest to
avoid harm and being dominated. It is the simultaneous expression of independence and weakness. As such, Tocqueville doubts complete equality

.gc.ca/aia/default.asp?Language=E&Page=pressroom&Sub=speeches&Doc=20000729_e.htm (last
accessed: February 9, 2006).

28. *DA* 2.2.5, 2.2.7. The literature on Tocqueville's ideas on religion and on associational life
is extensive. See Pierre Manent, *Tocqueville and the Nature of Democracy*, trans. John Waggoner
(Lanham, Md.: Rowman and Littlefield, 1996); Joshua Mitchell, *The Fragility of Freedom* (Chicago: University of Chicago Press, 1995); James Sloat, "The Subtle Significance of Sincere Belief:
Tocqueville's Account of Religious Belief and Democratic Stability," *Journal of Church and State*
42, no. 4 (Autumn 2000): 759–80. For their application to Canada, see Thomas L. Pangle, "The
Accommodation of Religion: A Tocquevillian Perspective," in *The Canadian and American Constitutions in Comparative Perspective*, ed. Marian C. McKenna (Calgary: University of Calgary Press,
1993), 3–24, and Anthony A. Peacock, "Strange Brew: Tocqueville, Rights, and the Technology
of Equality," in *Rethinking the Constitution: Perspectives on Canadian Constitutional Reform, Interpretation, and Theory*, ed. Anthony A. Peacock (Toronto: Oxford University Press, 1996), 122–60;
Heyking, "The Harmonization of Heaven and Earth," 663–97.

is possible because, for instance, people are unequal in intellects. Like the invisible God of the medieval mystics, "complete equality eludes the hands of the people at the moment when they believe they have seized it," which requires them to accept, with "singular melancholy," the equality they can achieve rather than the equality they desire (*DA* 1.2.5, 2.2.14). However, its logic induces a desire for homogenization and a built in diffidence and envy toward others that aggravates individualism, which undermines the people's ability to enjoy solidarity or friendship through their own efforts.

Conflicted between his belief in his own independence and his perception of his powerlessness, the democrat slouches toward the "immense being" that is the tutelary state:

As in centuries of equality no one is obliged to lend his force to those like him and no one has the right to expect great support from those like him, each is at once independent and weak. These two states, which must neither be viewed separately nor confused, give the citizen of democracies very contrary instincts. His independence fills him with confidence and pride among his equals, and his debility makes him feel, from time to time, the need of the outside help that he cannot expect from any of them, since they are all impotent and cold. In this extremity, he naturally turns his regard to the immense being that rises alone in the midst of universal debasement (*DA* 2.4.3).

Because of Tocqueville's emphasis on the psychological, moral, cultural, religious, and philosophical dimensions of this process, it is appropriate to refer to the subject of these pathologies as the "democratic soul."[29]

Tocqueville considers individualism *(individualisme)* to be one of the key vices of democratic equality. He distinguishes individualism from selfishness *(egoïsme),* which is rooted in blind human instinct and is "a vice as old as the world. It scarcely belongs more to one form of society than to another" (*DA* 2.2.2). Tocqueville found the origins of individualism in the nature of democratic societies: "Individualism is a reflective and peaceable sentiment that disposes each citizen to isolate himself from the mass of those like him and to withdraw to one side with his family and friends, so that after having thus created a little society for his own use, he willingly abandons society at large to itself" (*DA* 2.2.2). The individualist is one who withdraws from society into a private and isolated cocoon with those like him because, in part, the immensity of his society, "the public," overwhelms

29. Mitchell, *The Fragility of Freedom,* 78–87. See also Deneen, *Democratic Faith,* 214–38.

him. As a result, public opinion takes on greater authority than government or religion ever had in human history: "kings often make one obey, but it is always the majority that makes one believe; it is therefore the majority that one must please in all that is not contrary to the faith" (*DA* 2.1.5).

In addition to his shrunken spatial horizon, the individual also experiences a shrunken temporal horizon. Unlike ancient aristocrats who had a strong sense of ancestry and tradition, the democratic individual is rootless, which leads him to regard himself as an isolated atom in time, disconnected from heritage and progeny as much as from neighbor: "In democratic peoples, new families constantly issue from nothing, others constantly fall into it, and all those who stay on change face; the fabric of time is torn at every moment and the trace of generations is effaced. You easily forget those who have preceded you, and you have no idea of those who will follow you. Only those nearest have interest" (*DA* 2.2.2). Tocqueville anticipates the work of twentieth-century economists who find democracies particularly ill-equipped to make long-term decisions.[30] Examples include foreign policy, sacrifice of long-term environmental protection for short-term economic gain, accumulation of public debt that burdens future generations instead of the present one, and numerous issues involving "sexual politics" that result in inadequate replacement birth rates, which themselves require high immigration rates that require the state to take over an increasing amount of socialization functions in order to transmit cultural values.[31] However, Tocqueville identifies this as a problem of moral character among democrats, whether leader or citizen.

Individuals withdraw into themselves, giving them sovereign knowledge over their particular self-interest, which, ironically, makes them too reliant on public opinion as the source of their "hypergoods." However, their devotion to themselves and to equality leads them blindly to believe in pub-

30. Hans-Hermann Hoppe, *Democracy: The God That Failed: Studies in the Economics and Politics of Monarchy, Democracy, and Natural Order* (New Brunswick, N.J.: Transaction Publishers, 2001).

31. These pathologies of the democratic soul are prior to the economic reasons for the demise of marriage that critics of same-sex marriage legislation see articulated in the writings of Friedrich Engels (Douglas Farrow, "Facing Reality," in *Divorcing Marriage: Unveiling the Dangers in Canada's New Social Experiment,* ed. Daniel Cere and Douglas Farrow (Montréal-Kingston: McGill-Queens University Press, 2004), 156–57). Some proponents of same-sex marriage and the decriminalization of polygamy also regard them as steps toward abolishing the legal category of marriage altogether (see Martha Bailey, "Regulation of Cohabitation and Marriage in Canada," *Law and Policy* 26, no. 1 [January 2004]: 153–75; Angela Campbell et al., *Polygamy in Canada: Political and Legal Implications for Women and Children* [Ottawa: Status of Women Canada, 2005]).

lic opinion whose authority is even greater and pervasive than that of the church in medieval times: "but this same similarity gives them an almost unlimited trust in the judgment of the public; for it does not seem plausible to them that when all have the same enlightenment, truth is not found on the side of the greatest number" (*DA* 2.1.2). They rely inordinately on public opinion because they cannot imagine anything beyond it, including the foundation of their rights, which can no longer be grounded in nature, as it was for the founders of liberalism, because "nature" is lost on the empiricist individualist. Thus, their self-reliant individualism, combined with their blind faith in enlightened public opinion, according to which religion itself "reigns there much less as revealed doctrine than as common opinion" (*DA* 2.1.2), makes them especially hostile toward the claims of religion when those claims are expressed in terms of revealed doctrine: "Thus they willingly deny what they cannot comprehend: that gives them little faith in the extraordinary and an almost invincible distaste for the supernatural" (*DA* 2.1.1). Seen in this light, the democrat will necessarily view any arrangement between the state and religious associations as simply a compromise between reason and forces of irrationality, much in the same way that the Charter can be seen—within the ideology of liberalism—as a compromise between reason and the irrationality of particular identities that are mixed into the federal structure.[32]

Like a single particle in the ocean, democratic man is overwhelmed by the expanse of his society and even regards the human species as the object of his contemplation and allegiance. Equality suggests a cosmopolitanism wherein the individual identifies not with his nation but with the human species. Not everyone immediately feels this allegiance to the universal, but the feeling of being in a historical process owing to forces beyond human control—evolution, historical progress, globalization, democratization, technology, secularization—suggests sooner or later that everyone will feel it (*DA* 1.2.5, 2.1.20). For Tocqueville, the idea of equality suggests a belief in the indefinite perfectibility of the human race (*DA* 2.1.8). This is the object of "democratic faith," which is manifest in various ways in Canadian political society, including the view that the Charter is a "living tree" in constant

---

32. For instance, Pierre Trudeau, the key author of the Charter, had "reason before passion" as his key motto. Reason implied universal Enlightenment rationality, while passion meant irrationality, located in "particular" structures including the provinces and any other institution subordinate to the nation (see Kevin J. Christiano, *Pierre Elliott Trudeau: Reason before Passion* [Toronto: ECW Press, 1994]).

(and judge-led) evolution, and it also expresses itself in impatience against older faiths that do not necessarily share its Promethean aspirations.

While individualism and the "ephemeral monster" persist as an ever-present danger, Tocqueville thought that democracy contains moral, spiritual, and political resources within itself to counter the danger. However, the cost of utilizing those resources requires democrats to risk appearing antidemocratic because such resources are *extra res publicam*. He identified as the main resource the "holy enterprise" of cultivating "associations," including religious "associations" such as churches, schools, and more specialized bodies that play a key role in his story.

Associations, political and nonpolitical, are the means by which individuals, who are weak when alone and isolated, join together to act from strength for common projects. Tocqueville observes the multiplicity of associations and purposes: commercial, industrial, "religious, moral, grave, futile, very general and very particular, immense and very small," as well as those for various tasks such as founding seminaries, building inns, raising churches, building hospitals, and so on (*DA* 2.2.5). Where aristocratic societies depend on a few powerful individuals to perform such tasks, democratic societies have a more difficult task because they depend on isolated and weak individuals to form associations. Thus, associations must counter the prevailing tendency toward isolation and weakness that equality creates: "Unhappily, the same social state that renders associations so necessary to democratic peoples renders them more difficult for them than for all others." He thus refers to the science (other times, art) of association as the "mother science" (*DA* 2.2.5, 2.7): all other sciences/arts depend on the progress of that one. Even so, democratic states, tutored by the liberal axiom that law is about coercion, have an instinctive horror toward civil associations that might make a moral challenge to the state (*DA* 2.2.7).

Associations furthermore constitute "schools" that teach democrats to cherish their freedom and to identify their particular self-interest with the public interest. They cultivate what Tocqueville calls "self-interest well understood" (*DA* 2.2.8–9), which is so-called when individuals not only identify their self-interest with the common interest (and are willing to make small to medium sacrifices for the latter) and act in a field of action that is sufficiently large to lift their hearts, but not so large as never to see the fruits of their labors. Since the modern state is so large, and beyond the scope of most people's minds, associations provide a more human level of organization that enables individuals to identify their individual self-interest with that of the association, and enables them to regard the fruits of their labors more clearly than on the level of the state.

As a friendly critic of democracy, Tocqueville, therefore, enables us to understand how democratic principles themselves require moderation, and how religious groups and organizations are particularly well suited, but simultaneously are in a precarious situation, to correct some of democracy's vices. Primary is the ability to create, maintain, and cultivate religious communities that not only provide *good reasons* for members to join and remain, but also address the individualism and its effects that Tocqueville identified as corrosive of democratic life. Their mission is to offer a mirror to show the wider society a higher way of life to embrace, and to articulate sympathetically with the broader culture. In sum, the greatest counterbalance a religious group or organization can provide is to provide the fruits of friendship in the good that has always been the mission of the great world faith groups and their churches, and that cannot be obtained by the political realm.[33]

Freedom for Religious Associations under the Charter of Rights and Freedoms

Looking at how the Canadian Supreme Court handles the freedom of religious associations enables one to understand the degree to which the "mother science" of associational life is allowed to leaven the aspirations of democratic faith in the Canadian polity. Between 1982, the year the Charter was instituted, and the early 1990s, most Supreme Court cases involved the protection and accommodation of religious and nonreligious minorities from laws that were seen to have been based on religious or sectarian purposes. Charter jurisprudence in this area was originally characterized by the attempt to judge laws such as Sunday closing laws according to whether they were consistent with the secular purposes of the Charter or whether

---

33. For broader theoretical considerations on how the voices of revelation can converse with the broader culture in a way that respects both faith and reason, see David Walsh, *Guarded By Mystery: Meaning in a Postmodern Age* (Washington, D.C.: The Catholic University of America Press, 2002). See also my *Augustine and Politics as Longing in the World* (Columbia: University of Missouri Press, 2001) and "Disarming, Simple, and Sweet: Augustine's Republican Rhetoric," in *Talking Democracy: Historical Perspectives on Rhetoric and Democratic Deliberation*, ed. Benedetto Fontana et al. (University Park: Penn State University Press, 2004), 163–86.

their purpose was religious and thus discriminatory toward religious minorities. In recent years, however, the focus has expanded to include cases involving religious minorities petitioning to protect their associational life against the encroachment of the secular state, as well as the role of religious expression in a public space seen as becoming increasingly secular in such a way that removes religious voices from public debate.[34] The jurisprudence has been ably summarized and analyzed elsewhere,[35] but it is helpful here to focus on how the logic of some recent decisions makes associational life fragile. Especially in cases in which the freedom of a religious association confronts an equality right of some other minority seeking recognition (part of the expanded sense of harm, noted above), the Court (and lower courts) have attempted to promote the equality right, but not always at the expense of the religious association. Quite frequently the strategy has been to avoid substantive questions on how the rights of each rank in Charter jurisprudence. When the courts wish to promote the equality right at the expense of the right of the religious association, the courts have attempted to minimize, and even trivialize, the conflict between the competing rights, which undermines the Court's role in the nation-building process.

In *R. v. Big M. Drug Mart,* the Supreme Court set the tone for future freedom-of-religion cases by collapsing religion into conscience, despite the Charter's wording of "freedom of conscience and religion."[36] Then Chief Justice Dickson wrote: "What unites enunciated freedoms in the American First Amendment, § 2(a) of the *Charter* and in the provisions of other human rights documents in which they are associated is the notion of the centrality of individual conscience and the inappropriateness of governmental intervention to compel or to constrain its manifestation."[37] Freedom of conscience is fundamental because it accords with the ability of "each citizen to make free and informed decisions" and with "basic beliefs about human worth and dignity." While his definition of freedom of religion in terms of conscience is true as far as it goes, it is essentially an individualistic reading of freedom of religion, and ignores the communal aspect of reli-

34. See J. Gonthier's concerns over this view of secularism advocated by some litigants in his dissent in *Chamberlain v. Surry School District No. 36,* 2002 SCC 86 at 135.

35. David M. Brown, "Freedom From or Freedom For?: Religion as a Case Study in Defining the Content of Charter Rights," *University of British Columbia Law Review* 33 (2000): 551–616; Heyking, "The Harmonization of Heaven and Earth?" 676–95.

36. *Canadian Charter of Rights and Freedoms,* Schedule B of the *Constitution Act,* 1982 (U.K.), 2(a) [hereinafter *Charter*]. *R. v. Big M Drug Mart Ltd* (1985) 1 S.C.R., 295 [hereinafter *Big M.*].

37. *Big M.* at 346.

gion that is so important to many religions, including Judaism, Islam, and Roman Catholicism. Dickson's definition views religion as an essentially private matter, which informs the Charter's later decisions.

The pathologies of Tocqueville's democratic soul can be seen most clearly when the Supreme Court is faced with having to arbitrate between the rights of a religious group and an internal minority who invokes s. 15 of the Charter to contest the group's right to remove rights and privileges from that minority, as well as to set the terms of how a religious group engages with the broader society. The Court either has upheld the right of religious organizations to discriminate according to bona fide occupational requirements (BFOR), or has attempted to minimize the conflict between the two stake-holders in a way that diminishes the profundity with which each side regards its own position; it recognizes one by recognizing none. This strategy undermines the Supreme Court's role as a nation-building institution because it ends up draining the public sphere as a meaningful place where recognition can be owed.

The Court did not directly handle the problem of religious liberty in *Vriend v. Alberta,* in which the litigants were Mr. Vriend, a lab instructor who was fired by Kings College, a Christian college, for homosexual behavior, and the Alberta government.[38] Kings was not a party to the case, and the Court dealt mostly with the issue of whether the Alberta government should have included protections for homosexuals in its Human Rights Act. After reading homosexual rights into the Alberta Human Rights Act, the Court simply concluded that Kings would have its employee code of conduct accepted by a court as a BFOR.

Lower courts and tribunals have generally accepted BFORs by religious institutions, and their reasons for doing so have been largely consistent with the Supreme Court's prudential approach to religious liberties. For example, the Manitoba Human Rights Commission ruled in favor of a Mennonite College who fired a secretary after she converted to Mormonism.[39] However, as Alvin Esau observes, the BFOR approach insufficiently protects associations because BFOR depends on individual judges and not on law. Instead, he advocates statutory "exemptions to preserve religious associational life" over BFOR.[40] The idea of BFOR requires religious orga-

38. *Vriend v. Alberta* (1998) 1 S.C.R. 493 [hereinafter *Vriend*].
39. *Schroen v. Steinbach Bible College* (1999) 35 C.H.R.R. D/1 (Man. Bd. Adj.), Mr. Donald Knight, Q.C., Board of Adjudication, July 21, 1999 [hereinafter *Schroen*].
40. Alvin Esau, "'Islands of Exclusivity': Religious Organizations and Employment Discrimi-

nizations to put themselves before the bar of virtue in the modern republic, and, in that sense, it presupposes that the rights of those religious organizations flow from the state instead of presupposing that the individuals and groups (with the rights and commitments inherent to them) are prior to the state, as is the case of traditional liberal democratic theory. BFOR thus presupposes the existence of civic virtue that judges religious organizations.

BFOR is at the crux of how the Charter structures and hinders associational life in Canada. It has been noted that the logic of the Charter, which aspires to recognize the universality of human rights, suppresses particular cultural, regional, and religious practices by treating them as "irrational." Speaking of Trudeau's version of the Charter, Andrew Fraser observes that "[a]ccording to Trudeau's functionalist logic, the survival of any local, regional, or civic culture cannot be treated as an end in itself. . . . Trudeau's utilitarian and bloodless version of Canadian nationalism assumes that the function of language is to transmit standardized messages through a culturally homogeneous space altogether detached from the normative constraints of time and tradition."[41] Under these auspices, George Egerton argues that Trudeau intended the Charter to facilitate secularization in Canada, which meant not only disengaging laws such as those relating to sexuality from religious justifications and limitations, but going further by limiting their roles in participating in public debate: "[T]he Liberal government was facilitating a process of differentiation whereby religion would be divested of its former role as arbiter of public morals, with churches being transformed from the 'conscience of the nation' to privatized suppliers of spiritual services to consumers."[42]

Such standardized or instrumentalized speech conflicts with an associational life in which participation is seen as organic or holistic. While

---

nation," *University of British Columbia Law Review* vol. 33, special edition (2000): 722. See his more extended analysis in *The Courts and the Colonies: The Litigation of Hutterite Church Disputes* (Vancouver: University of British Columbia Press, 2004), 295–331.

41. Andrew Fraser, *The Spirit of the Laws* (Toronto: University of Toronto Press, 1990), 16. In this chapter, we are not juxtaposing "utilitarian and bloodless" with a society based on race, warrior ethos, or Schmittian friend-enemy distinction. It is rather juxtaposed with a society whose pre-political existence is based in its constitutive myths, stories, and constitutional pride in self-government; its politics is characterized more by a civil conversation shared by cives who continuously explore their relation with one another (Michael Oakeshott, *On Human Conduct* [Oxford: Clarendon Press, 1975], 122–23). See also William Mathie, "Political Community and the Canadian Experience: Reflections on Nationalism, Federalism, and Unity," *Canadian Journal of Political Science* 12, no. 1 (March 1979): 3–20.

42. Egerton, "Trudeau, God, and the Canadian Constitution," 96.

BFOR is meant to avoid trivializing the ways of life of minorities under the homogenizing, secularizing logic of the Charter (and so indicates the Charter's requirement of moderation), BFOR expresses the ambivalence of the regime toward religious associational life. As Esau observes, "the religious workplace is a church where people worship together, not just at work, but through work. . . . So long as the BFOR test is premised on showing that the particular job has explicit religious duties attached to it or that the job has a role model dimension, the test is fundamentally at odds with the nature of many religious workplaces or organic communities of faith."[43] BFOR, and associational freedom in general, works only when the practices not directly related to worship in the pews can still be understood by the secular state as related to religious purposes, and so that they are not treated as "privatized suppliers of spiritual services to consumers" who transmit "standardized messages through a culturally homogeneous space."

Trinity Western University v. the British Columbia Council of Teachers is so far the most significant case involving the rights of a religious organization that the Supreme Court has yet heard.[44] The BCCT had refused to accredit TWU's teacher program on the grounds that the code of behavior that all TWU students must sign was deemed discriminatory against homosexuals and thus made graduates of its teacher program ill-equipped to deal fairly with homosexual students in public schools. The Court ruled in favor of Trinity Western University on the grounds that the BCCT had been unable to find instances of discrimination committed by TWU graduates. In its 8 to 1 decision, the Court generally recognized the value of

43. Esau, "'Islands of Exclusivity,'" 734–35. Esau's point pertains whenever the Court distinguishes matters it views as central to religious faith versus those it views as periphery. This can be seen in its analysis of mandated versus voluntary religious practices of Orthodox Jews in *Syndicat Northcrest v. Amselem* (2004) 2 S.C.R. 551. David Brown criticizes the Court's distinction, which is based on the broader assumption of a distinction between sacred and secular, as unworkable ("Neutrality or Privilege?: A Comment on Religious Freedom," *Supreme Court Law Review* 29[2d] [2005]: 222–26). Consider also the tendency of courts to consider aboriginal spirituality not in terms of freedom of religion, but in terms of treaty rights. (Lori G. Beaman, "Aboriginal Spirituality and the Legal Construction of Freedom of Religion," *Journal of Church and State* 44 [Winter 2002]: 135–49). The difficulty of determining a role for Shari'ah-based arbitration for Muslims is another example (Marion Boyd, *Dispute Resolution in Family Law: Protecting Choice, Promoting Inclusion,* Report to Ontario Attorney-General and Minister Responsible for Women's Issues, Government of Ontario. 2004).

44. *Trinity Western University v. British Columbia College of Teachers* (2001) 1 S.C.R. 772 [hereinafter *Trinity*].

religious associations as genuine contributors toward meaningful pluralism within civil society. It also observed that TWU is a voluntary organization that will not appeal to everyone. They thus decided the case in terms analogous to the BFOR, on the basis that internal minorities have the right to join or leave the institution.

The Court's treatment of discrimination, or, more precisely, its failure to define it, is more troubling. The Court ruled in favor of TWU in part because the BCCT could not prove discrimination. However, the Court did not explain what it meant by discrimination. Inciting violence against and isolating homosexual students are blatant examples of unjustifiable discriminatory behavior. However, TWU, by setting up a code of behavior, views some forms of discrimination as justified. For instance, a graduate of TWU may well agree with its code of behavior and wish to act upon those beliefs in the classroom. One can imagine an example of a teacher or guidance counselor, out of sincere and thoughtful belief, counseling in a caring and inclusive way that respects the dignity of a homosexual student, while advising him or her of the teacher's opinion about the superiority of chastity and heterosexual relations. The BCCT would regard such behavior as unjustifiably discriminatory, but the Supreme Court left the issue hanging. By doing so, they failed to provide proper guidance on the extent of freedom of religious practices when those practices conflict with the Court's construction of selfhood for s. 15 rights.[45]

A 2002 Ontario Superior Court decision that required an Ontario Roman Catholic high school to permit a homosexual student to attend the prom with his same-sex partner sharply divided belief from action by treating the prom as having no connection whatsoever to the educational purposes of the Roman Catholic school.[46] Ironically, Justice MacKinnon's decision unintentionally separated belief from action also for the homosexual student even in deciding in his favor, because the Justice defined the prom exclusively as a "celebratory cultural and social event of passage from high school," and as having nothing to do with courtship or dating leading to

45. In a related case, the British Columbia Court of Appeal upheld the BCCT's disciplining of a teacher who wrote letters to a newspaper critical of homosexuals (*Kempling v. British Columbia College of Teachers* (2005) BCCA 327 [CanLII]).

46. *Hall v. Powers*, Ontario Superior Court of Justice, May 10, 2002, Court File No. 02-CV-227705CM3 [hereinafter *Hall*]. This case was later discontinued at the Ontario Superior Court of Justice (*Hall v. Durham Catholic District School Board* [2005] CanLII 23121 [ON S.C.]), available on-line at: http://www.canlii.org/on/cas/onsc/2005/2005onsc14089.html.

marriage or other intimate relations. His understanding of the prom (and the dating and courtship rituals contained within it) is based on the "fun" culture of the democratic soul. He ended up treating the social meaning of the prom as having no connection to the litigant's homosexuality, just as it was seen to constitute no significance for heterosexuals in that matter.[47] His reasoning meant the decision was only a Pyrrhic victory for the litigant and proponents of s. 15 equality rights, who wish to use the courts to obtain societal recognition. For homosexuals, as for religious associations, the jurisprudence of the democratic soul creates a homogeneous social space devoid of meaning, thus aggravating the isolation of those wishing to see a connection between themselves and their community.

The Supreme Court replicated the easygoingness of the democratic soul in *Chamberlain v. Surrey School District No. 36*,[48] which overturned a provincial court decision permitting the Surrey, British Columbia, school board to exclude books portraying homosexual parenting from elementary school libraries, where they would have been included as part of K–1 level education. The Court reversed the lower court's decision on the grounds that the board's decision, which was based in part on the religiously based objections of some of its members, excluded homosexual perspectives and was thus intolerant. The Court based its decision in part by rejecting arguments that such material is inappropriate for K–1 level children because it induces "cognitive dissonance." Whatever the theoretical difficulties with this category, the Court countered by portraying K–1 level children as quite capable of living with it. They did so even though some members of the majority opinion have used the potential for it in an earlier case when the rights of a Jehovah's Witness were in question, but there the Court ruled that the "cognitive dissonance" of having a Jehovah's Witness father and a Roman Catholic mother would upset the Jehovah's Witness's child.[49] However, in *Chamberlain*, the Court characterized the subject matter of the books in such reductionistic terms so as even to remove the potential for cognitive dissonance anyway: "But such dissonance is neither avoidable nor noxious. Children encounter it every day in the public school system as members of a diverse student body. They see their classmates, and perhaps also their teachers, eating foods at lunch that they themselves are

47. *Hall* at 25–26.
48. *Chamberlain v. Surrey School District No. 36* (2002) 4 S.C.R. 710.
49. *P. (D.) v. S. (C.)* (1993) 4 S.C.R. 141.

not permitted to eat, whether because of their parents' religious strictures or because of other moral beliefs. They see their classmates wearing clothing with features or brand labels which their parents have forbidden them to wear. And they see their classmates engaging in behavior on the playground that their parents have told them not to engage in."[50] While six-year-olds may view marital relationships and family structures in the same way they view clothing brand labels, the Court in this passage was making a general statement about the social space and civic obligations Canadians as a whole must have for one another. In doing so, the Court reduced marital relationships, which encompasses every strata of the human person, including the biological, sexual, rational, and spiritual realms, to a state of affairs indistinguishable from cafeteria behavior or the wearing of designer labels. Like the *Hall* decision, the Court removed the significance of sexuality, courtship, and marriage from consideration, which is a loss for both sides of the case regardless of which side wins in this particular judicial decision. The Court promotes "cognitive dissonance" by eliminating it with "utilitarian and bloodless" egalitarianism, and thus it declares: "tolerance is always age-appropriate."[51]

The 2004 case, *Syndicat Northcrest v. Amselem,* departs somewhat from the "utilitarian and bloodless" egalitarianism the Court has so far promulgated.[52] The Court ruled that a condominium board had to allow a group of Orthodox Jewish unit-owners to construct succahs on their balconies as part of the Jewish festival of Succot, despite the prohibition in their condominium contract prohibiting tenants from altering property. The Court took an expansive view of religious freedom and practices connected to it. Unlike the *Trinity Western* and *Chamberlain* cases, it neither dodged the question of a minority religion's interface with the larger society nor watered down that interface to the point of making it meaningless. Writing for the majority, Justice Iaccobucci viewed religious ritual and practice as being as important as religious belief. Religion gets protected as a matter of choice as well as cultural practice, based on the Charter's protection of religion and minorities. Richard Moon criticizes the decision because he sees the court incoherently trying to defend religious freedom on the basis of both individual autonomy and unchosen identity (i.e., that which gets

50. *Chamberlain* at 65.
51. *Chamberlain* at 67.
52. *Syndicat Northcrest v. Amselem* (2004) 2 S.C.R. 551.

"recognized"). The Charter protects rights on the basis of both principles, but Moon prefers it to protect religious freedoms on the basis of autonomy. His criticism of the Court's reasoning has a ring of truth to it, but, as David Brown responds, neither "choice" nor "identity" adequately explains religious phenomena.[53] Moreover, "autonomy" and "identity" are not mutually exclusive categories under the auspices of Charter liberalism. It seems, however, that the Court's conflation of the two is an attempt to defend religious freedom on the basis of a principle found neither in the Charter nor in the terminology of "hypergoods" found in Charter jurisprudence, but in the recognition that religious belief and practices precede the constitution and social contract both historically and ontologically. Since the Court prefers the language of Charter "hypergoods," it necessarily makes this recognition in a clumsy fashion. As such, the decision reflects a degree of practical judgment over mechanical legal rule-following that is especially appropriate for religious freedom cases.[54] The decision in many ways comports with Tocqueville's defense of religious associations, and by seemingly giving priority to religious over secular (i.e., property) values, it also comports with David Novak's insistence that religious groups are specially placed to defend rights because their communities precede political society, both historically and ontologically.[55] Even so, it is worth noticing that the Court decided in favor of the religious rights of a minority against the property rights of the condominium association; property rights are not in the Charter, anyway. Faced with a conflict of religious freedoms and other types of rights-claims, it may have dodged the fundamental issues as it did in *Trinity Western.*

This sketch of religious freedom cases shows that Canada has a court that wishes neither to trample religious freedoms, nor to hold them in highest esteem. It shows it is capable of preserving the rights of religious communities. However, it is inconsistent largely because it lacks a robust theoretical framework in which to ground religious freedoms in a genuinely pluralist society. Until it clarifies key concepts such as "secular" in the way it conceives political society, religious freedoms in Canada will remain fragile.[56]

53. Richard Moon, "Religious Commitment and Identity: *Syndicat Northcrest v. Amselem,*" *Supreme Court Law Review* 29(2d) (2005): 202, 216; Brown, "Neutrality or Privilege?" 222–26.
54. As argued by Heyking, "The Harmonization of Heaven and Earth?" 687, 696–97.
55. Novak, "Human Dignity and the Social Contract," 51–68.
56. As argued by Benson, "Considering Secularism," 83–98, and "Notes toward a (Re)Definition of the 'Secular.'"

Canada's Invisible Crown and Canada's Re-Founding

Numerous commentators use the language of nation-building and founding to describe the Charter's role in Canadian society. As Samuel LaSelva observes, the Charter's function of securing rights is based on it first having secured the sovereignty of Canadians.[57] Further, Alan Cairns notes that rights identify the character of Canadians when he observes that "[r]ights tell us who we are."[58] Roy Romanow, the former premier of the province of Saskatchewan, said of the Charter: "Building upon it, future generations of Canadians can strengthen the fabric of nationhood."[59] Cairns clarifies the soulcraft of this founding: "A citizenry seized of the constitutional recognition accorded by the Charter would be drawn out of provincialism into a pan-Canadian sense of self. . . . [T]he Charter was a nationalizing, Canadianizing constitutional instrument intended to shape the psyches and identities of Canadians."[60] This soulcraft is what CJ McLachlin refers to as the Charter's "hypergoods" and its "total claim" upon each individual. Former Chief Justice Antonio Lamer regarded the re-founding so momentous he proclaimed in 1992 that the Charter is "a revolution on the scale of the introduction of the metric system, the great medical discoveries of Louis Pasteur, and the invention of penicillin and the laser." Five years later he stated, "Thank God for the Charter. . . . [People] just don't realize what it would be like if we didn't have these rights."[61] The intimate connection of individual rights and nation-building is reflected in Knopff's observation that rights are no longer regarded as natural, but based on "con-

57. See Ian Greene, *The Charter of Rights* (Toronto: James Lorimer, 1989), 38; Samuel LaSelva, *The Moral Foundations of Canadian Federalism* (Montreal-Kingston: McGill-Queens University Press, 1996), 89.

58. Alan C. Cairns, *Reconfigurations: Canadian Citizenship and Constitutional Change* (Toronto: McClelland and Stewart, 1995), 203. For the contrary view, see Alexander Hamilton's characterization of the Bill of Rights as a monarchal device (*Federalist* no. 84).

59. Roy Romanow, "'Reworking the Miracle': The Constitutional Accord of 1981," 8 *Queen's Law Journal* 98 (1983).

60. Cairns, *Reconfigurations,* 197. It could be argued that "soulcraft," or civic education, is not a function of liberal politics, which seems to presuppose the autonomy of citizens and a view of law as procedural instead of educative. For the contrary view, see the essays in *Cultivating Citizens: Soulcraft and Citizenship in Contemporary America,* ed. Dwight D. Allman and Michael D. Beaty (Lanham, Md.: Lexington Books, 2002).

61. Quoted in Knopff and Morton, *The Charter Revolution and the Court Party,* 16. For an instance of the old Canadian Bill of Rights offering *superior* protection of religious freedoms to that of the Charter, see Heyking, "Harmonization of Heaven and Earth?" 684.

sensus," that is, on social and political conditioning.[62] Thus, the Charter's inauguration of an era of modern republicanism includes re-founding the regime, which includes "changing human nature, so to speak," to use the language of Jean-Jacques Rousseau on the Legislator's task of founding a regime.[63]

As seen in the discussion above on the Court's construction of freedom and human dignity, many view the Charter as the focus of their myth that Canada under the Charter is developing (perhaps indefinitely) toward ever-expanding inclusion, nationhood, and participatory democracy (republicanism). It is a quasi-teleological and historical myth, and one of liberation from the vestiges of past prejudices that supported "elitism" and exclusion, and also liberation from religious, metaphysical, and historical supports of the past. Thus, Cairns contrasts the future- and rights-oriented Charter with the more Spartan but more organic, quasi-Burkean Constitution Act of 1867, which was oriented toward history and to origins.[64] This change from a "dark" past to an enlightened secular future can be seen in the statements of Trudeau and others who viewed the Charter as a secular document to supersede the age of religion as encapsulated in the Constitution Act of 1867.[65] This change to a historical self-understanding is seen in the tendency of Supreme Court justices to provide a purposive reading of the Charter instead of one that focuses on original intent. Like a St. George in constant pursuit of the dragons of inequality, the purposive reading is meant to liberate various individuals and minorities from what the judges view as restrictions on autonomy.

The Charter myth as a myth of progress contains two immediate contradictions. First, just as Tocqueville noticed that democratic souls regard universal humanity as the object of action, so too does this Charter myth aspire to cosmopolitanism, which undermines the sense that one can have a particular nation or a particular people. Instead, it produces "utilitarian and bloodless" civic obligations among "autonomous" subjects, as seen in the religious freedom cases. Second, it is unclear that Canada has secularized, and can be secularized, to the extent that religious and otherwise metaphysical considerations of reality can be removed from political de-

62. Knopff, "Populism and the Politics of Rights," 699.
63. Rousseau, *Social Contract*, 2:7.
64. Cairns, *Reconfigurations*, 97–118.
65. Egerton, "Trudeau, God, and the Canadian Constitution," 96.

liberations and analysis. Indeed, the Charter may necessitate the Court to engage in even greater religious and philosophical discussion.[66]

While the "secular" status of the allegedly new Canada is open to question, so too is the belief that the Charter's modern republican aspiration fits with Canadian society. The Charter is purported to form a republican people, endowed with rights that their act of constituting itself as a people have recognized and secured. Yet, as Fraser tartly observes, "No republican could fail to notice that the Charter came into being as an Act of the Imperial Crown in Parliament. Never having been submitted to the Canadian people for ratification, the Charter would appear to have failed the most minimal test for republican legitimacy."[67] The deeper problem that Fraser's observation manifests has been the cause of eminent University of Toronto political scientist Peter Russell's "brooding" over the state of the Canadian constitution. He reports in the preface to the first edition of his book, *Constitutional Odyssey,* which is pointedly subtitled with the question, "Can Canadians Become a Sovereign People?" that his broodings were prompted by a remark that American political theorist Walter Berns posed to him: "Peter, you Canadians have not yet constituted yourselves as a people." Russell concluded that Berns was right, and observed the difficulties of moving from a Burkean and organic pre-Charter constitutionalism to the Charter, which reflects more the Lockean social contract constitutionalism.[68] Fraser and Russell cast doubt on the myth that the Charter has refounded or can re-found the Canadian polity. This inherent contradiction raises doubts about the workability of a style of constitutional interpretation that assumes a "way of life" when, in fact, there are multiple "ways of life," and where what is taken as the "Canadian" way of life is more often than not the central Canadian "Laurentian" way of life.[69]

---

66. Benson, "Considering Secularism," 83–98, and "Notes toward a (Re)Definition of the 'Secular,'" 519–50. According to Cairns: "'Rights' pushes university law faculties in the direction of legal theory and political philosophy" (*Reconfigurations,* 202).

67. Andrew Fraser, "Beyond the Charter Debate: Republicanism, Rights, and Civic Virtue in the Civil Constitution of Canadian Society," *Review of Constitutional Studies* 1, no. 1 (1993): 31.

68. Peter Russell, *Constitutional Odyssey: Can Canadians Become a Sovereign People?* 3rd ed. (Toronto: University of Toronto Press, 2004), ix, 10–11.

69. Barry Cooper, "Regionalism, Political Culture, and Canadian Political Myths," in *Regionalism and Party Politics in Canada,* ed. Lisa Young and Keith Archer (Toronto: Oxford University Press, 2002), 92–111; Cooper, "Theoretical Perspectives on Constitutional Reform in Canada," in *Rethinking the Constitution,* ed. Peacock, 217–32; Kim, "The Absence of Pan-Canadian Civil Religion: Plurality, Duality, and Conflict in Symbols in Canadian Culture."

The difficulty of envisaging a Canadian modern republic is that there is no meaningful unit that one can identify as a Canadian "people" that also carries out politics outside of the apparatus of the state. Instead, Smith observes how efforts to promote republicanism in Canada are hindered by the fact that Canada's state form is not republican. It is best understood in terms of the "invisible crown," whose authority emanates from the top down to the people. This differs decisively from republicanism, where authority flows from the people, who legitimate their regime. But a people must be a people to give their regime legitimacy. In Canada, there is no *populus* that corresponds to an envisaged *res publica*. Furthermore, the embedded Canadian state, which, despite the Charter, remains a monarchy, is charged with the responsibility of forging that people. Thus, freedom in Canada is attenuated by the fact that there is no Canadian "people" that exists as a corporate body capable—practically or theoretically—of transferring its rights to each other and of setting up a state that guarantees those rights, as is required by the basic precepts of liberalism.

Canadians want the freedoms and community spirit associated with a modern republic, but they, or their elites, want their monarchal forms to create it. However, the means of bringing about the goal has the effect of undermining the goal, as well as freedoms at the heart of that goal. The monarchal element of the Canadian state was expressed most bluntly by the Privy Council Office itself: "Constitutionally, the power of the state flows from the Crown and generally speaking may only be exercised by or on the authority of the Crown."[70] Thus, in Canada, politics is about partnership with the Crown. One thinks of the concentration of power in the prime minister's office, the difference between the inner- and outer-cabinet, the power of the civil service in initiating the law-making process, and the ability of political parties to constrain other forms of democratic expression. Also consistent with the "invisible Crown" is the politics of recognizing Charter Canadians—women, aboriginals, gays, and other groups who fall under the penumbra of s. 15 rights—through programs like the Court Challenges Program, not as autonomous, non-governmental "outside bodies," but as client agencies.

The Charter reflects a situation in which the state has become entangled

---

70. Canada, Privy Council Office, *Submissions to the Royal Commission on Financial Management and Accountability* (Ottawa: 1979, Submission 1: "Responsibility in the Constitution," 1–5). Quoted in C. E. S. Franks, *The Parliament of Canada* (Toronto: University of Toronto Press, 1987), 18. Franks notes that Parliament has a relatively small role if this viewpoint is accepted.

in society to the extent that "society has been constitutionalized, or the constitution has been socialized."[71] Thus, Canada, like many Western democracies, is an "embedded state" characterized by numerous interactions between a relatively diffuse civil society and a government where power is becoming increasingly concentrated into fewer and fewer hands. Politics becomes the self-legitimating activity of the executive whose authority, its "invisible crown," is ostensibly legitimated by ostensible civil society groups that are themselves created, funded, supported, and recognized by the executive itself. The primary checks on government are no longer Parliament, but the media and the government's own inefficiency.[72] Because the democratic soul is concerned foremost with its self-interest rather than its pride in self-government, it chooses to allow the state to define and defend its rights.[73]

The interweaving of a modern republican goal with the monarchal means to bring it about can also be seen in our articulations of citizenship, which symbolize the characteristic gathering together democratic souls seek and find. In fact, the democratic soul, which has no identity, can articulate neither itself nor togetherness, so, as Smith observes, the "invisible crown" attempts to manufacture it. Yet, every attempt to define the Canadian people has failed because such definitions evaporate in empty and overly abstract formulas about tolerance, multiculturalism, and so forth. For example, a Ministry of Citizenship and Immigration document lists Canadian values to be equality, respect for cultural differences, freedom, peace, and law and order. While those values are attractive especially for immigrants from coun-

71. Cairns, *Reconfigurations*, 201, 31–61.

72. *The Republican Option in Canada*, 143; *The Invisible Crown*, 148–55; Donald Savoie, *Governing From the Centre: The Concentration of Power in Canadian Politics* (Toronto: University of Toronto Press, 1999) and "The Rise of Court Government in Canada," *Canadian Journal of Political Science* 32, no. 4 (December 1999): 635–64. The literature on the political executive's role in establishing clientelistic relations with various minorities in its nation-building function is extensive. See Leslie A. Pal, *Interests of State: The Politics of Language, Multiculturalism and Feminism in Canada* (Montreal: McGill-Queen's University Press, 1993); Knopff and Morton, *The Charter Revolution and the Court Party;* Ian Brodie, *Friends of the Court: The Privileging of Interest Group Litigants in Canada* (Albany: State University Press of New York, 2002). Andrew Fraser traces this "self-legitimating" executive action of nation-building to eighteenth-century ideas about enlightened despotism (*The Spirit of the Laws*, 47). See also his application of this idea to Trudeau and the Charter (14–18).

73. See Harvey Mansfield Jr., *America's Constitutional Soul* (Baltimore: Johns Hopkins University Press, 1991), 214. According to Tocqueville, democrats "accept for a general principle that the public power ought not to intervene in private affairs, but each of them desires that it *aid* him as an exception in the special affair that preoccupies him" (*DA* 2.4.3, 644n1 [emphasis added]).

tries that lack them, the document fails to explain how they have been practiced in Canada's specific history. Neglecting one's history signifies lack of confidence in that history.[74] Similarly, Smith observes of a 1996 Canadian report on multiculturalism:

"[C]ore values" favor the abstract and the passive as witness the following list of values . . . : "a belief in equity and fairness; a belief in consultation and peaceful dialogue; a respect for diversity; a recognition of the importance of accommodation and tolerance; a spirit of generosity and compassion; and pride [in] and respect for the environment." The language of entitlement, the clientelistic relationship that the Charter creates for specific groups, and the dependency upon the executive for protection and advocacy are characteristic of the subject of citizenship in Canada.[75]

This is Trudeau's "utilitarian and bloodless" Charter nationalism.

For tolerance and multiculturalism to be meaningful for republicans, they have to point to an underlying substratum of civic virtue that is tied to a particular people with a particular history.[76] Both of these are elusive creatures in the Canadian experience. Only historical experience can build tolerant republican peoples. However, nation building and even much of rights-politics are conducted under the auspices of the self-legitimating executive action of the Crown. Thus, Smith observes that "citizenship [now] depends upon the arts and the academy, and 'particularly the structure of universities and their relationship to the larger society' for its propagation."[77] We have noted how the Charter's secularizing function shifted authority away from churches to the Court, the new "conscience of the nation," with references to the Court as "legal cardinals" now commonplace.[78] Even so, Egerton testifies to the "top-down" model of Canadian political authority

74. Citizenship and Immigration Canada, *A Look at Canada* (Ottawa: Minister of Public Works and Government Services Canada, 2005), 7, available at http://www.cic.gc.ca/english/pdf/pub/look.pdf. Father Raymond J. de Souza, "Dumbing Down 'Canadian Values,'" *National Post* (Don Mills, Ont.), March 9, 2006: A19.

75. Smith, *The Republican Option in Canada*, 194–95, citing Multiculturalism and Citizenship Canada (1991–92), "Citizenship Discussion Document."

76. See Hannah Arendt's invocation of Burke and the "rights of Englishmen" in her explanation of how notions of universalistic human rights failed to protect Jews from the Holocaust. To be meaningful, "human rights" must actually be "our rights" (Hannah Arendt, *Totalitarianism* (New York: Harcourt, Brace, Jovanovich, 2001), 172).

77. Smith, *The Republican Option in Canada*, 190–91, quoting Jean Leca, "Questions on Citizenship," in Chantal Mouffe, ed., *Dimensions of Radical Democracy: Pluralism, Citizenship, Community* (London: Verso, 1992), 22.

78. Egerton, 108, and Simpson, A15.

when he equates the acceptance of Trudeau's liberalism by elites with "[t]his ideological and social conversion of Canadians," despite "the unwillingness [among Canadians] to accord ruling elites much by way of honor, respect, or even legitimacy."[79] In contrast to a consociational identity derived from below and from robust, diverse, and self-organizing groups of civil society, citizenship now depends upon instruction and communication from above.

The vagueness of the meaning of Canadian citizenship can be seen as the result both of the regionalism and lack of pan-Canadian identity and of the inner vacuity of the democratic soul. The attempt to define citizenship for the democratic soul, which, in attempting to move beyond the Thrasymachean "justice is the interest of the stronger" to which it inclines, ends up identifying citizenship in terms of formalistic process and the negotiated relations among such selves, as Allan Gregg notices of "fundamentalist" secularists who rely on legalism and procedure to defend their moral claims.[80] Thus, contentless buzzwords such as "equity," "fairness," "dialogue," "respect," "diversity," "toleration," Tocquevillian "compassion," and, of course, motherhood issues like the environment abound.

Such buzzwords provide the veneer of the high-minded cosmopolitanism—a reflection of a society committed to universal human rights—which gives people the impression that more concrete articulations of virtue and self-hood (i.e., beliefs of religious associations) appear sectarian and rational, and are thus in need of being enlightened and relieved of their particularities. Ultimately, the progressive cosmopolitan myth of the Charter repudiates the Canadian experience of associational life: "The radicalism of the Trudeau option lay in several quarters, though nowhere more so than in its rejection of a consociational idea of citizenship secured from below, a conception rooted in the central experience of Canadian history."[81]

Conclusion

Through their elites, Canadians are in the midst of creating a cosmopolitan democracy under the Charter of Rights and Freedoms. The myth of equality and progress is seen as a means of legitimating this shift in its political existence. Progress is an article of faith in a perfectible future—no

79. Egerton, 108–9.
80. Gregg, "The Christian Comeback," 22.
81. Smith, *The Republican Option in Canada*, 189.

less an act of faith than faith in the Prophet Mohammed or in the Resurrection of Jesus—which is why it is appropriate to speak of this process as a civil religion. The purported re-founding of the regime therefore takes on cosmic significance for the adherents of this democratic faith. This democratic faith has the potential to challenge and marginalize those faiths whose practices run counter to the articles of the democratic faith in part because those faiths take their cues from ancient tradition, revelation, or revelation expressed through natural law. While the potential exists for democratic faith to proclaim *"non salus extra republicam,"* a combination of common sense among Canada's Supreme Court Justices and the inherent contradictoriness of the democratic faith's aspirations to secularize and unify Canada provides those faiths with breathing room. Whether those faiths respond constructively and provide coherent countercultural examples of the good life depends on their willingness and ability to engage and criticize the democratic faith, and to serve as the superior philosophically prophetic voices they were originally called to be.

Bibliography

Primary Sources

Antiquity

Cicero, Marcus Tullius. *The Nature of the Gods.* Translated by Horace C. P. McGregor. Penguin Classics. Harmondsworth: Penguin, 1984.

———. *The Republic. The Laws.* Translated by Neil Rudd. Oxford World's Classics. Oxford: Oxford University Press, 1998.

———. *The Speeches.* Translated by N. H. Watts. Loeb Classical Library. Cambridge and London: Harvard University Press/William Heinemann, 1965.

Livy, Titus. *Rome and the Mediterranean. Books XXXI–XLV of The History of Rome from Its Foundation.* Translated by Henry Bettenson. London: Penguin, 1976.

———. *Titi Livi Ab Urbe Condita Libri.* Vol. 9: Books XXXIX and XL. Edited by W. Weissenborn and H. J. Müller. 5th ed. Berlin, Dublin, and Zurich: Weidmannsche Verlagsbuchhandlung, 1965.

Plato. *Gorgias.* Translated by Donald J. Zeyl. Indianapolis, Ind.: Hackett, 1987.

———. *The Laws of Plato.* Translated by Thomas L. Pangle. New York: Basic Books, 1980.

———. *Platon: Oeuvres Complètes.* Edited and translated by Édouard des Places, S.J., and Auguste Diès. 4th ed. Vols. 11–12. Paris: Les Belles Lettres, 1992.

———. *The Republic of Plato.* 2nd ed. Translated by Allan Bloom. New York: Basic Books, 1991.

Medieval

Ambrose. *Some of the Principal Works of Ambrose.* Translated by H. de Romestin. Nicene and Post-Nicene Fathers, Second Series 10. Reprint. Grand Rapids, Mich.: Eerdmans, 1989.

Augustine. *City of God.* Translated by Henry Bettenson. New York: Penguin, 1984.

———. *Confessions.* Translated by Henry Chadwick. New York: Oxford University Press, 1991.

———. *Sermons.* Translated by Edmund Hill. Part 3, Vol. 3: *The Works of Saint Augustine: A Translation for the 21st Century.* Edited by John E. Rotelle. Hyde Park, N.Y.: New City Press, 2003.

Firmicus, Maternus. *The Error of the Pagan Religions.* Translated by Clarence A. Forbes. Ancient Christian Writers 37. New York: Newman Press, 1970.

Klein, Richard. *Der Streit um den Victoriaaltar. Die dritte Relatio des Symmachus und die Briefe 17, 18 und 57 des Mailänder Bischofs Ambrosius.* Texte zur Forschung 7. Darmstadt: Wissenschaftliche Buchgesellschaft, 1972.

Lactantius. *Epitome Divinarum institutionum.* Edited by Eberhard Heck and Antonie Wlosok. Stuttgart: Teubner, 1994.

———. *Institutiones Divines.* Vol. 5, 2. Edited by Pierre Monat. Sources Chrétiennes 204. Paris: Les Éditions du Cerf, 1973.

Minucius, Felix. *Octavius.* Translated by G. W. Clarke. Ancient Christian Writers 39. New York: Newman Press, 1974.

———. *Octavius.* Lateinisch-Deutsch ed. Edited by Bernhard Kytzler. München: Kösel, 1965.

Tertullian. *Apology.* Translated by S. Thelwall. Ante-Nicene Fathers 3. American ed. Grand Rapids, Mich.: Eerdmans, 1989.

Modern

Bacon, Francis. *The Essays or Counsels Civil and Moral.* Edited by Brian Vickers. Oxford: Oxford University Press, 1999.

———. *New Atlantis and the Great Instauration.* Revised ed. Edited by Jerry Weinberger. Arlington Heights, Ill.: Harlan Davidson, 1989.

———. *The Works of Francis Bacon.* Edited by James Spedding, Robert Leslie Ellis, and Douglas Denon Heath. Boston: Brown and Taggard, 1861.

Hobbes, Thomas. *Leviathan.* Edited by Edwin Curley. Indianapolis, Ind.: Hackett, 1994.

Kant, Immanuel. *Critique of Pure Reason.* Edited and translated by Paul Guyer and Allen W. Wood. New York: Cambridge University Press, 1998.

Locke, John. *Essay Concerning Human Understanding.* Vol. 1. Edited by Alexander Campbell Fraser. New York: Dover Publications, 1959.

———. *A Letter Concerning Toleration.* Edited by James H. Tully. Indianapolis, Ind.: Hackett, 1983.

Machiavelli, Niccolò. *The Prince.* 2nd ed. Translated by Harvey C. Mansfield. Chicago: University of Chicago Press, 1998.

Mill, John Stuart. *Three Essays on Religion.* Amherst, Mass.: Prometheus, 1998.

Montesquieu. *The Spirit of the Laws.* Edited and translated by Anne Cohler, Basia Miller, and Harold Stone. New York: Cambridge University Press, 1989.

Rousseau, Jean-Jacques. *Emile.* Translated by Allan Bloom. New York: Basic Books, 1979.

———. *The Essential Rousseau.* Translated by L. Blair. New York: Penguin, 1975.

———. *Social Contract, with Discourse on Virtue of Heroes, Political Fragments, and Geneva Manuscript.* Translated by Judith R. Bush, Roger D. Masters, and Christopher Kelly. Vol. 4 of *The Collected Writings of Rousseau,* edited by Roger D. Masters and Christopher Kelly. Hanover, N.H.: University Press of New England, 1994.

Smith, Adam. *The Theory of Moral Sentiments.* Indianapolis, Ind.: Liberty Classics, 1969.

Spinoza, Benedict. *A Theologico-Political Treatise.* Translated by R. H. M. Elwes. New York: Dover Publications, 1951.

Voltaire. *Philosophical Dictionary.* Vol 1. Translated by Peter Gay. New York: Basic Books, 1962.

United States

Bush, George W. *A Charge to Keep: My Journey to the White House.* New York: Harper Collins, 1999.

Franklin, Benjamin. *The Autobiography of Benjamin Franklin.* New York: Random House, 1950.

Jefferson, Thomas. "Autobiography." In *Thomas Jefferson: Writings.* Edited by Merrill Peterson. New York: Library of America, 1984 [1821].

———. *The Life and Selected Writings of Thomas Jefferson.* Edited by Adrienne Koch and William Peden. New York: Random House, 1944.

———. *The Papers of Thomas Jefferson.* 29 vols. Edited by Julian P. Boyd. Princeton, N.J.: Princeton University Press 1950–.

———. *The Portable Thomas Jefferson.* Edited by Merrill Peterson. New York: Viking Press, 1975.

———. *Thomas Jefferson: Writings.* Edited by Merrill Peterson. New York: Library of America, 1984.

Madison, James. "Memorial and Remonstrance Against Religious Assessments." In *Writings.* New York: Library of America, 1999.

Peterson, Merrill, and Robert Vaughan, eds. *The Virginia Statute for Religious Freedom: Its Evolution and Consequence in American History.* New York: Cambridge University Press, 1988.

Tocqueville, Alexis de. *Democracy in America.* Translated by Harvey C. Mansfield and Delba Winthrop. Chicago: University of Chicago Press, 2000.

———. *Oeuvres Completes.* Paris: Gallimard, 1961–1998.

Washington, George. *Writings.* Edited by John Rhodehamel. New York: Library of America, 1997.

Canada

Coffin, Charles Carleton. *The Seat of Empire.* Boston: Fields, Osgood, 1870.

Cook, Ramsay, ed. *French-Canadian Nationalism: An Anthology.* Toronto: MacMillan, 1969.

Elshtain, Jean Bethke. "A Response to Chief Justice McLachlin." In *Recognizing Religion in a Secular Society: Essays in Pluralism, Religion, and Public Policy,* edited by Douglas Farrow, 35–40. Montréal-Kingston: McGill-Queens University Press, 2004.

Forbes, H. D., ed. *Canadian Political Thought.* Oxford: Oxford University Press, 1984.

King, William Lyon Mackenzie. *Industry and Humanity.* Edited by David Bercuson. Toronto: University of Toronto Press, 1973.

McLachlin, The Right Honorable Beverley P.C. "Freedom of Religion and the Rule of Law: A Canadian Perspective." In *Recognizing Religion in a Secular Society: Essays in Pluralism, Religion, and Public Policy,* edited by Douglas Farrow, 12–34. Montréal-Kingston: McGill-Queens University Press, 2004.

Norman, R. W. *Our Duties and Opportunities.* Montreal: Gazette Printing House, 1877.

Ross, George W., ed. *Patriotic Recitations and Labor Day Exercises.* Toronto: Warrick and Rutter, 1893.

Ryerson, Egerton. *Annual Report of the Normal, Grammar and Common Schools in Ontario for the Year 1870.* Toronto: Hunter, Rose, 1871.

———. *First Lessons in Christian Morals for Canadian Families and Schools.* Toronto: Copp, Clark, 1871.

———. *Ontario for the Year 1870.* Toronto: Hunter, Rose, 1871.

Shortt, Jonathan. *The Gospel Banner! A Sermon Preached to the Loyal Orange Lodges, Assembled in St. John's Church, Port Hope, July 12th, 1853.* Montreal: Wilsons and Noland,1853.

Strachan, John. "On Church Establishment." In *Canadian Political Thought,* edited by H. D. Forbes, 10–17. Oxford: Oxford University Press, 1984.

———. "Pastoral Letter of the Bishops of the Ecclesiastical Province of Quebec." In *Canadian Political Thought,* edited by H. D. Forbes, 96–106. Oxford: Oxford University Press, 1984.

———. "The Programme Catholique: The Next Elections." In *Canadian Political Thought,* edited by H. D. Forbes, 93–95. Oxford: Oxford University Press, 1984.

Secondary Sources

General

Arendt, Hannah. *Totalitarianism.* New York: Harcourt, Brace, Jovanovich, 2001.

Berger, Peter L. *The Desecularization of the World: Resurgent Religion and World Politics.* Grand Rapids, Mich.: Eerdmans, 1999.

Deneen, Patrick J. *Democratic Faith.* Princeton, N.J.: Princeton University Press, 2004.

Elazar, Daniel J., and John Kincaid. *The Covenant Connection: From Federal Theology to Modern Federalism.* Lanham, Md.: Lexington Books, 2000.

Farrow, Douglas, ed. *Recognizing Religion in a Secular Society: Essays in Pluralism, Religion, and Public Policy.* Montréal-Kingston: McGill-Queens University Press, 2004.

Fraser, Andrew. *The Spirit of the Laws.* Toronto: University of Toronto Press, 1990.

Gebhardt, Jürgen. "Politische Kultur und Zivilreligion." In *Politik, Hermeneutik, Humanität—Gesammelte Aufsätze von Jürgen Gebhart,* edited by Clemens Kauffmann et al., 101–16. Berlin: Duncker and Humblot, 2004.

Gottfried, Paul. *Multiculturalism and the Politics of Guilt: Toward a Secular Theocracy.* Columbia: University of Missouri Press, 2004.

Heyking, John von. "Secularization: Not Dead Yet, But Never What it Seemed." *International Studies Review* 7, no. 2 (2005): 279–84.

Hildebrandt, Mathias. *Politische Kultur und Zivilreligion.* Würzburg: Koenigshausen and Neumann, 1997.

Hook, Sidney. *Religion in a Free Society.* Lincoln: University of Nebraska Press, 1967.

Hoppe, Hans-Hermann. *Democracy: The God That Failed: Studies in the Economics and Politics of Monarchy, Democracy, and Natural Order.* New Brunswick, N.J.: Transaction Publishers, 2001.

Jeffrey, David Lyle. *People of the Book: Christian Identity and Literary Culture.* Grand Rapids, Mich.: Eerdmans, 1996.

Norris, Pippa, and Ronald Inglehart. *Sacred and Secular: Religion and Politics Worldwide*. Cambridge: Cambridge University Press, 2004.

Pera, Marcello. "Letter to Joseph Ratzinger." In Joseph Ratzinger and Marcello Pera, *Without Roots: The West, Relativism, Christianity, Islam*. Translated by Michael F. Moore, 94–96. New York: Basic Books, 2006.

Solzhenitsyn, A. I. "Repentance and Self-Limitation in the Life of Nations." In *From Under the Rubble*. Edited by A. I. Solzhenitsyn and translated by A. M. Brock, et al., 105–43. Boston: Little, Brown, 1975.

Sowell, Thomas. *The Quest for Cosmic Justice*. New York: Free Press, 1999.

Voegelin, Eric. *History of Political Ideas*. Vols. 19–26 of *Collected Works of Eric Voeglin*. Columbia: University of Missouri Press, 1997–99.

———. *Modernity without Restraint*. In *Collected Works of Eric Voegelin*. Vol. 5. Edited by Manfred Henningsen. Columbia: University of Missouri Press, 1999.

———. *The New Science of Politics*. Chicago: University of Chicago Press, 1952.

———. *Order and History*. Vols. 14–18 of *Collected Works of Eric Voegelin*. Columbia: University of Missouri Press, 2000–2001.

Walsh, David. *Guarded by Mystery: Meaning in a Postmodern Age*. Washington, D.C.: The Catholic University of America Press, 2002.

Antiquity

Assmann, Jan. *Herrschaft und Heil: Politische Theologie in Altägypten, Israel und Europa*. München: Hanser, 2000.

Bauman, R. A. "The Suppression of the Bacchanals: Five Questions." *Historia* 39, no. 3 (1990): 342–43.

Beard, Mary, John North, and Simon Price. *Religions of Rome*. 2 vols. Cambridge: Cambridge University Press, 1998.

Bleicken, Jochen. *Verfassungs- und Sozialgeschichte des Römischen Kaiserreiches*. Vol. 2. 3rd ed. Paderborn: Schöningh, 1994.

Burkert, Walter. *Antike Mysterien*. München: Beck, 1991.

———. *Greek Religion*. Translated by John Raffan. Cambridge, Mass.: Harvard University Press, 1985.

Castel-Bouchouchi, Anissa. "L'Espace civique: le plan de la Cité des *Lois*." *Revue Philosophique* 190 (2000): 21–39.

Cochrane, Charles N. *Christianity and Classical Culture: A Study of Thought and Action from Augustus to Augustine*. Indianapolis, Ind.: Liberty Fund, 2003.

Dodds, Eric R. *The Greeks and the Irrational*. Berkeley and Los Angeles: University of California Press, 1951.

———. *Pagan and Christian in an Age of Anxiety: Some Aspects of Religious Experience from Marc Aurelius to Constantine*. Cambridge: Cambridge University Press, 1990.

Fuhrmann, Manfred. *Rom in der Spätantike. Porträt einer Epoche*. Munich: Artemis and Winkler, 1994.

Gould, John. *The Development of Plato's Ethics*. Cambridge: Cambridge University Press, 1955.

Grote, George. *Plato and the Other Companions of Sokrates.* 3rd ed. London: John Murray, 1875.

Klosko, George. *The Development of Plato's Political Theory.* London: Methuen, 1986.

Larivée, Annie. "Du vin pour le Collège de veille? Mise en lumière d'un lien occulté entre le Choeur de Dionysos et le *nukterinos sullogos* dans les *Lois* de Platon." *Phronesis* 48 (2003): 29–53.

Lee, Edward N. "Reason and Rotation: Circular Movement as the Model of Mind *(Nous)* in Later Plato." In *Facets of Plato's Philosophy,* edited by W. H. Werkmeister, 71–102. *Phronesis* Supplementary, vol. 2. Amsterdam: Van Gorcum, 1976.

Lewis, V. Bradley. "The Nocturnal Council and Platonic Political Philosophy." *History of Political Thought* 19, no. 1 (1998): 1–20.

———. "Plato's *Minos:* The Political and Philosophical Context of the Problem of Natural Right." *Review of Metaphysics* 60 (2006): 17–54.

MacDowell, Douglas M. *The Law in Classical Athens.* Ithaca, N.Y.: Cornell University

Momigliano, Arnoldo. "Introduction. Christianity and the Decline of the Roman Empire." In *The Conflict between Paganism and Christianity in the Fourth Century,* edited by Arnoldo Momigliano, 3–4. Oxford: Clarendon, 1964.

———. "The Disadvantages of Monotheism for a Universal State." *Classical Philology* 81, no. 4 (1986): 285–97.

Morrow, Glenn R. *Plato's Cretan City: A Historical Interpretation of the "Laws."* Princeton, N.J.: Princeton University Press, 1960.

Nightingale, Andrea. "Writing/Reading a Sacred Text: A Literary Interpretation of Plato's *Laws.*" *Classical Philology* 88, no. 4 (1993): 279–300.

Nippel, Wilhelm. "Orgien, Ritualmorde und Verschwörung? Die Bacchanalien-Prozesse des Jahres 186 v. Chr." In *Große Prozesse der römischen Antike,* edited by Ulrich Manthe and Jürgen von Ungern-Sternberg, 65–73. München: Beck 1997.

North, John A. *Roman Religion.* Oxford: Oxford University Press, 2000.

Pangle, Thomas L. "The Political Psychology of Religion in Plato's *Laws.*" *American Political Science Review* 70, no. 4 (1976): 1059–77.

Piérart, Marcel. "Les *euthunoi* athéniens." *Antiquité classique* 40 (1971): 526–73.

———. *Platon et la Cité grecque: Théorie et réalité dans la Constitution des "Lois."* Bruxelles: Académie Royale de Belgique, 1974.

Reverdin, Olivier. *La Religion de la Cité Platonicienne.* Paris: Boccard, 1945.

Saunders, Trevor J. *Plato's Penal Code: Tradition, Controversy, and Reform in Greek Penology.* Oxford: Clarendon Press, 1991.

Schofield, Malcolm. "Religion and Philosophy in the *Laws.*" In *Plato's "Laws": From Theory into Practice, Proceedings of the VI Symposium Platonicum, Selected Papers,* edited by Samuel Scolnicov and Luc Brisson, 1–13. Sankt Augustin: Academia Verlag, 2003.

Scolnicov, Samuel, and Luc Brisson, eds. *Plato's "Laws": From Theory into Practice, Proceedings of the VI Symposium Platonicum, Selected Papers.* Sankt Augustin: Academia Verlag, 2003.

Solmsen, Friedrich. *Plato's Theology.* Ithaca, N.Y.: Cornell University Press, 1942.

Sourvinou-Inwood, C. "Further Aspects of *Polis* Religion." *Annali, Instituto orientale di Napoli: Archeologia e storia antica* 10 (1988): 259–74.

———. "What Is *Polis* Religion?" In *The Greek City from Homer to Alexander*, edited by Oswyn Murray and Simon Price, 295–322. Oxford: Clarendon Press, 1990.

Stalley, R. F. *An Introduction to Plato's "Laws."* Oxford: Blackwell, 1983.

Strauss, Leo. *The City and Man*. Chicago: Rand McNally, 1964.

———. *The Argument and the Action of Plato's "Laws."* Chicago: University of Chicago Press, 1975.

Todd, S. C. *The Shape of Athenian Law*. Oxford: Clarendon Press, 1993.

Verboven, Koenraad. *The Economy of Friends: Economic Ascpects of Amicitia and Patronage in the Late Republic*. Brussels: Éditions Latomus, 2002.

Voegelin, Eric. *Order and History*. Vol. 3, *Plato and Aristotle*. Baton Rouge: Louisiana State University Press, 1957.

Yunis, Harvey. *A New Creed: Fundamental Religious Beliefs in the Athenian Polis and Euripidean Drama*. Hypomnemata 91. Göttingen: Vandenhoeck and Ruprecht, 1988.

Medieval

Becker, Carl. *Der "Octavius" des Minucius Felix. Heidnische Philosophie und christliche Apologetik*. München: Beck, 1967.

Bowersock, Glen W. "Symmachus and Ausonius." In *Colloque Genevois sur Symmaque à l'occasion du mille six centième anniversaire du conflit de l'autel de la Victoire*, edited by F. Paschoud, 1–15. Paris: Société d'Edition Les Belles Lettres, 1986.

Brown, P. R. L. "Political Society," In *Augustine: A Collection of Critical Studies*, edited by R. A. Markus, 311–24. Garden City, N.Y.: Anchor Books, 1972.

Campenhausen, Hans von. *Lateinische Kirchenväter*. Stuttgart: Kohlhammer, 1986.

Fortin, Ernest. *Classical Christianity and the Political Order: Reflections on the Theologico-Political Problem*.Vol. 2 of *Ernest L. Fortin: Collected Essays*. Edited by J. Brian Benestad. Lanham, Md.: Rowman and Littlefield, 1996.

Heyking, John von. *Augustine and Politics as Longing in the World*. Columbia: University of Missouri Press, 2001.

Klein, Richard. "Die Romidee bei Symmachus, Claudian und Prudentius." In *Colloque Genevois sur Symmaque à l'occasion du mille six centième anniversaire du conflit de l'autel de la Victoire*, edited by F. Paschoud, 119–38. Paris: Société d'Edition "Les Belles Lettres," 1986.

Maier, Franz Georg. *Die Verwandlung der Mittelmeerwelt*. Augsburg: Weltbild, 1998.

Markus, R. A. *Saeculum: History and Society in the Theology of St. Augustine*. Cambridge: Cambridge University Press, 1970.

O'Donnell, James J. *Augustine: A New Biography*. New York: HarperCollins, 2005.

Schall, James V. "The 'Realism' of Augustine's 'Political Realism': Augustine and Machiavelli." *Perspectives on Political Science* 25, no. 3 (1996): 117–23.

Modern

Anderson, Fulton. *The Philosophy of Francis Bacon*. Chicago: University of Chicago Press, 1948.

Beiner, Ronald. "Machiavelli, Hobbes, and Rousseau on Civil Religion." *Review of Politics* 55, no. 4 (1993): 617–38.

Chazan, Paul. "Rousseau as Psycho-Social Moralist." *History of Philosophy Quarterly* 10, no. 4 (1993): 341–54.

Farrington, Benjamin. *Francis Bacon, Philosopher of Industrial Science.* London: Lawrence and Wishart, 1951.

Faulkner, Robert K. *Francis Bacon and the Project of Progress.* Lanham, Md.: Rowman and Littlefield, 1993.

Ferrara, A. *Modernity and Authenticity: A Study in the Social and Ethical Thought of Jean-Jacques Rousseau.* Albany: State University of New York Press, 1993.

Fuller, Tim. "The Theological-Political Tension in Liberalism." *Philosophy and Theology* 4, no. 3 (1990): 267–81.

Grimsley, R. *Rousseau and the Religious Quest.* Oxford: Clarendon Press, 1968.

Hendel, C. W. *Jean-Jacques Rousseau Moralist.* London: Oxford University Press, 1934.

Hill, Christopher. *The Bible and the Seventeenth-Century Revolution.* New York: Penguin Press, 1993.

Innes, David C. "Bacon's *New Atlantis:* The Christian Hope and the Modern Hope." *Interpretation* 22, no. 1 (1994): 3–37.

———. "Francis Bacon, Christianity and the Hope of Modern Science." Ph.D. dissertation, Boston College, 1992.

Kries, Douglas. "Rousseau and the Problem of Religious Toleration." In *Piety and Humanity: Essays on Religion and Early Modern Political Philosophy,* edited by Douglas Kries, 259–86. Lanham, Md.: Rowman and Littlefield, 1997.

LePain, Marc A. "The Fruit of the Land: Biblical and Classical Allusions in Francis Bacon's *New Atlantis.*" Unpublished manuscript.

Mahoney, Daniel J., and Paul Seaton, eds. *Modern Liberty and Its Discontents.* Lanham, Md.: Rowman and Littlefield, 1998.

Masters, Roger D. *The Political Philosophy of Rousseau.* Princeton, N.J.: Princeton University Press, 1968.

McClay, Wilfred M. "Two Concepts of Secularism." In *Religion Returns to the Public Square: Faith and Policy in America,* edited by Hugh Heclo and Wilfred M. McClay, 31–62. Baltimore: Johns Hopkins University Press, 2003.

McGrath, Alister. *The Twilight of Atheism.* New York: Doubleday, 2004.

McInerny, Ralph, ed. *Modernity and Religion.* Notre Dame, Ind.: University of Notre Dame Press, 1994.

McKnight, Stephen. *The Religious Foundations of Francis Bacon's Thought.* Columbia: University of Missouri Press, 2006.

Melzer, Arthur. *The Natural Goodness of Man: On the System of Rousseau's Thought.* Chicago: University of Chicago Press, 1990.

———. "The Origin of the Counter-Enlightenment: Rousseau and the New Religion of Sincerity." *American Political Science Review* 90, no. 2 (1996): 344–60.

Mitchell, Joshua. *The Fragility of Freedom.* Chicago: University of Chicago Press, 1995.

Prince, Bronwen, ed. *Francis Bacon's New Atlantis: New Interdisciplinary Essays.* Manchester, UK: Manchester University Press, 2002.

Prickett, Stephen. *Origins of Narrative: The Romantic Appropriation of the Bible.* Cambridge: Cambridge University Press, 1996.

Proulx, Jean-Baptiste. *Le Canada, le Curé Labelle, et la colonization*. 1885. Reprint Saint-Jacques, P.Q.: Editions du pot de fer, 1992.

Rahe, Paul A. *Republics Ancient and Modern: Classical Republicanism and the American Revolution*. Chapel Hill: University of North Carolina Press, 1992.

Ripstein, Arthur. "The General Will." *History of Philosophy Quarterly* 9, no. 1 (1992): 69–84.

Schwartz, Joel. *The Sexual Politics of Jean-Jacques Rousseau*. Chicago: University of Chicago Press, 1984.

Sloat, James. "The Subtle Significance of Sincere Belief: Tocqueville's Account of Religious Belief and Democratic Stability." *Journal of Church and State* 42, no. 4 (Autumn 2000): 759–80.

Weinberger, Jerry. "Science and Rule in Bacon's Utopia." *American Political Science Review* 70 (1976): 865–85.

———. *Science, Faith, and Politics: Francis Bacon and the Utopian Roots of the Modern Age*. Ithaca, N.Y.: Cornell University Press, 1985.

White, Howard. *Peace among the Willows: The Political Philosophy of Francis Bacon*. The Hague: Martinus Nijhoff, 1968.

Whitney, Charles. *Francis Bacon and Modernity*. New Haven, Conn.: Yale University Press, 1986.

Zuckert, Michael P. *Launching Liberalism: On Lockean Political Philosophy*. Lawrence: University Press of Kansas, 2002.

———. "Locke and the Problem of Civil Religion." In *The Moral Foundations of the American Principle*, edited by Horowitz, 3rd edition, 202–3. Charlottesville: University Press of Virginia, 1979.

United States

Aikman, David. *A Man of Faith: The Spiritual Journey of George W. Bush*. Nashville, Tenn.: W Publishing Group, 2004.

Alley, Robert S. *The Supreme Court on Church and State*. New York: Oxford University Press, 1988.

Allman, Dwight D., and Michael D. Beaty, eds. *Cultivating Citizens: Soulcraft and Citizenship in Contemporary America*. Lanham, Md.: Lexington Books, 2002.

Banning, Lance. "James Madison, the Statute for Religious Freedom, and the Crisis of Republican Convictions." In *The Virginia Statute for Religious Freedom: Its Evolution and Consequence in American History*, edited by Merrill Peterson and Robert Vaughan, 109–38. Cambridge: Cambridge University Press, 1988.

Bellah, Robert N. "American Civil Religion in the 1970's." In *American Civil Religion*, edited by Russell E. Richey and Donald G. Jones, 255–72. New York: Harper and Row, 1974.

———. *The Broken Covenant: American Civil Religion in Time of Trial*. New York: Seabury Press, 1975.

———. "Civil Religion in America." *Daedalus* 96, no. 1 (1967): 1–21.

———. "Conclusion: Competing Visions of the Role of Religion in American Society." In *Uncivil Religion: Interreligious Hostility in America*, edited by Robert N.

Bellah and Frederick E. Greenspahn, 219–32. New York: Crossroad, 1987.

———. "Public Philosophy and Public Theology in America Today." In *Civil Religion and Political Theology,* edited by Leroy S. Rouner, 79–97. Notre Dame, Ind.: University of Notre Dame Press, 1986.

———. *Varieties of Civil Religion.* New York: Harper and Row, 1980.

Berg, Thomas C. "Minority Religions and the Religion Clauses." *Washington University Law Quarterly* 82, no. 3 (2004): 919–1000.

Berns, Walter. *The First Amendment and the Future of American Democracy.* New York: Basic Books, 1976.

Brant, Irving. 1951. "Madison: On the Separation of Church and State." *William and Mary Quarterly* 3rd ser., 8 (1951): 5.

Bryce, James. *The American Commonwealth.* Revised ed. Vol. 2. New York: Macmillan, 1911.

Buckley, Thomas E. *Church and State in Revolutionary Virginia, 1776–1787.* Charlottesville: University of Virginia Press, 1977.

———. "The Political Theology of Thomas Jefferson." In *The Virginia Statute for Religious Freedom: Its Evolution and Consequence in American History,* edited by Merrill Peterson and Robert Vaughan, 75–107. Cambridge: Cambridge University Press, 1988.

———. "The Religious Rhetoric of Thomas Jefferson." In *The Founders on God and Government,* edited by Daniel Dreisbach et al., 53–82. Lanham, Md.: Rowman and Littlefield, 2004.

Carter, Stephen L. *The Culture of Disbelief: How American Law and Politics Trivialize Religious Devotion.* New York: Harper, 1993.

———. *God's Name in Vain: The Wrongs and Rights of Religion in Politics.* New York: Basic Books, 2000.

Cohen, Naomi. *Jews in Christian America: The Pursuit of Religious Equality.* New York: Oxford University Press, 1992.

DeWolf, David K., et al. *Traipsing into Evolution: Intelligent Design and the Kitzmiller v. Dover Decision.* Seattle, Wash.: Discovery Institute Press, 2006.

Douthat, Ross. "Theocracy! Theocracy! Theocracy!" *First Things* 165 (August/September 2006): 23–30.

Dreisbach, Daniel. *The Founders on God and Government.* Lanham, Md.: Rowan and Littlefield, 2004.

———. "A New Perspective on Jefferson's Views on Church-State Relations: The Virginia Statute for Establishing Religious Freedom in Its Legislative Context." *American Journal of Legal History* 35 (1991): 172–204.

———. "Thomas Jefferson and Bills Number 82–86 of the Revision of the Laws of Virginia, 1776–1786: New Light on the Jeffersonian Model of Church-State Relations." *North Carolina Law Review* 69 (1990): 159–211.

———. *Thomas Jefferson and the Wall of Separation between Church and State.* New York: New York University Press, 2002.

Eckenrode, Hamilton James. *Separation of Church and State in Virginia: A Study in the Development of the Revolution.* Richmond, Va.: Davis Bottom, 1910.

Fish, Stanley. "Mission Impossible: Settling the Just Bounds between Church and State." *Columbia Law Review* 97 (1997): 2279–83.

———. *There's No Such Thing as Free Speech*. New York: Oxford University Press, 1994.

Freiling, Thomas M., ed. *George W. Bush on God and Country*. Fairfax, Va.: Allegiance Press, 2004.

Frost, Bryan-Paul, and Jeffrey Sikkenga, eds. *History of American Political Thought*. Lanham, Md.: Lexington Press, 2003.

Gaustad, Edwin. *Sworn on the Altar of God: A Religious Biography of Thomas Jefferson*. Grand Rapids, Mich.: Eerdmans Publishing, 1990.

Gebhardt, Jürgen. *Americanism: Revolutionary Order and Societal Self-Interpretation in the American Republic*. Translated by Ruth Hein. Baton Rouge: Louisiana State University Press, 1991.

Gedicks, Frederick Mark. *The Rhetoric of Church and State: A Critical Analysis of Religion Clause Jurisprudence*. Durham, N.C.: Duke University Press, 1995.

Goldberg, Michelle. *Kingdom Coming: The Rise of Christian Nationalism*. New York: W. W. Norton, 2006.

Hamburger, Philip. *Separation of Church and State*. Cambridge, Mass.: Harvard University Press, 2002.

Hamilton, Marci. *God vs. the Gavel: Religion and the Rule of Law*. New York: Cambridge University Press, 2005.

Heclo, Hugh, and Wilfred M. McClay, eds. *Religion Returns to the Public Square: Faith and Policy in America*. Baltimore: Johns Hopkins University Press, 2003.

Herberg, Will. *Protestant-Catholic-Jew: An Essay in American Religious Sociology*. Garden City, N.Y.: Doubleday, 1955.

Huntley, William B. "Jefferson's Public and Private Religion." *South Atlantic Quarterly* 79 (1980): 286–301.

Isaac, Rhys. "'The Rage of the Old Serpent Devil': The Dissenters and the Making and Remaking of the Virginia Statute for Religious Freedom." In *The Virginia Statute for Religious Freedom: Its Evolution and Consequence in American History*, edited by Merrill Peterson and Robert Vaughan, 139–69. Cambridge: Cambridge University Press, 1988.

Jeffries, John C., and James E. Ryan. "A Political History of the Establishment Clause." *Michigan Law Review* 100, no. 2 (2001): 279–370.

Kaplan, Esther. *With God On Their Side*. New York: New Press, 2004.

Karst, Kenneth L. "Religious Freedom and Equal Citizenship: Reflections on Lukumi." *Tulane Law Review* 6 (December, 1994): 335–72.

Kengor, Paul. *God and George W. Bush: A Spiritual Life*. New York: Regan Books, 2004.

Kessler, Sanford. "Locke's Influence on Jefferson's 'Bill for Establishing Religious Freedom.'" *Journal of Church and State* 25 (1983): 231–52.

———. *Tocqueville's Civil Religion: American Christianity and the Prospects for Freedom*. Albany: State University of New York Press, 1994.

Knippenberg, Joseph M. "Religion and the Limits of Liberal Pluralism." In *Democracy and Its Friendly Critics: Tocqueville and Political Life Today*, edited by Peter A. Lawler, 111–24. Lanham, Md.: Lexington Books, 2004.

Koritansky, John C. "Civil Religion in Tocqueville's Democracy in America." *Interpretation* 17, no. 3 (1990): 389–400.

Kramnick, Isaac, and R. Lawrence Moore. *The Godless Constitution: The Case against Religious Correctness.* New York: W. W. Norton, 1996.

Lawler, Peter Augustine. *The Restless Mind.* Lanham, Md.: Rowman and Littlefield, 1993.

———. "Tocqueville on Pantheism, Materialism, and Catholicism." *Perspectives on Political Science* 30, no. 4 (2001): 218–226.

———, ed. *Democracy and Its Friendly Critics: Tocqueville and Political Life Today.* Lanham, Md.: Lexington Books, 2004.

Levinson, Sanford. *Constitutional Faith.* Princeton, N.J.: Princeton University Press, 1989.

Linker, Damon. *The Theocons: Secular America under Siege.* New York: Doubleday, 2006.

Manent, Pierre. *Tocqueville and the Nature of Democracy.* Translated by John Waggoner. Lanham, Md.: Rowman and Littlefield, 1996.

Mansfield, Harvey. *America's Constitutional Soul.* Baltimore: Johns Hopkins University Press, 1991.

Mansfield, Stephen. *The Faith of George W. Bush.* New York: Jeremy Tarcher/Penguin, 2004.

Marty, Martin E. *A Nation of Behavers.* Chicago: University of Chicago Press, 1976.

———. *Religion and Republic: The American Circumstance.* Boston: Beacon Press, 1987.

———. "Two Kinds of Two Kinds of Civil Religions." In *American Civil Religion,* edited by Russell E. Richey and Donald G. Jones, 139–60. New York: Harper and Row, 1974.

Marty, Martin E. *Civil Religion, Church, and State.* Munich, Germany: K. G. Saur, 1992.

———. "Eight Approaches toward Understanding Public Religion and Politics in America." In *Politics, Religion, and the American Experience,* edited by Edith Blumhofer, 1–15. Tuscaloosa: University of Alabama Press, 2001.

Marty, Martin E., and Jonathan Moore. *Politics, Religion, and the Common Good: Advancing a Distinctly American Conversation about Religion's Role in Our Shared Life.* San Francisco: Jossey-Bass, 2000.

McBrien, Richard P. *Caesar's Coin: Religion and Politics in America.* New York: Macmillan, 1987.

McClay, Wilfred M. "Bush's Calling." *Commentary* 119, no. 6 (June 2005): 49–53.

———. "The Soul of a Nation." *Public Interest* 155 (Spring 2004): 4–19.

McGarvie, Mark. *One Nation under Law: America's Early National Struggles to Separate Church and State.* DeKalb: Northern Illinois University Press, 2004.

Mitchell, Joshua. "The Trajectories of Religious Renewal in America: Tocquevillean Thoughts." In *One Nation Under God?* edited by R. Bruce Douglass and Joshua Mitchell, 17–44. Lanham, Md.: Rowman and Littlefield, 2000.

Monsma, Stephen V., and J. Christopher Soper, eds. *Equal Treatment of Religion in a Pluralist Society.* Grand Rapids, Mich.: Eerdmans, 1998.

O'Malley, Deborah Ann. *The Dictates of Conscience: The Debate over Religious Liberty in Revolutionary Virginia*. Ashland, Ohio: Ashbrook Center, 2006.

Orwin, Clifford. "The Unravelling of Christianity in America." *Public Interest,* no. 155 (2004): 20–36.

Owen, J. Judd. *Religion and the Demise of Liberal Rationalism*. Chicago: University of Chicago Press, 2001.

Owens, Erik. "Taking the 'Public' Out of Our Schools." *Journal of Church and State* 44, no. 4 (2002): 717–47.

Pacelle, Richard L. *The Transformation of the Supreme Court's Agenda: From the New Deal to the Reagan Administration*. Boulder, Colo.: Westview Press, 1991.

Pangle, Thomas L. "Religion in the Thought of Some of the Leading American Founders." *Notre Dame Journal of Law, Ethics and Public Policy* 4 (1989): 37–50.

———. *The Spirit of Modern Republicanism: The Moral Vision of the American Founders and the Philosophy of Locke*. Chicago: University of Chicago Press, 1988.

Phillips, Kevin. *American Theocracy*. New York: Viking, 2006.

Pierard, Richard V., and Robert D. Linder. *Civil Religion and the Presidency*. Grand Rapids, Mich.: Zondervan, 1988.

Poelvoorde, Jeffrey. "American Civil Religion." In *How Does the Constitution Protect Religious Freedom?* edited by Robert A. Goldwin and Arthur Kaufman. Washington, D.C.: AEI Press, 1979.

Ponnuru, Ramesh. *The Party of Death*. Washington, D.C.: Regnery, 2006.

Rosen, Jeffrey. "Is Nothing Secular?" *New York Times Magazine,* January 30, 2000, 40–45.

Rutland, Robert. *George Mason: Reluctant Statesman*. Baton Rouge: Louisiana State University Press, 1961.

Sandoz, Ellis. *A Government of Laws: Political Theory, Religion, and the American Founding*. Columbia: University of Missouri Press, 2002.

———. *Republicanism, Religion, and the Soul of America*. Columbia: University of Missouri Press, 2006.

Sanford, Charles B. *The Religious Life of Thomas Jefferson*. Charlotteville: University of Virginia Press, 1984.

Shain, Barry Alain. *The Myth of American Individualism: The Protestant Origins of American Political Thought*. Princeton, N.J.: Princeton University Press, 1994.

Sheridan, Eugene R. "Introduction." In *Jefferson's Extracts from the Gospels,* edited by Dickinson Adams. Princeton, N.J.: Princeton University Press, 1983.

Sheldon, Garrett Ward. *The Political Philosophy of Thomas Jefferson*. Baltimore, Md.: Johns Hopkins University Press, 1991.

Shklar, J. *Men and Citizens*. London: Cambridge University Press, 1968.

Singer, Peter. *The President of Good and Evil: The Ethics of George W. Bush*. New York: Dutton, 2004.

Smith, Steven D. *Foreordained Failure: The Quest for a Constitutional Principle of Religious Freedom*. New York: Oxford University Press, 1995.

Swanson, James L., and Christian L. Castle, eds. *1990 First Amendment Law Handbook*. St. Paul, Minn.: West Group Publishing, 1990.

Tessitore, Aristide. "Legitimate Government, Religion, and Education: The Political Philosophy of Thomas Jefferson." In *History of American Political Thought,* edited by Bryan-Paul Frost and Jeffrey Sikkenga, 137–43. Lanham, Md.: Lexington Books, 2003.

Zuckert, Catherine. "The Role of Religion in Preserving American Liberty: Tocqueville's Analysis 150 Years Later." In *Tocqueville's Defense of Human Liberty: Current Essays,* edited by Peter Augustine Lawler and Jospeh Alulis, 223–39. New York: Garland Publishing, 1993.

Canada

Ajzenstat, Janet. *The Once and Future Canadian Democracy.* Montréal-Kingston: McGill-Queens University Press, 2003.

———. *The Political Thought of Lord Durham.* Montréal-Kingston: McGill-Queens University Press, 1988.

Benson, Iain T. "Notes Toward a (Re)Definition of the 'Secular.'" *University of British Columbia Law Review* 33, special edition (2000): 519–50.

Blumstock, Robert. "Canadian Civil Religion." In *The Sociology of Religion: A Canadian Focus,* edited by W. E. Hewitt, 171–94. Toronto: Butterworths, 1993.

Brown, David M. "Freedom From or Freedom For?: Religion as a Case Study in Defining the Content of Charter Rights." *University of British Columbia Law Review* 33 (2000): 551–616.

Cairns, Alan C. *Reconfigurations: Canadian Citizenship and Constitutional Change.* Toronto: McClelland and Stewart, 1995.

Cere, Daniel, and Douglas Farrow, eds. *Divorcing Marriage: Unveiling the Dangers in Canada's New Social Experiment.* Montréal-Kingston: McGill-Queens University Press, 2004.

Choquette, Robert. *The Oblate Assault on Canada's Northwest.* Ottawa: University of Ottawa Press, 1995.

Christiano, Kevin J. *Pierre Elliott Trudeau: Reason before Passion.* Toronto: ECW Press, 1994.

Christie, Nancy, and Michael Gauvreau. *A Full-Orbed Christianity: The Protestant Churches and Social Welfare in Canada, 1900–1940.* Montreal-Kingston: McGill-Queen's University Press, 1990.

Cook, Ramsay. *The Regenerators.* Toronto: University of Toronto Press, 1985.

Cooper, Barry. "Quebec Nationalism and Canadian Politics in Light of Voegelin's *Political Religions.*" In *Politics, Order, and History: Essays on the Work of Eric Voegelin,* edited by Glenn Hughes et al., 208–32. Sheffield: Sheffield Academic Press, 2001.

Côté, Pauline. "From Status Politics to Technocratic Pluralism: Toleration of Religious Minorities in Canada." *Social Justice Research* 12, no. 4 (1999): 253–82.

Dussault, Gabriel. *Le Curé Labelle: Messianisme, utopie et colonisation au Québec, 1850–1900.* Montreal: Hurtubise, 1982.

Egerton, George. "Trudeau, God, and the Canadian Constitution: Religion, Human Rights, and Government Authority in the Making of the 1982 Constitution." In *Rethinking Church, State, and Modernity: Canada between Europe and America,* edited by David Lyon and Marguerite Van Die, 90–112. Toronto: University of Toronto Press, 2000.

Emberley, Peter. *Divine Hunger: Canadians on Spiritual Walkabout.* Toronto: Harper-Collins Canada, 2002.

Flanagan, Thomas. *Louis "David" Riel: "Prophet of the New World."* Toronto: University of Toronto Press, 1979.

Forbes, H. D., ed. *Canadian Political Thought.* Oxford: Oxford University Press, 1984.

Gidney, R. D., and W. P. J. Millar. *Inventing Secondary Education: The Rise of the High School in Nineteenth-Century Ontario.* Montreal-Kingston: McGill-Queen's University Press, 1990.

Grant, John Webster. *Moon of Wintertime: Missionaries and the Indians of Canada in Encounter since 1534.* Toronto: University of Toronto Press, 1984.

Greene, Ian. *The Charter of Rights.* Toronto: James Lorimer, 1989.

Hébert, Bruno. *Monuments et patrie: Une réflexion philosophique sur un fait historique: La célébration commémorative au Québec de 1881 à 1929.* Québec: Les éditions pleins bords, 1980.

Heyking, John von. "Harmonization of Heaven and Earth?: Religion, Politics, and Law in Canada." *University of British Columbia Law Review* 33, special edition (2000): 663–98.

James, Patrick, Donald Abelson, and Michael Lusztig, eds. *The Myth of the Sacred: The Charter, The Courts, and the Politics of the Constitution in Canada.* Montréal-Kingston: McGill-Queens University Press, 2002.

Jones, Preston. *A Highly Favored Nation: The Bible and Canadian Meaning, 1860–1900.* Lanham, Md.: University Press of America, 2007.

Kim, Andrew E. "The Absence of Pan-Canadian Civil Religion: Plurality, Duality, and Conflict in Symbols of Canadian Culture." *Sociology of Religion* 54, no. 3 (1993): 257–75.

Knopff, Rainer. *Human Rights and Social Technology: The New War on Discrimination.* Ottawa: Carleton University Press, 1990.

Knopff, Rainer, and F. L. Morton. *The Charter Revolution and the Court Party.* Peterborough, Ont.: Broadview Press, 2000.

Knowles, Norman. *Inventing the Loyalists: The Ontario Loyalist Tradition and the Creation of Usable Pasts.* Toronto: University of Toronto Press, 1997.

Laforest, Guy. *Trudeau and the End of a Canadian Dream.* Montreal-Kingston: McGill-Queens University Press, 1995.

LaSelva, Samuel. *The Moral Foundations of Canadian Federalism.* Montreal: McGill-Queens University Press, 1996.

Lyon, David, and Marguerite Van Die, eds. *Rethinking Church, State, and Modernity: Canada between Europe and America.* Toronto: University of Toronto Press, 2000.

Marshall, David B. *Secularizing the Faith: Canadian Protestant Clergy and the Crisis of Belief, 1850–1940.* Toronto: University of Toronto Press, 1992.

Martin, Robert Ivan. *The Most Dangerous Branch: How the Supreme Court of Canada Has Undermined Our Law and Our Democracy.* Montréal-Kingston: McGill-Queens University Press, 2003.

McKillop, A. B. *A Disciplined Intelligence: Critical Inquiry and Canadian Thought in the Victorian Era.* Montreal-Kingtson: McGill-Queen's University Press, 2001.

McKillop, A. B., and Paul Romney, eds. *God's Peculiar Peoples: Essays on Political Culture in Nineteenth Century Canada.* Ottawa: Carleton University Press, 1993.

McLean, John. *The Indians of Canada: Their Manners and Customs.* London, England: Charles H. Kelly, 1892.

Moir, John S. *Church and State in Canada: 1627–1867: Basic Documents.* Toronto: McClelland and Stewart, 1967.

Murphy, Terrence, and Roberto Perin, eds. *A Concise History of Christianity in Canada.* Toronto: Oxford University Press, 1996.

Novak, David. "Human Dignity and the Social Contract." In *Recognizing Religion in a Secular Society: Essays in Pluralism, Religion, and Public Policy,* edited by Douglas Farrow, 51–68. Montréal-Kingston: McGill-Queens University Press, 2004.

Pagé, Norman. *La cathédrale Notre-Dame d'Ottawa: Histoire, architecture, iconographie.* Ottawa: Les presses de l'Université d'Ottawa, 1988.

Pal, Leslie A. *Interests of State: The Politics of Language, Multiculturalism and Feminism in Canada.* Montreal: McGill-Queen's University Press, 1993.

Pangle, Thomas L. "The Accommodation of Religion: A Tocquevillian Perspective." In *The Canadian and American Constitutions in Comparative Perspective,* edited by Marian C. McKenna, 3–24. Calgary: University of Calgary Press, 1993.

Peacock, Anthony A. "Strange Brew: Tocqueville, Rights, and the Technology of Equality." In *Rethinking the Constitution: Perspectives on Canadian Constitutional Reform, Interpretation, and Theory,* edited by Anthony A. Peacock, 122–60. Toronto: Oxford University Press, 1996.

Polka, Brayton. "The Supremacy of God and the Rule of Law in the Canadian Charter of Rights and Freedoms: A Theologico-Political Analysis." *McGill Law Journal,* 32, no. 4 (1987): 854–63.

Routhier, Adolphe-Basile. *Conférences et Discourse.* Montreal: Librairie Beauchemin, 1904.

Russell, Peter. *Constitutional Odyssey: Can Canadians Become a Sovereign People?* 3rd ed. Toronto: University of Toronto Press, 2004.

Sabetti, Filippo. "Covenantal Language in Canada: Continuity and Change in Political Discourse." In *The Covenant Connection: From Federal Theology to Modern Federalism,* edited by Daniel J. Elazar and John Kincaid, 259–83. Lanham, Md.: Lexington Books, 2000.

Samson, Jane. *The British Empire.* Oxford: Oxford University Press, 2001.

Savard, Pierre, ed. *Aspects de la civilisation canadienne-française.* Ottawa: Editions de l'Université d'Ottawa, 1983.

Savoie, Donald. *Governing from the Centre: The Concentration of Power in Canadian Politics.* Toronto: University of Toronto Press, 1999.

Semple, Neil. *The Lord's Dominion: The History of Canadian Methodism.* Montreal-Kingston: McGill-Queen's University Press, 1996.

Silver, A. I. *The French Canadian Idea of Confederation, 1864–1900.* Toronto: University of Toronto Press, 1982.

Smillie, Benjamin G., ed. *Visions of the New Jerusalem: Religious Settlement on the Prairies.* Edmonton: NeWest Press, 1983.

Smith, David E. *The Invisible Crown: The First Principle of Canadian Government.* Toronto: University of Toronto Press, 1995.

———. *The Republican Option in Canada.* Toronto: University of Toronto Press, 1999.

Stahl, William. "Symbols of Canada: Civil Religion, Nationality, and the Search for Meaning." Ph.D. thesis. Berkeley, Calif.: Graduate Theological Union, 1981.

Vaughan, Frederick. *The Canadian Federalist Experiment: From Defiant Monarchy to Reluctant Republic.* Montréal-Kingston: McGill-Queens University Press, 2003.

Wade, Mason. *The French Canadians.* Vol. 2. Toronto: Macmillan, 1975.

Woodley, Edward Carruther. *The Bible in Canada.* Toronto: Dent, 1953.

Contributors

DAVID J. BOBB is founding director of the Hillsdale College Allan P. Kirby, Jr. Center for Constitutional Studies and Citizenship, in Washington, D.C., from where he serves as lecturer in political science. He is writing a book on humility and politics.

JOHN VON HEYKING is associate professor of political science, University of Lethbridge in Alberta. He is the author of *Augustine and Politics as Longing in the World* (Missouri, 2001), along with articles on friendship, just war, Islamic political thought, deliberative democracy, Nicholas of Cusa, and religious liberties under Canada's Charter of Rights and Freedoms. He coedited volumes 7 and 8 of the *Collected Works of Eric Voegelin,* as well as *Friendship and Politics: Essays in Political Thought* (Notre Dame, 2008).

DAVID C. INNES is assistant professor at the King's College in New York City, where he teaches political theory. He is also the founder and a director of the Evangelical Political Scholars Association. He earned a B.A. at the University of Toronto, the Ph.D. at Boston College, and an M.Div. from Reformed Presbyterian Theological Seminary in Pittsburgh. He has published previously on Francis Bacon in *Interpretation.*

PRESTON JONES has been a U.S.-Canada Fulbright scholar and a fellow of the Pew Program in Religion and American History. He has published more than 200 articles for scholarly and general audiences, and he has published books with InterVarsity Press, the University of Alaska Press, and the Research and Education Association. He is professor of history at John Brown University in Arkansas.

JOSEPH M. KNIPPENBERG is professor of politics and director of the Rich Foundation Urban Leadership Program at Oglethorpe University in Atlanta, Georgia, where he has taught for more than twenty years. His scholarly work focuses on the intersection between religion, politics, and law, and his articles and reviews have been published in a wide array of edited volumes and journals. He is an adjunct fellow of the Ashbrook Center for Public Affairs at Ashland University in Ashland, Ohio. In that capacity, he contributes to the Center's No Left Turns blog and writes opinion pieces for a variety of outlets.

DOUGLAS KRIES holds the Bernard J. Coughlin, S.J., Chair in Christian Philosophy at Gonzaga University in Spokane, Washington. His most recent book is *The Problem of Natural Law*.

V. BRADLEY LEWIS is associate professor in the School of Philosophy of the Catholic University of America. He specializes in classical political philosophy and philosophical jurisprudence.

WILFRED M. MCCLAY is Sun Trust Chair of Excellence in Humanities at the University of Tennessee, Chattaooga, and he is coeditor of *Religion Returns to the Public Square: Faith and Policy in Modern America*.

THOMAS F. POWERS is assistant professor at Carthage College, where he teaches in the Great Ideas Program and in the political science department. His teaching and research interests lie at the juncture of constitutional law and political theory. He has written on the theoretical questions raised by constitutional debates about religious liberty, civil rights, and civil liberties and the war on terror.

MATTHIAS RIEDL taught political theory and philosophy at the University of Erlangen-Nuremberg, Germany, and Duke University, North Carolina. Currently he is assistant professor in the history department of Central European University, Budapest, and holds the chair of Comparative Religious Studies. His research focuses on the relation of religion and political thought in historical and intercivilizational perspective.

JEFFREY SIKKENGA is associate professor of Political Science at Ashland University in Ashland, Ohio. He is an adjunct fellow at the John M. Ashbrook Center for Public Affairs and senior fellow at the Program on Constitutionalism and Democracy at the University of Virginia. He is coeditor of *History of American Political Thought* (Lexington Press, 2003), and is currently completing a book on the debate over freedom of conscience as a natural right in the political thought of John Locke and the American founding.

TRAVIS D. SMITH is assistant professor of political science at Concordia University in Montreal.

RONALD WEED is assistant professor of philosophy at the University of New Brunswick. He specializes in ancient Greek philosophy, ethics, and political philosophy. He is the author of *Aristotle on Stasis: A Moral Psychology of Political Conflict* (Berlin: Logos Verlag, 2007) and articles on Aristotle, Rousseau, Kant, and contemporary philosophy. He has taught at Saint Louis University and Tyndale University College, Toronto, and was a visiting fellow at the University of Leeds in 2007.

Index

Abel, 69–70

Abraham, 140

Accommodationist, 238, 245, 247, 251, 253, 256–58

Adam, 140, 143

Adams, John, 207, 209n5, 213n17, 216n22, 219–22, 223n31, 225–27, 228n40

Agnosticism, 78, 92

Aid, 238n6, 240–41, 243, 247–49

Ambrose of Milan, 9

Ambrose, 48–49, 60–65

Amendment, 236–40, 242, 245, 249, 251, 254–57, 258n71, 261

America, 167–179, 180n12, 181–183, 185n16, 186n17, 187–202, 207–9, 210n7, 211n11, 212n15, 213–15, 219n27, 227, 232

Amour–Propre, 156

Amour–Soi, 147, 153

Andrews, Bishop, 123, 128

Anglicanism, 11, 13,

Apollo, 28, 33–34, 115

Apostle, 100

Aristocracy, 48, 62–63

Ark, 129n17, 131–32, 136–37

Arnobius, 9, 48, 59

Association: interest, 151; religious 152

Associations, 303, 305–7, 310–12, 314, 317–18, 320, 327

Atheism, 41–44

Athenian stranger, 21, 23–24, 27, 30, 34–36, 39, 41–45

Atlantis, 121, 122n1, 123–4, 125n9, 130, 132–33, 135–36, 138, 140n36, 141n39, 142, 144

Aubrey, John, 100, 101n12

Audit *(euthuna),* 34

Augures, 52

Augustine of Hippo: general, 1n1, 8–9, 48, 57, 59, 65, 66–92; *City of God,* 1n1, 9, 48, 57, 65

Authenticity, 145, 147–48, 149n9, 153n22, 154n26, 156, 160–66

Authority, 95, 98, 100–101, 107, 115–16, 117n27, 177, 184, 188–90, 196, 203, 300, 304–5, 309–10, 324–26

Authority: divine, 23, 27, 29, 30–31, 36; political, 22, 139; religious, 34

Autonomy, 300, 319–20, 321n60, 322

Bacchanals, 50–55

Bacchus, 51–52

Bacon, Francis: general, 2, 11, 121–28, 129n16, 130–35, 136n34, 138–44; *New Atlantis,* 11, 121, 122n1, 123–4, 125n9, 130, 132–33, 135–6, 138, 140n36, 141n39, 142, 144; *New Organon,* 130–31, 140n38, 142; *The Great Instauration,* 122, 123n6, 134, 143

Bartholomew, The Apostle (Bacon's *New Atlantis*), 132, 137

Beiner, Ronald, 6

Belief, 180–81, 183n14, 184–86, 189–90, 192–93, 196, 207–8, 210–12, 214n18, 215–16, 219n27, 224, 227n39, 234, 241–42, 247, 252–53, 258, 260, 267n23, 274, 299–300, 303, 307–8, 310, 313, 317, 319–20, 323, 326–7

Belief: moral–political, 2; private, 159, 160; privatization of, 160

Bellah, Robert, x, 3, 4n5, 239

Benjamin, 122, 123n3, 128n16

Bensalem, 121, 123–26, 128–32, 134–39, 140n38, 141–42, 144

Berger, Peter, vii

Berns, Walter, 245, 256n66, 257n67, 258n71

Bible, 262, 265, 268n26, 273n59, 278, 280–90, 294–97

Bill for Establishing Religious Freedom (1779), 207, 209–11, 214, 235

Black, Justice, 240

349

Thomas, Justice Clarence, 261
Thrasymachus, 97n7,
Tocqueville, Alexis de, 6, 7n13, 12, 15,
167–203, 298n1, 304n21, 305–12, 314, 320,
322, 325
Tolerance, 146–48, 150, 153, 156–66
Toleration: general, 2, 6–7, 11, 54, 62, 172,
195n27, 198; religious, 94, 97, 117n27
Totalitarianism: ideological, ix; theocratic, ix
Tradition: general, 213, 218, 221, 224, 234–35;
Judeo-Christian, 278; sacred, 277; secular,
277
Trevelyan, Sir Charles, 280
Trials, 32–34
Trinity Western University v. B. C. C. T., 298,
316, 319–20
Trudeau, Pierre Elliot, 300n7, 301, 310n32,
315, 322, 325n72, 326–27
Tuck, Richard, 94n4
Tyranny, 73, 86

Unitarianism, 189–90 (See also deism)
United States of America, 1–2, 4– 6, 7n13, 8,
12–15
Unity: general, 178, 183–84, 187, 199; political,
7–10; of the individual, 156–58; of the
state, 146, 148, 150–52, 156–57, 163–64
Universe, 121, 131, 143–4, 167, 169n3, 170n5,
178n10, 179n11, 188n22, 197n28, 199n31

Utilitarianism, 7
Utopia, 77, 79, 110, 119

Varro, 48, 57
Varro, Marcus Terentius, 1n1, 9, 74–76
Vengeance, 111, 120
Vera religio, 9
Virgil, 48
Virtue: civic, 9, 92; general, 54, 56
Visigoths, 66
Voegelin, Eric, 6, 21n7, 22, 31n26, 37n38,
39n43
Vriend v. Alberta, 314

Washington, George, 254n57, 259
Waterhouse, Benjamin, 219–21, 223, 226–27
"Way of Life": Canadian, 323
Will: collective, 157–58, 162; general, 149n9,
150–51, 157–58, 161, 163; unity of, 152
Winthrop, John, 295
Wisdom of the Ancients, 124
World–historic event, 2–3
Worship, 95–96, 97n6, 101, 106, 125, 131, 138,
140

Zeus, 23, 26, 27, 37
Zuckert, Michael, 5, 6n11

Civil Religion in Political Thought: Its Perennial Questions and Enduring Relevance in North America was designed and typeset in Adobe Garamond Pro by Kachergis Book Design of Pittsboro, North Carolina. It was printed on 60-pound Natures Book Natural and bound by Thomson-Shore of Dexter, Michigan.